# Problems, Promises, and Paradoxes of Aid: Africa's Experience

Edited by

Muna Ndulo and Nicolas van de Walle

CAMBRIDGE SCHOLARS

PUBLISHING

Problems, Promises, and Paradoxes of Aid: Africa's Experience,
Edited by Muna Ndulo and Nicolas van de Walle

This book first published 2014

Cambridge Scholars Publishing

12 Back Chapman Street, Newcastle upon Tyne, NE6 2XX, UK

British Library Cataloguing in Publication Data
A catalogue record for this book is available from the British Library



ISBN (10): 1-4438-6745-4, ISBN (13): 978-1-4438-6745-0

# TABLE OF CONTENTS

# LIST OF TABLES AND FIGURES

# CONTRIBUTORS

**Kojo Busia** is Chief of the African Peer Review Mechanism (APRM) Support Unit in the Governance and Public Administration Division (GPAD) of the UN Economic Commission for Africa (UNECA) based in Addis Ababa, Ethiopia. He also served as a member of the ECA technical team that conducted the review monitoring good governance in Africa, culminating in the publication of the first continent-wide study, the African Governance Report (AGR) in 2005. Prior to joining UNECA in 2003, Dr. Busia worked as a U.S. Foreign Service Officer with the United States Agency for International Development (USAID) and served as a Democracy and Governance Officer in parts of Africa and Eastern Europe including Kenya, Mali, and Romania. Dr. Busia completed his BA in international relations at George Mason University and received his MA in Africana Studies and a Ph.D. in International Development Planning from Cornell University.

**Aaron M. Chassy** is a specialist in good governance and civil society with twenty years of experience developing and managing programs in thirty countries worldwide as well as in the United States. His areas of technical expertise include decentralization and democratic local governance, implementing participatory policy reform, strengthening civil society, citizen advocacy promotion, and the rule of law. Mr. Chassy has served as a USAID Democracy and Governance Foreign Service Officer working in USAID/Washington and USAID/Guinea-Conakry. At present, he serves as Senior Technical Advisor for Catholic Relief Services.

**Nikolas Emmanuel** is an Assistant Professor in political science at the University of Copenhagen. He holds a Ph.D. in political science from the University of California, Davis. He also has a M.Phil. in political science and African studies from the Institut d'Études Politiques and the Centre d'Études d'Afrique Noire in Bordeaux, France.

**Esau Kaakunga** is a Senior Lecturer in Economics at the University of Namibia; he previously held a similar position at Polytechnic of Namibia. From 2001 to 2006 he served as Senior Economist in Research at the Bank of Namibia. He has been a consultant to international organizations including the African Development Bank, USAID, the Institute for Global Dialogue, the Electoral Institute of Southern Africa, UNDP, the Southern African Development Community, and the African Capacity Building Foundation. Dr. Kaakunga is a member of the Agricultural Economics Research Center network and the Poverty Economic Policy network.

**Moses Kiggundu** is Professor of Management and International Business at the Sprott School of Business, Carleton University, Canada. His research focuses on the challenges of managing globalization and creating conditions for a competitive economy in developing countries, with particular interest in the internationalization of business, foreign direct investment, and South-South economic engagements with Africa. He has worked with multinational companies, the United Nations and other international organizations.

**Howard Lehman** is Associate Professor of Political Science at the University of Utah, where he has been teaching since 1986. He holds a Ph.D. in Political Science from the University of Minnesota. He is the recipient of two Fulbright Lectureship awards, to Slovakia in 1994–95 and to Japan in 2002–03. In 2006, Professor Lehman was invited to be a Visiting Scholar at Kobe University and was selected to present his project on Japanese aid to Africa at a UN-sponsored conference in Helsinki.

**Cecelia Lynch** (Ph.D., Political Science, Columbia University) is Professor of Political Science and Director of the Center for Global Peace and Conflict Studies at the University of California, Irvine. She was the winner of the 1999 Furniss Award from the Mershon Center for International Security and co-winner of the 1998 Myrna Bernath Award from the Society for Historians of American Foreign Relations, both for *Beyond Appeasement: Interpreting Interwar Peace Movements in World Politics* (Cornell University Press). She has been awarded fellowships from the Social Science Research Council and MacArthur Foundation, and is completing a book on tensions in Western (Christian) religious ethics on violence, funded by the AAUW and Huntington Library. In 2006, she was awarded an Andrew W. Mellon New Directions Post-doctoral Fellowship for her current research on Islamic and interfaith religious ethics in world crises. She received her Ph.D. in Political Science from Columbia University in New York City.

**Daniel Maxwell** is the Research Director of Food Security and Livelihoods in Complex Emergencies at the Feinstein International Center, Tufts University. Prior to joining academia, he had over twenty years of leadership in NGO program development and management. He was the Deputy Regional Director (2003–2006) and Regional Program Coordinator (2002–2003) for CARE-International, East and Central Africa Regional Unit; the Regional Food Security Advisor, CARE-International, East Africa Regional Unit (1998–2002); and a Rockefeller Fellow at the International Food Policy Research Institute and Noguchi Memorial Institute for Medical Research (1995–1998).

**Muna Ndulo** (D.Phil., Oxford) is Professor of Law and Director of the Institute for African Development at Cornell University. He is also Honorary Professor of Law at the University of Cape Town, South Africa, Extraordinary Professor of Law, Free State University, South Africa, and a former Professor of Law and Dean of the Law at University of Zambia. He has extensive international and UN experience, having served as Legal Officer in the International Law Branch of the UN Commission on International Trade Law; as Legal Adviser and Political Advisor to the UN Observer Mission in South Africa; the UN Assistance Mission to East Timor; and the United Nations Missions to Kosovo and Afghanistan. He has consulted with the World Bank, the African Development bank, the Economic Commission for Africa, and the International Development Law Organization.

**Phyllis Pomerantz** is Professor of the Practice of Public Policy at the Duke Center for International Development, Sanford School of Public Policy, Duke University. Prior to Duke, Dr. Pomerantz was a staff member of the World Bank, beginning there in 1979 as an economist and rural development specialist on Latin America. She subsequently held a series of managerial positions, including Chief of Brazil Agriculture, Chief of Infrastructure Operations in Southern Africa, and Country Director of Zambia and Mozambique. In 2001, she became the World Bank's first Chief Learning Officer, a position she held until her retirement in 2005. Dr. Pomerantz holds two Masters and a Ph.D. in International Relations/International Development from the Fletcher School of Law and Diplomacy.

**Haley Swedlund** holds a Ph.D. in political science from the Maxwell School of Citizenship and Public Affairs, Syracuse University. She is currently an assistant professor at the Centre for International Conflict Analysis and Management, Radboud University, in Nijmegen, the Netherlands. She received her B.S. in political science and women's studies from Texas Christian University and her M.A. from Syracuse University. She also works with the Transnational Non-governmental Organization Initiative based at the Moynihan Institute of Global Affairs, Syracuse University.

**Finn Tarp** is Director of UN University-Wider; He is also Professor and Chair of Development Economics at the University of Copenhagen, where he completed his M.Sc. and Ph.D. in Economics. Professor Tarp has some thirty years of experience in academic and applied development economics research and teaching. His field experience covers numerous countries across Africa and the developing world more generally, including longer term assignments in Swaziland (two years), Mozambique (eight years) and Vietnam (three years). In addition to his university positions, Finn Tarp has held senior posts and advisory positions within government and donor organizations, and he is a member of numerous international committees and advisory bodies. These include the European Union Development Network (EUDN) and the African Economic Research Consortium (AERC).

**Nicolas van de Walle** (Ph.D., Princeton University) is Maxwell M. Upson Professor of Government at Cornell University. He has published widely on democratization issues as well as on the politics of economic reform and on the effectiveness of foreign aid, with special focus on Africa. In addition, van de Walle has worked extensively as a consultant for a variety of international and multilateral organizations, including the World Bank, USAID, and UNDP. From 2004 to 2008 he was Director of Cornell's Mario Einaudi Center for International Studies and Associate Dean for International Studies, College of Arts and Sciences.

# ACRONYMS

| | |
|---|---|
| AAA | Accra Agenda for Action |
| AAD-SAP | African Alternative Framework for Adjustment Programmes |
| ACC | All Africa Conference of Churches |
| ADF | Augmented Dickey-Fuller (test) |
| AIC | African Initiated (or Instituted) Churches |
| APRM | Africa Peer Review Mechanism |
| ARDL | Auto-regressive Distributed Lag |
| ATR | African Traditional Religion |
| BHN | Basic human needs |
| BOP | balance of payments |
| BSHG | Budget Support Harmonization Group |
| CAP | Country Assistance Program |
| CBO | Community-based organization |
| CCIC | Canadian Council for International Cooperation |
| CDF | Comprehensive Development Framework |
| CIDA | Canadian International Development Agency |
| CIVICUS | World Alliance for Citizen Participation |
| CPA | Country Programmable Aid |
| CPAF | Common Performance Assessment Framework |
| CSO | Civil Society Organizations |
| DAC | Development Assistance Committee |
| DfID | Department for International Development (UK) |
| DFI | Development Financial Institution |
| DPCG | Development Partners Coordination Group |
| ECHO | European Community Humanitarian Office |
| ECM | error correction model |
| EDPRS | Economic Development and Poverty Reduction Strategy |
| EHRC | Ethiopian Human Rights Council |
| EPLF | Eritrean People's Liberation Front |
| EPRDF | Ethiopian People's Revolutionary Democratic Front |
| EXIM | Chinese Bank for Exports and Imports |
| FASID | Foundation for Advanced Studies on International Development |

| | |
|---|---|
| FGC/M | female genital circumcision/mutilation |
| FOCAC | Forum on China-Africa Cooperation |
| FSNAU | Food Security and Nutrition Assessment Unit (Somalia) |
| GAVI | Global Alliance for Vaccines and Immunization |
| GBS | general budget support |
| GEF | Global Environmental Facility |
| GFATM | Global Fund to Fight AIDS, Tuberculosis and Malaria |
| G-JAS | Ghana Joint Assistance Strategy |
| GMB | Grain Marketing Board (Zimbabwe) |
| GNI | Gross National Income |
| GOS | Government of Sudan |
| GoR | Government of Rwanda |
| GPGs | global public goods |
| GPRS | Growth and Poverty Reduction Strategy |
| GPS | Ghana Partnership Strategy |
| HIPC | Heavily Indebted Poor Countries |
| HLF | Accra High Level Forum |
| ICU | Supreme Council of Islamic Courts Union |
| IDPs | Internally displaced persons |
| IDRC | International Development Research Centre |
| IFAPA | Inter-Faith Action for Peace in Africa |
| IMF | International Monetary Fund |
| IPC | Food Security and Humanitarian Phase Classification Map (of FSNAU) |
| IPRCC | International Poverty Reduction Centre in China |
| ISA | international strategic alliance |
| JBIC | Japan Bank for International Cooperation |
| JETRO | Japan External Trade Organization |
| JICA | Japan International Cooperation Agency |
| LDC | Less Developed Countries |
| LICUS | Low-Income Countries Under Stress |
| MCC | Millennium Challenge Corporation |
| MDC | Movement for Democratic Change (Zimbabwe) |
| MNCs | multinational corporations |
| MOFCOM | (China's) Ministries of Commerce |
| MONUC | UN Organization Mission in the Democratic Republic of the Congo |
| MOU | memorandum of understanding |
| NEPAD | New Partnership for Africa's Development |

| | |
|---|---|
| NGC | National Governing Council |
| NPoA | National Plan of Action |
| NRM | natural resource management |
| ODA | Official Development Assistance |
| OECD | Organization for Economic Cooperation and Development |
| OEEC | Organization for European Economic Cooperation |
| OFAC | Office of Foreign Assets Control (under U.S. Patriot Act) |
| OLS | Operation Lifeline Sudan (UN) |
| ONLF | Ogaden National Liberation Front |
| PAAERD | UN Programme of Action for African Economic Recovery and Development |
| PETS | Public Expenditure Tracking Survey |
| PFM | Public Financial Management |
| PMF | public financial management |
| PMMS | performance measurement and management systems |
| PPP | Purchasing Power Parity |
| PRIO | Peace Research Institute Oslo |
| PROCMURA | Programme for Christian-Muslim Relations in Africa |
| PRS | Poverty Reduction Strategy |
| PRSPs | Poverty Reduction Strategy Papers |
| PSNP | Productive Safety Net Programme |
| RGE | rural group enterprises |
| RWG | Redistribution with growth |
| SIDA | Swedish International Development Agency |
| SPA | Strategic Partnership with Africa |
| SPA-BSWG | Strategic Partnership with Africa Budget Support Working Group |
| SPLA | Sudan People's Liberation Army (Maxwell) |
| SWAp | sector-wide approaches |
| TFG | Transitional Federal Government |
| TNG | Transitional National Government |
| TPLF | Tigray People's Liberation Front |
| TRI | technical research institution |
| UCDP | Uppsala Conflict Data Program |
| UNECA | United Nations Economic Commission for Africa |
| UNMIL | UN Mission in Liberia |
| UNOSOM | UN Operation in Somalia |
| VCA | value chain analysis |

| | |
|---|---|
| WDI | World Development Indicators |
| WFP | World Food Programme |
| ZANU-PF | Zimbabwe African National Union–Patriotic Front |

# PREFACE AND ACKNOWLEDGMENTS

This book is the result of a conference titled "Problems, Promises, and Paradoxes of Aid: Africa's Experience," held at Cornell University, April 16–17, 2010. The conference was sponsored by Cornell's Institute for African Development in collaboration with the Cornell Center for a Sustainable Future, Cornell's Mario Einaudi Center for International Studies, and the Academic Network on Legal Empowerment of the Poor, University of Oslo. This is an interdisciplinary book looking at all aspects of aid including the delivery, impact, and effectiveness of aid.

The book considers the problems, effectiveness, and paradoxes of economic aid with special reference to Africa. The original aim of aid was to help alleviate a country's social problems without changing or altering basic social structures. Since then development aid has undergone a transformation from traditional aid to what is now termed development cooperation, partnership, or development assistance. With this transformation have come varied views surrounding aid effectiveness and the need for aid. In addition, the question of whether aid actually supports development has become a hotly debated topic.

With the signing of the Paris Declaration on Aid Effectiveness at the Paris High Level Forum II and the Accra Agenda for Action (AAA), the issue of aid has gained added prominence. The Paris Declaration is an unprecedented achievement for the international donor community and the partner governments committing themselves to key principles for aid reform. The AAA builds on the commitments agreed upon in the Paris Declaration.

Africa has, in recent years, joined the global search for mutually agreeable and workable aid relationships with the developed world. The New Partnership for Africa's Development (NEPAD) was adopted by the African Union in the quest for building new relationships with international partners based on mutual obligations, commitments, interests, and benefits. NEPAD places an emphasis on aid effectiveness, with a monitoring peer review mechanism to enhance mutual accountability of recipient countries and donors.

In light of the global economic downturn, the debate on aid has intensified. Aid skeptics claim that aid has failed or has achieved very little and that development aid has no effect on the speed with which countries develop. Aid advocates, however, argue that the role of aid in economic development is much more complex and multifaceted than the anti-aid advocates portray.

There is also argument about which form development aid should take in order to be effective. Should it, for example, focus on investing in infrastructure, health, training, and private activity? This would clearly be followed by the question: Is there any evidence that such aid-financed projects would be effective? A common criticism in recent years has been that rich countries have put so many conditions on aid (tied aid) that the conditions have reduced aid effectiveness; for example, some donor countries require the partner country to open up to foreign trade and investment, even though many of these countries may not be ready for it. In addition to country-to-country aid, development charities make up a vast web of non-governmental organizations, religious ministries, foundations, business donations, and college scholarships devoted to development aid. It has been observed that as the debate on aid ranges, an increasing number of African countries are beginning to step away from aid dependency as the domestic private sector becomes the engine of growth across much of Africa. Currently it is estimated that at least a third of African countries receive aid that is equivalent to less than 10 percent of their tax revenues (Gathigan 2012). On average, Africa has managed to raise an estimated $441 in taxes per person per year while receiving $41 per person per year in aid, according to *African Economic Outlook 2011* (African Development Bank Group 2011).

We begin this volume on aid by providing an overview of the academic literature that has evaluated the effectiveness of aid across countries. We then address the question: does aid support economic development? The chapters draw on a review of micro- and macroeconomic evidence, spanning four generations and decades of literature, including specific country studies. The volume examines the varied and evolving views and approaches to aid. It presents a comprehensive assessment of the role of aid in economic development, its approaches and its impact on development. The book offers recommendations on how aid can best be administered. In addition, some of the chapters provide country case studies illustrating how aid has worked in those countries. The chapters are written for the informed lay reader, with a minimum of methodological detail and a primary focus on descriptive, institutional, and policy factors. Each author has considerable knowledge and expertise in the subject matter of his or her chapter. The speakers' varied backgrounds reflect the conference's interdisciplinary focus; taken together the essays create an invaluable educational resource.

The conference could not have taken place and the book could not have been written without the help of many people. We would like to thank Ms. Evangeline Ray for her excellent editing and diligent preparation of the manuscript for publication, and Ms. Jackie Sayegh for her excellent work organizing the conference, without which this book would not have been possible. We also wish to thank research assistant Hanna Haile for the extremely helpful research she did for the book.

*—Muna Ndulo and Nicolas van de Walle*

# CHAPTER ONE

# INTRODUCTION

MUNA NDULO

Although the past century has marked great progress, ushering in the post-industrial digital age and greatly improved living standards in much of the world, Africa seems to lag behind the rapid advancements that have occurred in the rest of the world. Africa by and large continues to follow a vicious cycle of poverty and underdevelopment—in spite of its great natural resource base of petroleum, minerals, and other goods. This is as the result of a range of factors including the continent's political, economic, and social history. Many African states fall into a category of countries that Richard Miller defines as having "a substantial portion of inhabitants who are hard pressed to meet urgent material needs and with a technology of production which is as a whole significantly behind the world's most advanced countries (Miller 2010)." Wars, droughts, and other natural disasters, coupled with poor governance, corruption, and poor mitigation and adaptation capacities have exacerbated the situation.

More optimistic developmental trends have, however, been noted in recent years. According to an op-ed column in the *New York Times,* six of the world's ten fastest growing economies between 2001 and 2010 were in Africa (Kristof 2012). The International Monetary Fund forecasts that between 2011 and 2015, African countries will account for seven of the top ten spots (Kristof 2012). There are studies, for instance, that show a number of countries with a growth in GDP of about 6 percent per year, with the lowest point of inflation at below the two-digit level (Miller 2010). Although these rather recent improvements are taking place in less than half the continent, it is a positive step for sub-Saharan African countries, which had lagged behind on many economic indicators since attaining autonomous governance about a half-century ago (Arbache, Go, and Page 2008). The need to consolidate gains and to attain more rapid growth is clear as the recorded development still falls far short of what is required to lift the great majority of people out of poverty. We need to vigorously pursue more holistic, sustainable development programs, aiming not merely to increase GDP but also to ensure poverty reduction, environmental justice, respect for human rights, transparency, and accountability.

While there is general agreement that poverty reduction and achievement of development in sub-Saharan Africa are matters of great importance, there is no consensus with respect to the question of what the best means for achieving these ends are. Official development assistance or aid has been the default resort for a long time, not only to alleviate urgent stresses but also to provide capital for long-term development. It has, however, ignited controversies and debates. Many people believe that aid is either stolen by corrupt leaders or wasted on ineffective programs, while yet another argument holds that, for a variety of reasons, aid does not work even when it gets to its intended recipients. There is, however, no consensus on how huge investments could be financed in the short term other than by an increase in aid.

## What is Aid?

A working definition of aid is key to understanding the dynamics of aid architecture and the controversies surrounding it in the African context. Aid or official development assistance generally refers to the transfer of resources, capital, and/or technical assistance from a donor to a recipient country.[1]

Not everyone agrees on how the term aid should be defined. Is aid a tangible or an intangible item? Is it concrete, or should we focus on the abstract elements? Should we conceive of aid as the actual amount that was put to proper use, carving out whatever amount was not put to effective use? The classic approach is to define aid in broad terms, encompassing all of the resource flows from the developed world into the developing or underdeveloped world (Ryrie 1995). Others have suggested that "real aid" or aid that has brought about sustainable development or immediate welfare to the poor should be the focus (Thomas 2011, 7). There is also the tendency to regard aid given out of generosity as a dole or gift (Bauer 1972).[2] In addition, some insist that official development assistance comprises not only the actual object that is being transferred but also the relationship that has been forged between the developed world and the developing world as a result of this transfer of resources (Pomerantz 2004, 8). For this reason, the definition of aid would be incomplete without the intangible element.

Aid comes in several forms, such as money, subsidized loans, food, medications, technical assistance, and technology transfer. Categorization of aid assistance has a temporal as well as a functional element. Based on the purpose for which it is given, aid broadly conceived can be categorized into either development or humanitarian aid. Humanitarian aid is meant to relieve immediate stresses caused by sudden-onset humanitarian emergencies. It is given as a short-term response to prevent a humanitarian crisis in the wake of a natural or anthropogenic disaster and consists of providing bare necessities for survival, including food and medicine. Development aid has the end of fostering long-term socioeconomic development and independence. This type of assistance could be project-specific or program-specific.

## Arguments for and against Aid

Questions have been raised as to whether aid is really the answer to Africa's developmental needs. The concerns raised are three-fold: the reasons for the grant of aid, the conditionality attached to it, and its effectiveness—its administration and whether it actually benefits the populations it was intended to help.

*Motivations behind the Grant of Aid:* Realists and internationalists or liberalists offer contrasting explanations for the motivations behind aid allocations (Selbervik 1999, 30–31).[3] Realists and neo-realists agree that, with the exception of humanitarian aid, a donor country will offer aid only when the donor country has a certain interest in the recipient country and stands to gain from the creation of an aid relationship with that country (Omoruyi 2001, 29). The idea is that the donor country is motivated merely by the pursuit of security and strategic or political objectives (Selbervik 1999, 30–31). Therefore, the motives behind providing aid may be to maintain diplomatic relations, to encourage military allies, to exert political influence, to expand markets, to extend cultural influence, to pursue a religious agenda, to counter terrorism and fundamentalist Islam, and so on. The idea is that all sovereign states determine their national interests without any outside interference in the somewhat anarchic international system. However, the way in which sovereign states will act and influence the international system is different for realists and neo-realists.[4] For realists, the only sub-Saharan African countries that are of interest to donors are those either rich in natural resources or possessing geo-political strategic benefits to the donor countries. Policy/security motives (such as those of the U.S. and Russia during the cold war) need to be distinguished from commercial motives, which Lehman in this book argues shaped Japanese aid.

The liberal or internationalist counterpart to this theory on aid is predicated on the premise that state interests are determined by international as well as domestic conditions. For this reason, the liberalist emphasis is that aid assistance should be given because all regions of the world are important to states and humanity, and poverty is a common problem for all people (Omoruyi 2001, 30–31). Some, like philosopher Richard Miller, assert that developed countries have a responsibility to help developing and underdeveloped countries based on the "Principle of Sympathy" grounded in respect (Miller 2010).

On the ground, however, this realist-internationalist divide is not always clear-cut. Foreign aid policies are usually driven by motivations that have elements of both the internationalist and realist theories (Omoruyi 2001, 48). Omoruyi's study of motivations behind aid allocations in the post-cold war era, for instance, shows that internationalist theory is more evident as morality appears to be one of the driving forces for aid allocation, while the realist motivation based on national interest is less evident in the findings, but both are at play in the aid architecture. At the same time, it should not be forgotten that there are people in rich countries who are genuinely concerned about the welfare of those in low-income countries and who give aid for purely altruistic reasons. There are people who care about the suffering of others and who express their care by making significant donations (Gates 2012).

*Ineffectiveness of Aid:* Another argument against aid is that it is not designed to promote economic development. According to this argument, aid has been ineffective insofar as many of the communities it was targeted to help are still underdeveloped and still grapple with lack of infrastructure, disease, and food insecurity. Aid is seen by some as crippling the capacity of the recipient nation by fostering passive dependency and encouraging corruption. Instead, this argument goes, the focus should be on private investment and more work, which would lead to more ambition and growth. Some of the offered explanations for the ineffectiveness of aid are as follows.

Institutional pessimists argue that recipient country institutions are influenced by foreign aid through the interaction of political power and economic interest at play in the giving of aid. This results in corruption and ineffective use of aid. For instance, the argument is that foreign aid makes political institutions of recipient countries more dictatorial than they had been without the aid and fosters more corruption. The counter-argument offered by institutional optimists is that aid affects the institutions of recipient countries positively. For instance, aid could create democracy in places where it had not previously existed. Nabamita Dutta et al. (2011) offer a third alternative, which they call the "amplification" effect, signifying that foreign aid merely fortifies the political institutions that predated the grant of aid. If the institutions were previously democratic, they will become more democratic; if they were dictatorial, they will become even more dictatorial.

The structural position asserts that foreign aid causes underdevelopment because it strengthens the power imbalance between rich and poor countries. Dambisa Moyo (2009), for instance, concludes that the overreliance on aid has trapped African nations in a "vicious circle of aid dependency, corruption, market distortion, and further poverty, leaving them with nothing but the need for more aid." Gates (2012) argues that this claim is not convincing. He cites for example the fact that over the past fifty years, the number of children who die annually has been reduced from 20 million to fewer than 8 million. Meanwhile, the proportion of people living in extreme poverty has declined by more than half. He argues that these massive improvements are due in large part to aid-funded programs that, for example, buy vaccines and boost farmers' productivity. The Blair Commission on Africa points out that budget support to Tanzania has enabled the government there to double per capita spending on education. The same assistance made it possible for Tanzania to introduce in 2002 a policy of free and compulsory education benefiting 1.6 million children. Tarp observes in this book that the question of whether aid is or is not beneficial is not as simple as it may appear. He concludes that there is no indication of harmful effects from foreign aid and that on the whole aid does promote economic growth in the recipient countries.

*Conditionality:* Development assistance is seldom given without any strings attached. There are mixed views on whether this political conditionality is interference or "the legitimate support of budding democratic tendencies (Hofmeier 1991)." The conditionality that is attached to the grant of aid can be either political or economical, or a combination of both. Historically donors have used conditionalities to pursue their own security and commercial interests. While some emphasize the need to incorporate conditionalities that promote social objectives and human rights, others dismiss conditionalities as ineffective and useless for that reason (Burnell 1997).

## A Brief History of Aid

For much of the twentieth century, aid has been pumped into African economies. And although the ideas and institutions for aid to Africa can be traced to the European colonial period, for the purposes of this chapter, the history of aid can be classified into four periods: pre-World War II, World War II, post-World War II, and the post-cold war period.

## Pre-World War II

Although it is difficult to pinpoint a time in history when aid began, there is general agreement that prior to World War II, the types of foreign aid consisted mainly of military support. Donor countries gave their military support to a warring party that was of some strategic significance to the donor country.[5] In addition, European colonial powers shipped capital and finished products to their colonies. However, it is questionable whether this can be seen as foreign aid since these goods were sent in exchange for raw materials shipped to Europe; besides, the colonies were non-autonomous units that were administered by the European powers (Aid Watch n.d.).[6]

## World War II and the Cold War Period

A series of events of particular significance to the aid architecture narrative came about as World War II drew to a close. These included the creation of the United Nations, the establishment of global financial institutions—the World Bank and the International Monetary Fund—at Bretton Woods, and the United States' foreign policy known as the Marshall Aid Plan (Cumming 2001). These institutions have been major actors in international development as throughout the years they have overseen or made possible the international distribution of funds, whether in the form of loans, subsidies, or aid.

Following the Second World War, the U.S. formulated the Marshall Aid Plan, which provided more than US$12 billion in aid to war-shattered economies in Western Europe between 1948 and 1951 (Cumming 2001). This was the first large-scale foreign assistance program. Although aid was viewed as a means of reconstructing war-devastated countries economies and helping them to industrialize, another driving reason for this grant was to curb Soviet influence in Western Europe and to discourage the communist parties in recipient countries from becoming stronger.[7] Throughout the 1950s the cold war remained the driving force for aid relations. In the following decade the economies of Western Europe began to recover and the recipient countries were able to stand on their own feet.

In the 1960s, decolonization began to take place in much of Africa and Asia, and aid focus turned to the newly established states. These new states did not have the same level of development as their former colonial powers, and the importance of tackling poverty and promoting development became increasingly clear (Aid Watch n.d.). There are two conflicting views on what the driving force for aid relations between the West and the newly established states was. On the one hand, there are arguments that with the collaboration created by the UN, the World Bank, and the IMF, the grounds for which aid was given were mainly eliminating poverty and achieving development. Some argue, however, that the new relationship was tantamount to neo-colonialism. Western powers wished to provide aid to Francophone and Anglophone Africa lest they become Soviet satellites. At this point, although most Western European countries had fairly robust economies, lacking colonial or geopolitical interests in Africa they did not wish to participate in providing aid driven by cold war politics. France, Belgium, and Britain, however, continued to be involved with their former colonies in various ways, including the provision of aid.[8] The cold war continued to serve as the force behind development assistance agendas during the 1970s and 1980s. To some extent in recent times the cold war has been replaced by the fight against terrorism and the spread of political Islam.

The 1970s was marked by a shift in the approach to aid assistance. A more "human" approach focusing on social considerations such as health (life expectancy, infant mortality rates, and disease), education, income distribution, gender equality, and institutions and governance, rather than simply macroeconomic growth, were beginning to inform the decision to grant aid assistance (Aid Watch n.d.).

## The Post-Cold War Era

In the post-cold war era official development assistance (aid) continues to play a major role in international development. Most of the aid originates either from members of the Organization for Economic Cooperation and Development (OECD) or from a new entrant—China—which is becoming increasingly important. In post-conflict societies, aid has been given as part of some peacekeeping programs and to promote transitions to democracy and capitalism in former communist countries.[9] In post-conflict societies aid has the potential to contribute to conflict prevention through its effects on the growth and level of income, which are key factors in reducing the risk of renewed conflict. In the African context, humanitarian assistance continues to be provided through the present day as for example in Somalia, Durfur, and Eastern Congo.

## The Way Forward

This book is an anthology of essays contributing new scholarship to the contemporary aid discourse. It provides an interdisciplinary investigation of the role of aid in African development, compiling the work of historians, political scientists, legal scholars, and economists to examine the reasons for the failure of aid. It offers a new perspective into how aid can be made more effective so that African communities can actually reap the intended benefits. Questions regarding the effectiveness of aid are addressed by looking at specific case studies of donor as well as recipient countries. Questions of ownership are addressed and examined in the context of two debates. The first, addressed especially by Nic van de Walle and Phyllis Pomerantz in their respective chapters, is about "ownership": to what extent should aid be designed by the recipient country itself? This has especially been an issue in the years since the Paris Declaration. The second part of the ownership debate concerns whether aid should focus on "need" or "performance." In other words, should donors direct aid to the poorest countries, regardless of their policies and level of governance, or should aid "reward" countries who are doing the right thing? What would be the implications of such a policy for poor states considered undeserving of aid? What is the likelihood of such states falling into a deep hole as failed states? The future of aid is also addressed: should aid continue to be a part of the development agenda of developing/ underdeveloped countries in sub-Saharan Africa? If so, how much and what type of aid is needed, and how it can be made most effective?

The general refrain of the essays presented here is that economic indicators alone do not fully reflect a country's level of development. A range of factors that show the well-being of communities—such as the protection of human rights—should be taken into consideration when measuring the level of development that has been achieved. The major criticism against aid is that it cripples the recipient country's economic growth by turning it into a passive receiver; aid is seen as a disincentive for people to work. In addition, it has been noted that aid has been mostly supply-driven, not demand-driven. The availability of aid depends upon donors, not on the actual needs of recipients. For this reason, aid may not meet the desired goals in the society it was intended to help. The governments of donor and recipient countries also play a major role. Inefficient and corrupt governance will mean that aid does not always reach the targeted groups. It might also be that aid is an instrument for creating political alliances and not really given for altruistic reasons. Lack of public participation and lack of disclosure create little understanding of what is really happening, either among Africans or among Westerners. The attached conditions may not always be compatible with developmental agendas of the countries receiving the assistance. Moreover, aid donors may not take into account the sociocultural context in which aid is being given; assistance programs should seek not only to fix short-term problems but also to empower aid recipients through education, technical assistance, or technology transfer.

Hence, the themes that run through the chapters of the book are that donors ought to meet the needs of the communities they want to help, consulting with them and providing them with some measure of ownership and say in the assistance that is given. Donors need to understand the sociocultural context, to protect human rights, and to be guided by principles of social and environmental justice. Other suggested strategies for making aid more effective include peer review, self-assessment, empowerment of women, encouraging accountability, investing in agriculture, helping smallholder subsistence farmers, introducing ethical and professional standards for civil service, and raising the competence of civil servants.

## Organization of the Book

The book is comprised of thirteen chapters. Following this introductory chapter, Finn Tarp (chapter two) investigates the aggregate impact of aid on country-wide indicators, particularly economic growth. He warns that the question is not as simple as it may appear. Drawing on macroeconomic and microeconomic data spanning forty years, he concludes that there is no indication of harmful effects from foreign aid. He finds that aid does provide developmental benefits to the recipient countries, although these benefits are not as significant as they are claimed to be. He provides an overview of the academic literature that has evaluated the effectiveness of aid across countries. The focus is on the aggregate impact of aid; that is, its effect on country-wide indicators, particularly economic growth. The chapter first provides some essential background to these debates and then examines the question of whether aid supports economic development. Methodological difficulties mean that it is hard to provide a definitive and comprehensive conclusion. The chapter concludes that aid should never be considered to be a "solution" in itself to poverty.

In chapter three, Esau Kaakunga provides an empirical investigation of the impacts of foreign aid on economic development in Namibia through a simple endogenous growth model. He concludes that introducing more aid will contribute to economic development in Namibia as long as the government invests in infrastructure and education with a view to promoting economic growth.

In chapter four, Nicolas van de Walle explores the difficulties of implementing the Paris Declaration 2005 recommendations regarding recipient country ownership, particularly in those countries where there is low state capacity and a systematic deficiency in governance. Van de Walle notes that calls to promote country ownership were initially designed to reform aid modalities in countries with good governance and democratic politics, where, it was thought, greater responsibility should be taken in the design and implementation of aid in order to improve its effectiveness. The concept of ownership is ambiguous, however, and the chapter suggests that two distinctive definitions of ownership have often muddled the debate about the implications of ownership promotion by donors. Over time, moreover, the ambition to promote ownership has led donors to extend these new modalities to countries with many governance problems, and this has had predictably bad outcomes. The chapter concludes with the recommendation that we not give up on greater ownership, but pursue it only in countries that have demonstrated the capability and motivation to promote democratic development.

In chapter five, Phyllis Pomerantz notes that global programs have expanded dramatically over the past decade. In certain circumstances, they may be invaluable in the supply of underprovided global public goods. However in a number of cases, global programs are either creating additional difficulties for country-based programs or replicating problems that recent reforms in aid have sought to mitigate or eliminate. Also, many of these programs are mischaracterized as aid, adding to mounting confusion and contradictions on the aid scene. Phyllis Pomerantz compares global programs and local based programs with the finding that global programs are either creating additional difficulties for country-based aid programs or replicating problems that recent reforms in aid have sought to mitigate or eliminate. Drawing from the metaphor of the tortoise and the hare, she concludes that country-based programs are probably more effective in terms of poverty reduction.

In chapter six, Aaron Chassy reflects on the fact that bi- and multilateral donor support for strengthening civil society has not been examined in comparison to donor support for other development sectors. In recent years such support has been tied to civil society support for state-led programs and public sector reforms. Chassy discusses the bottom-up push for reform, a move among civil society organizations to counter the process controlled by state actors who are only going through the motions of reform to satisfy donors' conditions—now more fashionably referred to as performance milestones—for disbursement of funds. These state actors are for the most part unwilling to include civil society organizations in any meaningful way in design, implementation, or monitoring of reforms because most African states remain authoritarian and predatory to varying degrees. Many civil society organizations, which are chronically in need of operational and programming support, have little choice but to go along with the charade and participate in the policy reform process. In return for their willingness to raise public awareness about and mobilize public support for the reforms, they receive small grants that are usually limited to covering the costs associated with activity implementation. As a result empty shell reforms receive the patina of legitimacy from civil society participation without any measurable change in the levels of inclusion, competition, or the quality of governance. This chapter offers a strategy and sequence that is designed to enable donors and participants to design a more effective approach to strengthening civil society's institutional development.

Daniel Maxwell in chapter seven examines the politicization of humanitarian aid through a historical overview of instances where aid has been turned into a means of achieving political or security objectives. He examines four case studies from Sudan, Somalia, Ethiopia, and Zimbabwe.

In chapter eight, Kojo Busia looks into whether or not the African Peer Review Mechanism (APRM) could enhance democratic governance in Africa and whether it has the potential, in contrast to previous experiments with externally determined reform agendas foisted on African states, to improve state-society relations in Africa through a new approach to African governance capitalizing on African ownership in conception, design, roll-out, implementation, and ongoing evaluation. The chapter looks into issues around the creation of the APRM as a central component of Africa's new development agenda and the significance of APRM in the context of the new paradigm of development cooperation for aid effectiveness. Dr. Busia also looks at the transformation the APRM is bringing about in social and state relations of African countries—a transformation that will lead to emphasis on domestic accountability to citizens rather than external accountability to donors. He compares donor approaches to strengthening governance and looks at how the APRM is informing a perspective of domestic accountability. The discussion of governance is relevant to the theme of the book as one of the recurring challenges in most of Africa is lack of effective governance systems and accountable governance.

Nikolas Emmanuel examines the connection between foreign aid and peace implementation in chapter nine. He argues that aid offered in post-conflict situations can signify a peace dividend offered by the external power in exchange for terminating a war; this could serve as an incentive during the negotiation and implementation stages of the peace settlement. In addition, he examines the primary aid patterns that are used in post-conflict situations and intrastate conflicts as well as the theoretical and technical literature for alternative explanations concerning what may increase or diminish the ability of negotiated settlements to succeed and endure. He also provides a quantitative analysis of donor aid based on the success of peace settlements in Africa during the past fifteen years by looking at sixty-five negotiated settlements during that period.

In chapter ten, Haley Swedlund asks the question: Should we fund the state? Direct budget support, or aid disbursed directly into the general treasury of the receiving country, allows recipients to utilize their own allocation, procurement, and accounting structures. The chapter analyzes Rwanda's experience with direct general budget support, where aid is disbursed directly into the general treasury of the country, and poses the question of whether this increases coordination, ownership, and government capacity. Supporters argue that general budget support directly aligns with the Paris Declaration on Aid Effectiveness (2005) and the Accra Agenda for Action (2008). The chapter explores whether or not direct budget support actually increases coordination, government capacity, and ownership, with particular emphasis on how ownership plays out in practice.

In chapter eleven, Cecelia Lynch examines the way that faith-based groups provide aid and the ethical paradoxes they face in their work by analyzing the experiences in Kenya and Cameroon. She first maps the organizational trends of the two countries to find out the way in which aid organizations operate in Africa. Scholars are increasingly coming to grips with the role of faith-based organizations in providing humanitarian assistance, in terms of both emergency relief and development programs. The argument in favor of faith-based aid is that religious groups already exist in difficult-to-reach areas and are already trusted by their constituent members, while the argument against is that faith-based aid is either tied to proselytizing or promotes religious exclusivism and, potentially, conflict.

Moses Kigundu (chapter twelve) observes that although China and Canada share deep historical and institutional roots as major donors of aid and development assistance to Africa, their operations are conducted separately. He provides a brief overview of Canadian and Chinese aid programs in Africa and then examines how the two nations might cooperate. The chapter presents the concepts and applications of international strategic alliances, value chain analysis including hybrid value chains, and organizational cluster development as these apply to Africa's aid and development. Kiggundu concludes by examining the prospects for and challenges in making such alliances work as well as the possibility of aid agencies and investors using the model as a template for future collaboration with the Chinese in Africa.

In chapter thirteen, Howard Lehman compares Japan's lengthy relationship with African countries to the emergence of China's assertive foreign policy in Africa. He argues that China's active and extensive intervention on the continent has usurped Japan's distinctive approach to foreign aid. The second part of the chapter takes up Ghana as a case study. Lehman highlights the determinants, strategies, policies, and comparative advantages of Japanese aid to Ghana and Japan's position of supporting the strategic objectives and priorities of the Ghana Growth and Poverty Reduction Strategy Policy. He argues that Japan's official development assistance policy makes important departures from the widely accepted ideology and policy objectives of the Washington consensus. He first highlights the macro-level themes of Japanese national development and then examines the micro-level goals of its foreign aid policy in Ghana.

## Notes

[1] The Britannica Academica defines foreign aid as "the international transfer of capital, goods, or services from a country or international organization for the benefit of the recipient country or its population." http://www.britannica.com/EBchecked/topic/213344/foreign-aid/256255/History

[2] In the words of Bauer, foreign aid is the transfer of resources from the hands of the taxpayer of the donor country to the government of the recipient country.

[3] Hilde Selbervik focuses on two perspectives in international relations, the realist and internationalist (liberalist). While the realist perspective stresses that international relations is a question of self-interest and power, which is based in either human nature (classic realist thought, Morgenthau 1948) or the anarchy that exists in the international system (neo-realism, Waltz 1979), the internationalist perspective sees the state—which, realizing the importance of international interdependence, will seek peaceful conflict resolution and cooperation—as the principal actor.

[4] Conventional realism argues that states will provide aid so long as their interests are met in doing so, and neo-realists believe that a state will try to expand its economic, political and territorial control and rearrange the international system pursuant to its interests.

[5] www.britannica.com/EBchecked/topic/213344/foreign-aid/256255/History

[6] "However, the aid was not aimed at bringing about real economic development, rather it only benefitted urban elites and colonial business interests."

[7] At the end of World War II, the United Nations and international financial institutions (IFIs)—the International Bank for Reconstruction and Development (IBRD or World Bank) and the International Monetary Fund (IMF)—were founded to

raise capital for the reconstruction of Europe and Japan. The original aim of the IMF was to promote international monetary stability.

[8] The Britannica Online also asserts, "The postwar programs of the United Kingdom, France, and other European former colonial powers grew out of the assistance they had provided to their colonial possessions."

[9] www.britannica.com/EBchecked/topic/213344/foreign-aid/256255/History

## References

African Development Bank Group. 2011. "African Economic Outlook 2011."

Aid Watch. n.d. "A Brief History of Aid." Available at: http://aidwatch.org.au/where-is-your-aid-money-going/what-is-aid/a-brief-history-of-aid. Accessed June 27, 2012.

Arbache, J., D.S. Go, and J. Page. 2008. "Is Africa's Economy at a Turning Point?" In *Africa at a Turning Point: Growth, Aid and External Shocks,* eds. D. S. Go and J. Page. Washington DC: The World Bank, 13.

Bauer, P. 1972. *Dissent on Development.* Cambridge: Harvard University Press.

Blair Commission on Africa. 2010. "Commission on Africa Report: Still our Common Interest." Office of Tony Blair, September 20. http://www.tonyblairoffice.org/news/entry/commisison-for-africa-2010-still-our-common-interest/. Accessed July 9, 2012.

Britannica. n.d. Definition of "foreign aid." Available at: http://www.britannica.com/EBchecked/topic/213344/foreign-aid/256255/History. Accessed June 28, 2012.

Burnell, P. 1997. "The Changing Politics of Foreign Aid: Where to Next?" *Politics* 7:2, 117–125.

Cumming, G. 2001. *Aid to Africa: French and British Policies from the Cold War to the New Millennium.* Ashgate Publishing.

Dutta, N., P. T. Leeson, and C. R. Williamson. 2011. "The Amplification Effect: Foreign Aid's Impact on Political Institutions." Available at SSRN: http://ssrn.com/abstract=988841.

Gates, B. 2012. "The Truth About Foreign Aid." *New York Times,* January 26. Op-ed. http://www.nytimes.com/2012/01/27/opinion/the-truth-about-foreign-aid.html. Accessed July 9, 2012.

Gathigan, M. 2012. "Africa Begins to Rise Above Aid." *The Guardian,* January 19. Available at http://www.guardian.co.uk/global-development/2012/jan/19/africa-rising-above-aid-dependency. Accessed June 28, 2012.

Hofmeier, R. 1991. "Political Conditions Attached to Development Aid for Africa." *Intereconomics* 26:3, 122–127. Available at: http://dx.doi.org/10.1007/BF02926122.

Kristof, N.D. 2012. "Africa on the Rise." *New York Times,* June 30, Op-ed. http://www.nytimes.com/2012/07/01/opinion/sunday/africa-on-the-rise.html. Accessed July 9, 2012.

Mbeki, M. 2009. *Architects of Poverty: Why African Capitalism Needs Changing.* Picador, Africa.

Miller, R. W. 2010. *Globalizing Justice: The Ethics of Poverty and Power.* New York: Oxford University Press.

Moyo, D. 2009. *Dead Aid: Why Aid is Not Working and How There is a Better Way for Africa.* New York: Farrar, Strauss, and Giroux.

Omoruyi, L. O. 2001. *Contending Theories on Development Aid: Post-Cold War Evidence from Africa.* Ashgate Publishing Limited.

Pomerantz, P. R. 2004. *Aid Effectiveness in Africa: Developing Trust between Donors and Governments.* Lanham: Lexington Books.

Ryrie, W. 1995. *First World, Third World.* Houndmills, Basingstoke, Hampshire, and London: MacMillan Press Ltd.

Selbervik, H. 1999. "Aid and Conditionality. The Role of the Bilateral Donor: A Case Study of the Norwegian-Tanzanian Aid Relationship." *Norad,* July, 30–31.

Thomas, A. 2011. "Real Aid 3: Ending Aid Dependency." *ActionAid,* September 15.

# CHAPTER TWO

# AID EFFECTIVENESS

CHANNING ARNDT, SAM JONES
AND FINN TARP

## Introduction

The question of foreign aid's impact on economic growth is highly controversial and excites polarized opinions. Optimistic views of aid are exemplified by those of Jeffrey Sachs (2005), who calls for a doubling of worldwide aid flows as a moral obligation of rich countries that will "send forth mighty currents of hope" and lead to "the end of poverty." In contrast, William Easterly (2001, 2003, 2006) is a vocal skeptic, highlighting aid's apparent historic inability to buy growth. And today, in the midst of a serious global economic crisis, where aid is arguably more needed than ever, the attention of both the aid community and decision-makers is on "dead aid" (Moyo 2009), which argues for a complete cessation of aid flows to Africa.

This chapter provides an overview of the academic literature that has evaluated the effectiveness of aid across countries. Focus is on the aggregate impact of aid, that is, on its effect on country-wide indicators, particularly economic growth. Sections 2 and 3 of the chapter provide some essential background to these debates, while section 4 provides an answer to the core question: does aid support economic growth? Section 5 summarizes lessons from the literature, and section 6 concludes.

To answer the core question the authors draw on a review of both microeconomic and macroeconomic evidence spanning four generations and more than forty years of literature. The question in focus is not as simple as it may appear. Methodological difficulties are many, as carefully outlined by Temple (2010). Even so, there is very little to suggest that foreign aid has a consistent harmful effect across countries over time, and a balanced view of the literature and the data indicate that foreign aid does provide growth and development benefits to recipients. These benefits are not as large as sometimes argued, and they accrue over considerable time frames of thirty years or more. Thus, aid in itself should never be considered a “solution” to poverty.

## Why Are Some Countries Poor?

The disparities in living standards across countries in the world today are spectacularly large. Using per capita income figures, the average citizen of a wealthy country consumes about as much in a few days as the average citizen of many poor countries consumes in a year. Adjusted for differences in purchasing power, the gap narrows somewhat. Even so, the differences are so large that they defy precise measurement. Rough adjustments for purchasing power imply differentials in per capita income/consumption between wealthy and poor countries of about fifty times. Large differences also exist using other measures of well-being such as life expectancy, educational attainment, and infant mortality.

A proximate cause of this chasm in living standards relates to productive capacity. Poor countries simply do not produce very much. Economists typically view the productive capacity of an economy as being a function of stocks of factors of production, especially *physical capital* (factories, tools, computers, roads, etc.); *human capital* (workers with skills) and labor (workers without skills); as well as *technology*. Economists also posit a crucial role for *institutions,* which provide frameworks for organizing these factors in a manner that is productive. Poor countries lack physical capital, human capital, technology, and well-functioning institutions. This results in a poorly producing labor force, with negative implications for nearly all aspects of well-being.

There are some common elements to accumulating these four attributes that help to explain their relative absence in poor countries. First, they all accumulate through long-run processes. City buildings in most developed countries reflect more than a century of cumulative construction. Converting an infant into a highly skilled engineer takes at least two decades. While technological leaps are possible, technology improvement is mainly a slow evolutionary process conducted via repeated trial and error. Finally, institutions also evolve slowly over time; for example, British common law is based on centuries of case experience.

Second, accumulating physical and human capital, technology and institutions generally requires a forward-looking mind set; one must typically sacrifice something today in order to benefit in the future. This can be very difficult when current resources are highly constrained and people are unable to satisfy their basic needs. In this case there is no scope for saving.

Third, accumulation of these attributes relies on public-private partnerships. Even strongly market-oriented economies such as the United States rely on the public sector to educate the work force, to supply basic economic infrastructure such as roads and bridges, and to fund research and development for new technologies. This highlights the important role of institutions both for current and future production levels.

Finally, unless very well established, all four of these accumulation processes are highly vulnerable to disruption. At the extreme, years of effort can be wiped out in short order. As a prominent example, wars destroy both physical and human capital. More subtle disruptions can also have serious impacts. Experience indicates that nascent institutions are particularly vulnerable to disruption (Arndt 2000; Berg 1993). Even a relatively short period of neglect can substantially harm long-run efforts at institution building.

In summary, to improve living standards significantly, poor countries must produce more—much more. To produce more, poor countries must initiate and maintain long-run cumulative processes to build physical and human capital, acquire technology, and nurture institutions that facilitate growth. The role of aid for development, broadly conceived, is to support these long-run cumulative processes. The success of the aid enterprise in accomplishing this objective is the focus of this paper. However, before reviewing the debate about whether aid "works" from a broad macroeconomic perspective, it is helpful to start with some background about aid. The next section provides a definition of foreign aid, describes how it has changed over time, and indicates recent trends.

## What is Foreign Aid?

### Definitions

Foreign aid takes many forms. The most important in terms of its size and influence is official aid. The definition of official development assistance (ODA) is provided by the Development Assistance Committee (DAC) of the Organization for Economic Cooperation and Development (OECD). ODA is calculated as the sum of grants and loans that: (a) are undertaken by the official sector of the donor country on behalf of recipient countries; (b) have as the main objective the promotion of economic development and welfare in recipient countries; and (c) are on concessional financial terms (i.e., with a grant element equal to at least 25 percent of the total). In addition to these financial flows, technical cooperation costs are included in ODA, but grants, loans and credits for military purposes are excluded. Transfer payments to private individuals, donations from the public, commercial loans and foreign direct investment (FDI) are not counted. Moreover, while it is common to treat ODA and foreign aid as the same thing, this is misleading. Assistance funded by non-governmental organizations (NGOs), which is foreign aid but not ODA, has grown significantly in the past twenty-five years and now equals about one-third of official assistance.

The above definition indicates that foreign aid is not always a free resource transfer and often arrives with economic and political conditions. In many cases, official donors require that recipient countries pursue reforms or policies that the donors feel should promote economic growth or development, and aid may also be tied, which reduces its effectiveness. With respect to the multilateral development finance institutions, such as the International Monetary Fund (IMF) and the World Bank, these requirements are often known as stabilization and adjustment conditions. However, these conditions have been the source of much controversy. Some scholars have argued that the very policy reforms suggested by these institutions have been counterproductive and caused economic and social decline rather than growth.

One should also recognize that aid is often given for very different purposes—e.g., building infrastructure, expanding access to education, or responding to humanitarian emergencies. It is also the case that aid may be given primarily with an eye to the interests of donors (or firms from donor countries) rather than the interests of recipients. In a review of aid allocation patterns, for example, McGillivray (2003) finds that past colonial links and political alliances are major determinants of foreign aid and that such strategic factors are at least as important as variables that reflect recipient needs (see also Alesina and Dollar, 2000). At the same time, and as the next section demonstrates, official aid flows have not been static. Very different motives have driven aid relationships over time, particularly as global conditions and dominant ideas have changed.

## Foreign aid in historical perspective

In its modern form, foreign aid had its origins in the early 1940s and intensified after the disruption that followed World War II. The international economic system had collapsed, and war-ravaged Europe faced a critical shortage of capital and an acute need for physical reconstruction. The response was the European Recovery Program, commonly known as the Marshall Plan. During the peak years the U.S. transferred some 2–3 percent of its national income to help restore Europe (approximately 20–

30 times the foreign assistance the U.S. provides today as a share of national income). The Marshall Plan, which was administered by the Organization for European Economic Cooperation (OEEC), the predecessor of the OECD, was highly successful.

It is useful to highlight distinctions between post-war Europe and the developing countries that have been the focus of foreign aid for the past four decades. In the aftermath of the World War II, Europe primarily lacked physical capital. To be sure, the war killed a great many highly skilled people, damaged some institutions, and forced institutional change. Nevertheless, compared with the developing countries, post-war Europe was very well endowed with skilled people and institutional frameworks. Furthermore, before and during the War, European countries operated at the leading edge of technology. Hence, the fundamental missing element was capital, which foreign aid provided. The impressive results achieved by the Marshall Plan fuelled highly optimistic expectations about the future effectiveness of foreign aid.

After the success of the Marshall Plan, the attention of industrialized nations turned to the developing countries, many of which became independent during the 1960s. Economic growth in a state-led planning tradition became a key objective during the 1950s and 1960s, and it was widely believed that poverty and inequality would be quickly eliminated through growth and modernization ("trickle-down economics"). While the Marshall Plan was built around support to finance general categories of imports and strengthen the balance of payments (i.e., program aid), beginning in the early 1950s project aid became the dominant aid modality. Some donors continued to supply program aid, but aid was increasingly disbursed for the implementation of specific capital investment projects and associated technical assistance.

The multilateralism of aid became more pronounced after the mid-1970s. Multilateral channels were at the time seen as more efficient and less political than bilateral aid, so the UN, the World Bank, and other multilateral agencies expanded their activities considerably. The 1970s also saw an increased focus on employment, income distribution, and poverty alleviation as essential objectives of development and foreign aid. The effectiveness of trickle-down economics was widely questioned, and new strategies referred to as "basic human needs" (BHN) and "redistribution with growth" (RWG) were formulated and propagated alongside more radical "dependency" theories of development. Nevertheless, the typical project aid modality remained largely unchanged.

The "golden era" of the 1960s and 1970s came to an abrupt end at the beginning of the 1980s. The second oil shock, occurring in 1979, reversed economic conditions and brought on a large increase in interest rates due to economic stabilization policies adopted by developed countries. The international debt crisis erupted, and macroeconomic imbalances were widespread among developing countries. On the political scene, Ronald Reagan and Margaret Thatcher came to power in the U.S. and the U.K. respectively, and at the World Bank Anne Krueger became Vice President and Chief Economist, replacing Hollis Chenery. Economic circumstances in the developing countries and relations between the North and South changed radically. The crisis hit hard, especially in many African countries. The focus on development strategy and policy shifted to internal domestic policy failure, and achieving macroeconomic balance (externally and internally) became widely perceived as an essential prerequisite for renewed development. In addition, "trade not aid" became the dominant slogan among many leaders and economists.

During the 1980s, the goal of reducing the role of the state in the economy turned into a rallying call. Reliance on market forces, an outward orientation, and the role of the private sector—including NGOs—were emphasized by the World Bank and others. In parallel, poverty alleviation slipped out of view in mainstream agendas for economic reform, but remained at the centre of attention in more unorthodox thinking such as the "adjustment with a human face" approach of UNICEF. At the same time, bilateral donors and international agencies struggled with how to channel resources to the developing world. Quick-disbursing macroeconomic program assistance, such as balance-of-payments support and sector budget support (which were not tied to investment projects, and which could be justified under the headings of stabilization and adjustment), appeared an ideal solution to the dilemma of maintaining the resource flow and the desire to promote policy reform. Financial program aid and adjustment loans (and eventually debt relief) became fashionable, and policy conditionality was more widespread. In other words, a rationale that corresponded well with the orthodox guidelines for good policy (known as the "Washington Consensus") had been found for maintaining the aid flow.

By the early 1990s, a number of factors had fomented, raising skepticism about the benefits of foreign aid. These included: a) the persistence of economic crises in much of the developing world; b) geopolitical changes following the end of the Cold War, which weakened patron-client relationships between developing countries and former colonial powers; c) the perception that policy conditionality was failing to promote genuine policy reform; and d) a growing fear that aid was generating undesirable dependency relationships. Consequently, the traditional support given to foreign aid by vocal interest groups in the industrial countries receded.

Bilateral and multilateral aid institutions were subjected to criticism and at times characterized as blunt instruments of commercial interest in the industrial world, or as self-interested, inefficient, rent-seeking bureaucracies. Moreover, acute awareness in donor countries of cases of poor governance, corruption, and "crony capitalism" led to skepticism about the credibility of aid recipients.

Nevertheless, a resurgence of official development assistance, at least at the level of political rhetoric, occurred. During the late 1990s a consensus emerged among developed country governments that a renewed approach to development assistance—one that avoided the mistakes of the past—was warranted. In part this stemmed from recognition of the growing magnitude of global interdependencies (globalization), which meant that poverty and conflict in one corner of the globe could have implications for all. These views gave birth to the Millennium Development Goals (MDGs), directed explicitly at poverty reduction and addressing basic human needs such as access to education, health and water. The main focus was on the poorest countries and on Africa in particular. In this vein, then British Prime Minister Tony Blair launched his Commission for Africa in February, 2004, publishing its findings in 2005. Other initiatives, such as the Jubilee Debt Campaign to cancel third world debts, received a high profile. Thus, the plight of the poor became a part of popular discourse and a cause promoted by celebrities and politicians alike.

## Trends in foreign aid

In accordance with changes in motives and perceptions, aid volume has fluctuated over time. Total aid grew steadily in real terms until the early 1990s. After 1992, however, total aid flows started to decline in absolute terms until the turn of the millennium. Since then, there has been a modest upturn in aid flows, but not on a scale that corresponds either to estimates of the funds deemed necessary to meet the MDGs or to the promises made by developed country governments (such as those of the G8 at the Gleneagles summit in July, 2005).[1]

Two further points merit comment. First, while aid flows have grown slowly over the past decade, and in many cases have actually fallen in per capita terms due to consistent population growth, private flows expanded considerably until the international financial and economic crisis of 2008–09. Thus, despite the widespread perception that foreign aid amounts to a very significant resource, it is now the case that in many developing countries official assistance is dwarfed by other external capital inflows such as foreign direct investment (FDI) and remittances. However, this phenomenon does not apply equally to all countries. For many of the poorest countries, particularly those in sub-Saharan Africa, foreign aid remains highly significant and is a vital source of funds to support import purchases and government spending.

Secondly, and as a consequence of the foregoing, the allocation of aid (as measured by the aid to GNI ratio) is highly skewed. Based on data for 1996–2005, the largest number of recipient countries received aid on the order of 1.8 percent of their GNI (the mode) per year, and 50 percent of countries received aid at a rate of 3.2 percent of GNI or less (the median). This corresponds to a distribution of aid with a mode of US$17.9 per capita per year and a median of US$31.5. With this background, the next section turns to the issue of analyzing the overall impact of past aid on growth.

## Does Aid Support Economic Growth?

This section addresses a key policy question: does foreign aid raise economic growth rates in developing countries? As discussed in Section 2, economic growth is fundamental to achieving a range of development objectives. Although the above question may be simple, it is not easy to answer. This stems from methodological challenges as well as weaknesses in the available data. To properly measure the effect of aid, ideally the analyst would compare the value of a chosen indicator—growth in this case—in two strictly independent situations: with and without aid. To establish the "true" measure of aid impact, the importance of all other circumstances that have affected growth in a given country over time must be properly accounted for. As we cannot simultaneously observe the same country with and without aid, the fundamental evaluation challenge is to compare what actually happened with an artificially constructed counterfactual. In observational studies, there is no way of doing this without making assumptions that are bound to be debatable, both in theory and in practice. For this reason—as well as ideological reasons—the impact of aid remains highly controversial.

The past decades have witnessed a massive outpouring of studies on the effectiveness of foreign aid. Many development experts, subscribing to different paradigms of development thinking, have grappled with this topic; and methodologies have varied. More specifically: 1) the impact of aid has been evaluated at the micro- and macroeconomic levels; 2) cross-country comparisons as well as single-country case studies have been used; and 3) broad surveys of a qualitative and interdisciplinary nature, as well as more "hard core" quantitative work, have been pursued. A brief survey of the main findings of this large body of literature is attempted in the following sub-sections.

## Microeconomic evidence

While this chapter is chiefly concerned with the impact of aid on aggregate indicators, it is useful to begin with the microeconomic evidence (mainly from specific projects). This evidence paints a reasonably positive picture. The most rigorous evaluations in this area are done by the World Bank, and reports from the Independent Evaluation Group (IEG) of the World Bank are encouraging. Average rates of return to aid are generally above 20 percent, and decent project rates of return have been reported regularly over the years in one survey after another. Overall, a mass of project-based evidence has been collected, and few dispute that aid interventions have helped to bring about improved outcomes such as better health, improved access to education, and promotion of appropriate agricultural technology.

The evaluation of development interventions at the microeconomic level has been bolstered by the recent and rapid expansion of randomized program evaluation techniques, including experimental approaches (see Banerjee 2007; Duflo and Kremer 2005; and Langbein 2006). These seek to avoid potential sources of bias from earlier project evaluations, such as selection bias from choosing only completed (successful) projects, and rely on detailed data that is collected both before and after interventions. Moreover, to address the problem of confounding factors, random selection of beneficiaries is also often used in a manner similar to that of clinical trials for new drugs. Evidence from these studies has been positive in many instances (but not all), indicating that aid-financed interventions can generate substantial benefits for individuals. For example, randomized control trials of providing deworming treatments to school-aged children in Kenya have shown that highly cost effective drugs can reduce school absenteeism by 25 percent and increase school participation by at least 0.14 years of schooling per treated child (Miguel and Kremer 2004).

Despite the above, two fundamental challenges remain. First, it is problematic and often inappropriate to generalize the results from a specific evaluation to other contexts. In many cases, it is unclear how a particular effect was generated or what factors may constrain a putative causal mechanism from operating in other situations (for further discussion see Deaton 2009). Second, neither the results nor the techniques of (randomized) microeconomic evaluation can be directly translated to the aggregate level. The deworming treatments mentioned in the preceding paragraph are a good example. Microeconomic evaluations establish that the deworming programs studied increased the quality (through reduced absenteeism) and quantity (through increased years of schooling) of education. However, many years of continuous and broad-scale effort are required to significantly augment the average education level of the working age population. Hence, the growth benefits of the intervention are contingent upon continued success of scaled up programs and even then will only materialize through time.

## Three previous generations of macroeconomic studies

Rather than attempting to aggregate the impact of numerous microeconomic interventions, the approach to evaluating the macroeconomic impact of aid examines total aid flows and the economic growth rate. Normally, this has been done across countries with the expectation that, other things being equal, countries that receive more assistance would grow more rapidly. However, the *prima facie* evidence suggests that the countries who have received the most aid have also performed relatively badly in terms of economic growth. This implies a contradiction between positive microeconomic evidence and the disappointing aggregate performance of countries that have received substantial aid inflows, a paradox often referred to as the "micro-macro" paradox (Mosley 1987).

A large number of studies have attempted to shed light on this apparent paradox. Previous studies can be classified into three generations, each influenced by dominant theoretical paradigms as well as available empirical tools. The first two generations were inspired by relatively simple models of the growth process, such as the Harrod-Domar model and the two-gap Chenery-Strout extension. The underlying idea behind the Harrod-Domar model is of a stable linear relationship between growth and investment in physical capital. Assuming all aid is invested, it is straightforward to calculate how much aid is required to achieve a target growth rate. The impact of aid is assumed to be positive and helps plug either a savings or a foreign exchange gap. Empirical studies in this tradition consequently focused on the extent to which aid increases savings and investment in recipient countries. As the detailed survey in Hansen and Tarp (2000) testifies, first generation studies generally concluded that aid does tend to increase total savings/investment, but not by as much as the aid flow. Quite reasonably, this simply suggests a non-negligible proportion of aid is consumed rather than invested.

Retaining the focus on capital accumulation, the second generation of literature explored the impact of aid on growth via investment. Using data for a cross-section of countries, a large number of studies of this kind were produced during the 1980s and early 1990s. Hansen and Tarp (2000) conclude that the findings from these studies consistently indicate a positive link between aid and investment. While a majority of the aid-growth studies of this generation also suggested a positive impact, the result that captured attention was Mosley's micro-macro paradox. This puzzle raised doubts concerning the appropriateness of the underlying growth model and the empirical techniques used. Indeed, it is a tall order to expect both a constant output-capital relationship and that all aid is invested. A second line of critique of the Harrod-Domar and two-gap approach is the argument that growth is less related to physical capital investment than often assumed (Easterly 1999, 2003). If the productive impact of aid depends more on incentives and relative prices, as well as the policy environment more generally, then it becomes important to consider these broader effects.

The second generation of studies also introduced the problem that poorly performing countries may receive more aid precisely because of their poor growth performance (e.g., Mosley et al. 1992). There is no necessary logical inconsistency between low growth and high aid inflows. When countries have done well for a while, average incomes will have increased and donors tend to transfer less aid (at least relative to GNI) and may eventually withdraw. At the same time, donor nations have specifically sought to direct aid towards the poorest countries. This implies that, over time, there is a marked tendency for the best performing countries to receive less aid relative to GNI and for the worst performers to receive more. Empirical analyses that do not account for the two-way relationship between aid and growth (that is, the endogeneity of aid) will not reveal aid's 'true' impact. Most second generation studies, however, did not deal with this issue.

From the early 1990s a third generation of more sophisticated econometric studies came to dominate the academic and public discourse about aid. This was motivated by the availability of much better data, allowing analysts to look at changes both across and within countries over time (i.e., panel data became available). Insights from new theories of economic growth, as well as a rapidly increasing numbers of general empirical growth studies, also influenced the research literature. Mindful of the weaknesses of previous studies, the aid-growth relationship came to be perceived as (possibly) non-linear and the endogeneity of aid was taken more seriously. Among the numerous studies of this generation, a leading paper that also came to exert a significant influence on aid policy is the study out of the World Bank by Burnside and Dollar (1997, 2000). The authors argued that although aid has no impact on growth on average, it can work as long as recipients pursue 'good' policies. In their own words: "... aid has a positive impact on growth in developing countries with good fiscal, monetary and trade policies ... [but] ... in the presence of poor policies, aid has no positive effect on growth" (2000: 847).

These results, however, were subject to substantial criticism and were shown to be highly fragile. For example, Hansen and Tarp (2001) found that a story of diminishing returns to aid, captured by a squared aid term, best captures the non-linear relationship between aid and growth and is the empirical specification with most support in the data. They concluded that aid has a positive impact on growth but with diminishing returns. Alternatively, Dalgaard et al. (2004) found that variation across countries in the returns to aid seems to be related to their geographical location. Specifically, aid was found to be far less effective in tropical areas over the last 30 years. They also stress, however, that it is hard to believe that aid should be inherently less potent in the tropics. Thus, the real explanation for the aid-tropics link is likely to be elsewhere and the authors call for further research to help disentangle the channels through which aid matters for productivity and efficiency. In an empirical review of many of these contributions, Roodman argues that the results of this generation are extremely sensitive to methodological choices. He goes on to conclude that while some aid is likely to increase investment and growth, aid "is probably not a fundamentally decisive factor for development" (2007: 275). Moreover, due to the multiple kinds of aid, and differences in the efficiency with which it may be put to use, the noise in the data may mask any valuable information regarding the 'true' impact of aid.

## Recent contributions

Despite the methodological difficulties, a series of recent studies—a fourth generation—have taken a decidedly pessimistic stance. In particular, in their widely cited paper, Rajan and Subramanian (2008) conclude that aid has had no systematic effect on growth and assert that this conclusion holds across methodologies, time periods and forms of aid. Thus, and as advocated by the authors (2008: 660), an appropriate research agenda may be to unpack the different effects of aid on growth by focussing on intermediate outcomes which are proximate determinants of income growth.

A number of scholars have interpreted this agenda as being one of explaining why resource transfers in the form of aid, at least some of which are invested, don't lead to an overall increase in the growth rate. A leading explanation for a negative effect of aid that offsets the benefits of the resource transfer is that aid undermines or weakens governance by increasing the returns to corruption and/or increasing rent seeking activities. Djankov et al. (2008), for example, argue that aid has a statistically significant negative effect on changes in political institutions (specifically, democracy). Aid is likened to natural resource windfalls, which in principle could be used to boost growth, but in practice have often resulted in poor governance and a poor growth record over time. According to Djankov et al. (2008), the negative effect of aid on political institutions is larger in magnitude than that caused by natural resource windfalls. Similarly, in an earlier study, Rajan and Subramanian (2007) find that manufacturing sector growth in developing countries is undermined by a detrimental effect of aid inflows on governance.

Other scholars argue that, given that the association between income growth and investment in both human capital (skills, education, health) and physical capital appears to be fragile within countries over time (Kenny 2005), it is unsurprising that a robust relationship between aid and growth has been elusive. This accords with the view that growth is an extremely complex, idiosyncratic and open phenomenon that cannot easily be captured by simple empirical models (see Temple 2000). Indeed, in the wider development economics literature, there has been a shift away from grand theories of how developing countries grow, towards a more nuanced emphasis on binding constraints (Rodrik 2007) and varieties of coordination challenges. All-purpose explanations of growth that apply equally across countries over time are viewed with scepticism. Collier (2007), for instance, identifies numerous growth traps to which low income countries may be subject and each of which demands a different policy response. Accordingly, he argues that foreign aid is only likely to directly boost growth in a relatively small number of cases. In the remaining cases, it will often only sustain countries on a form of minimal life support.

In light of this increasing humility concerning what we know about how growth is initiated and then sustained, a set of recent papers focuses on the effects of aid on non-growth outcomes such as infant mortality, health, and education. Mishra and Newhouse (2007), for example, find a small but statistically significant effect of health aid on reductions in infant mortality. Masud and Yontcheva (2005) also find that some types of aid help reduce infant mortality.

Recent theoretical exercises give further weight to the need for modest expectations regarding the magnitude of the possible impact of foreign aid on growth. Rajan and Subramanian (2008) also contribute to this literature. Based on a standard neoclassical production function framework, and assuming that aid only increases physical capital investment, they estimate that the overall increase in the growth rate accruing from aid inflows of 10 percent of GDP may only lie in the range of 1 percent to 2.5 percent depending on the share of aid that is invested and on productivity impacts. Thus, at the levels of aid seen by most countries, which amounts to a few percent of GDP, these effects may be very difficult to distinguish from business cycle fluctuations and external shocks, especially when the endogeneity of aid and the quality of data on GDP and aid flows are considered. In fact, while Rajan and Subramanian emphasize that their estimates rarely have an effect on growth that is statistically different from zero, they are also unable to conclude statistically that the impact of aid on growth falls outside of the range suggested by theory. This is particularly true when longer time frames are considered. In these cases, the estimated parameters are much closer to the suggested ranges than they are to zero.

Furthermore, the range for the expected impact of aid on growth proposed by Rajan and Subramanian may be overoptimistic. Using a more sophisticated theoretical approach, Dalgaard and Erickson (2009) find that expectations with respect to the impact of aid on growth should be even more modest. They consider aid inflows to sub-Saharan Africa over the past thirty years, which averaged around 5 percent of recipient GDP, and calculate an expected annual increase in the growth rate from past aid flows of around 0.1 percent. This assumes that all aid is invested and there are no productivity impacts. An effect of this magnitude would be impossible to isolate from other factors affecting growth with existing data and methods. Whatever the expected reasonable range, a fundamental point is that, once one uses more realistic theoretical models compared to those used in the first and second generation literatures (see Easterly 1999), the expected potency of aid in stimulating growth declines. Given the ranges predicted by growth models, there may be no aid effectiveness puzzle after all.

Finally, research attention also has been given to long-run determinants of growth that have a cumulative but often not immediate impact on the rate of income growth. Changes in human capital, such as education and health, move only slowly at the aggregate level and exert a positive influence on economic growth with a substantial lag. This comes from simple demographics whereby improvements in schooling indicators, for example at the primary level, can take many years to translate into noticeable increases in average education levels among working age adults. Ashraf et al. (2008) demonstrate that the immediate economic impact of gains in life expectancy from disease eradication may be a reduction in per capita incomes due to increased child survival and the consequent increase in the ratio of the non-working age to the working age population. In short, as a result of these interventions, incremental growth in population can easily exceed the incremental growth in income for two, three or even more decades following interventions.

The impressive performance of many developing countries, including countries in sub-Saharan Africa, in improving social indicators such as expanding access to education, reducing infant mortality, and expanding access to health services over the past three decades may only now be translating into gains in per capita income. This reinforces the need for modest expectations regarding the effect of aid on observed income growth. Where aid has been used primarily to boost social spending, as advocated under the MDGs, it may be inappropriate to investigate the aid-growth relationship under anything other than a time horizon of thirty to forty years.

In response to these concerns, there have been calls for more detailed country case studies, which permit a more nuanced assessment. Arndt et al. (2007) provide a case study of Mozambique in which they attempt to evaluate the effects of aid across different proximate drivers of growth. Starting with long-run growth accounting estimates, they find that aid has played a crucial role in rebuilding infrastructure and expanding access to health and education. Aid has supported rapid reconstruction and seems to have crowded in private and foreign investment, but has also brought substantial governance and economic management challenges. This provides supporting evidence for Collier's (2007) argument that aid can be particularly beneficial in post-war environments but also brings new challenges.

Finally, in their recent up-to-date cross-country study, Arndt, Jones, and Tarp (2010) note that while the micro-macro paradox seems to have been revived, a balanced view of the evidence is that aid remains an important tool for enhancing the development prospects of the poor. Arndt et al. apply micro-econometric techniques from the program evaluation literature and lessons from the growth literature in a novel way, and their findings show that aid has a positive and statistically significant causal effect on growth over the long run, with point estimates at levels suggested by growth theory. Arguably, their approach represents the most carefully developed empirical strategy employed in the aid-growth literature to date, and the average treatment effect of aid on growth is positive in both the 1970–2000 and 1960–2000 periods. In fact, the statistically significant point estimates suggest that an inflow on the order of 10 percent of GDP spurs per capita growth by more than one percentage point per annum in the long run. These estimates are consistent with the view that foreign aid stimulates aggregate investment and also contributes to productivity growth, despite some fraction of aid being allocated to consumption. In the shorter term, however, the analysis by Arndt et al. indicates that the impact of aid is difficult to discern. Nevertheless, combining the longer run macro evidence with the evidence at the micro- and meso-levels, a consistent case for aid effectiveness emerges.

## Some Stylized Lessons

Despite what may be seen as the rather paltry fruits of hundreds of academic studies, a number of lessons have been learned. These can be summarized as follows:

We now have a better understanding of the difficulties involved in investigating whether aid stimulates growth on aggregate. In particular, we have a solid grasp of why empirical results are often biased towards zero (even if there is a positive true long-run relationship). The principal factors behind this are noisy and weak data; the high complexity and idiosyncratic nature of the growth process; the endogeneity of aid; and the demographic implications of gains in social indicators that may be driven by aid. Furthermore, methods that enable the analyst to deal with all of these factors simultaneously, and thereby tease out the "true" impact of growth, are only beginning to emerge.

Putting these methodological difficulties aside, it is essential that one maintain appropriately modest expectations about the magnitude of aggregate returns to aid. As discussed above, theoretical exercises built on realistic assumptions tend to indicate small growth gains from the average volumes of aid that have been donated in the past (and which are likely to continue). Such expectations are significantly smaller than those generated from the early generations of research on aid and growth. However, this message is not widely disseminated and needs to be absorbed by the wider policy community and general public.

It is important to recognize the multiple channels through which aid may have an impact on growth, as well as corresponding differences in the horizon over which aggregate effects may become apparent. Improvements in health, education, and institutions can take a very long time (up to a generation) to cumulate into potential growth effects. This indicates that non-growth aggregate outcomes associated with aid, such as changes in education or health indicators, can be usefully studied in their own right. At the same time, this also means that countries with very different initial conditions and/or aid profiles may see very different responses to aid over time.

Finally, an obvious but often forgotten point is that history matters. Aid has not been provided on a random basis, nor has there been any kind of stability in donor aid allocation strategies or views about what constitutes the "right" set of policies to induce growth. Consequently, one must exercise substantial caution in using past trends to inform about future possibilities. There is no doubt that during the Cold War, aid was often used as a geo-political tool of advanced countries. Today, the emphasis is on poverty, social welfare, and conflict (or terrorism) prevention. Of course, these shifts in donor behavior and global conditions further frustrate the methodological challenge, but they cannot be ignored. The point that political motives largely guide the size and the form of aid is of crucial importance. Clearly, if the motivation of donors is not growth and development, then it is not that surprising that the link between aid and growth is tenuous. A related point is that the lack of coordination among donors—and sometimes conflicting objectives as well—further reduce the impact of aid on growth. Still another issue—relevant in a number of circumstances including recent Chinese aid via-à-vis sub-Saharan Africa—is aid provided as a carrot to have access to natural resources.

So, where does this leave us? The tone of the very recent literature is pessimistic, but this literature comes nowhere near to confining the estimated causal impact of aid on growth to less than the range reasonable expectations would suggest. Moreover, the pendulum in the literature tends to swing slowly, with more critical assessments tending to follow more positive assessments and so forth. At the same time, methodological improvements are being realized by works on both sides of the debate. As shown in the study by Arndt, Jones, and Tarp (2010), "recent literature" is now introducing new methodological improvements that arrive at a more positive tone.

Overall, looking broadly across the full range of existing literature from microeconomic evidence to the cross-country macroeconomic analyses relating aid to growth, the balance of evidence indicates positive effects, particularly when longer time frames are considered. In this, Collier argues that over the past thirty years aid has probably increased the annual growth rate of the poorest countries by around one percentage point and adds that: "Without aid, cumulatively the countries of the bottom billion would have become much poorer than they are today" (2007: 100). These conclusions do not deny that aid can be inefficient or that negative side effects may arise from specific projects or relationships. Nor do they imply that we should stop learning about how aid works or how to do aid better. Here, on the contrary, much work remains to be done.

## Summary and Conclusions

Arndt, Jones, and Tarp (2010) begin their recent paper by noting that the extent to which foreign aid can be a decisive factor in the economic development of low-income countries remains controversial. In 1987, Paul Mosley suggested that while aid seems to be effective at the microeconomic level, any positive aggregate impact of aid is much harder to identify. He labeled this the micro-macro paradox, and it challenged the conclusions of the seminal works by Papanek (1972, 1973). After more than twenty years, Rajan and Subramanian (2008) concluded "it is difficult to discern any systematic effect of aid on growth." At the same time, microeconomic evaluations, including rigorous contributions to the program evaluation literature by development economists, have demonstrated the potential for well-designed interventions to achieve significant positive results.

Thus, after two decades of intense analytical work using new theory, new data and new empirical methodologies, it might appear that the micro-macro paradox has been revived. Other similarities with the late 1980s and early 1990s exist, not least with respect to policy. In 1994, the *Economist* magazine concluded from the results of Boone (1994) that "aid [goes] down the rathole." Today, in the midst of a serious global economic crisis, where aid is arguably more needed than ever, the attention of both the aid community and decision-makers is on "Dead Aid" (Moyo 2009), which argues for a complete cessation of aid flows to Africa.

So, has the aid and growth literature come full circle? The response of Arndt, Jones, and Tarp (2010) is "no." While the pendulum has swung to skepticism concerning the ability of aid to contribute to economic growth in the most recent literature, a series of important points of agreement have emerged. First, methodological advances have improved the profession's capacity to identify causal effects in economic phenomena. These advances in methods are beginning to be applied at the more aggregate level, and they underline that when proper analytical care is taken, pessimistic conclusions about the aid-growth link give way to more realistic assessments.[2] Second, these methodological advances highlight the serious challenges that must be surmounted in order to derive robust causal conclusions from observational data. In many important areas of inquiry, longstanding debates with respect to causal impacts persist despite improved methods and improved data availability. At the same time, we highlight in accordance with Temple (2010, 4448) that "an insignificant coefficient should usually be seen as absence of evidence, not evidence of absence, at least until the economic implications of a confidence interval have been explored."

Third, the formation of reasonable expectations about the likely returns to foreign assistance has been greatly facilitated by the application of modern growth theory. Finally, there is an increasing recognition that many of the key interventions pursued by foreign aid will only result in positive growth outcomes over long-term horizons.

Arndt, Jones, and Tarp (2010) also show that the average treatment effect of aid on growth is positive in both the 1970–2000 and 1960–2000 periods. The long run elasticity of growth with respect to the share of aid in recipient GDP appears to around 0.13. This is consistent with the view that foreign aid stimulates aggregate investment and also may contribute to productivity growth, despite some fraction of aid being allocated to consumption. In sum, when combined with the evidence at the micro- and meso-levels, a consistent case for aid effectiveness emerges. There is no paradox. Overall, the bleak pessimism of much of the recent aid-growth literature is unjustified and the associated policy implications drawn from this literature are often inappropriate and unhelpful. Aid has been and remains an important tool for enhancing the development prospects of poor nations.

Finally, nearly all participants in the aid-growth debate recognize the potential for aid to do better, particularly in fostering productivity growth. The evidence indicates that sustaining foreign assistance programs at reasonable levels can be expected to enhance the living standards of the world's poorest people. Abolishing foreign aid, or drastically cutting it back, would be a mistake and is not warranted by any reasonable interpretation of the evidence. The challenge is to improve foreign assistance effectiveness so that living standards in poor countries are substantially advanced over the next three decades. And that it can be done is evident from historical examples such as Taiwan, Korea and Mozambique where aid has made major contributions to growth and development.

*This chapter was prepared based on an unpublished report for NORAD and other joint work including several UNU-WIDER working papers. We are grateful for helpful comments from many colleagues including Erik Thorbecke of Cornell University.*

## Notes

[1] For further information on the commitments made at the Gleneagles summit see, for example: www.g8.utoronto.ca/summit/2005gleneagles.

[2] See for example Hansen and Tarp (2001) for a critique of Burnside and Dollar (2000); Arndt, Jones and Tarp (2010) for a re-examination of Rajan and Subrama-

nian (2008); and Mekasha and Tarp (2011) for a rebuttal of the meta-study by Doucouliagos and Paldam (2008).

## References

Alesina, A., and D. Dollar. 2000. "Who Gives Foreign Aid to Whom and Why?" *Journal of Economic Growth* 5:33–63.

Arndt, C. 2000. "Technical Cooperation." In Foreign Aid and Development: Lessons of Experience and Directions for the Future, ed. F. Tarp. London: Routledge.

Arndt, C., S. Jones, and F. Tarp. 2010. "Aid, Growth, and Development: Have We Come Full Circle?" *Journal of Globalization and Development* 1:2, Article 5.

Arndt, C., S. Jones, and F. Tarp. 2007. "Aid and Development: the Mozambican Case." In *Theory and Practice of Foreign Aid, Frontiers of Economics and Globalization, Volume 1,* ed. S. Lahiri. Amsterdam: Elsevier.

Ashraf, Q. and O. Galor. 2008. "Dynamics and Stagnation in the Malthusian Epoch: Theory and Evidence." Brown University Working Paper, 2008:14, Department of Economics.

Banerjee, A. V. 2007. *Making Aid Work.* Cambridge, MA: Boston Review/MIT Press.

Berg, E. 1993. "Rethinking Technical Cooperation: Reforms for Capacity Building in Africa." Technical report, Regional Bureau for Africa, UN Development Programme, New York.

Boone, P. 1994. "The Impact of Foreign Aid on Savings and Growth." London School of Economics CEP Working Paper 1994: 677.

Burnside, C., and D. Dollar. 2000. "Aid, Policies, and Growth." *American Economic Review* 90: 847–68.

Collier, P. 2007. *The Bottom Billion.* Oxford: Oxford University Press.

Dalgaard, C., and L. Erickson. 2009. "Reasonable Expectations and the First Millennium Development Goal: How Much Can Aid Achieve?" *World Development* 37: 1170–81.

Dalgaard, C.-J., H. Hansen, and F. Tarp. 2004. "On the Empirics of Foreign Aid and Growth." *The Economic Journal,* 114: F191–216.

Deaton, A. 2009. "Instruments of Development: Randomization in the Tropics and the Search for the Elusive Keys to Economic Development." National Bureau of Economic Research, Working Paper 14690.

Djankov, S., J. Montalvo, and M. Reynal-Querol. 2008. "The Curse of Aid." *Journal of Economic Growth* 13:3, 169–194.

Doucouliagos, H., and M. Paldam. 2008. "Aid Effectiveness on Growth: A Meta Study." *European Journal of Political Economy* 24:1, 1–24.

Duflo, E., and M. Kremer. 2005. "Use of Randomization in the Evaluation of Development Effectiveness." In *Evaluating Development Effectiveness,* ed. G. Pitman, O. Feinstein, and G. Ingram. New Brunswick, NJ: Transaction Publishers.

Easterly, W. 1999. "The Ghost of Financing Gap: Testing the Growth Model Used in the International Financial Institutions." *Journal of Development Economics,* 60: 423–38.

—. 2001. *The Elusive Quest for Growth*. Cambridge, MA: MIT Press.

—. 2003. "Can Foreign Aid Buy Growth?" *Journal of Economic Perspectives* 17: 23–48.

—. 2006. *The White Man's Burden: Why the West's Efforts to Aid the Rest Have Done so Much Ill and so Little Good.* New York: Penguin Press.

—. 2009. "How the Millennium Development Goals are Unfair to Africa." *World Development* 37:1, 26–35.

Hansen, H., and F. Tarp. 2000. "Aid Effectiveness Disputed." *Journal of International Development* 12: 375–98.

Hansen, H., and F. Tarp. 2001. "Aid and Growth Regressions." *Journal of Development Economics,* 64: 547–70.

Kenny, C. 2005. "There's (Much) More to Life than Income: The Weak Link Between Income, Health, and Education." Unpublished report, World Bank.

Langbein, L. 2006. *Public Program Evaluation: A Statistical Guide.* Armonk, NY: M.E. Sharpe.

McGillivray, M. 2003. "Modelling Foreign Aid Allocation: Issues, Approaches and Results." *Journal of Economic Development* 28:1, 171–188.

Mekasha, T. J. and F. Tarp. 2011. "Aid and Growth: What Meta-Analysis Reveals." WIDER Working Paper 2011/22, UNU-WIDER.

Miguel, E., and M. Kremer. 2004. "Worms: Identifying Impacts on Education and Health in the Presence of Treatment Externalities." *Econometrica* 72:1, 159–217.

Mishra, P., and D. Newhouse. 2007. "Health Aid and Infant Mortality." IMF Working Papers, 07/100, International Monetary Fund.

Mosley, P. 1987. *Overseas Aid: Its Defence and Reform.* Brighton: Wheatshead Books.

Moyo, D. 2009. Dead Aid: *Why Aid Is Not Working and How There Is a Better Way for Africa.* London: Allen Lane.

Papanek, G. F. 1972. "The Effect of Aid and Other Resource Transfers on Savings and Growth in Less Developed Countries." *Economic Journal* 82:327, 935–50.

—. 1973. "Aid, Foreign Private Investment, Savings, and Growth in Less Developed Countries." *Journal of Political Economy* 81:1, 120–30.

Rajan, R. G., and A. Subramanian. 2007. "Does Aid Affect Governance?" *American Economic Review* 97:2, 322–327.

Rajan, R.G., and A. Subramanian. 2008. "Aid and Growth: What Does the Cross-country Evidence Really Show?" *Review of Economics and Statistics* 90:4, 643–665.

Riddell, R. 2007. *Does Foreign Aid Really Work?* Oxford: Oxford University Press.

Rodrik, D. 2007. *One Economics, Many Recipes: Globalization, Institutions, and Economic Growth.* Princeton: Princeton University Press.

Roodman, D. 2007. "The Anarchy of Numbers: Aid, Development, and Cross-Country Empirics." *The World Bank Economic Review* 21:2, 255–277.

Sachs, J. 2005. *The End of Poverty: Economic Possibilities for Our Time.*New York: Penguin Press.

Tarp, F. 2006. "Aid and development." *Swedish Economic Policy Review* 13:2, 9–61.

Temple, J. 2000. "Growth Regressions and What the Textbooks Don't Tell You." *Bulletin of Economic Research* 52:3, 181–205.

—. 2010. "Aid and Conditionality." In *Handbook of Development Economics* (chapter 67), eds. D. Rodrik and M. Rosenzweig. Amsterdam: Elsevier.

Yontcheva, B., and N. Masud. 2005. "Does Foreign Aid Reduce Poverty? Empirical Evidence from Nongovernmental and Bilateral Aid." IMF Working Paper 05/100, International Monetary Fund.

# CHAPTER THREE

# FOREIGN AID AND ECONOMIC DEVELOPMENT IN NAMIBIA

ESAU KAAKUNGA

The purpose of this study was to investigate empirically the propositions regarding the effects of foreign aid on economic development. Using a simple analytical endogenous growth model we have identified the effects of overseas development assistance and foreign direct investment on economic growth in Namibia. Despite the overall downward trend in the levels of development assistance, foreign expertise and financial support still play an important role in Namibia. The results indicate that the shares of investment in gross domestic product positively influence the short run behaviour of the gross domestic product in Namibia. The level of government consumption ratio to GDP affects the real gross domestic product negatively. The findings show that the openness promotes economic activities in Namibia. Foreign aid, on the positive side, has helped in boosting the gross domestic product.

Given the results of the study, injection of more aid into the Namibian economy will hasten growth. Thus, there is a need for government to strengthen its effort in making Namibia more competitive. It should continue with the creation of a more investment-friendly environment, improving availability of infrastructure, and investing in education and promoting economic growth.

## Introduction

Foreign aid is a significant source of income to developing countries, especially in Africa, where it averages 12.5 percent of gross domestic product and establishes by far the most important source of foreign capital (Pallage and Robe 2001). In such an environment, foreign aid has the potential to play a key role in promoting developing countries' economic growth (Hatemi-J and Irandoust 2005). An important objective of official development assistance to developing countries is the promotion of economic development and welfare, usually measured by its impact on economic growth. The promise of foreign direct investment as an engine for economic development in developing countries has gained momentum over the past three decades. In the 1970s, many developing countries were mistrustful of multinational corporations (MNCs), fearing a loss of sovereignty and preferring to borrow from banks to finance development projects (Akinkugbe 2003). After the debt crisis of the 1980s, foreign direct investment became highly sought after, especially with the widespread embrace of export-oriented development strategies.

A large proportion of foreign aid has been directed toward helping developing countries to improve their policies and institutions. The World Bank (1998) reports that when countries reform their economic policies, well-timed assistance can increase the benefits of reform and maintain popular support for the reforms. In the early days of development assistance, development economists believed that the newly independent governments were positive agents for change. Thus government-to-government aid was considered the best way to promote development. However, in most instances, aid flow to developing countries got diverted to finance consumption rather than investment. Experience has shown that the rosy optimism of aid-financed, government-led strategies for development often ended in failure (Inanga and Mandah 2008). Part of the aid to developing countries, channelled mainly through development financing institutions (DFIs), was used to intervene in the financial sectors of these countries. DFIs were encouraged, sponsored, and supported by both governments and donors.

Developing countries have traditionally been net importers of capital. Their two main sources of supply are official financing, including official development assistance (ODA) and private capital. The effects of the debt crisis of the 1980s are evident in the private loans, which have declined substantially (Durbarry, Gemmel, and Greenaway 1998). On average, during the period from 1970 to 1993 developing countries received 9.8 percent of their GDP annually as foreign aid, with a slowly rising trend in both real and nominal terms. However, the share of aid in total resource transfers fell between 1970 and 1984, increased during 1985 to 1987, and fell again thereafter. These declines reflected both a fall in the volume of foreign aid from donors and the relatively rapid expansion of private capital flows, the other major financing source. The overall net resource flows have been affected by major episodes in the world such as the two oil price shocks (1973–81), the international debt crisis (1982–87), and the recent period of liberalization in Less Developing Countries (LDCs) from 1988 onwards (Durbarry, Gemmel, and Greenaway 2006).

Africa has continued to make progress in many areas. Sixteen out of forty-seven countries achieved on average more than 4 percent growth over the past decade. Investment and trade trends have been steady. Net foreign direct investment (FDI) to Africa rose to N$6.8 billion in 2001 but was heavily concentrated in oil-exporting countries and South Africa. Africa had the highest returns on FDI in the world, and the flow of workers' remittances back to the continent doubled in only two years, reaching N$4 billion in 2002 (Ikhide 2006).

Nevertheless, the continent continues to face enormous development challenges. Half of the population lives on less than US$1 a day. The share of poor population remains unchanged over the period 1987–1998. This is the region with lowest income per capita and highest population growth. Overall GDP growth is roughly 3 percent, almost equalling the population growth. Even though the donor community has been providing huge amounts of aid to this region, its economic performance is still very poor.

Namibia is not an exception. After gaining independence in 1990, it opened its borders to foreign aid that same year. Namibia has witnessed an increase in overseas development assistance (ODA) since 1990. Immediately after independence, a huge amount—N$102 million—was recorded in government grants, increasing to N$104.3 million in 1991. However, overseas development assistance decreased significantly, to N$27.0 million in 2000, before rising to N$46.9 million in 2001. On average, ODA inflow was N$59.8 million and N$49.7 million for the period 1990–2000 and 2001–2007, respectively. Free-standing technical cooperation accounts for more than 50 percent of committed funds since independence. The next most significant types of ODA in Namibia are investment project assistance and investment related to technical cooperation. Investment project assistance (IPA) was the second largest type of assistance (NPC 2005). There have been huge fluctuations in the IPA between the years. However, the trend has been upward since 2001.

Program/budgetary aid or balance of payment support was the second largest type of assistance during the period under review. Like investment project assistance, this type of investment has fluctuated considerably since 1998. Another important type of assistance, the third largest during the period under review, is investment-related technical assistance. These resources are directly aimed at strengthening the capacity to execute specific investment projects. Items included under investment-related technical assistance include pre-investment activities directly related to the implementation of an approved investment project. Most funds committed since independence were destined for the education sector, with about a 20 percent share of total commitment. Agriculture, forestry and environment attracted 11.45 percent of commitments; while health, transport, and water supply recorded less than 10 percent during the period under review. The least commitments were made to Ministries of Home Affairs, Woman Affairs and Child Welfare, Safety and Security, and Labor and Social Welfare.

The remainder of the chapter is outlined as follows: section two surveys the literature; section three considers the methodology. Estimation and analysis of regression results are also discussed in this section. Section four gives conclusions and policy guidelines.

## Literature Review

In this section we review the literature with a view to identifying the causal relationship between foreign aid and economic growth. Most of the theoretical and empirical literature looks at the relationship between macroeconomic policies and economic growth. Yet this literature is essential for evaluating the relationship between foreign aid and economic development. The role of foreign economic assistance in economic development and growth remains contentious in economic literature. Some studies proved its positive impact on the economic development empirically, while other studies highlighted its negative effects as well. In general, aid is found to have a positive impact on economic growth through several mechanisms: 1) aid increases investment ; 2) aid increases the capacity to import capital goods or technology; 3) aid does not have an adverse impact on investment and savings; 4) aid increases the capital productivity and promotes endogenous technical change (Morrissey 2001).

On the empirical front, a number of studies have evaluated the effect of foreign aid on economic development in various countries. These studies have mainly used time series econometric analyses. Past studies of the aid-growth relationship have produced mixed results and have been criticized for methodological shortcomings associated with cross-country studies. Country-specific studies have also failed to produce any conclusive results. Ajetomobi et al. (2007) have found that development assistance to Nigeria has contributed positively to output growth. The impact was found to be stronger when in association with the exchange rate—one of the key variables of interest in structural adjustment policy. It is further found that development assistance is more effective when devaluation of the national currency has progressed further. In other words, aid and currency devaluation are mutually reinforcing.

Mallik (2008) in his study on foreign aid and economic development in the six poorest African Countries—namely the Central African Republic, Malawi, Mali, Niger, Sierra Leone, and Togo—has found that in five out of the six countries, the natural log of foreign aid as a percentage of real GDP has a significant negative long-run effect on the natural log of real GDP per capita. In the short run, aid growth has no significant effect on economic growth per capita for most of the countries except for Niger.

Dibeh (2007) found that after the war in Lebanon, foreign aid was mainly channeled toward providing resources for postwar reconstruction projects during the first phase, from 1992 to 1997. However, the second phase, from 1997 to the present, witnessed a qualitative shift in foreign aid utilization, from reconstruction toward financial stability and balance-of-payments (BOP) equilibrium. This shift allowed the government to intervene in the foreign exchange market, maintained balance-of-payments surpluses during this period, reduced interest rates on public debt instruments, and finally provided the necessary liquidity and "confidence" for the government to continue borrowing funds from local commercial banks and foreign investors. More importantly, this shift in foreign aid allowed the government to avoid financial and currency crises in 2002.

Ghulam (2005) in his paper on the Impact of Foreign Aid on Economic Development in Pakistan, found that foreign aid has helped boost GDP growth through structural transformation of the economy; laid foundations of the industrial and agricultural sectors; provided technical assistance, policy advice, and modern technology; assisted in overcoming budget deficits and BOP deficits; and funded projects for social sector development. As the regression analysis of GDP and the ODA confirms, Official Development Assistance (ODA) has a positive effect on GDP. GDP increases at the decreasing rate as the flow of foreign capital increases. Thus, the overall impact of aid on economic development is positive. Burhop (2005) examined the causal relationship between time series of foreign aid, income per capita, and investment for forty-five developing countries. The results indicate that eleven countries exhibit a causal relationship running from aid quota to income per capita. An impulse-response analysis reveals a positive relationship for only four countries. Once more, the effect of a positive aid shock is negative in seven countries. Chile, Mali, Haiti, and Syria successfully transformed aid into per capita growth.

A bivariate Granger causality test by Dhakal et al. (1996) involving four Asian countries (India, Nepal, Pakistan, and Thailand) and four African countries (Botswana, Kenya, Malawi, and Tanzania), using data from 1960 to 1990, failed to find any causal relationship between foreign aid and economic growth in any of these countries. On the other hand, Levy

(1988) found aid to be positively and significantly correlated with investment and economic growth in Africa. Using the Autoregressive Distributed Lag (ARDL) model, Gounder (2001) found that aid has a positive and significant effect on growth in Fiji.

Burnside and Dollar (1997), in their well-known paper "Aid, Policies, and Growth," find that aid has a positive impact on growth in developing countries with good fiscal, monetary, and trade policies but has little impact in countries where such policies are poor. The study uses data from fifty-six countries for six four-year periods beginning with 1970–1973 and ending with 1990–1993 and constructs a growth convergence model in which growth depends on the logarithm of real per capita GDP at the beginning of the period, incorporating the ratio of aid over GDP and an index measurement for macroeconomic policies in the right-hand side of the equation. The authors explain that "aid can affect output only through its effect on the stock of capital, that is, to the extent that it is used for investment rather than consumption." They argue that aid itself has a small and insignificant impact, but that aid interacting with good policy has a significant positive impact on growth. In fact, policy seems more important for aid effectiveness in lower-income countries. Moreover, the authors show that aid follows diminishing returns to scale. Another finding is that there is no tendency for total aid or bilateral aid to favor good policy, while multilateral aid is allocated in favor of good policy.

Papanek (1973), in a cross-country regression analysis of thirty-four countries in the 1950s and fifty-one countries in the1960s, treating foreign aid, foreign investment, other flows, and domestic savings as explanatory variables, finds that foreign aid has a substantially greater effect on growth than the other variables. He explains that "aid, unlike domestic savings, can fill the foreign exchange gap as well as the savings gap. Unlike foreign private investment and other foreign inflows, aid is supposed to be specifically designed to foster growth and, more importantly, is biased toward countries with a balance-of-payment constraint."

Fayissa and El-Kaissy (1999), in a study of seventy-seven countries over the sub-periods 1971–1980, 1981–1990, and 1971–1990, show that foreign aid positively affects economic growth in developing countries. Using modern economic growth theories, they point out that foreign aid, domestic savings, human capital, and export are positively correlated with economic growth in the studied countries. This is consistent with the economic theory of foreign aid, which asserted that overseas development assistance accelerates economic growth by supplementing domestic capital formation (Chenery and Strout 1966).

Pedersen (1996) asserts that it is still not possible to conclude that aid affects growth positively. Using game theory, he argues that the problems lie in the built-in incentive of the aid system itself. The aid conditionality is not sufficient and the penalties are not hard enough when recipient countries deviate from their commitments. In fact, there are incentives for aid-donating agencies to disburse as much aid as possible. This hinders the motivation of recipient countries and raises aid dependency, which in turn distorts development. Leff (1969) and Griffin and Enos (1970) have analyzed aid's negative impacts on growth. They argued that foreign aid could adversely affect economic growth by substituting domestic savings. So the literature on effectiveness of foreign aid shows positive as well as negative effects on economic development. Hansen and Tarp (2000) run a regression between aid and growth, where it is shown that aid increases the growth rate, and this result is not conditional on "good" policy.

## Methodology and Data

Earlier models for the determination of the aid-growth link were based on the Harrod-Domar growth model. The earliest of these models was developed by Chenery and Strout (1966). These models assume that there is an excess in the supply of labor, and growth is only constrained by the availability and productivity of capital. Three gaps were identified as constraints to growth, and these need to be filled by foreign aid to enable investment. The three gaps are: 1) savings gap, 2) trade balance gap, and 3) fiscal gap. In general most poor countries have inadequate levels of savings, and foreign aid can supplement those savings, which could then be directed to investment. In this case we assume that all foreign aid will be allocated for investment purposes. It is thus assumed that foreign aid will assist those countries to fill this gap, thus supplementing export earnings required to import capital goods. Most of the developing, underdeveloped, and especially the poor countries do not have the revenue-raising capacity to cover a desired level of public investment. Therefore, foreign aid is seen as essential to fill this gap.

One of the problems is that most studies of the aid-growth relationship are based on cross-country regressions, which lump together countries of heterogeneous characteristics and size. There are very few studies of the poorest African countries that examine the issue using single-country, time-series data. There is also the problem of reverse causality. For example, aid may follow in response to poor growth (and saving) performance, producing a high correlation between low growth and high aid flows. In order to avoid the problems of heteroskedasticity and the non-normality of distribution associated with cross-country studies, and the specification problems arising from simultaneity (endogeneity), we use co-integration analysis. Our variables of interest are: real gross domestic product, foreign direct investment as a percentage of gross domestic product, domestic investment as a percentage of gross domestic product, overseas development assistance, and openness. The essence of a co-integrating relationship is that the variables in the system share a common unit-root process. This methodology is also particularly suitable in this context because it provides a flexible functional form for modeling the behavior of the variables under the long-run equilibrium condition.

In the present study, the Augmented Dickey-Fuller (ADF) and Phillip-Perron tests were used to test for stationarity of the data. Both the constant and trend were included in the testing of the stationarity. The ADF test shows that all the variables except for the share of domestic investment in GDP are non-stationary. Having confirmed that most data series are non-stationary in levels, tests were further conducted to establish whether the data series are stationary in first difference or not. The results show that the variables with exception of investment are stationary in first difference when constant and trend are included. Thus, each of the original variables is integrated of order one. Furthermore, a test for co-integration using the Augmented Dickey-Fuller test revealed that the dependent variable is co-integrated with the independent variables.

| | ADF | I(d) |
|---|---|---|
| ΔFDIGDP | -4.9314 | I(1) |
| ΔODA | -4.5565 | I(1) |
| ΔRGDP | -4.3213 | I(1) |
| ΔOPEN | -3.5917 | I(1) |
| IGDP | -3.6846 | I(0) |
| ΔGCON | -3.98 | I(1) |

**Table 3.1. Unit Root Tests**

Source: Regression results. I(d) refers to the order of integration.

| | |
|---|---|
| Residuals | -4.6979 |

**Table 3.2: Co-integration Test using ADF**

Source: Regression results. I(d) refers to the order of integration.

## Model Specification

For the empirical testing, we follow the econometric specification of Mallik's (2008) endogenous growth model,[1] and thus consider the following specifications.

$$\Delta logRGDP_t = \beta_0 + \beta_1 \Delta logOPEN_t + \beta_2 \Delta logODA_t + \beta3 \Delta logFDIGDPt +$$

$$\beta_4 logIGDP_t + \beta_5 \Delta logGCON + U_t \quad (1)$$

Where RGDP is the real gross domestic product, openness is the share of the sum of exports and imports in the GDP, ODA is the ratio of overseas development assistance to the gross domestic product, FDIGDP is the share of foreign domestic investment in GDP, IGDP is the ratio of gross fixed capital formation to the gross domestic product, GCON is the share of government consumption in GDP, and $U_t$ is the random term assumed to be Gaussian white noise. All variables were entered in logarithmic form. The equations were estimated using the ordinary least square (OLS) regression method, and the data (for the period 1990–2007) was analyzed using EVIEWS 5.0, an econometric software package. The foreign direct investment, gross fixed capital formation, and overseas development assistance have been lagged for one year due to the fact that investments often take time before their effect on output can be registered. The fiscal data were converted into calendar form.

## Sources and Nature of Data

Usually secondary data in a developing country like Namibia have problems. But until these problems are solved we do the best we can with what we have. Availability of data has been a main constraint on the study. The primary source for data on foreign direct investment and overseas development assistance was the "Annual Report and Quarterly Bulletin" published by the Bank of Namibia. The data on government consumption and gross domestic product is obtained from national accounts published by the Central Bureau of Statistics in Namibia.

## The Empirical Results

In this section we have estimated three regression equations. The first regression equation includes all the explanatory variables, while in the second equation we have excluded overseas development assistance, and in equation 3 the ratio of foreign direct investment to GDP was left out. The exclusion of these variables in equations 2 and 3 was due to high correlation as depicted by the correlation matrix. However, it should be noted that the results are not significantly influenced by the exclusion of these variables in the respective equations. The estimated results are presented in Table 3.3. Regressions (1) to (3) in Table 3.3 show the results of the error correction model (ECM) and short-run dynamic models. A first conclusion from regression (1) is that foreign aid as proxied by overseas development assistance and foreign direct investment has a positive but insignificant effect on economic development in Namibia. When ODA was excluded from regression (2), the coefficient of foreign direct investment was still positive but insignificantly associated with economic development.

In regression (3) the results indicate that overseas development assistance is positively correlated with economic development, although the relationship turned out to be insignificant. In Table 3.3 the sign of the explanatory variables, share of government consumption in gross domestic product, ratio of gross fixed capital formation to GDP, and openness are basically consistent with the theory. The regression results indicate that government consumption share in GDP affects growth negatively and that this effect is significant at one percent in all the regression equations. The sign of the coefficient of the variable conformed with the traditional theory that consumption does not lead to economic growth. An increase in consumption implies a reduction in savings only for a given level of national income, which will slow the growth rate of investment and thus lower the rate of economic growth. The share of gross domestic fixed investment in gross domestic product relates positively to economic growth in all the regression equations. Finally, the results support the proposition that openness affects growth positively.

## Conclusions

The purpose of this study was to investigate empirically the propositions regarding the effects of foreign aid on economic development. Using a simple analytical endogenous growth model, we have identified the effects of overseas development assistance and foreign direct investment on economic growth in Namibia. The main findings of the econometric estimation of the impact of foreign on economic growth can be summarized as follows. The results show that the first differences of all variables, with the exception of ratio of investment to gross domestic product, are stationary when constant and trend are included. A test for co-integration using the Augmented Dickey Fuller test revealed that the explanatory variables identified in this study are co-integrated with gross domestic product.

| | **Equation number** | | |
|---|---|---|---|
| **Explanatory Variable** | **1** | **2** | **3** |
| Constant | 0.2210<br>(0.1564) | -0.3267<br>(-0.2453) | -0.1975<br>(-0.1383) |
| $\Delta FDIGDP_{t-1}$ | 0.3676<br>(1.1023) | 0.3751<br>(1.1762) | ----<br>---- |
| $logIGDP_{t-1}$ | 0.0991<br>(0.2103) | 0.1325<br>(0.2980) | 0.0885<br>(0.1860) |
| $\Delta logODA_{t-1}$ | 0.0647<br>(0.4206) | ----<br>---- | 0.0738<br>(0.4758) |
| ΔlogOPEN | 0.4240<br>(0.5594) | 0.4821<br>(0.6752) | 0.6361<br>(0.8583) |
| ΔlogGCON | -2.4974<br>(-2.9683) | -2.5833<br>(-.3.3040) | -2.0999<br>(-2.7332) |
| ECM(-1) | -0.5490<br>(-1.7561) | -0.5484<br>(-1.8313) | -0.3566<br>-1.3604 |
| $R^2$<br>F<br>DW | 0.5569<br>1.8850<br>1.6173 | 0.5481<br>2.4263<br>1.5670 | 0.4970<br>1.9764<br>1.7874 |

**Table 3.3: Regression results: Growth equations with Real GDP (ΔlogGDP) as a Dependent Variable**

Source: Regression Results.

Despite the overall downward trend in the levels of development assistance, foreign expertise and financial support still play an important role in Namibia. The results indicate that the shares of investment in gross domestic product positively influence the short run behavior of the gross domestic product in Namibia. The level of government consumption ratio to GDP affects the real gross domestic product negatively. The findings show that the openness promotes economic activities in Namibia. Foreign aid, on the positive side, has helped boost GDP growth through structural transformation of the economy; laid foundations of the industrial and agricultural sectors; provided technical assistance, policy advice, and modern technology; assisted in overcoming the budget deficits and the BOP deficits; and funded projects for social sector development. As the regression analysis of GDP, foreign direct investment, and ODA confirms, the effect of Official Development Assistance (ODA) on GDP is positive. Thus the overall impact of foreign aid on the economic development is positive.

Our econometric analysis has relied on aggregate FDI data. A more disaggregated analysis of FDI into its various sectors of destination would certainly have shed more light on the impact of FDI in the Namibian economy. The policy implications of the exercise are not straightforward due to the weak relationship we found in the econometric estimation. The policies are also important in the effectiveness of foreign aid, as aid has a more positive impact on growth where there are good fiscal, monetary, and trade policies in place (Ghulam Mohey-ud-din 2007). In the presence of poor policies, on the other hand, aid has no positive effect on growth. Accordingly, there is a need not only for good policies but also for the implementation of these policies as well as the proper monitoring of aid-utilizing projects to avoid the misutilization and mismanagement of foreign capital resources. Consequently we can say that aid may help boost economic growth only under the presence of appropriate monetary, fiscal, and trade policies. Given the results of the study, injection of more aid into the Namibian economy will hasten growth. Thus, there is a need for government to strengthen its efforts to make Namibia competitive. The Namibian government should continue with the creation of a more investment-friendly environment, improving availability of infrastructure, and investing in education and promoting economic growth.

## Notes

[1] An economic theory which argues that economic growth is generated from within a system as a direct result of internal processes. More specifically, the theory notes that the enhancement of a nation's human capital will lead to economic growth by means of the development of new forms of technology and efficient and effective means of production.

# CHAPTER FOUR

# THE DONORS AND COUNTRY OWNERSHIP IN AFRICA'S WEAK STATES

NICOLAS VAN DE WALLE

## Introduction

Critics have long argued that foreign aid to Africa has not proven to be effective because it has fostered programs and policies that were not widely supported within the region itself (Berg 1997; Booth 2003; van de Walle and Johnson 1997; and World Bank 1998). Dissatisfaction with the impact of aid led to a process of reform a decade ago, resulting in the donors agreeing to the Paris Declaration on Aid Effectiveness (2005) and the subsequent Accra Agenda for Action (2008). Both these resolutions identified *country ownership* as a key ingredient for successful foreign aid programs that would spearhead sustainable economic development. Both Paris and Accra defined ownership as the key principle that developing countries must lead their own development policies and strategies and manage their own development work on the ground for foreign aid to be effective in promoting development. More specifically, recipient governments should be fully committed to the modalities and objectives agreed to with donors in specific projects or aid programs, including policy formulation, program implementation and monitoring and evaluating results. The lack of recipient country ownership has been widely viewed as a reason why so much of aid is poorly implemented and/or not sustained following the termination of donor support.

How has the implementation of the country ownership principle of the Paris and Accra Declarations changed donor programs? This chapter seeks to critically take stock of the progress made since the mid 2000s, focusing in particular on the relationship between governance and country ownership, notably in Africa's so-called fragile states. Such principles as encouraging dialogue on aid matters between donors and recipient governments, hashing out a framework of mutual accountability, integrating aid into government budgeting and planning processes, and encouraging a more participatory process which consults with legislatures, local government and civil society will all improve aid efficiency and sustainability in some countries, if they are judiciously undertaken. The early evidence from various evaluations of the implementation of the Paris Declaration suggests that ownership can play a useful role in improving aid effectiveness.

However, this chapter argues, the new practices being developed today to promote aid ownership are at best problematic for many African countries that lack several requisite characteristics: good governance, relatively high state capacity and a general commitment to economic development. In countries without these characteristics, country ownership remains desirable but is likely to be quite elusive, with much of the new aid modalities of recent years unlikely to help develop ownership, and it may indeed prove counterproductive. In fact, I argue that some of the donors have lost sight of the Paris Declaration's explicit recommendation to combine selectivity principles with the implementation of an ownership strategy.

The argument proceeds in the following manner. The next two sections define the concept of country ownership more carefully and trace its origins to debates about aid effectiveness in the mid 1990s. Distinct definitions of the concept exist within the policy community, with different implications for governance and donor-recipient relations. Significantly, the initial call for modalities that promoted ownership was typically accompanied by calls for greater aid selectivity as well. Over time, and perhaps because of the disbursement pressures faced by the donor community in the wake of the Monterrey Consensus and the Millennium Development Goals campaign, the emphasis on selectivity has been attenuated and only the focus on ownership has remained.

Section 4 assesses the progress on the ownership agenda announced by the Paris and Accra resolutions and initially carried out through the World Bank's Poverty Reduction Strategy Papers (PRSP) process. It argues that the donors have made significant progress on implementing several new aid modalities, most notably the systematic resort to the PRSP documents and to sectoral program aid and direct budget support for recipient governments, but that there is little evidence so far that these initiatives have actually had much of an impact on promoting ownership, particularly in the poorest and most fragile low-income states of the region.

Section 5 identifies four prerequisites for the comprehensive implementation of an ownership agenda and suggests these are likely to be absent in many of the poorest countries most in need of foreign aid. Section 6 discusses the implications of regime type for country ownership. Section

7 discusses the implications for donors and for Democracy and Governance programming in particular. The chapter concludes by suggesting some simple ways to assess the extent of country ownership that is present or possible, depending on the nature of the political regime and the degree of state capacity, and it suggests ways in which USAID Democracy and Governance (DG) programs can contribute to the medium- to long-term enhancement of country ownership.

## The Paris Declaration and Ownership

Several studies of aid effectiveness during the 1990s (World Bank 1998; Berg 1997; van de Walle and Johnston 1997) argued that foreign aid's impact on poverty reduction and economic growth in low-income countries was undermined by donor practices and aid modalities that negatively affected the incentive structure for local actors. In particular, the proliferation of donors and projects, the poor integration of donor activities with other developmental actions of recipient governments, and the limited role of recipient governments in the design and implementation of aid projects was viewed as undermining the incentives to local officials to value the aid resources and seek to maximize their developmental impact. In sum, this literature argued that greater aid effectiveness would result if different measures were undertaken to increase the sense of *ownership* of aid resources by local officials. Aid would have a greater impact if it was better aligned with local policies and preferences, and if local officials took a greater role in the design and implementation of aid activities.

The advocacy for greater ownership was usually accompanied by a call for greater *selectivity* of aid, whereby the policy and governance performance of aid recipients would substantially determine how much aid they received. The call for greater selectivity was reinforced by studies that suggested that aid was more likely to have a positive effect on growth if it was provided in contexts of "good" macro-economic and sectoral policies (for instance, Burnside and Dollar 2000). Thus, countries that pursued these policies were designated to receive more aid, with a greater role in its disbursements, but at the same time, in order to sharpen the incentives to recipients, more problematic performers would simultaneously receive less aid. Indeed, many observers noted that this new aid reform agenda would be likely to result in a slowdown in the growth of aid volume, as selectivity criteria would result in fewer recipients and ownership dynamics would, at least initially, create disbursement bottlenecks (see Joseph and Gillies 2009).

The reforms pursued in the aid community during the last decade and encapsulated in the Paris Declaration of 2005 reflect the reform agenda laid out in these aid effectiveness studies. The end-product of a series of meetings of the High-Level Forum on Aid Effectiveness, the Declaration committed donor countries belonging to the Organization for Economic Cooperation and Development (OECD) to increasing their volumes of aid with the recognition that improving aid effectiveness was central to the goal of meeting the Millennium Development Goals. The Declaration itself centers around five related principles:

- Developing countries exercise leadership over their development policies and plans *(ownership).*
- Donors base their support on countries' development strategies and systems *(alignment).*
- Donors coordinate their activities and minimize the cost of delivering aid *(harmonization).*
- Developing countries and donors orient their activities to achieve the desired results *(managing for results).*
- Donors and developing countries are accountable to each other for progress in managing aid better and in achieving development results *(mutual accountability)* (OECD 2005).

The rest of this essay focuses on the first of these objectives, but it must be said that in the logic of the Paris Declaration, all of the objectives were designed to help increase the recipient government's commitment and capacity to undertake economic development, so in many respects, country ownership was the cornerstone concept of the Declaration.

## Variations in the Definition of Ownership

The Paris Declaration's original text called for "partner countries to exercise effective leadership over their development policies and strategies and [to] coordinate development actions" (OECD 2005, 5). Specifically, this required recipient countries to effectively take over the formulation of national development strategies, turn these strategies into operational programs linked to the national budget, and work to coordinate aid in partnership with donors, civil society, and the private sector (OECD 2005, 5). This formulation combined two distinct conceptions of ownership that in fact have important implications for donor-recipient relations, and about which the aid community has never been in complete agreement.

First, there is a "technocratic" version of ownership, in which the central government officials working closely with the donor community are encouraged to exhibit commitment to the development process and leadership over its implementation (for instance, see Best 2007, and Boughton and Mourmouras 2002, on the IMF's evolving conception of ownership). Second, however, discussions of ownership also put forward what might be called the "participatory" view of country ownership, in which ownership develops when the donors and government consult broadly with civil society, the private sector, and other non-governmental actors over aid and development policy. Ownership cannot really be sustained, it is argued, if the development process is not broadly participatory. As Meyer and Schulz (2008) point out, participatory ownership evokes both a means and an end: development policy that emerges out of democratic dialogue is a means to aid effectiveness while at the same time democratic participation is an end in and of itself (2008, 8; see also Entwistle and Cavassini 2003).

Over time, the OECD has tended to focus more on the participatory dimensions of ownership. For instance, the Accra Agenda for Action defined ownership as the process wherein developing countries will take "stronger leadership of their own development policies, and will engage their parliaments and citizens in shaping those policies" (OECD 2008c, 15). Central among the debates in Accra were questions of how to broaden the concept beyond its narrow focus on the central government to involve parliaments, local government, and civil society (OECD 2008a, 10–11), although as this essay argues below, it is easier to evaluate the technocratic definition of ownership.

The policy literature often fails to appreciate the extent to which these two definitions are in tension with each other. Since recipient governments and civil society organizations sometimes compete for donor support, they may have quite different policy preferences or differing views on what constitutes meaningful participation. Broad participation is clearly desirable in certain circumstances. When recipient governments are unresponsive to societal needs or uncommitted to poverty reduction, giving voice to the poor or to underserved communities can only help to improve policy making, and it would probably be counter-productive for donors to shield government officials from their own populations. Most observers agree that aid is improved when the recipients themselves have been involved in its design and implementation.

On the other hand, some areas of policy are probably not improved by broad participation. For instance, a long-standing conventional wisdom argues that monetary policy is improved when it is made by insulated, autonomous officials who are not pressured by societal forces. In addition, in practice, participation may introduce or exacerbate certain biases in development policy. In some countries, for instance, the civil society organizations that are likely to benefit from opening up the aid process may over-represent certain interests at the expense of others. Some critics have argued that much of civil society is too dependent on donor support to be considered an autonomous indigenous actor (Hearn 2007). There is some evidence, furthermore, that civil society often over-represents urban populations and thus perpetuates the urban bias in government policy. In Mali, for instance, most civic associations supported the donor-led efforts to reform the national Family Code, even though it turned out that a strong majority of the population was against it (Bleck and van de Walle 2011).

Finally, in liberal democracies, in which elections are free and fair and legislatures can be said to be truly representative, outsiders giving voice and resources to civil society actors may not necessarily advance either democratic governance or real participation, as it is far from clear that specific civic organizations are more representative than elected officials. Furthermore, donor support for non-state actors may in some cases undermine democratic consolidation, if the resulting increase in participation puts stress on fledgling democratic institutions.

It is thus important to assess the relationship between states and societal forces and between central state officials and the non-governmental sector to fully understand whether or not broad-based and equitable development will be abetted by broader participation. This point is discussed at greater length below.

## Progress on the Paris Declaration Ownership Objectives

Over the course of the past decade or so, donors have sought to carry out many of the principles embodied in the Paris and Accra documents. This has in particular taken the form of two new types of aid modality. First, the World Bank's implementation of the Poverty Reduction Strategy Papers (PRSP), an early attempt to promote local ownership around an integrated anti-poverty national strategy, has now been extended to the enormous majority of developing countries, with ninety completed strategies formally accepted by donors as of 2009. Most low-income countries now have some ongoing PRSP process at some stage of negotiation with donors. To be sure, some countries have not yet managed to complete a PRSP process, and enthusiasm for this modality appears to have waned in the donor community as a result of many of the issues discussed in this essay (Booth 2005; Driscoll and Evans 2005; World Bank Operations 2008). However, the PRSP provided the template for a host of sector-specific program aid efforts involving multiple donors and formally putting into place mechanisms for recipient accountability and participation that remain in place today.

The second new type of aid modality being put into practice is direct budget support to low-income governments, and this too has increased substantially in recent years. For the nineteen countries receiving systematic budget support, such assistance constitutes on average 19 percent of these countries' Official Development Assistance or ODA (SPA 2007). A 2007 survey by the Strategic Partnership with Africa (SPA) estimated that some $2.4 billion in budget support was given in 2005 to the fifteen countries it surveyed. That year, Rwanda received the equivalent of 8.4 percent of its national GDP in budget support, Sierra Leone 7.9 percent, Malawi 6.3 percent, and Mozambique 5.3 percent.

Budget support has the advantage of allowing rapid disbursement of funds, and it facilitated the ability of donors to increase their aid quickly following the emergence of the Millennium Development Goals Campaign in the 2000s. However, the donors sought to accompany budget support funding with clear policy and implementation conditionality. Thus, most budget support programs came with fairly detailed conditions, which usually required the creation of new structures to monitor implementation of the government programs made possible by budget support. In many cases, budget support was devoted to sector-wide programs, so the degree of government discretion over the funds was *a priori* limited (see Sridhar 2009 for the case of health-sector support). In Mali, for instance, a number of donors have provided budget support to the education sector for almost a decade now. There is a clear division of labor among the donors regarding the technical assistance that accompanies the funding, and a complex decision-making structure in which the donors are well represented designs, monitors, and evaluates implementation of the program that the donors agreed to with the Government, formally integrated into the ministry, but largely supplanted in the policy-making process (van de Walle, 2013, forthcoming). In sum, it should be understood that new modalities such as budget support, initially designed to promote country ownership, have not reduced either the level of conditionality or the involvement of the donors in day-to-day implementation issues (Molenaers and Nijs 2009).

Numerous studies have similarly evaluated progress toward the Paris Declaration's goals on country ownership since 2005. By the OECD's own standards, ownership is measured by the presence of an operational development strategy—a national strategy that establishes long-term development goals linked to national budgets. By the time of the OECD's 2008 monitoring assessment of the Paris Declaration, only 24 percent of participating countries had implemented such a strategy, far short of the

Declaration's goal of 75 percent by 2010. Donor support for country-owned development processes, measured by donor use of partner-country procurement and financial management systems similarly fell short of the Declaration's 2010 goals, with only 43 and 45 percent of aid channeled through each of these, respectively (OECD 2008b, 13).

On balance, thus, progress has been uneven and halting for the objectives of country ownership. The annual evaluations by the OECD (for instance, OECD 2008b) suggest only modest progress in terms of the quantitative measures that are supposed to measure progress on the Paris Declaration objectives, and not much momentum. OECD's 2008 report (OECD 2008b) examines progress for a number of indicators between 2005 and 2007, and typically finds self-reported forward progress in roughly half to two-thirds of the recipient countries. For instance, on average, 43 percent of donor procurement followed country systems in 2007, up from 39 percent in 2005, but this percentage had actually declined in seven countries. (OECD 2008b, 83).

The World Bank's evaluations of the PRSPs (for instance, World Bank 2009) suggest the extent to which the process remains poorly integrated with national development efforts and largely dominated by the donors and a small cadre of government officials. In their comprehensive review for the World Bank, Entwistle and Cavassini (2005) show how little progress has been made in integrating PRSPs with national planning and budgeting efforts. Only three out of the fifty-nine PRSPs they examined had a ministerial monitoring and evaluation system to track implementation of PRS, and in only about half of the countries had sectoral ministries aligned their policies with those of the PRSP. The problems were even greater once the participatory dimension was taken into account: in only seven of the fifty-nine countries had national parliaments been involved in the design and/or monitoring of the program.

How much have these new modalities actually promoted country ownership? Measuring the change in ownership over time is a difficult task. As Boughton and Mourmouras (2002) observe in relation to the IMF's attempts to promote ownership, assessing the concept is inherently subjective due to its inability to be directly observed by donors, its dynamic nature, and debates over *who* the owner of a policy is or should be (2002, 3–4). While the OECD clearly provides an indicator for assessing ownership's technical dimensions, the broader, participatory understanding of the term is neglected in the OECD monitoring survey that raises difficult questions about levels of democracy and ownership quality.

Measurement has, in fact, emerged as one of the most problematic and contentious areas surrounding the Paris Declaration, notably concerning country ownership. A report by the OECD itself admitted that ownership is "the most poorly defined of the Declaration's principles" (2008d, 12). In large part, this critique is rooted in the fact that the national development strategies required to meet the OECD's ownership indicator are contingent upon the production of a Poverty Reduction Strategy Paper, a project undertaken by partner countries that requires the approval of the World Bank. Donor influence on the "production of development knowledge" is then seen as interfering in the ability of a state to "own" its development plan in even a technical sense (OECD 2008d, 12).

In sum, the Paris Declaration's objectives regarding ownership have made some progress, even though significant roadblocks remain. What about its goals regarding selectivity? Given the original twin concerns for selectivity and ownership, one might have assumed that donors would have sought to implement the ownership agenda more comprehensively in better performing states. In fact, though, this does not appear to be the case. Strikingly, it has proven easier for the donor community to focus on ownership issues than on selectivity. In the United States, the emergence of the Millennium Challenge Corporation (MCC) in the early 2000s reflected the dual concerns of promoting greater selectivity and ownership at the same time (Radelet 2003; Lucas 2011). The MCC has largely met its mandate to select a small number of states that met fairly tough policy and governance criteria, and then grant them substantial aid packages in a process that would emphasize local ownership. On the other hand, the MCC's attention to the other aspects of the Paris Declaration has clearly not been a mandate and has not shaped its programming (Molenaers and Nijs 2009; Molenaers and Renard 2011).

The MCC experience is fairly unique. For other donors, the new aid modalities—including PRSPs, sector program aid, direct budget support and various donor alignment mechanisms—have been pursued in some of the poorest countries with histories of poor performance. The World Bank has actually targeted the category of several dozen countries it labels LICUS countries (Low Income Countries Under Stress) for PRSPs, under the argument that such a process will help build ownership. This approach has resulted in the formulation of PRSPs in post-conflict states such as Sierra Leone or, outside of Africa, in Cambodia. Also noteworthy are the current efforts to develop a PRSP in Afghanistan.

To be sure, the donors have moved away from the complete absence of selectivity that existed in an earlier period, in which aid was not withheld from even the most corrupt and incompetent governments (van de Walle 2005; Alesina and Dollar 2000). Still, the paragraphs below should make clear the extent to which the implementation of the Paris Declaration has disengaged from the original concern with greater aid selectivity. Instead, and despite a new terminology that emphasizes terms like "partnership" and "mutual accountability," these new modalities have been implemented with considerable amounts of old-fashioned conditionality. Resources, for instance, have been distributed in tranches that are subject to review of recipient country performance; donor-driven monitoring and evaluation processes have been emphasized and donor-funded expertise has played a key role in the design and implementation of aid activities to enhance quality controls. The language of partnership is somewhat disingenuous when only one partner can ever be held accountable or sanctioned.

The problems with the implementation of the ownership agenda have typically been most pronounced in the poorest countries and LICUS countries, according to considerable evidence that decisions by specific donors to interrupt the implementation of the new modalities has typically resulted from governance breakdowns and local capacity inadequacies. In the early 1990s, for instance, Malawi's direct budget support was interrupted several times because of accusations of high-level corruption. In August 2010, a consortium of donors announced it was reducing its budget support to Uganda by 10 percent to protest slow progress in combating graft. In 2011, several donors suspended their assistance to Mali because of a scandal involving the Minister of Health.

## Problematic Assumptions

The early evidence thus suggests that implementation of the ownership agenda has been uneven and particularly halting in the poorest and most fragile low income states. Why is this? In this section, it is argued that the new aid modalities to promote ownership described above make several overlapping assumptions about recipient governments that are often unrealistic, and when and where they are, the pursuit of greater "ownership" may be problematic for development outcomes. Four such assumptions in particular need to be examined:

### Governments actually have stable policy preferences

It is possible to imagine several situations in which this is likely to be a problematic assumption:

- Governments may lack the capacity to develop, articulate and carry out policy preferences. Very low capacity governments that have become highly aid-dependent may not really know what they want or have the ability to help carry out and evaluate donor projects. Thus, in recent years, donors that have sought to build ownership by having low-income governments design policy themselves have found this entails lengthy delays and special attention to capacity-building within key policy-making departments. Governments that lack the capacity to fully implement their own tax policies, for instance, or provide basic services to their populations are unlikely to be able to take full ownership of the development process.

- Governments may be more focused on power and wealth maintenance of the ruling elite than on development and as a result subordinate all development policies to the purpose of staying in power and preserving elite wealth. This can result in an absence of policy preference, or (see below) in a preference for anti-developmental policies. In some countries, the government exempts key elites from tax collection efforts or provides lucrative import licenses to political supporters that in effect undermine its official trade policies. Kleptocratic regimes such as Mobutu's Zaire, or the Equatorial Guinea of Nguema are the most extreme form of such regimes, where the government's predatory behavior all but entirely displaces developmental policy.
- Elections or regime change may introduce substantial changes in policy preferences that are at odds with agreements the previous government made with donors. The electoral victory of the Sandanistas in Nicaragua, for instance, democratically brought to power a government that rejected many of the policy choices the previous government had agreed to with donors (Schulz 2007).

## Governments have policy preferences that have the potential to contribute to broad-based development

This may not be the case. For example:

- A government may have substantial policy differences with donors, or some subset of donors, in which case ownership may lead to the implementation of policies the donors do not want carried out. In some cases, these policies are clearly wrong-headed. One can imagine, for instance, a government policy of collectivization of agricultural production. In the recent past, some low-income countries have pursued disastrous macro-economic policies for short-term political gain that strongly undermined long-term development; in other cases, the merits of the policy are more ambiguous and contentious. Some recipient countries have sought to maintain unsustainable subsidies with the help of donor resources. In Malawi during the late 2000s, for instance, the donors and government disagreed on the need for fertilizer subsidies, which amounted to as much as 16 percent of the government budget. The government's decision to restore the program in 2007 was contested by many donors.

- More commonly, part of or all of the government may lack the commitment to promote development at all. As noted above, some governments are entirely motivated by the need to stay in power, and this leads them to prefer policies that increase rents and discretion, rather than policies that promote growth and poverty alleviation. Or in some cases power maintenance leads the government to favor (or ignore) a region of the country or a specific ethnic group, even if this makes little sense from a growth/poverty alleviation dimension. Successive governments in Cameroon, for example, did not want to rebuild the Douala-Bafoussam road in the 1970s and 1980s because the southern/northern-led governments feared the economic power of the Bamileke ethnic group in the west of the country, which would have benefited from such a road. In a number of countries, economic policy has been used to punish a region that did not support the government in recent elections.

Too often, the ownership paradigm has been viewed as a mechanism for policy learning by recipient countries that leads them to adopt donor policy preferences. But it must be recognized that this is both simplistic and ethnocentric: simplistic because governments that are motivated by political logics rather than by the promotion of economic development may not be amenable to rational policy learning; ethnocentric because in some cases it is the donors who presumably would benefit from policy dialogue.

## Recipient governments are democratic enough that their policies are representative of the population and subjected to some degree of accountability

Clearly, if a government is deeply and completely unrepresentative, then government ownership of the aid process is not necessarily desirable. Likewise, accountability mechanisms are likely to be weak or nonexistent. In a country such as Zimbabwe, in which surveys suggest President Mugabe retains the support of only a small minority of the population at this point, granting the government greater discretion over donor resources and programs would hardly advance the objectives that motivate the ownership agenda. On the contrary, advancing the ownership agenda probably implies finding ways to empower the civil society that opposes the government.

### Governments are unified actors and bureaucracies and/or sub-national governments necessarily will comply with national political leadership

This, too, is often not the case.

- In democratic governments, the executive may be at odds with the legislature or extreme partisanship may distort or undermine policy implementation. Likewise, whether out of lack of capacity or because of differing motivations, bureaucracies may not be responsive. And in countries where there is a strong regional, ethnic or tribal element to politics and governance, the application of national policies may range from selective to non-existent.
- Government may be divided—either at the national level or between the center and regional or sub-national governments, where fundamental disagreements may exist. In federal states as diverse as South Africa, Nigeria or Ethiopia, state governments may have policy priorities very different from those of the central government, even when these are not mediated by political partisanship.

## Implications of Regime Type, Commitment and Capacity for Ownership

In sum, these critical assumptions hold in some cases, but not in others, which enormously complicates the implementation of an ownership agenda. Indeed, the problems identified by evaluations of the Paris Declaration discussed above almost invariably have their origins in one or more of these assumptions not being met by the recipient country. Even within a single country, differences in capacity and across sectors and regions have important implications. Democratic governments may be elite-dominated and/or have bureaucracies propelled by rent-seeking and patronage, even though political and civil rights are respected. National governments may lack democratic legitimacy, even as local governments are adequately democratic and/or representative. Even the most neo-patrimonial governments are likely to include pockets of technocratic capacity and developmental ambition.

The broad set of new modalities of the ownership agenda is likely to prove problematic when governance issues, serious capacity problems, and internal dissensions and divisions exist within the recipient country. Careful analysis is needed to understand better the trade-offs that are likely to exist among the different dynamics present in different types of recipient countries. Ownership difficulties differ across countries, depending on the nature of the regime, the extent of sub-national variation, the degree of state capacity, and the economic ideologies of policy elites. In the analysis below, we can identify three overlapping types of problematic recipient countries: non-developmental, low-capacity states, countries with authoritarian or non-representative governments, and finally fragile states, which can be defined as unstable non-developmental states, which typically include elements of both low capacity and authoritarian governance, and fragile states which include all of these negative elements. In each case, specific implications for aid can be identified.

## Non-developmental/Low-capacity countries

These are countries that exhibit very low capacity and little progress on economic development, despite the absence of significant internal violence. They are often characterized by poor governance, including significant corruption and political clientelism, despite the fact that many have moved to multi-party electoral politics in recent years, and many are not particularly authoritarian. The category includes such African countries as Benin, Central African Republic, Malawi and Mali.

This categorization reflects the view that very low capacity results from the lack of developmental ambition within the government. Even the poorest countries have the ability to develop the human capital to devise and implement development policies, but in a number of recipient countries, governments clearly have a hard time mobilizing this capital, which does not appear regularly available to it for a wide variety of reasons. In many settings, policy capacity can be understood to be endogenous to political and broader governance dynamics, which are discussed below. In other words, capacity is not an independent variable, over which recipient countries have no control, such as the weather or the absence of natural resources. Instead, governments choose to systematically under-invest in capacity-building for political reasons, so that over time low capacity results. For example, many countries have allowed the politicization of the promotion process within the civil service, so that in time, the top of the civil service is of inconsistent quality, and many top civil servants have then left public service. As a result, state capacity does not improve, despite the existence of an increasing pool of well-trained professionals. It is in this sense that these countries can be understood to be non-developmental.

The new aid modalities imply the capacity on the part of the government to undertake and sustain a "policy dialogue" with the donors. It is important to distinguish between dialogue and what might be called a "master class," in which the recipient government learns from the donors, as a dialogue suggests that at least some of the policy choices originate within the recipient country. For even minimal policy learning to take place requires the capacity and motivation to design, monitor, and evaluate policy, to collect adequate statistics and so on. Yet, as Jerven's (2010) review of African economic statistics suggests, the data available to decision-makers in many African countries does not readily allow them to reach even straightforward conclusions as to whether the economy is growing or not. For instance, in a careful examination of Tanzanian statistics, Jerven (2011, 392) cautiously concludes, "there is considerable uncertainty and room for misinterpretation regarding the Tanzanian growth record. The data are seemingly malleable; thus, claims of causal relationships between policy variables and periods of economic growth should be treated with caution."

Low capacity has proven problematic for many of the new aid modalities. For instance, the PRSP and MCC ideal of strategy papers and compacts being more or less completely devised by the recipient government requires a fairly high level of local capacity and developmental motivation. In their absence, the evidence suggests that donors or experts hired by the donors account for much of the policy inspiration in these documents (de Renzio 2006), which are not locally owned in any meaningful sense. In the past decade, such weak and low capacity states as the Central African Republic, Cameroon, Chad, and Guinea all had ongoing PRSPs with the donors, espousing the language of country ownership and structured by the different agreements, consultations, and roundtables that were meant to facilitate dialogue between partners. The evidence suggests that, in fact, such PRSPs were mostly or even entirely inspired and designed from the donor side, and implemented with the help of donor-funded technical expertise.

At the very least, one cost of the ownership agenda in such countries almost certainly includes a slowdown of aid disbursements, as local institutions are likely to lack the experience and general capacity of donor institutions, and building them up seriously takes time. There is thus a pretty clear trade-off between aid flows and ownership in many low-income countries with low capacity, and effective capacity-building seems like a prerequisite to a successful ownership approach in the medium term. The Millennium Challenge Corporation experience is interesting here, since this body has perhaps proceeded further than most donors in trying to forge local ownership and in establishing mechanisms of mutual accountability. For a long time, this resulted in a slowdown in disbursements—for which the MCC came under serious political criticism in Washington. Most other donors could not withstand the pressure to disburse and have preferred to risk undermining long-term ownership development.

Yet recipient governments will lack the incentive to promote greater capacity if they believe that the aid spigot will never be turned off no matter how poor their performance in managing the aid. In the present situation, governments too often pay no penalty for their low capacity, and so are content with the present deficiencies, regardless of the number of times donor documents formally advocate the importance of capacity building.

The dilemma for the donors is that the need for aid in these countries is particularly strong, given persistent problems of absolute poverty and economic stagnation. It is this need that primarily sustains aid flows, despite the persistent dissatisfaction within the donor community regarding governance issues. In Malawi, donors have interrupted assistance several times, threatened to do so more often, and increased conditionalities attached to aid disbursements, yet aid flows continue to be quite high. Problematically, high levels of aid have provided valuable discretionary resources to governments and lessened their motivations to escape the low-level equilibrium in which they find themselves. There is no escaping this dilemma, but the current blank check of direct budget support seems like a recipe to sustain the current stagnation as well as waste limited development resources.

In sum, the key challenge in these states is altering the incentives to ruling elites and steering them into a more developmental path that includes greater ownership, without punishing their neediest citizens. That there are no easy solutions to this will surprise no one who works on development assistance programs.

## Non-democratic countries

Virtually all aid recipient countries now convene regular elections and at least tolerate some form of opposition. Still, one can distinguish a class of countries in which it is largely inconceivable that the incumbent president would lose an election and in which civil liberties and political rights are tolerated only to the extent that they do not impinge on the political elite's privileges and hold on power. Such aid recipients would include Ethiopia, Cameroon, Angola, and Burkina Faso. In such authoritarian political regimes with weak mechanisms of accountability and a history of participation repression, the more ambitious ownership instruments such as budget support seem misguided, even if capacity is not in question (though often it can be).

The recent literature (Moss et al 2008; Morrison 2009) argues that budget support can act much like oil revenues or other kinds of rent income to shield governments from both their own incompetence and popular accountability, helping them to maintain the political status quo but delay growth and poverty alleviation. Aid reduces the need for the government to collect local taxes, and as a result, governments lack the incentive to develop greater taxation capacity. In addition, and more seriously, the literature posits that without the need to garner a minimum of popular acquiescence in order to collect tax revenues from the population, governments are more likely to entirely eschew representative and legitimate institutions of participation. In effect, aid revenues protect them from their own mistakes and the need to gain and retain general legitimacy.

Some of these governments have developmental aspirations. Authoritarian countries such as Uganda under Museveni and Kagame's Rwanda have promoted significant efforts in economic development. But experience suggests that governments that do not face criticism and that escape the consequences of their actions are more often than not likely to underperform. Without either horizontal or vertical accountability, corruption and cronyism is more likely to flourish, and political elites are likely to abuse their discretion over state power and resources. That is indeed the overwhelming experience of authoritarian governments during the course of the past several decades, particularly when leaders (for instance, Museveni) are allowed to remain in power for a long time (van de Walle 2005).

In such circumstances, a large volume of aid of any kind represents a political choice on the part of the donors in favor of the status quo (Hyden 2008). Buttressed by aid, governments are more likely to survive in power because they ask little of their citizens, who are less likely to voice their disapproval of the government as a result. Limiting aid to projects and putting strenuous conditions on aid are at best palliative, but these measures do allow donors to somewhat limit the discretion of the political elites. Donors can maintain some discretion over the regions and segments of the population that will benefit from the aid that may be important in countries with ethno-regional divisions. One can argue about how much support of any kind donors should proffer to such governments, but it seems incontrovertible that program support and direct budget support enhance the discretion of the government over aid resources and are likely to comfort the status quo considerably more than project assistance (Faust 2010).

As a result, in the absence of representative institutions, the ownership agenda needs to focus on enhancing participation and accountability to try to bring the government to a greater developmental commitment in the long run. Increasing participation in aid processes can serve to promote vertical accountability in a way that is not the case in democratic countries, where mechanisms of accountability are already embedded in the political institutions. So involving civil society or aggressively promoting transparency in the aid process actually promotes greater democracy in a way that is not necessarily true in an already thriving electoral democracy. In the latter, on the other hand, strengthening the non-executive parts of the state may similarly promote democratic accountability mechanisms. In sum, while all forms of accountability are important to good governance, it seems to be the case that on the spectrum of regime type from authoritarian state to democracy, donors should prioritize vertical accountability for countries residing closer to the authoritarian end of the spectrum, while horizontal accountability becomes more appropriate the more a country is on the democratic side. Few low-income democracies could not stand to have their judiciary and legislative branches reinforced. On the other hand, promoting checks and balances in authoritarian states may have much less impact than promoting mechanisms of vertical accountability, such as a freer press or a stronger civil society.

## Fragile states

The most serious problems with the ownership paradigm appear most clearly in the so-called "fragile states," which combine low capacity and authoritarian governance with significant sub-national divisions, and thus, political and social instability. This category would include such countries as Sudan, Chad, and the Central African Republic, states in which the development process has essentially broken down because of a combination of ethno-regional divisions, very low levels of state capacity, and poor governance. In some cases, there are regular multi-party elections, albeit highly flawed, but in effect governments are essentially authoritarian, while governance remains highly clientelistic and corrupt. There may be elections, but of very uneven quality and with the potential to bring about spikes in violence and political instability. Many of these states have recently suffered from significant internal conflict and/or face the imminent possibility of conflict. Some are mired in significant persistent conflict.

In these states, building country ownership is urgently needed, yet much of the ambitious ownership agenda that can work in stable middle-income countries would not be realistic. The most urgent question is typically *whose* ownership needs to be promoted. Not only are these regimes typically authoritarian and non-participatory, and not only is state capacity in short supply, but in addition, perhaps their signal characteristic is that they are divided along some combination of ethno-linguistic, regional, ideological, or racial lines. As a result, any kind of external support is politicized, as it is in effect appropriated by one group, or believed to be so by marginalized groups.

Donors can claim they are promoting institutions and palliating individual needs and are thus "apolitical," but this is naïve since putting resources into a divided political space invariably has implications for the distribution of power in the country (Hyden 2008; Faust 2010). In fragile states, moreover, even state institutions are viewed as factionalized and not benefiting the entire population. Thus, Roberts (2009) argues that all aid to Afghanistan is tarnished by the widespread sense that it is not a national resource, but a group resource, to be monopolized by some at the expense of others. When this happens, aid may exacerbate political rivalries and conflict.

This is a real dilemma for all forms of aid in such countries—and one that donors traditionally have too often ignored. But the characteristic of the ownership agenda is that it aims to give more discretion to the government, and in a divided polity this implies a much starker political choice on the part of the donor in the eyes of the population. When the government is not only divisive, but also corrupt and not terribly competent, the results are also likely to prove disappointing from an economic development point of view.

One solution for donors is to direct more of the aid through impartial civic organizations and technocratic project structures. This may not be a step forward in terms of the development of ownership, but it may be a necessary short-term measure given the divisions in the country. Experience suggests that such project structures are not sustainable and encourage little capacity development, but they may be viewed as a lesser ill and necessary to attend to urgent welfare needs. Still, even this solution, if it is to ensure that projects are not captured by interests linked to a specific faction, requires considerably more knowledge of local politics than most donors typically possess.

## Implications

Perhaps the main implication of this chapter is that aid should never be viewed as non-political. Aid resources invariably have a political effect within the recipient country. This is true of all aid modalities, and the claim of political neutrality made in the past for the most traditional forms of conditional project aid ring hollow, as such aid still provided extra finite resources to some local actors and institutions and not to others, thus having an impact on the local balance of power. But the ownership agenda, which provides larger amounts of discretionary resources to local actors in often highly divided societies, is unambiguously political; it is crucial that donors be aware of this and able to deal with it. If nothing else, this puts a huge premium on having aid programs informed by greater knowledge of the local socio-political dynamics than is the case at present.

Donor evaluations of the Paris Declaration tend to blame recipients for shortfalls in implementation since 2005. Yet some of the Paris Declaration recommendations that have not been implemented primarily concern the donors themselves (see Sridhar 2009). So, for instance, the importance of *donor coordination* is, if anything, greater in countries with poor governance and low developmental capacity. In such countries, the absence of coordination is likely to exert a greater relative cost, given their unusually low level of capacity and, typically, the high levels of aid dependence. In addition, greater donor coordination is likely to increase the leverage donors have in promoting good governance and development in these countries, since it will make it harder for recipient governments to play donors off each other. Unlike many of the issues discussed in this chapter, the difficulties inherent in promoting donor coordination have little to do with recipient country characteristics and everything to do with bureaucratic and political exigencies within the donor countries. Most donors relish coordinating, but few enjoy being coordinated.

In some cases, implementation of a new modality is possible and desirable, but only if donors are willing to slow down aid disbursements considerably. Thus, in low capacity states that nonetheless have significant pockets of developmental commitment, the principle of alignment remains a useful one, but only if donors are willing to wait for local policy preferences to assert themselves. As MCC has learned, it takes time and effort to get governments to develop clear policy preferences. This takes time largely because recipient governments lack aid management capacity and are not used to making complex policy choices. Too often, disbursement pressures on the donor side preempt alignment as attempts at alignment overwhelm the fragile management systems on the recipient side, but this is the fault of impatient donors, not of the recipient governments. Having said that, if donors continue to lack the self-discipline to carry out alignment strategies, then they should entirely avoid the concept in fragile states, for which a phony alignment policy may be worse than none at all.

Evaluations of the Paris Declaration and of attempts to carry out an ownership agenda often suggest that a recurring obstacle to program success has been the lack of political expertise within donor agencies regarding local socio-political dynamics that have implications for the development commitment of recipient country institutions. In his review of budget support programs and the reasons for inconsistent results, Gerster (n.d., 6) notes dryly that "the donors' understanding of the political context in the partner countries often left much to be desired." Similarly, a recent review of the implementation of the Paris Declaration principles in Afghanistan (Roberts 2009) repeatedly notes that the ownership agenda implies significant political choices, about which the donors are usually poorly informed (see also Faust 2010).

One implication for donors is that significantly greater resources will have to be devoted to acquiring knowledge about local politics and societies, institutional dynamics, and the impacts of programs on different interests for successful implementation of the new aid modalities to take place. This suggests that a heightened role for DG country research is a pre-requisite of a more effective ownership agenda, particularly in the fragile states. This research should go beyond traditional risk assessment and focus attention on the processes of decision-making, the impact of policies on the politicized social cleavages within society, and more generally the relationships between the state and key social groups.

DG assistance has an important role to play in the implementation of the ownership agenda and in the promotion of mutual accountability systems. As this chapter has argued, there is a strong correlation between poor governance and the absence of ownership. DG activities that improve governance will typically have at the very least an indirect impact on ownership, since better governed countries, where governments also better represent the aspirations of their citizens, are more likely to have effective development policies and programs and make better use of foreign aid.

As discussed above, more successful aid to semi-authoritarian recipient countries requires greater attention to mechanisms of *vertical accountability*. Putting a premium on increasing real effective participation in developmental policy both builds ownership in the long term and increases the sustainability of aid activities, but it also promotes democracy and democratic consolidation. Such classic DG activities as civic education, civil society strengthening and media support are all critically important to the long term agenda of ownership development in these countries, particularly when development commitment lags within the state itself.

One symptom of low ownership of aid is the almost complete absence of a public discourse on aid issues, despite the fact that aid may account for a fifth of the national economy and is often the biggest employer in the country other than the government itself. Promoting a public discourse on aid would help to promote local ownership of aid. This could include encouraging governments to create opportunities for dialogue with citizens and mechanisms to learn about citizens' preferences. Another instrument might be the local press, which today too rarely pays attention to aid. DG programs of support to the media might specifically include activities that educate and sensitize the journalist to aid issues. This recommendation is not offered as a panacea, and its effects are likely to be diffuse and not immediately obvious.

In divided countries, as argued above, economic development and aid activities are commonly believed to favor some groups in the population at the expense of others. The non-transparency of much of the development portfolio is in part to blame for this (Hubbard 2007). The absence of public information about development activities promotes the poor implementation of policies and greater corruption, and it also leads to broad misconceptions of the objectives of development activities. This provides another reason to encourage greater media attention to and the training of journalists on development activities.

As countries democratize, the focus of DG activities designed to improve local ownership need to shift progressively to the mechanisms of *horizontal accountability*. Once democracy has advanced to the point where there is real opposition within the legislature, political party support activities become more useful. DG activities of legislative strengthening are also likely to prove beneficial, so that legislatures can become an effective mechanism of horizontal accountability. Supporting economic policy units within the legislature and even aid monitoring units that would help start national debates on aid would increase government accountability for its role in the aid process, adding to the quality of aid programs and the ownership of national actors over it.

A number of changes in aid implementation processes have been introduced in recent years to promote ownership, including greater donor alignment with national development priorities and a greater role for the recipient country state bureaucracy in the design and implementation of aid programs. Too often, it is argued, aid is ineffective because recipient country governments do not actually fully support the policies and programs carried out by donors, or the state's central bureaucracy is not involved in them. Simply put, aid programs that are not integrated into the state's planning and budgeting are less likely to be "owned" by the government and thus are less likely to survive the end of donor funding. Thus, to build ownership, it is argued, the central government must be given a broader role in the full cycle of the aid process, from the design to the implementation and evaluation of aid. Under disbursement pressures, given the rapid increases in aid flows during the past decade, some donors have aggressively moved toward direct budget support for governments, which, it is argued, is the aid modality that best advances country ownership. However, the record of the implementation of the Paris Declaration analyzed above suggests that low capacity and various governance deficiencies have often undermined the development of ownership. Since these low capacity countries are often the neediest, these breakdowns are particularly unfortunate. After all, an aid system that does not work in the least developed states would not be useful. This essay has briefly assessed the reasons for this and suggested some remedies.

Recognition of the problems in the implementation of the ownership agenda, notably in the poorest and least developmental recipient countries, does not mean that the aid ownership paradigm is useless for most low-income countries. Clearly, nonetheless, the way in which ownership is understood and promoted has to be different depending on the national context. At present, unfortunately, the ownership agenda often seems to ignore this variation and assumes the virtues of a one-size–fits-all strategy. The risk is that the inevitable failures of the agenda in certain types of countries will lead to the proverbial throwing the baby out with the bath water, with a wholesale rejection of country ownership.

*The author wishes to thank David Booth, Liz Hart, Danielle Resnick, David Timberman, and Pablo Yanguas for useful comments on earlier drafts. All remaining flaws are the responsibility of the author. This chapter is based on an earlier paper prepared for and funded by the U.S. Agency for International Development. The views expressed are the author's alone and do not necessarily reflect the views of USAID or the U.S. government.*

## References

Alesina, A., and D. Dollar. 2000. "Who Gives Foreign Aid to Whom and Why?"*Journal of Economic Growth* 5:1, 33–63.

Best, J. 2007. "Legitimacy Dilemmas: The IMF's pursuit of Country Ownership." *Third World Quarterly* 28:3.

Berg, E. 1997. "Dilemmas in Donor Aid Strategies." In *Perspectives on Aid and Development,* eds. C. Gwin and J. Nelson. Washington, DC: Overseas Development Council.

Bleck, J., and N. van de Walle. 2011. "Parties and Issues in Francophone West Africa: Towards a Theory of Non-Mobilization." *Democratization* 185: 2011; 1125–1145.

Booth, D., ed.. 2003. *Fighting Poverty in Africa: Are PRSPs Making a Difference?* London: Overseas Development Institute.

Boughton, J., and A. Mourmouras. 2002. "Is Policy Ownership an Operational Concept?" *IMF Working Paper WP/02/72.*

Buiter, W. 2004. "Country Ownership: A Term Whose Time Has Gone." Speech at the Development Policy Forum, "Conditionality Revisited." Paris France, June 5, 2004.
Burnside, C., and D. Dollar. 2000. "Aid, Policies, and Growth." *American Economic Review* 90 4: 847–68.
Driscoll, R., and A. Evans. 2005. "Second-Generation Poverty Reduction Strategies: New Opportunities and Emerging Issues." *Development Policy Review* 23:1 January, 5–25.
Easterly, W., ed. 2007. *Reinventing Foreign Aid*. Cambridge: MIT Press.
Entwistle, J., and F. Cavassini. 2005. "Country Ownership: What Does it Really Mean?" *PRS Implementation Series Presentation*. Washington DC: World Bank.
Faust, J. 2010. "Policy Experiments, Democratic Ownership, and Development Assistance." *Development Policy Review* 285, 515–534.
Hannan, A. 2007. "The Paris Declaration and National Ownership: From de Jure to de Facto." *United Nations Development Program Staff Opinion Paper* No. 1, October.
Hearn, J. 2007. "African NGOs: The New Compradors?" *Development and Change* 38, 1095–110.
Hyden, G. 2007. "The Challenges of Making Governance Assessments Nationally Owned." Paper Presented at the Bergen Seminar *Governance Assessments and the Paris Declaration,* September 24–25.
—. 2008. "After the Paris Declaration: Taking on the Issue of Power." *Development Policy Review* 263: 259–274.
International CSO Steering Group ISG. 2008. "From Paris 2005 to Accra 2008: Will Aid Become More Accountable and Effective?"*Position Paper* 16, January.
Jerven, M. 2010. "The Relativity of Poverty and Income: How Reliable Are African Economic Statistics?" *African Affairs* 109: 77–96.
Jerven, M. 2011. "Growth, Stagnation, or Retrogression? On the Accuracy of Economic Observations, Tanzania, 1961–2001." *Journal of African Economies* 20:3, 377–394.
Joseph, R. A., and A. Gillies. 2009. *Smart Aid for African Development*. Boulder: Lynne Rienner Publishers.
Lucas, S. T. 2011. "Principles into Practice: Country Ownership." Washington, DC: Millennium Challenge Corporation, November.
Meyer, S. and N-S. Schulz. 2008. "Ownership with Adjectives: Donor Harmonisation: Between Effectiveness and Democratisation. Synthesis Report." *Fundacion para les Relaciones Internationales y el Dialago Exterior FRIDE.* Working Paper 59, March.

Molenaers, N. and L. Nijs. 2009. "From the Theory of Aid Effectiveness to the Practice: The European Union's Governance Incentive Tranche." *Development Policy Review* 275, 561–580.

Molenaers, N., and R. Renard. 2011. *Budget Support and Political Conditionalities.* Policy Brief 1. University of Antwerp, Institute of Development Policy and Management, Antwerp.

Morrison, K. M. 2009. "Oil, Nontax Revenue, and the Redistributional Foundations of Regime Stability." *International Organization* 63:107–138.

Moss, T., G. Pettersson, and N. van de Walle. 2008. "An Aid-Institutions Paradox? A Review Essay on Aid Dependency and State-Building in Sub-Saharan Africa." In *Reinventing Foreign Aid,* ed. W. Easterly. Cambridge: MIT Press, 255–282.

OECD. 2005. *The Paris Declaration on Aid Effectiveness.* Paris: OECD.

—. 2008a. "Chair's Summary: Third High Level Forum on Aid Effectiveness."Accra, Ghana: September 2–4, 2008.

—. 2008b. "Making Aid More Effective by 2010: 2008 Survey on Monitoring the Paris Declaration."

—. 2008c. *Accra Agenda for Action.*

—. 2008c. "Financing Development 2008: Whose Ownership?" *OECD Development Centre.*

—. 2009. "Development Cooperation Report 2009."*OECD Journal of Development* 101.

Rakner, L., and V. Wang. 2007. "Governance Assessments and the Paris Declaration."*CMI Issue Paper* 10.

SPA. 2007. *Survey of Budget Support*, 2006. April 4, 2007. London: ODI.

Sridhar, D. 2009. "Post-Accra: Is there Space for Country Ownership in Global Health?" *Third World Quarterly* 307.1363-77.

van de Walle, N. 2012. "Foreign Aid in Dangerous Places: The Donors and Mali's Democracy." Unpublished paper. Cornell University.

van de Walle, N. 2005. *Overcoming Stagnation in Aid-Dependent Countries*. Washington, DC: Center for Global Development.

van de Walle, N., and T. A. Johnson. 1996. *Improving Aid to Africa.* Washington, DC: Overseas Development Council, Policy Essay 21, distributed by Johns Hopkins University Press.

World Bank Operations Policy and Country Services. 2008. "Following Up on Accra: A World Bank Action Plan on Aid Effectiveness." Washington, DC: The World Bank. February 26, 2009.

World Bank. 1998. *Assessing Aid: What Works, What Doesn't, and Why.* New York: Oxford University Press.

# CHAPTER FIVE

# GLOBAL PROGRAMS, AID EFFECTIVENESS, AND POVERTY REDUCTION

PHYLLIS R. POMERANTZ

## Introduction

Over the past decade, global public goods (GPGs) and global programs have occupied a growing space in development discourse. A reflection of this is that the provision of GPGs was made one of the World Bank's six strategic themes (World Bank 2009). This seems almost inevitable in an increasingly globalized world. A financial crisis originating in the United States' home mortgage industry developed into a worldwide recession. A new strain of flu, first detected in Mexico and the United States in April 2009, quickly became a worldwide pandemic (World Health Organization 2010). Global climate and terrorism concerns in 2010 reached from the island nations of the South Pacific to the Olympic Games in Canada.

There is a relationship between the provision of GPGs and development assistance. However, the two concepts are not synonymous. Nor is the provision of GPGs a subset of aid. Yet the financing for global programs is increasingly tallied as part of the Organization for Economic Co-operation and Development's Development Assistance Committee (OECD-DAC) statistics on aid. If it were simply a matter of global program funds accounting for part of the recent increase in overseas development assistance (ODA), that would hardly be a cause for concern. However, some of the reasons global programs have succeeded in attracting donor support and some of the issues surrounding global programs raise "caution flags" for those interested in improving aid effectiveness with a focus on poverty reduction.

This chapter explores global programs from an aid and development perspective. It begins with a brief summary of the definition, origin, and basic theory underlying the concept of GPGs. This is followed by an outline of the various definitions of global programs, their expanding scope and numbers, and the reasons for their popularity. The bulk of the paper is devoted to taking stock of issues raised by global programs, particularly when juxtaposed with country-focused strategies and programs. A short conclusion reviews some recommendations on global programs and points to further work to analyze the issues and implement recommendations.

## Providing Global Public Goods: the Challenge of Collective Action

The concept of GPGs emerged in the 1990s from work by the United Nations Development Program (Kaul, Grunberg, and Stern 1999a). Building on economic work on public goods and collective action in the national context, GPGs were similarly identified as goods subject to market failure and provision difficulties. Public goods are non-rivalrous and non-excludable (Samuelson 1954; Olson 1971; Hardin 1968). Non-rivalrous means that one person's consumption or enjoyment of a good does not affect another's. Non-excludable means that once the good is provided, no one can be prevented from enjoying it. The classic examples are air and peace.

Exactly what makes a public good "global" is less clear. Kaul, Grunberg and Stern have perhaps the most demanding definition: "for a public good to be global, its benefits must reach not only a broad spectrum of countries but also a broad spectrum of the global population" (Kaul, Grunberg, and Stern 1999b, 11). In addition, it needs to meet current needs without harming those of future generations.

Even with a less restrictive definition (e.g., defining global as limited to more than one country in more than one geographical region), there are few pure GPGs.[1] There are six types of GPGs that are generally recognized:

- Preventing the emergence and spread of infectious disease;
- Tackling climate change and protecting biodiversity;
- Promoting financial stability and preventing financial crises;
- Promoting international trade and traffic;
- Achieving and maintaining peace and stability;
- Generating knowledge (International Task Force on Global Public Goods 2006, 16).

How a global public good is best supplied varies according to the number of countries involved, the timeframe for provision, and what is known as the technology of supply (Sandler 2001; Barrett 2006). A few examples can illustrate the differences. Developing a vaccine to prevent or cure HIV/AIDs is a distinct activity: a tested vaccine either exists or it does not. Also, developing a vaccine is a specialized activity; it is best handled by those few with the requisite expertise and resources. So an HIV/AIDs vaccine is called a binary, "best shot" global public good. It does not require an international agreement. Someone like Bill Gates can decide he is prepared to finance the vaccine's development on behalf of mankind.

In contrast, mitigating and adapting to climate change comprise a set of actions that cannot be resolved with a single successful effort; continuous global cooperation is required. However, since not all countries play a similar role in the production of greenhouse gases, not all countries are willing to make equal contributions to the reduction of greenhouse gases and other activities that could slow or mitigate climate change. Further, countries are reluctant to contribute without being sure that others are contributing their due share. Without that assurance, contributions will not necessarily yield a satisfactory level of benefit for all. So, in contrast to the HIV/AIDS vaccine, climate stability actions require formal international agreement, specifying the level and nature of each country's contribution, along with a process for monitoring compliance and imposing sanctions for non-compliance. The difficulties in achieving that kind of international agreement were highlighted in the United Nations' Copenhagen Conference in December 2009.

As these contrasting examples illustrate, in the absence of global government, providing GPGs is strictly voluntary, with some types of goods more difficult to supply. Today, the options for supplying GPGs are fairly limited. First, there is cooperation via international treaty (with or without enforceable sanctions) or through United Nations' General Assembly or Security Council approval. Second, international institutions (e.g., the World Bank, the International Monetary Fund, the World Health Organization) provide some of these goods either by bureaucratic action or regulation. A third option is when a single country or a group of countries assumes leadership in providing a GPG on behalf of the international community (either absorbing the costs or charging members of the "club" of users). Recently, this third option has also seen public-private partnerships involving governments, non-governmental organizations, foundations, and private companies.

## The Rise of Global Programs

Ideally, the definition of a global program would be a program involved in the provision of GPGs. While the undersupply of these goods has provided an impetus for some programs, many global programs provide a mixture of GPGs, national public goods, and even private goods. The World Bank's definition of a global program allows for considerable latitude:

Global programs are defined as partnerships and related initiatives whose benefits are intended to cut across more than one region of the world and in which the partners:

- reach explicit agreement on objectives
- agree to establish a new (formal or informal) organization
- generate new products or services
- contribute dedicated resources to the program (World Bank Operations Evaluation Department, 2004, p. 2)

How many global programs exist today? It is safe to say that there are upwards of two hundred global and regional programs and partnerships. As of 2008, the World Bank alone was involved in about 160 global and regional programs and partnerships (World Bank Independent Evaluation Group 2008, 54). There are now more than one hundred global partnerships in health alone (Aid Effectiveness Portal 2009). Total expenditures under global programs are not tagged separately in aid statistics, so it is impossible to have a precise estimate of the resources involved. Some specialists have estimated that nearly one-third of all official development assistance is now being delivered through global and regional programs, as opposed to more traditional country-based aid (Lele, Sadik, and Simmons 2007, 1). Most estimates are lower, but there is consensus that this is a rapidly growing area of development finance.

Table 5.1 shows 2008 expenditures for some of the larger programs.

| Program | Expenditures (US$millions) |
|---|---|
| GFATM | 2168 |
| GEF | 814 |
| CGIAR | 542 |
| GAVI | 736 |
| PEPFAR | 4140 |
| Education for All | 161 |
| Total: | 8561 |

**Table 5.1: 2008 Expenditures of Some Major Global Programs**

Sources: for the Global Fund to Fight Aids, Tuberculosis, and Malaria (GFATM); the Global Alliance for Vaccines and Immunization (GAVI); and the Global Environment Facility (GEF): *OECD 2010, 6.* For the President's Emergency Plan for Aids Relief

(PEPFAR), the table reflects the approved FY08 budget for country activities and central programs (does not include funding for UNAIDs, the Global Fund, the International Aids Vaccine Initiative (IAVI), or National Institute of Health (NIH) international research: *PEPFAR 2008, 11.* For CGIAR: Consultative Group on International Agricultural Research 2009, 1. For Education for All (table includes Fast Track Initiative and Education Program Development): *World Bank 2008a, 39.*

There are varied reasons for the impressive growth in global programs over the past decade (Lele, Sadik, and Simmons 2007, among others). First, thanks to an international communications revolution, the past decade witnessed increased understanding of the need to provide GPGs (e.g., climate stability) and avoid "global bads" (e.g., the spread of infectious diseases such as SARS, Avian Flu, HINI). Also in evidence was the need to help low-income countries provide GPGs since most did not have the capacity nor the incentive to provide them on their own. This is particularly so when incremental global benefits are large, but the costs to the individual country exceed the perceived or real benefits to the country. An example is Global Environmental Facility (GEF) funding to support biodiversity through a project protecting endangered species in a developing country.

Global programs have also been created where public and private donors identified some critical gaps in development funding, sometimes related to GPGs, sometimes not. For example, over the past several decades, research focused on developing country needs in agriculture and health has been significantly underfunded. The CGIAR and the Bill and Melinda Gates Foundation's Global Health Program were developed with a view toward filling these gaps. While some of what both programs fund are GPGs (e.g., CGIAR's basic research and Gates' quest for an HIV/AIDS vaccine), other activities are not (e.g., CGIAR's support of local natural resource management efforts or Gates' funding of a Canadian hospital to support tobacco control policies in India (Bill and Melinda Gates Foundation 2009).

There are also increasing numbers of global programs created where one or more donors wants to shine a global spotlight on a specific problem or accelerate actions that are not necessarily linked to global or even regional public goods. The Global Partnership for Education (formerly the Education for All – Fast Track Initiative), which has broad donor support, is arguably an example of that type of program.[2]

Closely related to the above are the cyclical donor fatigue and doubts that surround the effectiveness of the country-based model of development assistance, particularly in Africa (Pomerantz 2004, 2–3). Global programs, especially those that are private or public-private partnerships, carry the expectation that they will be more agile, faster and more effective, with less bureaucracy, than the country-based assistance provided by official bilateral and multilateral donors. Because most global programs are sectorally or "vertically" focused, supporters anticipate clear objectives, measurable indicators, and evaluations focused on outcomes. In an era of performance-based aid, where newly important donors such as China are challenging traditional aid programs and funding is constricted even for domestic programs, donors are anxious to show "results."

Tied to this has been the worry by some donors that commitments to increase ODA and to double the amount of aid provided to Africa will be met by limitations in absorptive capacity and "leakages" caused by neo-patrimonial politics or corruption. Since many global programs have developed their own delivery mechanisms and funding channels, donors share optimism that the programs can circumvent constraints and increase impact on the ground. Also, administration costs and other expenditures, such as research focused on developing countries, do not have to take place *in* developing countries to be counted as ODA. Thus new global programs can absorb incremental ODA without necessarily exposing donors to increased risk. Global programs represent a "safe haven" for donors.

Global programs have also been attractive in the changing relationship between bilateral and multilateral aid agencies and middle-income countries. With an increased focus on African countries and other low-income aid recipients,[3] some donors have cut back their aid programs to middle-income countries. A number of middle-income countries also have developed a reluctance, outside of emergencies, to keep borrowing from international development agencies such as the World Bank. Consequently, global program funding, usually in the form of grants and technical assistance, has become an attractive concessional source for middle-income countries. At the same time, managing global programs has been an important avenue for the World Bank "to keep a foot in the door" in middle-income countries, allowing it to maintain country relationships and knowledge. That is important for its potential role in an emergency and for its continuing role as disseminator of global development practice to low-income countries. For bilateral donors, participating in a global program allows them to retain some limited influence in countries where bilateral aid programs have been curtailed.

Global programs have also provided a new sense of mission for international agencies and potentially given them an extended "lease on life." While some global programs have created their own governance structures, others have sought out existing international agencies for administrative and financial support. As a consequence, the World Bank has been strengthening its capacity to manage global programs and provide advice and funding related to global and regional public goods (World Bank and International Monetary Fund Development Committee 2007, 21). In addition, the World Bank acts as the financial agent for some of the largest global programs. Two of the largest, the Global Fund to Fight AIDS, Tuberculosis and Malaria (GFATM) and the Global Environment Facility (GEF), alone accounted for over US$7 billion held in trust by the Bank in 2008 (World Bank, 2008a, p. 35). Calls for the World Bank to increase its involvement in the provision of GPGs and global programs have come from a number of sources (Birdsall 2006).

Finally, the increased reliance on the private sector to provide goods previously in the public domain, along with the recent wave of corporate social responsibility, has added a new set of actors to development finance. Global programs are appealing to the private sector because they appear to be attractive vehicles for getting things done with a broad reach and without getting too mired down in the complexities of developing country governments. Participation is good for reputation without a tremendous time commitment from corporate management.

To summarize, the rise of global programs is due to several factors. The chronic undersupply of GPGs and limited supply options have been an important impetus. Even more importantly, the programs are distinctly attractive to a diverse set of actors—weary and impatient bilateral aid donors; multilateral and international agencies in search of continuing relevance; cash-starved low-income countries; increasingly influential middle-income countries; and the international private corporate sector—all of whom see advantages in supporting global programs.

## Issues—Potential and Actual—with Global Programs

The increased focus on GPGs and global programs brings with it opportunities. Accomplishments over the past decade speak for themselves. A recent study by the Institute of Health Metrics and Evaluation in Seattle and the Harvard Initiative for Global Health found that development assistance for health had quadrupled from 1990 to 2007. A big factor in the increase, particularly in the 2000–2007 period, was the emergence of large global health programs (e.g., GFATM, the Global Alliance for Vaccines and Immunization [GAVI], and PEPFAR—a Global Program funded by one donor, the United States Government) (Ravishankar et al. 2009). As just one example, by the end of 2009, seven years after GFATM was founded, the organization had spent more than US$10 billion, funding more than 2.5 million people on anti-retroviral treatment for HIV/AIDS, distributing over 100 million insecticide-treated nets for malaria control, and providing treatment to six million people with active tuberculosis (GFATM 2010). Considering how long it takes for many international programs to be up and running, this is impressive.

At the same time, when viewed from a development and poverty reduction optic, global programs raise issues. In some cases, the benefits associated with global programs bring with them negative consequences or "side effects". In the following section, the issues are divided into four categories: issues with potentially negative aspects for low-income countries; issues with possible adverse impact on recent aid reform initiatives; issues that may lessen the effectiveness of global programs; and finally, issues related to the long-term impact of global programs on the global governance system.

## Global Programs and Low-Income Countries

*Agenda setting and who gets to decide.* In the absence of global government, there is no representative mechanism or forum that determines global priorities. Global programs have had a variety of beginnings. Some have originated with international agencies, others with one or more donor countries, and still others out of private sector/foundation interests. CGIAR, for example, grew out of a Mexico-Rockefeller Foundation program that established an international research center in Mexico and a joint Ford-Rockefeller rice research program in the Philippines. Years later, the two foundations, together with three international agencies—the Food and Agriculture Organization (FAO), the United Nations Development Program (UNDP), and the World Bank—joined forces to convince industrialized country donors to support an expanded international agricultural research effort (CGIAR n.d.). In contrast, the GEF got its start at the urging of the French Government, supported by the German Government, as a three-year Pilot Program within the World Bank (Clemencon 2006).

There is no mechanism for choosing among or prioritizing global programs. In reality, anyone with funding, a good idea, and some powers of persuasion can start a global program. While developing countries are loathe to reject "free money," it is far from clear that the preference set of today's aid programs matches that of either the preferences or needs of most low-income countries. This is a question even *within* a single sector, let alone *among* sectors. Referring to a study by McCoy et al. (2009) on the Gates Foundation's support for global health, a *Lancet* editorial noted:

Their study shows even more robustly that the grants made by the Foundation do not reflect the burden of disease endured by those in deepest poverty….

> *The concern expressed to us by many scientists who have long worked in low-income settings is that important health programmes are being distorted by the grants from the Gates Foundation. For example, a focus on malaria in areas where other diseases cause more human harm creates damaging perverse incentives for politicians, policy makers, and health workers (Lancet 2009, 1577).*

If a global program is financing a global (or regional) public good, some divergence from a country's priorities may be expected. That is precisely the reason incremental grant funding and special efforts are needed. However, resources and a country's ability to absorb them are not infinitely elastic. Efforts involving substantial human or financial resources preclude or harm the effectiveness of other efforts. In health, funding has been skewed toward specific diseases, stretching the capacity of health systems. As Ravishankar et al. (2009, 2118) note: "Although donors have made arguments emphasising the importance of funds providing general health-system support that are not linked to specific programmes or diseases, the volume of these flows remained low." Trade-offs exist, yet are neither explicit nor clear. This is even more of an issue when a global program does not provide GPGs or mobilize significant incremental resources.

Within specific global programs, the question of who gets to decide and whether recipients are adequately represented is also present. Early global programs such as CGIAR and many of the smaller programs today can be characterized as "shareholder organizations," where funders make the decisions. Increasingly, global programs have characterized them selves as "stakeholder organizations" with governance mechanisms that include wider representation and attempt to balance funders and recipients. The GEF Council and GFATM Board, for example, largely work by consensus, but formal approval rules call for double majorities of both funders and participants or funders and recipients.[4] CGIAR, which had become a largely donor-driven organization, has recently been reorganized to create more space between those who determine the scientific priorities and those who provide the funds.

While this is an improvement over donor-driven governance, these arrangements do not guarantee adequate representation for low-income countries. Low- and middle-income countries are generally lumped together as developing countries. Increasingly, the interests of low-income and middle-income countries diverge, as seen in recent international climate change meetings. Some of the fastest growing middle-income countries' interests are becoming more aligned with industrial country concerns and positions, e.g., reluctance to commit to specific targets for greenhouse gas reductions and increased priority for trade and financial stability measures. Moreover, possessed with greater planning, implementation, and coordination capacity, middle-income countries welcome the concessional funding and are able to adapt global programs to their needs.

Chasek and Rajamani (2003), looking at multilateral negotiations, report that developing countries attend many international meetings at a disadvantage because they are not adequately represented or even present at the issue-definition and fact-finding stages. This is more acute in the case of smaller, low-income countries. Even when low-income countries are formal participants in governing bodies for global programs, their ability to adequately prepare and actively participate varies. While delegations may attend major international meetings or formal board meetings, many low-income countries do not have the resources to participate extensively in key preparation meetings.

Low-income countries can potentially overcome these problems by joining together in strategic alliances or strengthening regional organizations. To date, these methods have been underutilized, in part because of collective action issues within these alliances. Even where joint representation exists, there is still under-representation within larger organizations. Over the past several years, an animated discussion has taken place about the need to expand developing countries' "vote and voice" within many international programs and organizations, including the World Bank. As part of the World Bank discussion, there was an acknowledgement that African countries, in particular, needed more resources to bolster their participation in Board discussions, including those related to global programs. As a result, a third African Executive Director (out of a total of twenty-five) was added to the Board. Nonetheless, it is recognized that complementary measures are still needed (World Bank 2008c).

To summarize, global programs have been largely supply-driven, many without significant low-income country participation in their conception. Despite attempts to include developing countries on some executive boards and councils, there are continuing questions about the extent of low-income countries' participation in their governance.

*Relationship to Aid.* OECD-DAC donors report contributions to large global programs as part of their aid totals. The question is how much of those contributions are incremental to what donors would have given in the absence of global programs. Total aid from OECD-DAC donors has risen over the past few years following the G8 commitments to increase aid from US$80 billion in 2004 to US$130 billion in 2010 (in constant 2004 terms). While OECD-DAC aid fell short of the 2010 goal by about US$19 billion, aid increased to about US$129 billion (in current prices) in 2010.[5] Global program financing accounts for part of that increase. What is not known is, without global programs, how much of those funds would have gone through other channels or for different purposes; in other words, how much global program funding is being substituted for more traditional aid.

What is clear is that some of those resources are misidentified as aid. Many GPGs are important for development and poverty reduction. The Millennium Development Goals (MDGs) reflect this (e.g., Goal 6: combat HIV/AIDS, malaria and other diseases), and many global programs reference the MDGs. Two issues arise from the vantage point of low-income countries. First, programs such as the GEF aim to provide incremental global environmental benefits. This is not aid—it is compensation to developing countries for the differential between national and global net benefits in the provision of GPGs. Second, because of the governance issues described above, low-income countries have less say in global programs and may have different priorities when it comes to sequencing and magnitude of effort under global programs and the MDGs. In addition, using the MDGs as justification for a global program is problematic from the point of view of a low-income country. The MDGs were not supposed to be a "one size fits all" effort to be automatically implemented at the country level and were not meant to result in increased donor control over the development agenda (Vandemoortele 2009). As the World Bank noted, "In many cases, it is likely [that Global Program Funds] are substituting highly targeted funding in place of general multilateral and bilateral assistance" (World Bank 2008b, 9).

*Fragmentation and "Capacity Mining."* Some might argue it does not matter under what rubric or through which channel the money comes, as long as it is forthcoming. Also, some of the funds under global programs, including those from private sources as well as from the largest donor—the U.S. government—might not have been forthcoming in any other form or for any other purpose. This needs to be weighed against the growing burden on low-income countries to manage and coordinate the various funding channels. The OECD's Development Cooperation Report for 2009 concluded that: "Fragmentation is a serious obstacle to making aid more effective. In essence, fragmentation describes aid that comes in too many small slices from too many donors, creating high transaction costs and making it difficult for partner countries to effectively manage their own development" (OECD 2009b, 35). Mozambique, for example, in 2007 had over 2,400 projects; Uganda, over 2,100 (Frot and Santiso 2009, 18). Fragmentation, already deemed excessive by OECD, may be underestimated since OECD measured fragmentation using the concept of Country Programmable Aid (CPA), aid that could be included within recipients' budgets. A portion of Global Program funding continues to be off budget and not captured within CPA.

It is worth reiterating some of the effects of the proliferation of funding channels, mechanisms, modalities, and donors. First, it makes government coordination and control over a country's development agenda a daunting task. Coordinating multiple activities (e.g., projects, technical assistance, global programs, sector-wide approaches, and general budget support) across a wide spectrum of sectors operating in varied geographic spaces and involving at least thirty official bilateral and multilateral donors would be challenging for any government. Second, the proliferation of channels diverts time and attention of government officials toward dealing with donors and an increasing load of monitoring and administrative reports. This is exacerbated in the case of global programs since monitoring and other systems are geared in substance and timing more to providing comparable cross-country data than to integrating with country systems (Learning Group of Global Programs 2008). Third, since donors need capable country nationals to manage their programs and offices in-country—and generally offer better pay and employment conditions—some of the best staff leave government service. In the end, new funding channels are part of a discouraging picture that ends up consuming country capacity without any guarantee of commensurate effectiveness on the ground.

## Global Programs and Implementation of the Paris Declaration on Aid Effectiveness

The Paris Declaration on Aid Effectiveness and the Accra Agenda for Action highlight five areas where reforms are needed to make aid more effective (High Level Forum on Aid Effectiveness 2005, 2008). These are: *ownership* (by recipient country); *alignment* (with recipient country policies and systems); *harmonization* (among aid agencies with respect to policies and processes); *managing by results* (recipients and aid agencies); and *mutual accountability* (between aid recipients and aid agencies). The record of global programs on the Paris/Accra agenda is mixed.

*Ownership.* Some global programs have succeeded in mobilizing strong support from civil society and the private sector at the country level. For example, many of the GFATM Country Coordination Mechanisms include NGOs, persons living with the diseases, and the private sector. Also, because of their focus, usually involving only one sector ministry, some global programs have generated strong support from those ministries. Ownership from central coordinating bodies such as Ministries of Finance is much weaker. As Lele et al. (2007, 7) note: "Issues of ownership, ever-present in country assistance programs, have become more acute as a result of the proliferation of global programs. To ensure accountability the rules and procedures of global programs tend to reflect the preferences of donors and staff of international agencies to a greater extent than do rules of country-focused assistance programs." If one takes ownership to mean country-driven formulation and implementation as opposed to participation as a result of persuasion and incentives (funding), then ownership in global programs is clearly an issue. This, combined with the limited participation of low-income country governments in program design and governance, suggests that incomplete country ownership is a limiting factor for the effectiveness of global programs.

*Alignment and Harmonization.* Alignment with country policies and systems and harmonization with other donors have been equally problematic. Because global programs have a limited breadth of action within each country, taking into account other sector activities at the country level is a challenge. The programs also have had difficulties in connecting to overall country strategy, policies, processes and priorities (Working Party on Aid Effectiveness 2008, 144). The guidance has been to at least try to align funding cycles with country budget cycles, and some funds have attempted to do this.

Another attempt at alignment has been to encourage global programs to participate in SWAps (sector-wide approaches) at the country level. SWAps are government-led sector programs that attempt to bring all major donors under the same policy and strategy framework, and to encourage the use of common procurement, auditing, monitoring and evaluation systems. SWAps are meant not only to strengthen donor alignment with government policies and systems, but also to bolster harmonization among donors. Global programs face challenges in participating in SWAps because of their specific objectives and processes (Working Party on Aid Effectiveness 2008, 144). Despite the challenges, GFATM is participating in health SWAPS in Mozambique, Malawi, and Rwanda. In the case of Mozambique, GFATM agreed to use the health sector budget instead of its own system for tracking funds for the three diseases it targets and to use country monitoring and reporting systems. It also agreed to subsume its Country Coordinating Mechanism under the broader coordination arrangements for the SWAp. A study of the arrangement concludes:

*The process of integrating the Global Fund into Prosaude [the health SWAp] has been mutually reinforcing, with the Global Fund acting as a more harmonized development partner and the SWAP process gaining from the Global Fund's sharper focus on technical and clinical priorities and use of more rigorous indicators as evidence of results. There is also a perception that Global Fund involvement has been useful in bringing about greater civil society representation within SWAP structures (Dickinson et al. 2007, 5).*

Elsewhere in the same study:

*This is not to say that transaction costs have reached an ideal minimum level yet or that the Global Fund-financed initiatives are fully integrated. The inherent tension between the Global Fund's vertical approach and the SWAp's horizontal approach has been successfully managed to date, but by no means eliminated (ibid, 3).*

What makes this situation somewhat baffling is that there is considerable overlap between the bilateral donors of the GFATM and those of the SWAp. If the best approach is to integrate within a horizontal SWAp, it calls into question the rationale for the vertical program in the first place.

*Managing by Results.* In contrast to the alignment and harmonization issue, some of the largest global programs have led the way in establishing a strong "results culture" and performance-based funding practices. While varying from program to program—and because it has been demanded by some of their funders—programs have spent considerable effort on developing *results* frameworks and monitoring and evaluation systems. In many cases, however, this effort has not used government systems, nor has it permeated back into government systems. Global funds are not reviewing, reforming, or using country monitoring systems and procedures to the extent possible. Reporting is geared more to the global programs' external audiences than to the recipient country (The Learning Group of Global Programs 2008).

*Mutual Accountability.* Accountability starts with transparency. Several of the global programs, e.g. GFATM and CGIAR, have set good standards on transparency by having extensive, user-friendly websites, with timely, public availability of key internal documents and studies.[6] As the Learning Group of Global Programs (2008, 7) noted: "Global Programs tend to have strong accountability to their international constituencies." At the country level, accountability is much weaker. Some programs involve the private sector and civil society and thus add new dimensions to the concept of mutual accountability. In general, though, accountability to country governments has been weak because of the programs' global mandates and their lack of direct representation on the ground (Learning Group of Global Programs 2008, 7). While mutual accountability is fragile throughout the aid architecture, it is perhaps a structural weakness for global programs. If a global program is providing a GPG because of relatively stronger international interests rather than country interests, incentives for mutual accountability are anemic at best.

Global programs generally profess support for the principles embodied in the Paris Declaration and the Accra Agenda for Action, and some, such as GFATM, are formal signatories. However, operating procedures and incentives are not conducive to upholding several of the principles, in particular *alignment, harmonization,* and *mutual accountability,* as noted above. The Accra Agenda for Action, while welcoming all development partners, had the following special mention of global programs:

> *We call upon all global funds to support country ownership, to align and harmonise their assistance proactively, and to make good use of mutual accountability frameworks, while continuing their emphasis on achieving results. As new global challenges emerge, donors will ensure that existing channels for aid delivery are used and, if necessary, strengthened before creating separate new channels that risk further fragmentation and complicate co-ordination at country level (High Level Forum on Aid Effectiveness 2008, 4).*

In the polite language of diplomacy, this is faint praise indeed.

## Global Program Effectiveness

Apart from the challenges that global programs pose for low-income countries and for aid reform efforts, there are other issues that potentially constrain the effectiveness of global programs. These include: global programs' fundamental dependence on country-level services and systems; uncertainties surrounding sustainability; the need for effective governance and evaluation; and the quest for efficiency. While none of these concerns is unique to global programs, they are more conspicuous in this environment.

*Dependency on Country Systems.* The fundamental dependence of global programs on country systems is prominent throughout the spectrum of global programs and explains some of the "mission creep" and periodic makeovers that beset global programs. CGIAR's basic agricultural research is of little use unless national research systems are able to adapt that research to a developing country's specific conditions. GEF efforts to preserve biodiversity are fraught with difficulties unless they are paired with efforts to improve livelihoods of local populations that depend on the source of biodiversity for their incomes. Disease-specific efforts ultimately are constrained by the limitations in national health systems: planning capabilities; trained medical personnel; infrastructure; supply chains and other logistics. In the case of both CGIAR and GEF, this has led to an expansion of objectives and activities over time, complicating the clarity of focus that is a strength of "vertical" global programs. In contrast, GFATM has tried to hold the line and limit its involvement in health system strengthening, focusing exclusively on the three diseases in its mandate. In practice, this has meant that countries need planning and technical support from other international agencies (e.g. the World Bank and the World Health Organization) in order to provide an adequate platform for GFATM efforts. It has also meant that in some countries, increased attention to the GFATM diseases, especially HIV/AIDS, has captured a disproportionate amount of available health system resources (World Bank 2008b, 21; Oomman, Bernstein, and Rozenzweig 2008).

The fundamental dependence of global programs on national systems leads to a paradox. Global programs were created to be more agile and effective than traditional, country aid channels and development systems. However, in many cases, global programs' agility and effectiveness are constrained by the capacity and quality of those same country systems. Improved governance, capacity development and system strengthening at the country level are not a global program's comparative strength, and as discussed earlier, the use of parallel systems may serve to undermine existing public capacity.

*Sustainability.* That leads directly to the question of sustainability. In the first instance, most global programs are dependent on official donors' continued funding. Global programs are competing with each other, as well as with multilateral and bilateral aid programs, for funds. What would happen if the U.S. government decided to reduce its commitments to PEPFAR and GFATM? As climate change concerns grow, will that affect commitments for global health? Also of concern is the heavy reliance on the Gates Foundation in the health sector. A 2007 study reported that out of a sample of eleven global health partnerships, seven relied entirely on the Gates Foundation for funding, and nine listed the Gates Foundation as their single largest donor (Buse and Harmer 2007, 266–67).

Some global programs, notably GAVI and UNITAID, have moved toward ensuring sustainability through innovative financing mechanisms that decrease their dependence on the aid budgets of donors in the near to medium term. GAVI, for example, is receiving funds from the International Finance Facility for Immunization (IFFIm), which raises money through issuing bonds guaranteed by donor governments. GAVI is also encouraging private sector research and development through an advance market commitment to pharmaceutical companies, stipulating that it will purchase a certain amount at a certain price if the specified drug or vaccine is developed. Both of these may eliminate funding uncertainty in the near term, but imply expanded donor commitments in the future. In contrast, UNITAID's airline tax, a small tax collected by thirteen countries whenever an airline ticket is purchased, and Product Red, in which businesses donate a small percentage of sales of designated products, raise money directly from consumers and businesses. Nonetheless, as Douste-Blazy and Altman (2010, 6) make clear,

> *All innovative financing mechanisms...were intended as supplements, not replacements, to help close the gap between official aid and the huge sums necessary to turn the tide against the three epidemics once and for all. If governments invoke these financing schemes as substitutes for official aid, then those funds' very purpose will be defeated.*

Consequently, the issue of sustainability remains. In addition, if the funds are off budget and/or reporting is deficient, recipient governments have no way to prepare themselves for contingent liabilities should the funding cease or to factor in recurrent cost obligations. Sustainability, always a problem for aid efforts, may well be worse in the case of global programs because of the weakness in country ownership.

*Governance and Evaluation.* As with all aid programs, global programs require clarity of goals and targets, effective governance, efficient operations, and meaningful and timely monitoring and evaluation. The largest programs (e.g., GEF, CGIAR, GFATM) have had extensive and, in some cases, multiple evaluations. Many of the smaller, newer programs have not, although the World Bank's Independent Evaluation Group has conducted a number of reviews of programs with World Bank involvement.[7]

A 2004 Global Programs evaluation by the World Bank's Operations Evaluation Department said that Bank management needed to work with its other partners in global programs "to develop and apply universally accepted standards of good governance, management, results orientation, and evaluation" (World Bank Operations Evaluation Department 2004, 89). It specifically mentioned written charters, transparent selection criteria, and clear terms of reference for board members, more voice for developing countries, guidelines on conflicts of interest and on the roles of NGOs and the private sector, and ensuring high-level oversight of evaluations with results shared with stakeholders.

Evaluation of some of the older and larger programs has posed additional challenges. Programs such as GEF and CGIAR have had evolving and expanding goals, based largely on donor preferences. As goals widen, evaluating efficiency and impact becomes more difficult. For example, CGIAR's contribution to basic plant breeding and germplasm improvement has been measured and is substantial. In contrast, its contribution to natural resource management (NRM) research is nebulous. A CGIAR review noted that the reasons for scant results in NRM are not yet clear. It could be a problem of insufficient effort and investment in NRM research, inappropriate methods of measuring NRM research, or simply a lack of impact (Pingali and Kelley 2007, 2396). Evaluating GEF's impact is similarly difficult. Much of what GEF does is not short-term, quantifiable, or large in relation to the host of environmental issues it covers. Consequently, there is a tendency to fall back on efficiency measures, an area where GEF has had some difficulties, as noted by CEO and Chair Monique Barbut when she took office in 2006 (Barbut, 2006).

*Efficiency.* Many global programs have been justified on the grounds that they are more agile than traditional aid programs, with lower administration and transaction costs. Over time, this seems to be less true for at least two reasons. First, many of the larger programs have undergone one or more significant "makeovers" to respond to concerns. CGIAR, GAVI, and GEF have all modified governance arrangements, funding procedures, and administrative processes over time. GFATM appears to be in "continuous improvement" mode, with changes in proposal procedures and grant approval criteria. On the one hand, this is a positive characteristic: the ability to incorporate lessons and adapt to new developments. On the other, every change initiative is disruptive and entails significant transaction costs for the recipients as they adjust to new processes and requirements. The "learning by doing" approach of many global programs is not without cost.

Secondly, as global programs mature, they go through a natural aging process and trend towards higher administrative costs. Unless the program transfers much of the planning and implementation responsibilities to others, bureaucratic growth is almost inevitable. As an example, GFATM , which prides itself on being a financing rather than an implementation agency, has gone from 135 secretariat staff in Geneva at the start of 2006 to 470 staff in January 2010 to 568 staff in April 2010 (an increase of 250 percent and 320 percent, respectively, compared to 2006). During the same period, total disbursements rose from US$1.3 billion in 2006 to US$2.6 billion in 2009 —an increase of 100 percent (GFATM n.d, staff numbers; GFATM 2009a, disbursement data). It should be noted that grant commitments, as opposed to disbursements, per full-time employee did rise during the period (GFATM 2009a). Nonetheless, the sharp rise in GFATM staff was noted in the recent comprehensive GFATM evaluation:

> *The failure of partnership reflects a failure of governance in the Global Fund Board and in the broader international system more than a failure of any particular partner. One striking consequence has been the dramatic growth of the Secretariat. In the first several years of the Fund, the staff size at any time was a third to twice the size planned a year or two previously....*
>
> *What followed was a continuous cycle of Global Fund hiring in Geneva to catch up with the oversight requirements of the Fund's expanding portfolio, with the Secretariat to take on functions that arguably other partners were in a better position to execute on the Global Fund's behalf (GFATM 2009a, 36).*

Over time, global programs, given difficulties with harmonization and alignment, may not be able to avoid bureaucratic entrenchment and growth. This could signficantly jeopardize their justification and donor support.

Issues related to effectiveness and efficiency are not unique to global programs. The difference is that at least some of these issues have been worked out and resolved over time in traditional aid programs. For the newer global programs, there is much less data and analysis of the arrangements currently in place (with the possible exception of the health sector where there is a growing body of data and analysis). There is little to suggest that global programs have made serious inroads yet in resolving the array of funding, governance, management, and evaluation difficulties that typically accompany development partnerships.

## Global Programs and Global Governance

Global programs bring up a number of challenging issues for the global governance system and architecture. Global programs are one way of providing GPGs that would be undersupplied if left only to individual nation states. Given the wide spectrum of issues surrounding them, global programs cannot help but call into question the efficacy of the current nation-state dominated system, where international cooperation is mainly voluntary and not well organized. Scott Barrett has argued that given the alternatives, the present system may well be the best:

> *Sovereignty, for all its faults, offers protections to individual societies and their governments. If the supply of GPGs is diminished as a consequence—well, that may be the price we have to pay for this freedom (Barrett 2007, 190).*

The question is—the best for whom? Despite the adoption of stakeholder systems by some leading global programs, the role of low-income countries in decision-making is muted. This is contradictory to current trends where traditional aid programs are calling for increased "voice" and ownership by recipient countries. Accomplishing that goal may recede farther into the future if global programs occupy a growing space in development finance.

At the same time, the growth in global programs may be strengthening the hand of middle-income countries. Cooperative solutions to global problems—related to climate change, financial stability, and infectious diseases, among others—will be impossible without the active engagement of middle-income countries. Global programs have sought to engage middle-income countries, and they, in turn, have reaped substantial benefits. The way things have evolved in global programs mirrors the growing predominance of the G-20 in international affairs. The problem is that the construct of "developing countries" as a single grouping is no longer valid, and is leaving out the poorest and weakest states.[8]

Global programs also highlight one of the fundamental dilemmas within the current international system: what to do about fragile states. Is it permissible, or even desirable, to intervene to provide GPGs directly to people without the explicit agreement of a barely functioning or malicious state? If global programs do intervene, for better or worse, they are contributing to a growing body of contradictions within the present system.

The growth of global programs may also produce fundamental changes in the aid architecture. Increased involvement of the World Bank in the provision of GPGs, for example, could reduce its role in providing country-based assistance, with those responsibilities transferred to others, including regional development banks. Alternatively, adding a significantly stronger role in GPGs while maintaining country-based programs would create a super-institution, but one with significant internal and external difficulties and divisions, as the supporters of each approach vie for resources and institutional prominence (World Bank Independent Evaluation Group 2008, 51). This is already happening to a certain extent, as evidenced by the Bank's admission of the need for incentives to encourage better linkage among country, regional, and global issues and responses (World Bank Independent Evaluation Group 2008, 73).

There are other potential changes to global governance institutions as a result of global programs. Calls for a World Health Organization with a stronger mandate to enforce global health regulations and coordinate actions led to the first substantive revision in 2005 of the 1969 International Health Regulations, which are binding on 194 nations. The WHO's ability to coordinate the myriad of global health initiatives continues to be severely constrained. Similarly, there have been calls for a World Environment Organization capable of putting order into an increasingly chaotic environmental funding situation. For the moment, stronger international organizations do not appear imminent, but the continued growth in global programs could have considerable impact on how that evolution proceeds.

## Conclusion

GPGs are, by definition, good. So how can global programs be problematic? To start off, not all global programs actually deliver GPGs. Instead, many global programs deliver what funders think countries should have: they are supply-driven. Even when GPGs are being delivered, there are a number of concerns. As this chapter has discussed, there are issues of particular relevance to low-income countries: the countries' lack of effective participation and decision-making; the possible substitution of earmarked funds for more flexible aid; and increased fragmentation and administrative burdens, depleting country capacity. Global programs are also problematic from the standpoint of the Paris Declaration on Aid Effectiveness. In particular, country ownership, alignment, harmonization, and mutual accountability pose challenges for global programs, and global programs have likely made progress on the Paris targets more difficult. There is another set of issues related to global programs' effectiveness. Global programs are fundamentally dependent on country-level services and systems—and therefore, in many low-income countries, dependent on the effectiveness of country-based aid programs. There are also questions surrounding sustainability of efforts and funding, the quality of governance, the challenge of impact evaluation, and the efficiency of operations. Sustainability, effectiveness, and efficiency issues are not unique to global programs, but traditional aid programs have had the opportunity to work out some of these issues over time.

At the same time, given the nature of GPGs, many will continue to be undersupplied unless global programs close the gap between country needs and country supply or between global benefits and country benefits. So it is important that the issues surrounding global programs are successfully tackled. The World Bank, in preparation for the 2008 Accra meeting, provided succinct guidance (Box 1).

*Box 5.1. World Bank Guidance on Global Program funds*

*When there are new initiatives...*

- Think twice about whether a separate new funding channel is needed.Strengthen the voice of partner countries.
- Maintain balance between vertical and horizontal approaches.
- Avoid intense verticality.
- Contribute to the provision of Global Public Goods.

*When implementing existing or new GPFs...*

- Funding should be on plan, on budget.
- Align to country systems and harmonize approaches.
- Ensure sustainability and predictability
- Integrate into sector strategies and measure sector results

Source: (World Bank 2008b, 34)

An OECD report on the health sector, while not referring only to global programs, went a bit farther:

> *A sound sector strategy, embedded in a broad national strategy and linked to financing through a medium-term expenditure framework and annual budget reviewed regularly by stakeholders, is needed not just for government's management of development, but as a means of inducing best-practice behaviour changes among donors.*

Increasingly, the default position is to "think twice" before creating a new initiative or instrument rather than using existing ones. Certainly there is more to be done to rationalize the multiple initiatives. But is that enough? Perhaps there is a case for a more radical pruning to reduce the number of players: the very long tail of small health projects in many countries suggests that there is scope for doing this without drastically reducing the funds available for health (OECD 2009a, 12). The guidance reveals the problem more than it provides concrete steps toward a solution.

This chapter is not the place either for a detailed roadmap—that will require a concerted effort with key stakeholders present. As a basis for further work and discussion, however, the following agenda could serve as a starting point to initiate a serious debate and work program.

- There needs to be a strong GPG rationale for providing funds through a global program. The first vehicle of choice for providing assistance to low-income countries should continue to be country-based aid. In any event, without strong country sector strategies, systems and involvement, global program effectiveness is likely to be compromised.

- A temporary , and obviously voluntary, moratorium on new global programs could be put into effect while three activities take place:
  - A comprehensive survey is carried out—and made public—of existing global programs, identifying sources of funds, amounts, recipients, and key activities.
  - A detailed plan of action, starting with the ten largest global programs, is established to address key issues. This is an activity that needs to be carried out at the country, individual program, and global levels jointly by the ten programs. The work of the Learning Group on Global Programs provides a starting foundation for this.
  - Based on the analysis of survey results and other data, and agreed criteria among a group of funders and recipients, a decision could be made to phase out (through merger or termination) at least twenty global programs (less than 10 percent of the total). As part of this, the reallocation of funds would be delineated.

Without a concerted effort, the number, diversity, and magnitude of issues surrounding global programs will continue to raise serious concerns and likely hamper aid effectiveness and poverty reduction efforts for the foreseeable future. In the absence of progress and with continued rapid growth, global programs could well constitute "the straw that broke the camel's back" for the current international aid and governance framework. Yet actions to bolster the roles of low-income countries, to improve the effectiveness of both country-based aid and global programs, and to better balance national and global benefits could transform global programs into effective allies in the struggle for aid effectiveness and poverty reduction.

## Notes

[1] Some argue that definitional problems could or do make the concept of global public goods of limited use as an analytical tool. (Long & Woolley, 2009; Benzanson, 2002).

[2] I say "arguably" because there is both support for and opposition to considering education as a global public good. See for example Bang 2007.

[3] At least in theory this is so. Easterly and Pfutze (2008, 42) argue that the share of aid going to low-income countries has remained relatively constant since the late 1960s.

[4] In the case of the GEF, the double majority is a 60 percent majority of the actual cumulative contributions to the program and a 60 percent majority of all member

states (Global Environment Facility 2007, 16). In the case of the GFATM, the double majority is a two-thirds majority of those present from a) the group representing donors and the private sector; and b) the group encompassing developing countries, NGOs, and affected populations (GFATM 2009b).
[5] All aid data is from OECD-DAC.
[6] Not all Global Programs pass this transparency test. At least some of the smaller programs have limited and outdated websites, and on Easterly and Pfutze's transparency index for bilateral and multilateral agencies, GEF (the only distinct Global Program in the index) was ranked in last place (Easterley and Pfutze 2008, 35).
[7] For a list of the completed evaluations, see World Bank Independent Evaluation Group, 2010.
[8] India is the only member of the G-20 that is considered to still be a low-income country.

## References


Aid Effectiveness Portal. 2009. "Current Debates: Reforming the International Aid Architecture." Accessed March 8, 2010, at: http://www.aideffectiveness.org/Current-debates-Reforming-the-international-aid-architecture.html

Bang, D. 2007. "Education as a Global Public Good." In *Towards New Global Strategies: Public Goods and Human Rights,* eds. E. A. Andersen and B. Lindsnaes. Leiden, Netherlands: Martinus Nijhoff Publishers, 345–367.

Barbut, M. 2006. "The New GEF: A Proving Ground for our Sustainable Future." Speech to the GEF Council Meeting, December 5, Washington, DC.

Barret, S. 2007. *Why Cooperate? The Incentive to Supply Global Public Goods.* New York: Oxford University Press.

—. 2006. "Critical Factors for the Successful Provision of Transnational Public Goods." In *Expert Paper Series Seven: Cross–Cutting Issues.* Stockholm: International Task Force on Global Public Goods, 1–53.

Benzanson, K. A. 2002. "Global Public Goods: Opportunities and Threats." *EU–LDC Network* , July, 2–5.

Bill and Melinda Gates Foundation. 2009. "Grants—St. Michael's Hospital." July. Accessed April 9, 2010 at: http://www.gatesfoundation.org/Grants-2009/Pages/St-Michael-s-Hospital-OPP51447.aspx.

Birdsall, N. 2006. "A Global Credit Club, Not Another Development Agency." In *Rescuing the World Bank,* ed. N. B. Washington DC: Center for Global Development, 69–85.

Buse, K., and Harmer, A. 2007. "Seven habits of highly effective global public-private health partnerships: practice and potential." *Social Science and Medicine*, 64: 2, 259–71.

CGIAR. 2009. "Financial Report 2008." Accessed April 11, 2010, at: http://www.cgiar.org/Publications/annual/pub_ar2008/cg_ar09_final_files/cgiar_annual_report/2008_CGIAR_Full_Financial_Report_FINAL.pdf

—. n.d.. "Who We Are: History of the CGIAR." Accessed April 9, 2010, at: http://www.cgiar.org/who/history/origins.html

Chasek, P., and Rajamani, L. 2003. "Steps Toward Enhanced Parity: Negotiating Capacity and Strategy of Developing Countries." In *Providin g Global Public Goods: Managing Globalization,* eds. I. Kaul, P. Conceicao, K. Le Goulven, and R. U. Mendoza. New York: Oxford University Press, 245–62.

Clemencon, R. 2006. "What Future for the Global Environment Facility?" *The Journal of Environment and Development,* March, 151 , 50–74.

Dickinson, C., J. Martinez, D. Whitaker, and M. Pearson. 2007. *The Global Fund operating in a SWAp through a common fund: issues and lessons from Mozambique.* London: HLSP Institute.

Douste-Blazy, P., and D. Altman. 2010. "A Few Dollars at a Time." *Foreign Affairs,* 89: 1, January/February, 2–7.

Easterly, W., and T. Pfutze. 2008. "Where Does the Money Go? Best and Worst Practices in Foreign Aid." *Journal of Economic Perspectives, 222* , 29–52.

Frot, E., and J. Santiso. 2009. "Crushed Aid: Fragmentation in Sectoral Aid." Accessed March 13, 2010, at: http://www2.hhs.se/site/home pages/EmmanuelsPDFs/WP6.pdf.

GFATM. 2009a. "The Five-year Evaluation of the Global Fund to Fight AIDS, Tuberculosis, and Malaria: Synthesis of Study Areas 1, 2, and 3." Geneva, March.

—. 2009b. May 5. "Board Operating Procedures, as Amended." May 5. Accessed March 10, 2010, at: http://www.theglobalfund.org/documents/board/Board_Operating_Procedures_en.pdf.

—. 2010. "The Global Fund 2010: Innovation and Impact—Results Summary." Accessed March 9, 2010, at http://www.theglobalfund.org/documents/replenishment/2010/Progress_Report_Summary_2010_en.pdf.

—. n.d.. "Secretariat—Core Structures." Accessed 2006, 2007, 2008, 2009, 2010, at: http://www.theglobalfund.org/en/secretariat/?lang=en.

Global Environment Facility. 2007. "Rules of Procedure for the GEF Council." Accessed March 10, 2010, at: http://www.gefweb.org/

uploadedFiles/External_Affairs/Publications/Rules_of_Procedure2007.pdf.
Hardin, G. 1968. "The Tragedy of the Commons." *Science*, 162: 1243–48.
High Level Forum on Aid Effectiveness. 2005. "Paris Declaration on Aid Effectiveness: Harmonization, Alignment, Results, and Mutual Accountability." March 2, Paris, France.
—. 2008. "Accra Agenda for Action." September 4. Accra, Ghana.
International Task Force on Global Public Goods. 2006. "Meeting Global Challenges: International Cooperation in the National Interest." Final Report. Stockholm, Sweden.
Kaul, I., I. Grunberg, and M. A. Stern. 1999a. *Global Public Goods: International Cooperation in the 21st Century.* New York: Oxford University Press.
—. 1999b. "Defining Global Public Goods." In *Global Public Goods: International Cooperation in the 21st Century,* eds. I. Kaul, I. Grunberg, and M. A. Stern. New York: Oxford University Press, 2–19.
Lancet, The. 2009. "What has the Gates Foundation done for global health?" Editorial, May 9. *The Lancet, 373*, 1577.
Learning Group of Global Programs. 2008. "Actions for Aid Effectiveness." Accessed March 11, 2010, at: http://siteresources.worldbank.org/ACCRAEXT/Resources/4700790–1210008992554/4968817–1218029841627/2008_GlobalPrograms LearningGroup_ActionsforAidEffectiveness.pdf.
Lele, U., N. Sadik, and A. Simmons. 2007. "The Changing Aid Architecture: Can Global Initiatives Eradicate Poverty?" Accessed March 10, 2010, at: http://www.oecd.org/dataoecd/60/54/37034781.pdf.
Long, D., and F. Woolley. 2009. "Global Public Goods: Critique of a UN Discourse." *Global Governance* , 15: 107–122.
McCoy, D., G. Kembhavi, J. Patel, and A. Luintel. 2009. "The Bill and Melinda Gates Foundation's grant-making programme for global health." *The Lancet, 373*, 1645–53.
OECD. 2009a. "Aid for Better Health – What Are We Learning About What Works and What We Still Have to Do?" Accessed April 8, 2010, at: http://www.oecd.org/dataoecd/32/6/43947784.pdf.
—. 2009b. "Rebalancing the World Economy: Development Cooperation Report 2009." Paris: OECD.
—. 2010. "Development Aid at a Glance: Statistics by Region—2010 Edition." February 8. Accessed April 11, 2010, at: http://www.oecd.org/dataoecd/59/5/42139479.pdf.
Olson, M. 1971. *The Logic of Collective Action.* Cambridge, MA: Harvard University Press.

Oomman, N., M. Bernstein, and S. Rozenzweig. 2008. "Seizing the Opportunity on AIDS and Health Systems." Washington, DC: Center for Global Development.

PEPFAR. 2008. "Fiscal Year 2008: PEPFAR Operational Plan." June. Accessed April 11, 2010, at: http://www.pepfar.gov/documents/organization/107838.pdf.

Pingali, P., and T. Kelley. 2007. "The Role of Agricultural Research in Contributing to Global Food Security and Poverty Alleviation: The Case of the CGIAR." In *Handbook of Agricultural Economics* Vol. 3, eds. R. Evenson and P. Pingali. London: Elsevier, 2381–2418.

Pomerantz, P. R. 2004. *Aid Effectiveness in Africa.* Lanham, MD: Lexington Books.

Ravishankar, N., P. Gubbins, R. J. Cooley, K. Leach-Kemon, C. M. Michaud, and D. T. Jamison. 2009. "Financing of Global Health: Tracking Development Assistance for Health from 1990–2007." *The Lancet,* 373, June 20, 2113–24.

Samuelson, P. A. 1954. "The Pure Theory of Public Expenditure." *Review of Economics and Statistics*, 11:387–89.

Sandler, T. 2001. "On Financing Global and International Public Goods." Policy Research Working Paper 2638, March. Washington DC: World Bank.

Vandemoortele, J. 2009. "The MDG Conundrum: Meeting the Targets without Missing the Point." *Development Policy Review* 27: 5, 355–71.

Working Party on Aid Effectiveness. 2008. "Aid Effectiveness: A Progress Report on Implementing the Paris Declaration." Third High Level Forum on Aid Effectiveness, September 2–4. Accra, Ghana.

World Bank. 2008a. "2008 Partnership and Trust Fund Annual Report." June. Accessed April 11, 2010, at: http://siteresources.worldbank.org/CFPEXT/Resources/TFAR_2008.pdf.

World Bank. 2008b. "Global Program Funds at Country Level: What Have We Learned?" Global Programs and Partnership Group. Washington, DC.

World Bank. 2008c. "Enhancing Voice and Participation of Developing and Transition Countries in the World Bank Group: Options for Reform." Development Committee of the Board of Governors, October 12. Accessed March 10, 3010, at: http://siteresources.worldbank.org/DEVCOMMINT/Documentation/21949668/DC2008–0013EVoiceandParticipation.pdf.

World Bank. 2009. "To Meet Global Challenges: Six Strategic Themes." Accessed March 7, 2010, at: http://go.worldbank.org/56O9ZVPO70.

World Bank and International Monetary Fund Development Committee. 2007. "Global Public Goods: A Framework for the Role of the World Bank." September 27, Washington, DC.

World Bank Independent Evaluation Group. 2008. "Annual Review of Development Effectiveness 2008: Shared Global Challenges." Washington, DC.

World Bank Independent Evaluation Group. 2010. "Global and Regional Partnership Reviews: Completed and Forthcoming Reviews." Accessed April 5, 2010, at: http://go.worldbank.org/3AS9R002M0.

World Bank Operations Evaluation Department. 2004. "Addressing the Challenges of Globalization." Washington, DC.

World Health Organization. 2010. "Pandemic H1N1 2009—Update 90." March 5. Accessed March 7, 2010, at: http://www.who.int/csr/don/2010_03_05/en/index.html.

# CHAPTER SIX

# CIVIL SOCIETY AND DEVELOPMENT EFFECTIVENESS IN AFRICA

AARON CHASSY

## Introduction

> *The only real test of the effectiveness of aid is its development impact — real changes in the lives and rights of millions of people affected by poverty and inequality."* [1]
>
> —Brian Tomlinson, Canadian Council for International Cooperation

Civil society can and has made meaningful contributions to addressing development challenges and to advancing democratic transitions in several African countries. The more innovative donor-funded civil society development programs are those that enable civil society organizations (CSOs) to do both.[2] CSOs are more credible when they are able to ground their calls for greater inclusion in decision-making, access to public resources, protection of rights, etc. in efforts to improve the quality of life of the people they serve. This approach does away with forcing Africans to choose between bread and the ballot, a false dichotomy often used by those with little interest in supporting either development or democracy.

A more balanced approach places the onus on CSOs to generate concrete benefits to their members and beneficiaries. If CSOs can do so consistently, they will represent their members' interests more effectively, especially before state actors. Nested in this theory of change is another one: if CSOs adopt democratic management practices, they will deliver more benefits to their members. In other words, a transparent and democratically-managed organization is a well-managed and *better-governed* organization.

This last point is crucial, because CSOs must model good governance internally if they are to credibly demand that state authorities do the same. In sub-Saharan Africa, depending on the country's regime type, modeling democratic practices alone is unlikely to provide civil society with sufficient leverage to force the state to adopt democratic reforms.[3] It can, however, protect CSOs from elites' efforts to "kill the messenger," painting CSOs broadly as corrupt, elitist, and therefore illegitimate representatives of citizens' voices.[4] Moreover, this approach can socialize CSOs' members around democratic values, contributing to the slow process of building a critical mass or constituency for democratic governance.

Civil society's adoption of this inside-out approach to promoting good governance is especially critical for membership-based organizations such as self-help groups, community-based organizations, and federations of CSOs. The two theories of change described above combine to form the central hypothesis of this essay: Donor-funded civil society development programs are more effective when they enable CSOs to practice internal democracy, i.e., to operate transparently, equitably, accountably and with integrity.

Moreover, as one considers the empirical evidence concerning donor-funded aid projects' ability to improve the quality of governance, it becomes even more apparent why local CSOs—and not external donors—must assume this role. According to some observers, "while aid has little impact on governance, governance has a substantial impact on aid effectiveness (Collier and Dollar 2001)."[5] Donors have sometimes responded to the challenge of promoting democracy by shifting their programmatic approaches to include at least a partial focus on strengthening CSOs to adopt this role. The question of how to improve effectiveness of such donor-funded efforts remains.

The second section of this chapter offers a strategy and sequence that will enable donors and practitioners to design more effective approaches to strengthening civil society's institutional development.[6] The chapter focuses specifically on how to build the capacity of membership-based CSOs acting either singly, in coalition with other CSOs, or collaboratively with like-minded state and private-sector actors to generate a bottom-up push for reform. In pursuing this strategy, donors must also be more intellectually honest with their civil society partners about the support they receive. Such support, like all aid, is contingent on how much it contributes to advancing the donor's national interests. When a donor's foreign policy pursues objectives inconsistent with the recipient country's development and democratic governance program goals, that incoherence sends mixed signals to African civil society actors.

Still, no matter how daunting these challenges may be, Africans must ultimately assume responsibility for overcoming them. African civil society leaders, like their state counterparts, do themselves no service by externalizing blame for their countries' continued struggles for democracy and development (Mills 2010). Some African civil society leaders and activists considered the Paris Declaration of March 2, 2005 and its proposed policy reforms to be useful in this respect. The Declaration produced a series of high-level forums with dialogues focused on how recipient countries could assume greater responsibility for overcoming their development challenges. African civil society activists were hopeful that these dialogues would contribute to creating a more enabling environment for democracy in their own countries.

Nonetheless, a few African civil society leaders remain skeptical, because they see these policy discussions and reforms as more of a distraction—technocratic fixes to existing aid delivery systems that maintain a highly unequal status quo. They would prefer to focus instead on engendering greater citizen-led, civic-driven change that has the potential for transforming societies (Fowler and Biekar 2008). Seen in this light, many in the worldwide civil society movement believe that a focus on aid delivery mechanisms may be inadequate or at best misplaced. Instead, they believe that people in developing countries would be better served by donor-funded assistance that supports democratic development.[7] For that reason, this chapter will focus on *development effectiveness* rather than aid effectiveness.

These issues are fundamentally ones of power: the nature and dynamics of African civil society actors' relationships not only with their own governments but also with their "partners," international donors and non-governmental organizations (NGOs). To be fair to donors, it is no easy task striking the balance between satisfying the demands of domestic stakeholders on the one hand and operating consistently with best development practices on the other. Donors attempt to strike this balance by directly awarding international NGOs grants and then directing them to competitively solicit, award and manage sub-awards to local CSOs. These local CSOs run the gamut from informal rural farmers' cooperatives to urban-based, highly professionalized associations.

Donors choose this approach for three types of reasons: 1) political—to build domestic support for otherwise misunderstood if not unpopular government spending on foreign assistance; 2) programmatic—to increase the likelihood of achieving project objectives; and 3) fiduciary—to assure accountability for the use of taxpayers' funds and to satisfy the demands of those responsible for oversight of foreign assistance in the donor country's legislative branch. Regardless, in most cases, the donor's intention is also three-fold: to promote greater local "ownership" over the project objectives, to build local CSOs' institutional capacity, and to avoid the appearance of interfering in the host country's domestic politics.

These sometimes competing rationales help explain the distinction donors make between NGOs and CSOs. Donors consider NGOs, usually based in their home countries but sometimes based in the host country or the region, to be organizations that have attained a sufficient level of institutional capacity to produce project deliverables consistent with the donor's financial and program audit requirements. On the other hand, CSOs are viewed more as the organizational platform for building local social capital, a means for achieving both developmental and democratic outcomes. Since the early 2000s calls for greater host country ownership have led donors to begin direct funding urban-based "local" CSOs, which donors view as more professionalized and "audit-able," based on their successful past performance using donor funds. This trend parallels a similar one of donors direct-funding development assistance to host country governments with non-projectized mechanisms, either directly with treasury-to-treasury transfers or more indirectly with multi-donor basket-funding.

Understandably, some local African CSOs have chafed at this approach, viewing international NGOs as donor-appointed minders or gatekeepers rather than as true development partners. Beginning in the late 1980s and early 1990s, regional umbrella groups of African CSOs began to demand greater equality in relationship to their Northern (U.S. and other OECD-member nation) partners (Ingersoll and Ingersoll 1990).[8] At the same time they began to reach out to sister groups in Latin America, Asia and even Eastern Europe and the former Soviet Union to form a much more inclusive platform for *global* civil society, *independent* of donor policy agendas. Since 1996, the World Alliance for Citizen Participation (CIVICUS), based in South Africa, has represented the nexus for this global civil society movement, organizing an annual world assembly that brings together civil society leaders and activists from around the world.

Ideally, the relationship between African CSOs and international NGOs should be one based on partnership. Partnership principles should include the following: shared vision; devolution of authority, autonomy and accountability; respect for and mutuality of interests; equality and transparency in all decision-making; commitment to mutual institutional capacity-building and eventual organizational transformation; ownership by each organization's respective constituencies; and sustainability (Catholic Relief Services n.d.).[9]

Most international NGOs now generally accept these principles or some version of them, because they recognize that local communities and their institutions are best placed to bring about social change. By concurrently partnering with and strengthening the capacity of African CSOs, international NGOs are learning that strong organizations with capable staff can design, implement, evaluate, and sustain effective development interventions. This capacity strengthening approach is vital, because people and organizations are active participants in their progress rather than passive beneficiaries. This approach achieves the intended results required by the donor and satisfies the preferences of the people whom international NGOs and their African CSO partners both hope to serve.

Even with this evolution in NGO-CSO relationships, among donors and practitioners alike there is still debate on what civil society does and whether or not it contributes to effective development. Some see civil society as an essential conduit for citizen voice, a civic watchdog or even guard dog to confront the repression of less-than-democratic regimes. Others view it as a fad, the result of ill-informed aspirations that Western donors have projected onto African societies where there is little historical or socio-cultural basis for their adoption. Similarly, some of the harshest critics view civil society as a meaningless residual sector, neither the market nor the state, comprised mostly of a grab bag of ineffective individual and organizational actors. Finally, some donors and practitioners conceptualize civil society as a space where individuals and interest groups interact non-violently to work towards the common good.

## Definitions of civil society

To gain greater clarity on these and other questions, a quick literature review shows that definitions and interpretations of civil society have changed, mainly to keep pace with the emergence and evolution of the Weberian bureaucratic state. Most of the current definitions include elements from the foundational definitions of Locke, Hegel and De Tocqueville and draw from the following (Paffenholz and Spurk 2010):

- *Habermas* focused on civil society's role in the public sphere. The polity requires the articulation and inclusion of diverse interests beyond those held by politicians and political parties. Marginalized groups in particular need to organize to articulate and channel their interests into institutional arenas where they can influence decisions that impact their lives.
- *Gramsci* underscored how civil society empowered citizens to mobilize around issues of shared interest and to confront elites, seeking to exclude them from governance and deliberation.
- *Walzer* viewed civil society as a space of uncoerced human association and relational networks formed for the sake of family, faith, in-

terest and ideology for the purpose of promoting common interests. The groups and networks may be formal or informal, are voluntary and essentially non-profit.

From the field of peace-building comes a more operational definition for civil society, which is outlined below and which forms the backbone of this chapter's analytical framework. The framework is formed to respond to the question: what exactly does civil society do? At a very general level, civil society can serve as a catalyst for citizen action, either individually through civic engagement or collectively through efforts organized by formal CSOs or less-structured social movements. For that reason, the framework is adaptable and applicable to the African context inasmuch as it expands on the two basic areas of intervention, focusing more on what civil society actors *do* than on who or what civil society *is*. In addition, the framework's authors, Paffenholz and Spurk (2006), point how out how "traditional" African civil society actors, whether they are chiefs, elders, peer, or affinity groups, and comprised of men, women, or youth, often perform similar if not the same functions as CSOs in non-African contexts.

## Seven-functions model of civil society

Paffenholz and Spurk disaggregate individual and collective action into *seven functions,* which civil society performs for peace-building and democratic governance. For the purposes of this chapter, the framework has been modified to apply more to the activities of governance and poverty alleviation (Paffenholz and Spurk 2010). Admittedly, certain approaches and activities might fall into multiple functional areas, but the distinctions remain useful. The seven functions are defined as follows:

1. Socialization: These activities demonstrate the value of adopting democratic principles, values and practices. A civic education project in a democracy and governance program will describe the roles, rights and responsibilities of citizens and those who govern them. More integrated approaches, nested in other technical sectors' projects, will transfer democratic management practices to membership-based organizations, such as grassroots or community-based organizations (CBOs). Examples of CBOs include health center management committees, microfinance solidarity groups, natural resource user groups, farmers associations, cooperatives, or parent-teacher associations (PTA).
2. Building social cohesion: Whereas socialization helps bind members of a single group internally, social cohesion bonds citizens horizontal-

ly across ethnicity, gender and religion with individuals and groups externally (Paffenholz and Spurk 2010). Civil society-led activities seek to orient citizens away from gaining access to resources doled out by "big men" in patron-client networks (Chabal and Daloz 1999) and toward collaboration on issues of shared interest with each other as well as toward a rules-based relationship with the state to increase its responsiveness and accountability.

3. Service delivery: The direct provision of services forms an important part of CSO strategy to generate value and become more economically viable as an organization. Where the state has shed its responsibility to provide social welfare and public services (e.g., shelter, health, education, etc.), civil society has often filled the gap.
4. Monitoring for accountability: Here, civil society monitors the state apparatus, gathering information so that, where the political space exists to do so, it checks state authorities, holding them accountable with the information gleaned.
5. Advocacy and public communication: Civil society efforts empower citizens, especially marginalized groups, to reclaim their rights before elected and appointed state officials. In addition, urban-based CSOs can undertake higher-level policy advocacy with national government officials. Finally, ad hoc or formal coalitions may organize a larger effort to build a mass-based constituency for political reforms.
6. Protection of citizens: This includes activities that protect lives, freedom, and property against attacks or oppression by state authorities. It focuses on human, political, and civil rights.
7. Intermediation and facilitation among citizens and between citizens and the state: Civil society undertakes two important tasks. First, it mediates among diverse, often competing agendas of various interest groups within civil society. Second, it channels citizen voice to state structures so that citizens can gain access to information and resources or participate in decision-making in policy and governance.

The seven functions model offers a useful way of looking at the approaches to strengthening programs (and potentially making them more effective) used in donor-funded civil society. Section 2 will use these seven functions to outline a strategy and sequence for generating bottom-up demand for democratic governance through membership-based CSOs adopting democratic practices. Each stage of the strategy's sequence includes descriptions of specific challenges as well as responses for developing programs at one or more of the following three levels:

- *Grassroots*: Creating more meaningful opportunities for citizens to

participate, both within CBO internal governance and externally with locally-elected or appointed officials.
- *Middle*: CSO efforts to build alliances, participate in networks with other civil society and political actors, and eventually generate a critical mass, or constituency, for change.
- *Top*: Civil society-led activities that increase political will among state actors so that they respond to civil society demands with improved developmental performance and more effective, equitable, and inclusive governance in targeted institutional arenas.

Where possible, we will draw from examples of programs implemented by CRS and other international NGOs and African CSOs in sub-Saharan Africa. These programs either strengthened civil society's institutional capacity or integrated capacity strengthening into programs in other technical sectors: agriculture, microfinance, health, education, etc. In Section 3 we will address some broader challenges and consider some responses at the policy, programmatic, and operational levels.

## Analysis of Civil Society Functions and Programmatic Recommendations

In very general terms, this strategy begins by strengthening membership-based community-based organizations (CBOs) *internally* so that they gain sufficient levels of credibility to advocate for their members' interests *externally*. CBOs can incorporate and apply democratic management principles *(socialization)* by making their financial management more transparent and accountable and their internal governance more equitable, responsive, and inclusive. As they elect members to leadership positions freely and fairly and manage internal finances transparently, CBO members realize that democratically-managed CBOs are better-managed CBOs. They are more capable of delivering benefits to their members through activities that contribute to improving their quality of life (*internal* service delivery).

Better-performing, more viable CBOs will have greater confidence, credibility and competence to reach out to and engage with other CBOs, local-level private sector actors, and government officials, especially on issues of collective interest. These issues include increased food security, access to critical public services, more equitable resource governance, and broad-based local economic development. Such efforts have the potential to bridge horizontal divisions rooted in socio-cultural identity politics (social cohesion) and to engender cooperation among local stakeholders. As a result, civil society can assume greater responsibility for fulfilling core local governance functions where decentralization laws allow for outsourcing and contracting to local service providers (*external* service delivery).

Where offers of partnership and cooperation prove insufficient, civil society actors can increase their members' awareness of the need for change and their willingness to advocate for it *(advocacy and public communication).* These efforts may include a variety of participatory monitoring mechanisms to collect and analyze local governments' performance, providing a more empirical basis to their demands for change *(monitoring and accountability).* This process will inevitably generate some conflict among competing interest groups as well as with subnational government officials, who may or may not be willing to respond to civil society demands. CSOs, either singly or as members of ad hoc coalitions, can help resolve such conflicts *(intermediation)* and reduce the likelihood of conflicts turning violent.

CBOs and middle-level CSOs can expand their coalitions outward through partnerships and strategic alliances to form a broad-based constituency for democratic governance or reform. They may form federations, umbrella groups, or networks of CSOs, which will help provide greater political clout to civil society actors when they push upward for reforms with top-level decision-makers *(advocacy and public communication).* Such reforms, in theory, will help remove the constraints that inhibit local communities' access to markets and decision-making in local governance institutional arenas.

The strategy articulated here is highly idealized. Besides simply ignoring calls for change, state actors may react by attacking civil society leaders and citizen activists, using violence as well as hamstringing CSOs with politically-motivated legal, fiscal, and administrative restrictions. In such scenarios, middle- and top-level CSOs will need to confront this behavior and provide CSOs and individual activists with the means to defend themselves (protection). Here again, civil society umbrella groups and federations, with the assistance of legal societies, may provide greater political clout by pooling their collective resources and mobilizing broad constituencies. Together, they will more likely be able to fend off state efforts to constrict the space available for legitimate civic participation.

## Socialization

The entry point for this strategy is CBO promotion of internal democracy. Over the past fifteen years, donor-funded democracy and governance programs have begun to adopt a more "applied" or "integrated" approach (Groelsema, Ott, and Muncy 2000), which has tied adoption of democratic management practices to the pursuit of development objectives such as access to potable water; better quality, more affordable healthcare and education; and opportunities for revenue generation, etc. This approach to socialization offers greater incentives for changing behavior than moral exhortations to assume one's civic duty.

*Specific challenges.* Many donors assume civil society instills the kinds of positive values that help citizens to bond together, initially within their own socio-cultural identity groups. Civil society, by its inherently associative nature, *will* instill values and attitudes—but not necessarily the values donors had hoped to promote. Depending on the context, civil society can also work *against* more positive forms of socialization.

For example, ongoing conflicts in Sudan and the Great Lakes in Central Africa, as well as recently concluded conflicts in Sierra Leone, Liberia and Angola, were fueled less by ideology or ethnic division than by contestation over access to renewable and non-renewable natural resources. In each of these examples, peer group members that would otherwise have formed strong bonds of internal cohesion to support each other were instead isolated from their extended families and communities and forced into serving as agents, slaves and concubines for warlords and elites. These elites and warlords then manipulated the same intra-group bonds by deeply traumatizing individuals and severing traditional ties of affection to form violent militias.

Donor-funded efforts to support socialization frequently ignore the fact that most Africans acquire their values through the complex web of social obligations in their societies' "economy of affection" (Hyden 1983). Without conducting a rigorous social sensitivity analysis to begin to untangle these relationships, the resulting donor-funded programs do little to enable Africans, as individuals, to develop their own strategies for socialization. Many of the donor-funded socialization activities focus on individuals' rights to differentiate and assert themselves from the larger whole. This is not to say it is unimportant to empower individuals or to address inequalities. However, given that most Africans view themselves as connected inextricably in their relationships to others, donors must try to develop approaches that reinforce and validate these communitarian values, not work against them.

*Response.* Socialization activities at the *grassroots* level should begin by first identifying "traditional" African values consistent with, or at least adaptable to, developing relationships based on tolerance, trust, and mutual respect. These values, including the social nature of humanity (e.g., *Ub-*

*untu* in South Africa, *Utu* in Eastern Africa, *Adamadenya*[10] in the Mandé culture of West Africa, etc.) and the obligation of leaders to assure the welfare of those whom they serve, exist across diverse cultures. CBOs can help instill and reinvigorate these values by adopting democratic management practices, an assertion supported by a conclusion in a study of Nigeria's civil society: "Strikingly, the only organizations in our sampling that performed the socialization function were democratically structured groups…This finding underscores the importance of democratic structures in inculcating democratic political culture with (civil society) groups" (Kew and Obi 2010).

This finding is consistent with some of the more successful socialization programs used in integrated democracy and governance programs, as documented by the U.S. Agency for International Development (USAID) in the late 1990s in Mali, Guinea, Madagascar, Zambia, and Zimbabwe (Groelsema, Ott, and Muncy 2000). The most successful civil society initiatives were those that encouraged civil society actors, especially CBOs at the grassroots, to employ a strategy of adopting democratic practices acquired through capacity-building activities for use *internally*. Later, they used the resulting improved ability to serve their members as a source of credibility *externally* for demanding that subnational government authorities adopt similar practices in their governance systems.

This approach begins by strengthening CBOs and their internal operational capabilities. Strong operational capabilities concretize democratic principles and form the foundation for developing sound management systems that can deliver benefits to members efficiently and consistently. Operational capabilities also include internal governance. If designed well, capacity-building activities encourage CBO members to articulate the qualities they expect from their leadership, the criteria used to elect leaders, the authorities and responsibilities assigned to them, and their relationships with individual members. Building these relationships on a foundation of democratic principles will reorient members away from vertical patron-client relationships, which remain prevalent in Africa's civil society. The relationships should instead be such that CBO members base their loyalty and support for leadership on leaders' willingness to embrace and put into practice the following principles:

- *transparency* in access to and dissemination of information important to CBO members;
- *accountability* in designing and operating administrative and financial management systems;
- *integrity* established by using merit-based criteria and processes to nominate and elect CBO officers;

- *competition* established by building internal checks and balances into the CBO constitution and bylaws; and
- *equality* established by opening up participation in CBO internal governance to all members without prejudice.

One positive example of how socialization contributes to robust development outcomes comes from Mali. Without prompting or encouragement from CRS or its local CSO partner, members of the Koulou community school cafeteria management committee purchased foodstuffs from small, mostly female cereal producers to fulfill their commitment for a local school feeding program rather than from the considerably better off local (mostly male) merchants. They expressed their commitment to the value of economic justice by ensuring that the least advantaged benefited the most from the purchase of local products (Chassy 2010).[11] All of the local purchases met the quality standard set by the prefectoral agricultural extension agent and far exceeded the minimum quantity set by CRS and its local partner.

## Service delivery

Once a project has established itself by gaining the trust and buy-in of local participants, the next step in this strategy is to anchor the project by delivering concrete benefits to participants through *internal* service delivery. Membership-based CSOs, whether they are informal self-help groups, CBOs, or more mature, professional NGOs, need to generate value for their members if they are to remain viable. They often do so through delivering services initially only to their own members. Increasing this capability is important if CSOs intend to build on this experience to eventually become contractors for subnational governments where they will be responsible for service delivery to the broader community.

*Specific challenges.* Starting in the 1980s, as a result of structural adjustment programs, many African states began to shed their responsibility for delivering public goods and services to their citizens (Kasfir 1998). Civil society, not the private sector, filled this gap, providing services directly to citizens, especially in remote rural areas where access to them was much more limited. Faith-based organizations operating through extensive grassroots structures functioned as *de facto* service providers for marginalized communities. Since the 1990s, poverty reduction plans have begun to reverse this trend through sector reform strategies that have included decentralized service delivery. While efforts to decentralize state authority down to the lowest level have increased levels of access (e.g. in Mali, Ghana, Uganda, and Rwanda), such efforts have produced mixed and not always sustainable results in terms of quality and equity of services delivered.

Francophone countries, whose reforms have followed the French model of *la tutelle*, have undergone a process more of deconcentration than of devolution or democratic decentralization.[12] Even in Uganda, the move to multiparty politics was accompanied by a *re*centralization of key administrative and financial functions (Manyak 2010). Decentralization is no panacea for reducing poverty and improving the quality of governance. It can replicate the same exclusion and inequalities found at higher levels of government as well as reinforce inter-identity group divisions over access to public resources and decision-making.

*Response.* Participating in implementation of decentralization reforms poses significant challenges, and if a CSO cannot first demonstrate its ability to consistently deliver quality services to its own members, it is unlikely to perform well as a contractor for local government. Therefore, the first step at the *grassroots* level is to approach CBO and CSO organizational capacity-building through the lens of small business development. Several U.S.-based international NGOs, cooperative development agencies, and for-profit contractors have created fairly rigorous models of organizational development for micro- and small enterprises, owned and run by individual entrepreneurs as well as by groups. Many of their models utilize the democratic management practices described above *(socialization),* reinforcing group solidarity in cooperative enterprises and employer-employee loyalty in individually-owned firms.

In Guinea, for example, the Cooperative League of the USA strengthened the internal democracy of rural group enterprises (RGE). RGE members demanded the same transparency and accountability from local government leaders as they had become accustomed to in managing their RGEs. Local officials, who lacked similar knowledge and skills, asked the RGE members to share their management expertise with them and include them in the RGEs' capacity-building. As a result, rural group enterprises figured prominently in helping local councils identify and collect taxes from markets, truck stops, timber harvests, and gravel pits. With their organizational strength and management capacity, the RGEs provided oversight in allocating and programming those tax monies. They insisted that revenues be invested in schools, health clinics, and other infrastructure according to law. In a few instances, they removed corrupt officials from office (Groelsema, Ott and Muncy 2000).

More importantly, contextualized adaptations of management, production, marketing and sales techniques help build *economically viable* organizations. The combination of these techniques and democratic management practices enables CSOs to operate more as social enterprises—organizations that use business management systems to achieve a social mission. CSOs learn to use these systems through internal resource mobilization and service delivery. Later, as they gain more experience they apply tools like feasibility studies, business plans, marketing strategies and competitive analysis to increase their capabilities to access external credit and to position themselves as potential service providers for local governments.

A brief field visit will provide many useful examples of how CBOs have applied democratic management practices to deliver services not only to their members but also to the rest of the community. These services include:

- opening a village store to supply the community with food staples and sundries;
- selling the village's food crop harvest to a wholesaler at a higher, negotiated price;
- co-managing a community forest or other renewable natural resource; and
- allocating a portion of the organization's revenue for social investments, such as building a new classroom or renovating the community health center.

Building on these experiences, CBOs (and CSOs) can negotiate contracts or enter into public-private partnerships with government agencies for service delivery on a more level playing field at the *middle* level. In particular, they can insist on a more equal say in decision-making. They can build on solid performance as a contractor to demand greater participation in local economic planning, development and monitoring for performance. Local governments in turn will enjoy improved public perceptions of their performance.

## Building social cohesion

The third step in the strategic sequence focuses on building social cohesion to expand the "constituency" for reform or democratic governance outwards. Overcoming identity politics and strengthening horizontal social cohesion is an enormous challenge. Even at the grassroots level, such efforts are extremely labor-intensive and time-consuming. John-Paul Lederach, one of the leading thinkers in the field of peace-building, has told colleagues that he was thinking about calling his next book, "The Magic of

Ten," because unless donors and practitioners think in terms of decades, they aren't really engaged in peace-building (Lederach 2007).

Ten years is much longer than most donors are willing to commit to; most projects last two to three years on average. Still, forging such horizontal bonds is essential for creating a critical mass in support of democratic governance. It also offers one of the few feasible approaches to overcoming the powerful grip neo-patrimonial regimes continue to exert over many African societies (Chabal and Daloz 1999b).

*Specific Challenges.* Research by Frances Stewart has demonstrated that horizontal inequalities remain one of the major drivers of violent civil conflict in Africa (Stewart 2008). African elites have repeatedly demonstrated their willingness to exploit social cleavages, especially those based on socio-cultural identity, to advance their individual agendas. They manipulate long-held resentments of opposing sides, instrumentalizing violent conflict to skew political processes and secure a tighter hold on the administrative structures of the state. Recent spates of violence in central Nigeria were initially reported as religious in nature, but further analysis revealed the root causes of the conflict to be inequitable access to land, public resources, and decision-making in the governance structures of Jos state (Nossiter 2010b).

These significant challenges have begun to unravel many practitioners' idealized images of grassroots communities as places where everyone lives together harmoniously. They soon realize that relationships among interest groups in these communities are far more complex. In fact, they are responding to the same incentives found in patron-client networks. These networks' affective ties influence the dynamics of individuals' relationships with each other and with state structures.

*Response.* It is unwise to apply community-level strategies that rely solely on working within individual CBOs, because their membership tends to be homogenous in terms of socio-cultural identity. Initially, CBOs may provide an entry point, as described above *(socialization),* but to generate social cohesion it will be important at the *grassroots* level to apply a "people-to-people" or "healthy relationship" approach. A people-to-people approach enables individuals from separate, opposing groups to identify the prejudices and stereotypes that divide them as well as the issues of shared interest that connect them (Church and Rogers 2006).

Through facilitated dialogue individuals begin to resolve their differences while refocusing their efforts on what connects them. Often they share common concerns such as meeting their basic daily needs, especially livelihood security, and access to public services, natural resources, economic opportunities, etc. As they identify these shared interests, they can apply newly acquired conflict prevention and democratic management skills to bridging their differences and achieving shared goals.

Shared goals generally provide tangible incentives to help reinforce the need to co-exist non-violently. These incentives are effective only insofar as social cohesion activities contribute to reorienting relationships toward trust, tolerance, mutual respect, and equality. CBOs, which ostensibly focus on serving and representing their members' interests, can apply what they learned in developing healthy relationships internally to dialogue with other CBOs comprised of opposing identity groups. On this basis, they can apply democratic management practices to serve the interests of the rest of the community. In this sense, CBOs serve a critical role: they elevate their members' level and scope of concern. As CBO members learn how their participation in CBO activities benefits both them and the CBO, they will also see how CBO activities, such as service delivery, can benefit the greater community as well. Thus, CBOs contribute to overcoming one of the biggest challenges to community development: providing individual citizens with a concrete *private* benefit for addressing a public, *social* concern.

The Democratic Republic of Congo (DRC) provides a stark example of the importance of building social cohesion. The conflict there has taken the lives of millions of innocent people. In the Maniema Province of the DRC, faith-based organizations including the Catholic Church's parish networks have lessened the impact of rape as a weapon of war by bringing opposing sides together in the Connect People to Peace project. This project helped resolve longstanding conflicts through dialogue, negotiations, community activities, reconciliation ceremonies and greater participatory decision-making in community development (Catholic Relief Services 2009).

At the *middle* level it is possible to apply a "middle-out" approach as described by John-Paul Lederach in his model for supporting organic networks of civic-driven change (Lederach 2005). In some African contexts, such networks continue to exist, having originated in the pre-colonial period. In West Africa, the *Kafo* (*Mandé* for county) system of social organization was based on connecting people from a particular region horizontally on issues of collective interest.[13] The *Kafo* closely resembled a "special district," operating as a semi-autonomous body responsible for managing communal goods and governing common resources (Baker et al. 2002). Special districts offer a potential way to fuse service delivery and social cohesion functions at progressively larger scales, depending on their compatibility with the country's decentralization framework.

## Intermediation and facilitation

While expanding the constituency for reform outwards to include more, diverse stakeholders, civil society project implementers and their partners must also foster greater programmatic coordination and linkages through intermediation, the next stage in the strategic sequence. This functional area is cross-cutting, as many CSOs engage with the government officials in various institutional arenas—local councils, members of parliament and deliberative bodies, frontline ministry technical services, electoral commissions, courts, etc.—to serve their members' interests.

*Specific challenges.* In many African countries, individual and organizational capacity tails off at the subnational levels of government. Weak administrative structures have little ability to respond to civil society demands and initiatives and suffer no penalty for ignoring them. For this reason, CSOs have stepped in to serve as interlocutors for citizens and communities, with varying degrees of success. They are hampered by their own limited knowledge of how governance systems function.

Besides their limited knowledge, CSOs' inability to move beyond self-promotion and preservation to construct solid working relationships with potential partner organizations hampers their effectiveness in the area of intermediation. They are hesitant to cooperate with peer groups in meaningful ways because they are uncertain whether such cooperation will limit their access to potential or actual funding opportunities. Not only in Africa but worldwide, CSO umbrella groups or federations will sometimes compete with their own member organizations for funding opportunities, generating more resentment and disunity. Weak state structures, already insecure from public perceptions of their ineffectiveness, are only too happy to exploit CSOs' inability to cooperate and coordinate among themselves.

*Response.* At the *grassroots* level, alliances of CBOs can collectively enjoin civic engagement and mobilization efforts around a shared agenda to sharpen their message, increase coordination, and eliminate "over-organizing" community members. A major source of frustration for many civil society project "beneficiaries" is the tendency for donor-funded program implementers to insist on creating yet another structure, usually a committee, for implementing each new project. Channeling CBO-led civic participation across multiple sector programs into the locally elected councils will help increase program quality and strengthen public perceptions of local councils' credibility.

This will require that practitioners learn to collaborate more effectively across their own "identity groups," i.e., technical sector stovepipes, and encourage participants to reach agreement on a shared agenda and present it to local councils.[14] Such collaboration presents its own challenges, because of the highly competitive nature of securing donor funding. Even post-award, many donor-funded implementers, usually international NGOs and contractors, are reluctant to cooperate with each other because of potential problems of attribution in reporting results from their activities and what they consider to be the proprietary nature of the technical approaches and deliverables (e.g., training methodologies, assessments, analytical tools, etc.) they produce.

Local councils, even those that are less than democratically governed, can help synthesize and prioritize citizens' diverse needs, whether they involve access to education, allocation of the local tax revenues, dispute resolution, or the location of a borehole well. Civil society-strengthening projects that attempt to increase citizen participation should include members of local councils in their capacity-building and technical assistance efforts, as described in the Guinea RGE example above, so that local councils will be more receptive to CBOs' and citizen groups' demands for good governance. One potential benefit is that local council members often wear many hats and frequently are already active members of CBOs. Such players may demand better organizational capacity-building and request that CBOs be included as key partners in government projects.

At the *middle* level, donor-funded programs should focus on strengthening deliberative bodies' and political parties' capacities to "govern out," including outreach to higher-level CSOs. The civic-driven change school (Fowler and Biekar 2008) cautions that civil society should maintain its distance from political society, but it is highly unlikely that civil society alone will bring sufficient pressure to bear on elites without support from political actors. Some of the more mature donor-funded parliamentary strengthening programs in East Africa (Uganda, Tanzania, and Kenya) have included the promotion of such linkages among institutional actors.

Donors have hoped the resulting alliances would create a countervailing force to the countries' respective executive branches. At a minimum, civil society actors could coordinate more with political parties and politicians so that they would not inadvertently work at cross-purposes. Among other things, civil society actors can help expand and diversify the base of support for political parties so that parties are less prone to serve the interests of Big Men in the political party leadership. In exchange, political parties can pursue a more constituent-driven agenda in deliberative bodies, an agenda that responds more to citizen demands.

Pre-independent South Sudan offers an example of such civil society intermediation and facilitation. UNDP, PACT and CRS collaborated together with the Government of South Sudan's Local Government Board (LGB) to set up County Development Committees (CDCs), the forerunners of the current system of local government in the newly independent South Sudan. In the Local Government Recovery Program (LGRP), CRS produced recommendations that the LGB adopted as policy to promote robust engagement between civil society and local government structures. The LGRP supported a comprehensive capacity development approach, including not only technical assistance and support to physical facilities, but also building greater social cohesion, accountability and participatory governance (Catholic Relief Services 2009).

One of the more exciting opportunities at the *top* level to institutionalize participatory mechanisms for civil society intermediation includes high-level accountability mechanisms such as the Africa Peer Review Mechanism (APRM). The APRM is carried out by multi-disciplinary teams of both government technocrats and civil society policy experts. Both the process and final product demand a substantial degree of civic participation. Some civil society actors, upon their governments' agreeing to the APRM process, follow up by pressing for more consistent adherence to APRM standards of participation. Similarly, civil society in partnership with the private sector has participated actively in other accountability mechanisms, such as the Kimberley Process and the Extractive Industries Transparency Initiative, to monitor their governments' compliance with international standards on the commercial exploration, exploitation and exportation of non-renewable resources.

## Monitoring and Accountability

The next step in this strategic sequence, balancing the state-society relationship through monitoring and accountability, is one of the more challenging ones. The state-society relationship is unbalanced by its very nature. Checks and balances remain weak within the African state, and civil society lacks *de jure* authority. The executive branch continues to dominate other branches at all levels of government, with most power concentrated at the central level. This stage in the strategy offers a few suggestions on how civil society might overcome these constraints, using monitoring to promote greater accountability.

*Specific challenges.* Civil society actors face four interrelated challenges in performing the "watchdog" function of monitoring public officials and holding them accountable. First, it is often extremely difficult to access the public information needed to monitor public institutions' performance and state authorities' behavior. Second, many African countries lack the legal structure that might support greater access to public information, such as a freedom of information act, public disclosure regulations or right-to-know mechanisms. Third, few rules exist or are applied consistently by government officials to classify whether or not information is too sensitive to be in the public domain. Fourth, in cases when authorities are more willing to share such information, public information dissemination systems operate in a shambolic state.

Besides limiting citizens' access to public information, Africa's political elites have little tolerance for anyone they consider to pose a serious political threat. They have harassed and even killed civil society activists and opposition party members, as was seen in 2010 with the "mysterious" death of a leading human rights activist in the Democratic Republic of Congo (Nossiter 2010a), and that of an opposition leader (Kron 2010) in the run-up to Rwanda's elections. Political elites need not always resort to violence; they can, for example, mobilize the machinery of the state to harass civil society activists.

They may invoke arbitrary tax inspections, wage unwarranted searches of offices, and confiscate CSO property and files. These tactics are often legalized through overly restrictive NGO registration laws, such as those recently enacted in Ethiopia, Uganda, and Rwanda. Ostensibly drafted for assuring accountability among NGOs, these new laws and regulations appear to uphold the rule of law while conveniently reducing political competition. They limit citizens' voice and right of association by shrinking the space available for civil society to function legitimately. Donors rarely apply diplomatic pressure to prevail on host country governments to amend such legislation, despite their reliance on civil society "partners" for many of their projects.

*Response.* One area where civil society has successfully undertaken monitoring and held public officials accountable has been at the *grassroots* level through the use of social accountability mechanisms. These participatory tools use either qualitative or quantitative assessment methods. Both approaches measure government performance against public expectations, financial commitments, and legal requirements. Qualitative methods include the use of citizen satisfaction and public service delivery report cards. These perception-based surveys measure the level of citizen ("customer") satisfaction with government performance in a range of operational areas.

Another tool used in some countries is the public expenditure tracking surveys (PETS) incorporated into the monitoring and evaluation system of the country's Poverty Reduction Strategy. CBOs applied such tools for tracking education sector reforms in Uganda, Tanzania, and Zambia and for health sector reforms in Rwanda, Ghana, and Nigeria as part of World Bank sector reform programs (Utstein Anti-corruption Resource Center n.d.). PETS allow CSOs and citizens to monitor the flow of budgeted resources from allocation by the central government authorities through expenditure and, in some cases, eventual liquidation of development projects by their subnational counterparts. PETS help identify where misadministration and malfeasance have diverted public resources and reduced the quality of public goods and services.

Using PETS and other social accountability tool results for evidence-based analysis helps institutionalize citizen oversight of government performance, especially in service delivery. As more CSOs become involved in service delivery as contractors to subnational government authorities, other civil society actors, such as national-level advocacy NGOs, can play the watchdog role. This division of labor may help service-delivery CSOs avoid "biting the hand that feeds them," which occurs when state authorities penalize them for criticizing government actions by taking away their contracts, an important source of revenue (Twijukye 2005). Specialization also insulates service-delivery CSOs from having to evaluate their own work, a potential conflict of interest.

Many national and some pan-African NGOs have worked at the *middle* level to promote aggregating social audit results as a way of increasing and deepening public participation in governance. This approach helps create greater linkages among donor-funded programs that otherwise concentrate on strengthening the performance of the government in one particular sector (e.g., natural resource management, agriculture, health, education, etc.). Following the money, whether it is allocated directly from the Ministry of Finance or indirectly via the Ministry of Local Government and technical line ministries, allows citizens and government officials alike an opportunity to determine whether or not development objectives are being achieved, and if not, to identify the reasons behind the shortfall.

In natural resource governance, Publish What You Pay, a coalition of over 280 African CSOs and International NGOs, has demonstrated that when they work together African CSOs can exert leverage on national governments and transnational corporations. The coalition has increased the transparency and accountability among governments, oil companies, and civil society for the management and allocation of extractive industry revenues. Mining, gas, and oil companies cannot and should not control how governments spend taxes, royalties, and fees, but they do have a responsibility to disclose the payments they make so that citizens can hold their governments accountable for the revenues from assets that the government manages on behalf of its citizens (Catholic Relief Services 2009).

At the *apex* level, the challenge remains how to engender greater downward political accountability for national-level public officials. Certainly much has already been said about the "culture of impunity" in Africa and the largely misdirected and unsuccessful approaches to transform it. While acknowledging the magnitude of the challenges posed (Chabal and Daloz 1999b), some approaches have offered some promise. For example, CSOs have negotiated with state authorities to draft, enact and monitor "integrity pacts," a useful tool for civil society-led efforts to demand greater accountability from public officials. Integrity pacts tend to work better when other accountability mechanisms—including whistle-blower protection, mandatory disclosure of public officials' income and assets, codes of conducts, public service commissions, etc.—are also in place and functioning effectively as part of the national integrity system.

## Communication and advocacy

Increasing citizen demand for change without generating a commensurate state response risks frustrating activists and reducing incentives for participation. Thus the next step in the strategic sequence must be using public communication and advocacy to engage state actors. Civil society actors rely largely on their ability to influence public opinion and raise public awareness of issues. In doing so they must balance their desire for change with the very real threat they face from elites, some of whom view public confrontation as a personal insult or threat. Civil society actors and journalists can reinforce this tendency with overly confrontational advocacy campaigns and less-than-balanced investigative reporting, respectively. Both are now learning to nuance their messages, in both substance and delivery, while testing new media freedoms to reach a broader audience.

*Specific challenges.* The challenges confronting civil society in this functional area resemble those described for monitoring and accountability: limited access to public information, few incentives for state authorities to respond to civil society demands, and the willingness of political elites to use the coercive powers of the state to marginalize, if not eliminate, perceived opponents. Rather than using violence, ruling politicians sometimes co-opt civil society leaders by offering them high-level posts in government. Some civil society activists' integrity is not so easily compromised. In Kenya, John Githongo, who had run the country's Transparency International chapter, was appointed President Kibaki's permanent secretary for ethics and governance. After only eighteen months, he had to flee for his life to the UK after disclosing the Anglo Leasing phantom deal, among others, in his report on "Findings of Graft in the Government of Kenya," which implicated several high-ranking administration officials (Gifford 2009).

In the media, levels of circulation for most print media remain small due to low literacy rates, and journalistic quality is inconsistent at best. Investigative reporting is frequently compromised by newspaper owners' political ambitions, and civil society activists usually have to pay newspaper reporters to cover their activities. Still, it is hopeful to see the rise of private broadcast media outlets reaching out and drawing in larger audiences with popular call-in talk shows. More recently, information communication technology has offered innovative means to engage citizens and form networks of activists, potentially beyond the reach or control of state authorities. Besides cell phones with SMS texting capability, the extension of internet access to secondary cities might increase the use of social media as an organizing tool, as seen in the recent Arab Spring. Still, the question remains—why should state authorities respond to civil society-led demands for change?

Some of the more creative responses to this dilemma have originated at the *grassroots* level. As described above, when CBO members are already empowered by more democratic internal management, they leverage their CBO's improved organizational performance to engage with external actors more successfully. The more successful CBO advocacy approaches are those constructed around defense or consolidation of these achievements, rather than some abstract set of "rights." It's not much of a stretch for CBO members to recognize that just as the CBO generates and manages its revenues to address issues of mutual interest, so too government structures should collect and manage tax revenues transparently and accountably.

Working at the *middle* level, strengthened, more democratically managed CBOs will have greater confidence to form strategic alliances with local council members. Together, they can build on their experiences as partners in promoting local economic development. They can approach higher-level subnational (district or provincial) or central government officials in ministry agencies responsible for allocating resources to local communities and for assuring delivery of technical advisory services. CBOs may federate to form regional and national-level CSOs. Similarly, local council officials and mayors may form associations of local governments, mayors, and municipal managers, etc. In partnership with each other, and later, as part of larger coalitions, they can help form a constituency for reform, providing the political clout needed for working at the top level.

In another example from Guinea, local FM radio stations harnessed the power of indigenous communication strategies (songs, proverbs, drama, skits, etc.) and the penetrative force of local radio broadcasts to bring the messages of democracy, civic rights, and peace-building to a large number of people. The population in the two regions targeted by the project was reported by the Independent National Elections Commission to have an average registration rate of 84.25 percent (Catholic Relief Services 2009).

At the *top* level, civil society-led confederations or umbrella groups, including private sector trade associations, can help aggregate their constituency's local-level initiatives and represent them before targeted decision-makers in national-level policy-making arenas. Confederations of PTAs, microfinance networks, and faith-based organizations' Parliamentary Liaison Offices are all good examples of influential, national-level CSOs that can advocate for their constituencies' interests at the highest levels. Since the early 2000s, South African NGOs have achieved some success using this approach to advance the "People's Budget," including the establishment of the Basic Income Grant for all children, and for people living with HIV/AIDS (O'Leary 2009).

## Protection of citizens

The last step in the strategic sequence focuses on "protecting" the gains achieved by civil society actors in their efforts to bring about socio-political change. With a few notable exceptions, justice sector institutions in Africa remain weak, presenting challenges and opportunities to civil societies seeking to consolidate their gains by institutionalizing democratic governance.

*Specific challenges.* Civil society actors struggle to assure that citizens enjoy more equitable access to justice and protection from abuse by security sector personnel. African judiciaries, along with being notoriously inefficient and backlogged with heavy case loads, remain subordinate to the executive branch. They lack trained, capable personnel, institutional autonomy, and the resources needed to operate independently and impartially. As a result, some observers have remarked that the systemic rigging of the justice sector—"telephone justice" being the most extreme example—creates conditions for the rule *by* law, rather than the rule *of* law.[15] Rule by law is used primarily by ruling elites to institutionalize limiting political competition and civic participation while maintaining the appearance of legality and due process.

From the perspective of those African citizens who are illiterate, with little or no formal education, much of the legal structure and system remain inaccessible and out of reach. Legal proceedings are usually held in the colonial European language, which few citizens speak either at all or well enough to understand the legal texts and procedures. In sub-Saharan

Africa, where 70 percent of the population continues to live in rural areas (World Bank n.d.), citizens must travel large distances at great personal expense to reach a justice facility. Once there, they encounter many of the same difficulties they confront elsewhere in public administration: corruption by poorly paid, disrespectful civil servants who often "misplace" case folders, causing untenable delays.

Nonetheless, civil society actors can and do attempt to extend greater, more equitable, access to justice to citizens through a variety of approaches. At the *grassroots* level, professional associations of lawyers and other civil society activists have formed human rights clinics that provide paralegal and legal assistance *pro bono* to those who otherwise would have limited access to similar services offered by the state. NGO-provided services sometimes involve representation in court, but more often they involve accompaniment and advice in resolving administrative legal concerns, such as access to public registries.

Second, some NGOs develop and publish national language-based materials to increase citizens' awareness about their legal rights. More innovative approaches include forms of functional literacy so that participants have the tools they need to learn how to apply their legal rights to more tangible daily livelihood concerns such as access to social and welfare services as well as business permits and licenses. Some NGOs have used broadcast media, including call-in radio talk shows, community radio broadcasts, panel discussions, round tables, and even soap operas and improvisational theatre to expand the reach of their public legal education programs.

At the *middle* level, NGOs may attempt to mainstream restorative justice into formal (legal) justice sector structures and systems. Customary forms of alternative dispute resolution (ADR) often involve consultation and facilitated dialogue between the plaintiff, defendant, and communal leaders. Civil society interventions strengthen and legitimize such practices by improving their compliance with existing legal frameworks. In this way, customary ADR contributes to a resolution that will not only be recognized and sanctioned by the state, but also contributes to more cohesive communal relations.

In an example from Southern Africa, the Diocesan Commission for Justice and Peace in Mzuzu, Malawi trained paralegals to work with traditional leaders to prepare and implement plans for discouraging practices that infringed on women and children's rights to inheritance and freedom from domestic violence. Paralegals brought cases of property grabbing and domestic violence to traditional leaders' attention and educated community members in human rights, inheritance rights and freedom from domestic violence (Catholic Relief Services 2009).

Finally, at the *top* level, national-level NGOs will push for greater enforcement of international laws and conventions, signed and ratified by their government. Civil society has enjoyed some success with this strategy, urging greater compliance with international legal norms and standards. Such opportunities have increased over the years with various UN summits and conventions, including the International Criminal Court (ICC). African countries' support was crucial for the ICC's creation, even though some African commentators complain that it focuses disproportionately on pursuing African suspects rather than those from the more powerful (Western) regions and countries.

## Remaining Challenges, Conclusions, and Recommendations

Donors and development practitioners confront several challenges and dilemmas in designing programs and projects that contribute to the institutional development of African civil society. This chapter has offered one possible response: strengthen the internal democracy of CSOs. If CSOs adopt democratic management practices, they will generate more benefits for their members. A better performing, more viable CSO possesses greater credibility and confidence to empower its members and beneficiaries to articulate their priorities and then effectively advocate for them before decision-makers. We conclude with a brief discussion of some of the broader challenges in applying this approach along with recommendations at the policy, programmatic, and operational levels.

### Policy challenges

In sub-Saharan Africa, besides revamping the way development assistance is delivered to conform to the Paris Declaration principles, donors should also consider that changes may be needed in their respective foreign policies. The U.S. has sought over the past ten years to integrate development with the defense and diplomacy streams of its foreign policy, and some European donors are contemplating a similar shift.[16] These donors should recognize that tying development to foreign policy may risk undermining not only development effectiveness but also their development programs' credibility.

While intended to increase policy coherence, coupling development with foreign policy sometimes achieves the opposite because of the compromises donors must inevitably make while pursuing higher priority commercial and geopolitical objectives. Sub-Saharan African governments, most of which have yet to fully transition to open societies and democracies, readily embrace donors' inconsistencies to justify eliminating political competition. By appealing to donors' higher priority concerns, they are able to close the political space available to African civil society actors with relative impunity even while donors rely on CSOs for participating in and implementing their programs. Not surprisingly, civil society actors, when confronted with such state behavior and tacit donor approval of it, will occasionally stop participating in donor-funded democratic governance programs.

Similarly, despite the rhetoric about the need for recipient governments to adopt sound policies and nurture democratic institutions, the Paris Declaration remains notably silent on poor performers. Donors argue that citizens in these countries should not be penalized for their governments' dysfunctions. Yet donors' continued steady stream of financial resources *does* penalize these citizens, because their assistance props up corrupt rulers and predatory states.[17] As it becomes obvious that citizens benefit little from whatever aid manages to trickle down to them, donors pivot to base their support for the government on maintaining the country's or region's stability.

The logic is reasonable enough: a penny of conflict prevention is worth a pound of peace-making cure. However, elites will stand this logic on its head to justify their authoritarian tactics as necessary to prevent instability. Paradoxically, rulers' heavy-handed tactics destabilize their countries and regions, because elites close off what little space remains for genuine citizen voice and political competition, eventually driving opponents out of the civic arena and into more violent approaches to resolving conflicts. The resulting instability only reinforces their policy and shifts donor concerns further away from improving development outcomes and more towards maintaining stability. What remains stable is the status quo, and while it is tenuous at best it is no less brutal for the very people who are supposed to benefit from donor-funded assistance.

*Policy Response.* Donors should adopt a more coherent foreign policy, or, at a minimum, implement their foreign policy more consistently. If donors are committed to promoting democratic governance only when doing so does not interfere with protecting their higher-level priorities, then they should state as much publicly. Otherwise, Africans will continue to view them as hypocrites due to their inability to balance meeting short-term foreign policy objectives with adhering to (stated) national values and international norms. African civil society leaders do not begrudge donors' need to promote their national interests through their foreign policy. They only want a more transparently, consistently applied policy so that they can manage their expectations accordingly.

## Programming challenges

Donor funding often steers civil society actors away from confronting regimes in direct political ways. Instead, donors often encourage a more technocratic approach to civil society public communication and advocacy, an approach based on top-down techniques such as social marketing, national "cascading" advocacy campaigns, etc. This tendency is due in part to donors' understandable attempt to reach the largest possible audience with limited resources. A more effective approach is one based on transformation, which empowers individuals and communities to recognize, articulate and demand change on their own terms. This approach has its own challenges: it requires significant resources for replication and scaling up and, more critically, recipient governments may perceive its overtly political nature as a potential threat.

At higher levels, instead of catalyzing broad-based constituencies for reform from the bottom up, donor programs promote a more expedient, instrumental form of participation. Typically "consultation" with civil society is limited to "key" civil society stakeholders who speak the same language as donors and are willing to validate rather than challenge donors' assumptions. Even within this relatively exclusive group, African states can minimize participation. For example, in the Uganda Anticorruption Threshold Program (2006–08), the Ugandan government allowed only five national advocacy NGOs to participate in a consultative group. In theory, the group should have offered inputs to developing and monitoring implementation of targeted reforms. In practice, the government's Director of Ethics and Integrity wielded veto power over which NGO recommendations could be presented to the monthly meeting of policy-makers responsible for overseeing the reforms' implementation. As a result, there was very little interaction between civil society and these policymakers, and even less input from the former in designing the public procurement, audit, administration of justice, and other important policy reforms.

*Programming Response.* Programs should follow the inside-out strategy and sequence outlined in this essay and focus particularly on supporting platforms where more equitable partnerships can be forged between civil society actors and their allies in the private sector and political society. These partnerships should extend both horizontally, to support greater networking, and vertically, to develop a constituency. The operating principle connecting efforts in both directions must be a commitment to infuse all of the platform's relationships, systems and structures with democratic practices.

## Operational challenges

Membership-based CSOs at all levels struggle to institutionalize democratic management practices. In fact, they often mirror the same behaviors they seek to change among the political elite. Not surprisingly, CSOs are dominated by leaders and leadership styles found in the rest of African society. The CSOs' lines of authority and communication perpetuate unequal power relationships among ethnic, gender, age, and caste groups. These structures channel loyalty vertically bottom up from clients to patrons, rather than building greater internal cohesion horizontally among members. In the African context, the natural tendency of any organization to suffer from "founderitis" is compounded by Africans' deference to patrons and reinforced by their allegiance to group identities.

*Operational Response.* Civil society actors can and must do their part by continuing to adapt democratic practices to the African context and to institutionalize them in their organizations. This might be one way to generate citizens' ownership for their country's democratic transition. It might also contribute to building a critical mass of civically-engaged citizens who will provide civil society leaders with the power and credibility they need to eventually force the state to begin responding to citizens' demands.

Several African CSOs have made such contributions in their own countries and elsewhere on the continent. A few examples include the West African Network for Peace-building, the Institute for Democracy in Africa, the Publish What You Pay-Africa coalition, and the African Centre for the Constructive Resolution of Disputes, among others. These organizations have established themselves on equal footing with international NGOs, strengthening not only their own institutional capacity but that of their sister CSOs in countries throughout the continent. They have helped build strong in- and cross-country networks of CSOs as well as platforms where civil society professionals can collaborate to pursue their shared agenda of advancing and consolidating democratic transition non-violently.

*The author wishes to thank Mr. Ben Lentz, Dr. Steven Snook, and Mr. Paul Miller for sharing their reflections on managing and implementing civil society-strengthening programs in sub-Saharan Africa. They also provided invaluable feedback on the essay's earlier drafts. Many thanks also to Dr. Phyllis Pomerantz, a fellow presenter at the Cornell symposium on which this volume is based, for her review of the first draft.*

## Notes

[1] Taken from Tomlinson, 2008
[2] By donor, I refer primarily to the U.S. government and the several dozen departments, agencies and bureaus within the U.S. government responsible for funding and administering U.S. development assistance, chief among which is the U.S. Agency for International Development (USAID). USAID continues to be responsible for the design and management of the majority of civil society programs funded by the U.S. government.
[3] Sub-Saharan Africa and its various states and civil societies are incredibly diverse. By taking such a broad view, this essay may be missing out on a far richer analysis that reflects on Africa's heterogeneity to draw out some explanations for its differences. Such an analysis, while intriguing, is beyond the scope of this chapter. Instead, we will attempt here to identify some common threads through the analytical framework presented.
[4] By elites, I refer to political, financial, and cultural elites. Per Chabal and Daloz (1999a), the borders between state and society (and between the political, economic and social spheres) remain largely fluid and permeable.
[5] The authors assess the quality of governance across three variables: preventing corruption, promoting popular participation, and democratization.
[6] By development practitioners, I mean professional staff, working as employees and consultants for international and African for-profit enterprises and faith-based and nonprofit organizations.
[7] In the recently released international framework draft formulated in anticipation of the First Global Assembly, Open Forum for CSO Development Effectiveness, several CSO delegates presented the following principles of development effectiveness: 1) Pursuing human rights and justice; 2) embodying gender equality and promoting women's rights; 3) focusing on people-centered empowerment; 4) practicing CSO transparency, openness, and good governance; 5) strengthening autonomy, local ownership, and participation; 6) pursuing equitable partnerships and solidarity; 7) creating knowledge and mutual learning; 8) committing to realization of sustainable outcomes (Open Forum for CSO Development Effectiveness 2010).
[8] In the Ingersolls' volume of collected essays, the American Council for Voluntary Action (InterAction) and the *Forum des Organisations Voluntaires Africaines de Développement* came together to address many of the challenges in the areas of development education, field programs, and leadership.
[9] As adapted from Catholic Relief Services brochure on Partnership and Capacity Building (Catholic Relief Services n.d.)
[10] *Adamadenya* literally means "the nature of being a child of Adam," and is the expression used most often to describe humanity in Mandé culture.
[11] As adapted from author's trip report to CRS/Mali.

[12] "Decentralization is the transfer of power and resources from national governments to subnational governments or to the subnational administrative units of national governments… Deconcentration may be defined as the national government reassigning responsibilities to the field offices of national ministries without placing these offices under the control of subnational governments" (Eaton et al. 2009).

[13] This brief discussion on the Kafo system is based on my personal conversation with Chéibane Coulibaly, Professor and President at Université Mandé Bukari, in January 2010.

[14] "The ways that donors and practitioners organize themselves tend to work against multi-sectoral integration. In the case of USAID, the disaggregation of funding by sector stems from Congressional appropriation structures, i.e., different funding "spigots," and sector-specific earmarks, e.g., child survival. USAID programming rules differ for each spigot and earmark, isolating technical sectors from each other through every level of program management thereafter. Integration requires more flexible rules with greater discretion for human catalysts to actualize their vision. Despite such structural rigidities, better information-sharing at the field level, co-location of activities and requiring technicians to work together in teams have been effective methods contributing to integration." As taken from the to-be-published CRS Report on Integrating Peace-building (Rogers, Bamat and Chassy 2010).

[15] Telephone justice refers to the phenomenon of a court decision resulting purportedly from a telephone call from the executive branch to the chambers of the presiding judge, informing the judge of the appropriate ruling he or she must take.

[16] The UK and Germany continue to keep development assistance separate from foreign policy; nonetheless, they have demonstrated a willingness to promote democracy and governance even in those African countries where rulers view these programs, often channeled through civil society organizations, as contrary to achieving other foreign policy objectives.

[17] Chabal's (2002) analysis of how African leaders have managed to game the international financial institutions' structural adjustment programs provides useful insights into the durability of neo-patrimonial regimes and the duplicity of donors.

## References

African Union. 2000. *Rwanda: The Preventable Genocide.* Addis Ababa: AU-IPEP.

Baker, M., R. Clausen, R. Kanaan, M. N'Goma, T. Roule, and J. Thomson. 2002. *Conflict Timber: Dimensions of the Problem in Asia and Africa, Volume III: Africa Cases.* Biodiversity and Sustainable Forestry (BIOFOR) IQC Task Order Final Report, ARD, Inc. Washington, DC and Burlington, VT: USAID.

Bassoon, A., and S. Sole. 2010. "Fresh arms probe ... maybe." *Mail & Guardian Online*, February 12: http://www.mg.co.za/article/2010-02-12-fresh-arms-probe-maybe.

Better Aid. 2010. *Civil Society Voices for Better Aid.* Statement to the UN-DCF in New York. June 29. http://betteraid.org/en/betteraid-policy/betteraid-publications/statements/349-betteraid-statement-to-the-un-dcf-in-new-york.html Accessed August 11, 2010.

Blair, H. 2010. E-mail message. Yale University Department of Political Science, September 7.

Bratton, M., and N. van de Walle. 1994. "Neo-patrimonial Regimes and Political Transitions in Africa." *World Politics* 46: 4. July: 453–489.

Catholic Relief Services. n.d. Partnership and Capacity Building. Unpublished brochure.

Catholic Relief Services. 2009. Past Performance Report Summary Table. Past Performances. Baltimore, Maryland: Catholic Relief Services.

—. 2011. *Catholic Relief Services Program Quality Support Department.* http://www.crsprogramquality.org/publications/2011/3/15/partnership-and-capacity-strengthening-sustainable-developme.html. Accessed August 23, 2011.

Chabal, P. 2002. "The Quest for Good Government and Development in Africa: Is NEPAD the Answer?" *International Affairs* 78, 3: 447–462.

Chabal, P., and J-P. Daloz. 1999a. "The Illusions of Civil Society." In *Africa Works: Disorder as Political Instrument*, eds. P. Chabal and J-P. Daloz, 17–30. Bloomington, IN: The International African Institution / Indiana University Press.

Chabal, P., and J-P. Daloz. 1999b. "W(h)ither the State." In *Africa Works: Disorder as Political Instrument*, eds. P. Chabal and J-P. Daloz, 3–16. Bloomington, IN: The International African Institution / Indiana University Press.

Chassy, A. 2007. Interview with anonymous East African expert in governance. *Proposal Strategy Session,* April 2007.

—. 2010. *Technical Support to CRS/Mali.* Trip Report, Baltimore, MD. Unpublished report.

Church, C., and M. Rogers. 2006. Designing for Results: Integrating Monitoring and Evaluation into Conflict Transformation Programs. Washington, DC: Search for a Common Ground.

CIVICUS. 2010. *Development Cooperation: The Aid Effectiveness International Dialogue.* http://www.civicus.org/development-cooperation-/aid-effectiveness-int-dialogue. Accessed June 14, 2010.

Collier, P., and D. Dollar. 2001. *Development Effectiveness: What Have We Learnt?* Washington, DC: The World Bank Development Research Group.

Eaton, K., T. Dickovick, P. Smoke, J. Larios, and L. Siegel. 2009. *Democratic Decentralization Programming Handbook.* ARD, Inc. Technical Publication, Washington, DC: USAID.

Fowler, A., and K. Biekar. 2008. "Civic-driven Change: Implications for Aided Development." In *Civic-driven Change: Citizens' Imaginations in Action*, by A. Fowler and K. Biekar. The Hague, Netherlands: Institute of Social Studies.

French, H. 2010. "UN Congo Report Offers New View on Genocide." *New York Times*, August 27.

Gettleman, J. 2010a. "Kenyans Approve New Constitution." *New York Times*, August 5.

—. 2010b. "Rwandan Leader Heads to New Term Under Shadow of Repression." *New York Times*, August 10. http://www.nytimes.com/2010/08/11/world/africa/11rwanda.html?ref=africa.

Gifford, P. 2009. *Christianity, Politics, and Public Life in Kenya.* New York: Columbia University Press.

Gregersen, H., A. Contreras-Hermosilla, A. White, and L. Phillips. 2004. "Forest governance in federal systems: an overview of experiences and implications for decentralization." *Workshop on Decentralization in Forestry.* Interlaken : UN Forum on Forests, CIFOR, Inter-Cooperation, SDC, 12.

Groelsema, R., D. Ott, and D. Muncy. 2000. *Synthesis of Democracy and Governance Cross-Sectoral Case Studies.* Synthesis, Washington, DC: USAID.

Herzenberg, C. S. (ed.). 2010. *Player and Referee: Conflicting Interests and the 2010 FIFA World Cup.* Corruption and Governance Program Report, South Africa. Johannesburg: Institute of Security Studies.

Hyden, G. 1983. *No Shortcuts to Progress: African Development Management in Perspective.* Berkeley: University of California Press.

Ingersoll, T.G, and P.W. Ingersoll (eds.). 1990. *Toward Partnership in Africa.* Leonminster, MA: Eusey Press.

InterAction. 2010. *Interaction: A United Voice for Global Change.* http://www.interaction.org/search/apachesolr_search/%22%20Africa%20Liaison%20Program%20Initiative%22. Accessed August 11, 2010.

Kasfir, N. (ed.). 1998. *Civil Society and Democracy in Africa: Critical Perspectives.* London: Frank Cass & Co., Ltd.

Kew, D., and C. Obi. 2010. "Nigeria: Dilemmas of Militarization and Co-optation in the Niger Delta." In *Civil Society & Peace-building: A Crit-*

*ical Assessment*, ed. T. Paffenholz. Boulder: Lynne Renner Publishers, 351–380.

Korir, B. C. 2009. *Amani Mashinani (Peace at the Grassroots): Experiences at Peace-building in the North Rift Valley in Kenya.* Eldoret: Catholic Diocese of Eldoret.

Kron, Josh. 2010. "Rwanda Opposition Figure Found Dead." *New York Times*, July 15.

Lederach, J. P. 2005. *The Moral Imagination.* Oxford: Oxford University Press.

—. 2007. Interview by Tom Bamat. *Personal conversation with J.P. Lederach.*

Lewis, D. 2002. "Civil Society in African Contexts: Reflections on the Usefulness of a Concept." *Development and Change*, 569–586. London School of Economics. http://personal.lse.ac.uk/lewisd/images/Lewis-D%26C2002.pdf. Accessed May 29, 2012.

Manyak, T.G. & I. W. Katono. 2010. "Decentralization and Conflict in Uganda: Governance Adrift." *African Studies Quarterly*, 1–24.

Mills, G. *Why is Africa Poor?* 2010. Development Policy Briefing Paper, Center for Global Liberty & Prosperity. Washington, DC: The Cato Institute.

Nossiter, A. 2010a. "Lifetime of Tracking Killings Ends in Activist's Own." *New York Times*, June 27.

—. 2010b. "Toll from Religious and Ethnic Violence in Nigeria Rises to 500." *New York Times*, March 9.

O'Leary, Fr. S. 2009. "New World Disorder – Civil Society Engagement: A Case Study of the People's Budget Campaign in South Africa." 2008 Summer Institute of Peace-building Learning Document. Working on Equity: Lumuru, Kenya. Baltimore, MD: Catholic Relief Services, 17–19.

Open Forum for CSO Development Effectiveness. 2010. "A Draft International Framework for CSO Development Effectiveness." First Global Assembly, Open Forum for CSO Development Effectiveness. Istanbul, Turkey, 3–7.

Paffenholz, T., and C. Spurk. 2006. *Civil Society, Civic Engagement, and Peace-building.* Working Paper, Sustainable Development Network, Conflict Prevention and Reconstruction. Washington, DC: World Bank.

Paffenholz, T., and C. Spurk. 2010. "A Comprehensive Analytical Framework." In *Civil Society & Peace-building – A Critical Assessment*, eds. T. Paffenholz and C. Spurk. London: Lynne Rienner Publishers, 65–76.

Putnam, R., R. Leonardi, and R. Nanetti. 1993. *Making Democracy Work: Civic Traditions in Modern Italy.* Princeton, NJ: Princeton University Press.

Rogers, M., T. Bamat, and A. Chassy. 2010. *Integrating Peace-building into Humanitarian and Development Programming.* Program Quality Support Department Learning Document. Baltimore: Catholic Relief Services.

Skapinker, M. 2010. "Chilling Assault on South Africa's Press." *Financial Times*, August 17, 9.

Smith, D. 2010. "Tutu: 'South Africa has lost its Pride.'" *Mail & Guardian Online*, May 6: http://www.mg.co.za/article/2010-05-06-tutu-south-africa-has-lost-its-pride.

Stewart, F. 2008. *Horizontal Inequalities and Conflict: Understanding Group Violence in Multiethnic Societies.* Hampshire, UK: Palgrave Macmillan.

Tomlinson, B. 2008. "Special Issue: Civil Society and Development Effectiveness: North/South Challenges." *Reality Check: The Reality of Aid, Civil Society, and Development Effectiveness: Another View*. August: 3–11.

Twijukye, G. 2005. "Biting the hand that feeds you? Examining subcontracting and accountability mechanisms between civil society organisations and local governments in Arua and Kabale Districts." Kabale District Farmers' Association, CARE-Uganda, Community Empowerment for Rural Development. Kampala, Uganda : Community Development Resource Network.

Utstein Anti-corruption Resource Center. n.d. *PETS - Examples and major findings.* http://www.u4.no/themes/pets/petsfindings.cfm. Accessed September 13, 2010.

World Bank. n.d. *Agriculture and Rural Development.* http://web.worldbank.org/WBSITE/EXTERNAL/TOPICS/EXTARD/0,,contentMDK:20445375~menuPK:1308541~pagePK:148956~piPK:216618~theSitePK:336682,00.html. Accessed September 14, 2010.

Young, Crawford. 2004. "The End of the Post-Colonial State in Africa." *African Affairs* 103, no. 410: 23–49.

# CHAPTER SEVEN

# THE POLITICIZATION OF HUMANITARIAN FOOD ASSISTANCE: USING FOOD AID FOR STRATEGIC, MILITARY, AND POLITICAL PURPOSES

DANIEL MAXWELL

## Introduction

On October 24, 1984, Michael Buerk of the BBC reported on a famine "of biblical proportions" in northern Ethiopia, bringing to the attention of the world the extent of human suffering in that famine. And the world responded: in 1985, efforts led by singer Bob Geldof raised millions of dollars for famine relief. Some twenty-five years later, the BBC ran another report, one about the diversion of that famine assistance to other purposes, including the financing of weapons purchases by rebel groups in Ethiopia at the time. There ensued a ferocious argument, live and on-air, between (now) Sir Bob Geldof and senior editors at the BBC about the accuracy of the 2010 BBC story alleging the diversion. In 1985, much of the relief was provided through cross-border operations into Tigray and Eritrea from eastern Sudan. The aid had been delivered semi-covertly because of government restrictions in wartime. Monitoring the end-use of the assistance was often not possible, and the aid was being funneled through the humanitarian wings of the rebel movements. It should hardly have come as a surprise that some of the aid money might have been used for other purposes. Nevertheless, Geldof called the BBC report "disgracefully poor reporting" and threatened lawsuits. Oxfam—a major player in the 1985 response—called it "palpable nonsense." The BBC stuck by its story for several months (BBC News 2007).

Four months previously, in November 2009, the U.S. had shut down its food aid pipeline to Somalia—which was by then arguably the world's worst humanitarian crisis. The U.S. justified this shutdown based on the threat of food falling into the hands of the *al-Shabab* movement, which controlled much of southern and central Somalia and was believed to have links to al-Qaeda. The shutdown was further justified as compliance with the regulations of the Office of Foreign Assets Control (OFAC). At the time, the World Food Programme (WFP) was investigating some of its transporters on corruption charges—diverting food aid—providing some legitimacy to U.S. suspicions.

However, several facts about this story could hardly escape the notice of observers: First, *al-Shabab* had been on the OFAC list for nearly two years by the time food aid was shut off. Second, some food aid had long been diverted from its intended recipients, and given the security situation, agencies have limited ability to monitor end use. So the possible diversion of WFP food was not new news.

Third, this move coincided with the run-up to an intended offensive by the Transitional Federal Government (TFG), using counter-insurgency lessons learned in Afghanistan and Iraq, and the U.S. was doing all it could to enlist humanitarian agencies to play a back-up role by quickly providing support to civilians in areas retaken by the TFG. The motive for the U.S. move mattered little to people on the ground: WFP's pipeline was cut by 40 percent overnight. As it happened, the TFG offensive never really materialized. But in early 2010, lacking international support, the WFP pulled out of southern and central Somalia after stepped-up threats from *al-Shabab*. This ended almost all food assistance in an area where the Food Security and Nutrition Analysis Unit for Somalia estimated 600,000 people were in need at the time, and it severely curtailed assistance in an area including several million people requiring food assistance (Food Security and Nutrition Analysis Unit [FSNAU] 2010). Though WFP itself sought to downplay the cut-off of funding from its major donor, the UN Humanitarian Coordinator for Somalia subsequently accused the U.S. of deliberately politicizing its food assistance, making it practically impossible to operate even in places still reachable by the UN or other humanitarian agencies (Gettleman 2010). In 2010, with much better than average rainfall, the food security impact of the cut-off was minimized. In 2011, in the face of one of the worst droughts in recent memory, the situation in Somalia deteriorated into a famine, and many of the agencies that would normally respond to a famine have not been able to access the area because of the events of 2009 and early 2010.

This chapter briefly reviews the background literature and the normative guidelines governing humanitarian food assistance. It then examines four cases, all in Africa over the course of the past decade or so, in which humanitarian food assistance has been used for political or security purposes by various constituencies. Two of these cases (Sudan and Somalia) are about humanitarian food assistance in the context of warfare; two (Zimbabwe and Ethiopia) consider the question in the context of electoral processes. The paper concludes with a synthesis of the findings and suggestions for policy, practice, and further research.

## A Humanitarian Perspective on the Politicization of Food Aid

Humanitarian assistance is increasingly allocated in accordance with political and security concerns, rather than on the basis of need.[1] It was classically intended to be provided solely based on time-honored humanitarian principles: humanity (protecting human life and dignity), impartiality (based only on need), independence (free of political interference), and neutrality (provided in such a way as to avoid favoring any side in a political or military conflict).

In the recent past, with the broad reorientation of counter-insurgency strategies by the U.S. and its allies, the merging of humanitarian, development, and strategic/military goals has become an increasingly explicit part of U.S. foreign policy.[2] The current government in the UK announced in 2010 that henceforward, British aid would also be allocated according to security considerations *(The Guardian* 2010). Recent reports from security think tanks advocate "humanity as a weapon of war (e.g. Brigety 2008)." And the examples above show that others besides donors use food aid for political or strategic purposes.

This paper examines the consequences of the deliberate politicization of food assistance, which remains the most common form of humanitarian aid. The arguments in response to this "securitization of aid" phenomenon have been two-fold. On the one hand, classic humanitarians have cried foul, noting that this is in direct violation of humanitarian principles, international agreements such as International Humanitarian Law (IHL), and other normative agreements to which most countries are signatory (though non-state actors or insurgent groups such as *al-Shabab* are not signatories). From a principles viewpoint, tying humanitarian assistance to security objectives puts at risk not only genuinely disaster-affected populations, but also the organizations that have traditionally provided such assistance, and indeed the foundations on which humanitarian action is predicated (Donini 2008). On the other hand, a more pragmatic critique focused on the question of aid effectiveness asks whether tying aid to political objectives actually has the intended result of addressing both humanitarian *and* political or security objectives—a topic on which there is a lot of rhetoric, but surprisingly little evidence (Wilder and Gordon 2009).

## Food Power and the Politicization of Food Aid—A Foreign Policy Perspective

In an influential 1985 book, Robert Paarlberg described "food power" as an attempt to "exercise political influence through the manipulation of food production or distribution" within states or between states by both state and non-state actors (Paarlberg 1985). After examining a number of historical cases, including food aid to India in the 1960s and the attempts to punish the Soviet Union for its invasion of Afghanistan in 1980, Paarlberg concluded that achieving strategic objectives through the exercise of "food power" was difficult if not impossible because manipulating access to food is not easy to do. There are too many players in the market, too many alternative sources of food supplies to make the manipulation of food aid a viable instrument, and, in the case of commercial food exports, too many alternative exporters as well as vehement opposition from U.S. exporters.

Even in cases where the manipulation of markets or access to humanitarian food assistance is possible, Paarlberg concluded that little real political influence would be gained. Poor people might suffer the consequences of sanctions, but political elites, policy makers, and (critically) militaries would not suffer. Indeed, political elites in targeted countries would blame foreign manipulation—possibly leading to an effect opposite of the intended one. Paarlberg's 2010 book, based on more recent examples, reiterates these findings (Paarlberg 2010).

The use of food as a weapon of war has been clearly established as a causal factor in contemporary famine. But it is one of many causal factors—it rarely stands alone. Macrae and Zwi (1991) noted that food has been used as a weapon of war, either indirectly through political and economic manipulation, or directly by diverting it to feed militias or to sell to get money for weapons purchases. While food has long been used as a weapon, the sheer amount of food aid—and specifically humanitarian food aid—has increased substantially.[3] Hence there has been increased scope for the manipulation of food aid—or its use as a weapon—as well.

Critics have noted that humanitarian assistance is seldom distributed in a manner completely devoid of political considerations and often has unforeseen consequences (de Waal 1997; Maren 1997). Since the time these critiques were offered, however, numerous efforts have put into place normative guidance to ensure that food is not misused and that unintended consequences are minimized, monitored, and corrected. These are reviewed in the next section.

## Normative Guidance on Humanitarian Food Assistance

Humanitarian assistance and humanitarian action generally are intended for conflict- or disaster-affected people in a manner that is somewhat isolated from the political circumstances of the disaster. While actual practice often falls short of this norm, a number of international instruments have been designed to protect it.

### Humanitarian principles

Humanitarian assistance is guided by a set of principles, widely held to include *humanity* (or the humanitarian imperative), *impartiality* (the provision of assistance solely on the basis of need—not provided or withheld on the basis of other criteria such as race, religion, political creed, or nationality), *neutrality* (provided in such a way as to avoid favoring one side or another in an armed conflict), and *independence* (free from the interference of non-humanitarian actors, particularly belligerents in a conflict). While these principles have no enforcement mechanism, in a recent unequivocal statement specifically on humanitarian food assistance, the European Community Humanitarian Office (ECHO), formally committed all its humanitarian aid to all four core principles (ECHO 2010). The Good Humanitarian Donorship Initiative also reaffirms commitment to these principles.

### Red Cross/Red Crescent NGO Code of Conduct

Perhaps the most fundamental of contemporary normative guidelines is the code of conduct for the International Red Cross and Red Crescent Movement and the NGOs in Disaster Response adopted in the aftermath of the Rwanda genocide in 1994. The first four articles are the most applicable to this case. These reiterate that aid (of any kind, food or otherwise) is provided impartially—based on need only. The Code is very clear on the separation of aid from politics—humanitarian aid will not be used to promote any "religious or political standpoint" —and on the separation of humanitarian objectives from foreign policy objectives: aid agencies "shall endeavor not to act as instruments of government foreign policy (IFRC 1994)." The Code has been signed by 436 humanitarian agencies—northern and southern, faith-based and secular, including all major humanitarian agencies and alliances with the exception of the Médecins sans Frontières (Doctors without Borders) alliance.

## International Humanitarian Law (IHL)

The 1949 Geneva Conventions and their Additional Protocols make it clear that the state has the primary responsibility for the well-being (including access to adequate food) of the population within its border .[4] Mourey (1991) outlined quite clearly the provisions of International Humanitarian Law regarding the politicization of food and food assistance in warfare.

He notes the following relevant articles:

- Starvation of civilians as a method of warfare is prohibited (Additional Protocol I, Article 54 (1));
- It is prohibited to attack, destroy, remove or render useless objects indispensable to the survival of the civilian population, such as foodstuffs, agricultural areas for the production of foodstuffs, crops, drinking water (Additional Protocol I, Article 54 (2));
- Relief actions that are exclusively humanitarian and impartial should be accepted when these people lack supplies essential for their survival (Additional Protocol I, Article 70; Additional Protocol II, Article 18).
- Parties to an armed conflict must allow humanitarian and impartial relief operations—including those aimed at providing food—when supplies essential for the civilian population are lacking.

Compared with other normative codes or guidelines, IHL is less restrictive of belligerent action with regard to food. For example, IHL doesn't explicitly say that food can't be manipulated—it simply makes it clear that starvation cannot be used as a method of war, or that aid cannot be interfered with when people "lack essential supplies for their survival." Nevertheless Mourey concludes that donors and governments cannot withhold food aid as a means of putting pressure on authorities or belligerents. Not all countries have signed on to all the additional protocols in which some of the above articles are found. Nevertheless, legal experts note that the entire corpus of IHL is considered to be international "customary law," whether or not individual states have signed individual protocols (Mourey 1991). The Genocide Convention could be interpreted as proscribing the use of food or food aid as a weapon, if the purpose of such usage was to eliminate, in part or in whole, an identified group of people.

## The Sphere Charter and minimum standards for disaster response

The Sphere Project, an initiative launched in 1997 to develop a set of minimum standards in core areas of humanitarian assistance, aims to improve the quality of assistance provided to people affected by disasters and to enhance the accountability of the humanitarian system in disaster response.[5]The Sphere standards probably represent the most ambitious interagency attempt at voluntarily enforced, industry-wide guidelines on how humanitarian assistance should be delivered and what principles should underlie it. Sphere reaffirms IHL in prohibiting the use of starvation as a method of war and notes that "where there is a risk of food aid being commandeered or used by combatants in an armed conflict, measures [should be] put in place to avoid it fueling the conflict (The Sphere Project 2004)."

## Other codes of conduct

Various other codes of conduct govern the distribution of humanitarian food assistance. These include the Euronaid Code of Conduct on Food Aid and Food Insecurity (Euronaid 1995), the Food Aid Charter of the Club du Sahel (Club du Sahel 1990), and the more recent Charter for Food Crisis Prevention and Management (Food Crisis Prevention Network and OECD 2007) based on the earlier Food Aid Charter of the Club du Sahel. The latter does begin to incorporate language around access to food as a human right, but otherwise, beyond affirming the general principles found in the IFRC Code and the Sphere Standards, these codes don't speak to the question of the politicization of humanitarian food aid *per se.*

## The Good Humanitarian Donorship Initiative

The GHD Initiative was formed by a group of donor agencies committed to improving the practice of financing humanitarian assistance. According to the GHD's *Principles and Good Practice of Humanitarian Donorship,* humanitarian assistance is subject to "the principles of humanity, impartiality, neutrality, and independence (GHD Initiative 2008)." Regarding the latter two (neutrality and independence), this means that "humanitarian action must not favor any side in an armed conflict or other dispute where such action is carried out, and [there must be] *autonomy of humanitarian objectives from the political, economic, military or other objectives that any actor may hold with regard to areas where humanitarian action is being implemented"* (emphasis added). Seventeen donor agencies, including the governments of the U.S. and the UK, endorsed the GHD Initiative.

## Summary

Several observations come out of this review. First, there is little doubt that a formal international consensus on the proper conduct of humanitarian food assistance operations exists: all revolve fundamentally around humanitarian principles and IHL. Agencies, governments, and donors have recently and explicitly reiterated their commitments to this consensus. But some actors in contemporary humanitarian crises—recipient country governments and non-state actors—are not part of this consensus. And formal consensus or not, actual practice on the ground is often very different from what is described above. The following case studies illustrate the point.

| Country | 2005 | 2006 | 2007 | 2008 | 2009 | Total |
|---|---|---|---|---|---|---|
| Ethiopia | 1,027,025.30 | 32,000.00 | 577,421.10 | 932,152.10 | 798,067.20 | 3,366,665.70 |
| Sudan | 907,027.10 | 586,242.50 | 485,908.40 | 666,304.50 | 493,965.80 | 3,139,448.30 |
| North Korea | 697,322.80 | 307,453.70 | 320,526.20 | 324,920.90 | 304,497.30 | 1,954,720.90 |
| Somalia | 39,294.80 | 203,192.40 | 92,350.80 | 364,507.80 | 313,450.30 | 1,012,796.10 |
| Afghan-istan | 164,008.40 | 147,368.00 | 204,696.40 | 304,180.50 | 179,447.10 | 999,700.40 |
| Kenya | 99,009.00 | 260,327.20 | 170,605.50 | 185,647.30 | 236,119.00 | 951,708.00 |
| Uganda | 223,835.00 | 197,457.80 | 234,087.70 | 155,155.60 | 88,450.60 | 898,986.70 |
| Zimbabwe | 71,552.80 | 134,487.40 | 145,523.50 | 336,949.60 | 209,070.00 | 897,583.30 |
| Georgia | 11,199.60 | 661,728.60 | 6,613.50 | 794.3 | 13,301.40 | 693,637.40 |

**Table 7.1. Top Ten Recipient Countries of Food Aid: 2005-2009 (Metric Tons)**

Source: WFP/FAIS

# Four Cases on the Manipulation of Aid

Four cases of the manipulation of humanitarian food assistance for political or military purposes are analyzed below. All are in Africa, and all involve major food aid recipients—two are about the use of food aid in militarized conflict; the other two are more about the uses of food aid to influence electoral processes. Table 8.1 provides information on the top ten recipients of food aid globally over recent years. All four case study countries are included in the top ten (highlighted in Table 7.1).

## Sudan: Civil war, Counter-insurgency and Politicized Food Aid

Sudan has had multiple conflicts over the past thirty years—particularly a two-decades-long civil war between the north and the south, and a counter-insurgency war in Darfur now in its seventh year. Sudan has been a major recipient of food assistance, surpassed only by Ethiopia in terms of total tonnage of humanitarian food aid delivered (Table 7.1). Food aid has been too valuable a commodity for belligerents, local leaders, and external actors in conflict to ignore. This case study examines only three specific issues or incidents related to the politicization or manipulation of food assistance—there were many, many more.

### OLS flight bans and "aid magnets" during the 1998 Bahr al-Ghazal famine

Food aid was manipulated to influence civilian movement and humanitarian response during the Bahr al-Ghazal famine in 1998. Though the causes of the famine included a range of factors, specific actions taken by the government of Sudan (GOS) in 1998 included the banning of relief flights into the region. In the end, the famine claimed the lives of an estimated 78,000 people (Deng 2002). Drought conditions set the stage, but in 1997, as the Sudan People's Liberation Army (SPLA) made gains in government areas of the south, the GOS intensified efforts to prevent further advances. This included stepped up raiding by *murahaleen* militias and successful attempts (at least in the short run) to split the SPLA. By early 1998, much of the civilian population of Northern Bahr al-Ghazal was displaced (Deng 1999).

The SPLA had long relied on guerilla tactics in Northern Bahr al-Ghazal—controlling the civilian population and their movement became a significant component of GOS strategy (Rhodes 2002), including displacing the population and destroying their assets. Local militias were drafted into the fight against the SPLA. One of these militias, led by Kerubino Bol, abruptly switched allegiances in early 1998, joining the SPLA in attacking the GOS garrison town of Wau. The fighting that followed displaced some one hundred thousand more people (Deng 1998). The government set about controlling the whereabouts of these and other people displaced from the fighting with renewed seriousness as other factors that led to the famine intensified (Drumtra 1998).

Food aid flights and airdrops were a carefully negotiated part of the UN's Operation Lifeline Sudan (OLS) agreement (Deng 1999). Granting or not granting flight permissions was one way in which the GOS controlled the movement of people. The flight bans were probably overemphasized at the time as a major cause of the famine, but they had a significant impact on the movement of people on the ground, and they certainly exacerbated the famine's impact.

In 1997, the government imposed about ten flight bans per month as a means of harassing OLS. In February and March, 1998, however, this figure jumped up to nearly 60 a month, in response to the offensives against Wau. This caused the migration of extremely hungry people on the ground to those sites where deliveries were permitted, environments without access to clean water, sanitation, or health facilities (Griekspoor and Collins 2001). For most of February 1998, airdrops were halted in Bahr al-Ghazal and the rainy season had nearly arrived before flights resumed their normal frequency. This crippled the early response to the growing famine conditions, as OLS was unable to react quickly even when the ban was lifted. The gap between planned and actual food deliveries was the same in March (when the bans were in effect) and April (when they were lifted) (Deng 2001). It wasn't until August that OLS finally met its targeted tonnage of food aid deliveries.

The flight bans highlight one of the underpinnings of famine laid out by Howe (2010). As bans were imposed and lifted for different places in the region, word of mouth generated migration of affected populations in search of relief, causing drop sites to become what Howe terms "aid magnets." At these sites, lack of hygiene and safe drinking water in combination with compromised immunity due to malnutrition led to the transmission of diarrheal disease, one of the main causes of the extremely high mortality (Howe 2010). Global acute malnutrition prevalence was to reach 60 percent at the peak of the famine in mid-1998—among the highest figures ever recorded. By May word had spread that both relief food and an acceptable level of security had been restored to Wau, attracting a daily influx of one to two thousand people (Rhodes 1998). By July and August, there were 50 to 100 deaths per day as people attempted to reach feeding centers and distribution sites in Wau (Griekspoor and Collins 2001). This corresponded to a crude mortality rate in excess of 25 people/10,000 population/day (Deng 1998).

The impact of the flight bans on the Bahr al-Ghazal famine has been the subject of a long debate. The bans were a tool used to undermine the relief effort, and their effect was increased vulnerability on the ground (Deng 1998). Restricted access meant that the GOS could control and manipulate the flow of aid—and hence the movement of people. Deng points out a more direct impact on a famine-affected population in the Nuba Mountains, also as a result GOS-imposed flight bans in 1998. The famine in the Nuba Mountains killed an estimated 5 thousand people—and the flight bans were the primary driver of that crisis (Deng 1998, 66). Yet despite the desperate conditions that prevailed on the ground, evidence is scarce that the flight bans did anything to serve the strategic interests of the GOS in the counter-insurgency campaign in either Bahr al-Ghazal or the Nuba Mountains (Deng 1998).

## The U.S. Government and the provision of food through the SPLA

Towards the end of 1999, the U.S. government passed legislation that all food aid for Southern Sudan (the biggest emergency operation in the world at the time) would be funneled not through Operation Lifeline Sudan, but directly through the humanitarian arm of the SPLA. The U.S. legislation authorizing the provision of food aid (and "non-lethal" forms of assistance) to the SPLA was the so-called Brownback amendment to the Sudan Peace Act, after its main sponsor, Senator Sam Brownback of Kansas. Brownback framed the provision of food aid directly to the SPLA in terms of a "religious war" being waged by Khartoum against the south. Humanitarian agencies on the ground in particular vehemently objected. A consortium of NGOs crafted a joint statement condemning the manipulation of humanitarian aid in support of combatants, arguing that the amendment created a dangerous ambiguity between humanitarian and military aid that would put at risk genuine aid efforts as well as the agencies responsible for delivering the aid.[6]

The UN agencies behind Operation Lifeline Sudan feared that the U.S. plan would disrupt the impartial distribution of humanitarian aid to civilians in both government- and rebel-controlled areas (Agence France Presse 1999). From the perspective of the WFP, there was a danger not only of disrupting the distribution of aid, but also of compromising the safety of the agency and NGO staff on the ground in this deliberately partisan approach to providing food aid (IRIN 1999). Counter-terrorism was certainly part of the rationale for the Brownback amendment—but it was couched in terms of concern about human trafficking and human rights violations on the part of the government of Sudan. Mainline human rights organizations were opposed to—not supportive of—the Brownback amendment (Human Rights Watch 1999).

Ultimately, the Clinton administration never adopted the policy. Bradbury et al. argued that, without explicitly funneling aid through the SPLA, the U.S. government met the same objectives more discreetly, and at a smaller political cost, though the methods adopted still had the effect of politicizing aid (Bradbury, Leader, and MacIntosh 2000). The objectives included keeping the Government of Sudan "off balance" and stemming the spread of fundamentalism that was believed to be part of the Khartoum government's plan. This was not the only time the U.S. Congress supported funding to Southern Sudan outside the framework of Operation Lifeline Sudan (U.S. House of Representatives 2001).

## Darfur

In Darfur, even humanitarian organizations have used food aid to serve security or other objectives. A recent study on the targeting of food assistance in complex emergencies highlighted practices of providing food assistance to aggressors threatening humanitarian convoys, personnel, or other recipients—practices referred to by aid workers as "food for access" or "food for protection (Young and Maxwell 2009)." Groups or communities not scheduled for food distribution arranged for groups of armed youth to stop food convoys, demanding that their communities be included if food was to pass through their areas. Alternatively, armed groups would demand payment in food in exchange for a guarantee that they would not attack neighboring communities receiving food aid once the humanitarian agency distribution teams left the area. The aggressors were usually portrayed as nomadic groups, but other rebel groups were also implicated. The food donated to these armed groups was clearly being used by militias as well as by the omitted communities, although exactly how it was used was never clear—it was obviously not subject to the usual post-distribution monitoring (Young and Maxwell 2009).

While this practice is not an official category of food aid, it was the manner in which agencies approached (or were forced to approach) the prevailing security situation for both themselves and their clientele in western Sudan at the time. Essentially a form of "protection racket" or security guarantee using food as the payment, the practice undermines impartiality. But it shows how food aid has been used to serve security objectives, even by humanitarian agencies—both their own security ("food for access") and that of the intended recipients ("food for protection"). Agencies operating on the ground at the time argued that they had little choice. The government of Sudan, local rebel commanders, and the African Union force could not guarantee security for the passage of truck convoys or for recipient communities (Young and Maxwell 2009).

### Conclusions

Nearly all actors in the conflicts in Sudan over the past thirty years have used, or attempted to use, food aid for political and security purposes. These include the government, rebel movements, donors, and even humanitarian agencies. These practices clearly undermined humanitarian principles and had devastating impacts on populations caught in conflict. There is, however, little evidence of the impact this had on achieving security objectives, beyond very short-term tactical gains. Certainly manipulating access to food, airdrops and IDP movements were insignificant in affecting the outcome of the fighting in Bahr al-Ghazal or the Nuba Mountains in 1998; neither was the overt American attempt to keep the government "off balance" by channeling food aid through their SPLA allies (or the less obvious ways they tried to accomplish this goal after OLS protested this politicization of food aid) any more effective. And though the use of food to buy safe passage for convoys or protect recipients may have prevented an immediate attack on either, this practice probably contributed to the *deteriorating* security situation faced by humanitarian agencies in 2008 and 2009.

## Somalia: Terrorism, Protracted Crisis, and the Politics of Response

### Background

Since the overthrow of the former president Siad Barre in 1991, Somalia has been in protracted conflict. Major fighting in 1992 combined with two bad harvests plunged much of the southern part of the country into famine (de Waal 1997). After lobbying from humanitarian organizations, a peacekeeping operation—UN Operation in Somalia (UNOSOM)—was formed to ensure the security of convoys delivering food assistance to famine-affected areas, supported in part by the U.S. military. But the U.S. effort rapidly turned into a conflict with specific warlords, culminating in the infamous "Black Hawk down" incident in 1993. Though subsequent UN missions attempted to regain lost momentum, Somalia was largely ignored for most of a decade.

The Transitional National Government (TNG) was formed in 2000—the first attempt at national government in Somalia after the overthrow of Siad Barre. However, it was dominated by a few major clans, which only served to intensify the problem. Opposing groups aligned with regional rivals (some receiving support from Ethiopia, others from Eritrea) and the conflict took on aspects of a proxy war. With the TNG unable to rally much support, groups allied to Ethiopia set up the Transitional Federal Government (TFG) in 2004. Though the TFG included some technocrats unaligned with the militias, much of its membership was the same well-known warlords. Islamist groups not affiliated with specific clans began to take shape during this period, mostly in opposition to the TFG. By the mid-2000s, it was clear that the only ideology able to compete with clanism—and thus lead to any transformation of Somali politics—was Islam. But some of the Islamic militias in Somalia had links to terrorist groups (Marshall 2009).

## The rise of Islamist forces

For a short period in 2005, an Islamist group in Mogadishu achieved relative security under the "Mogadishu Security and Stabilization Plan." By mid-2005, the Islamists had organized the Supreme Council of Islamic Courts Union (ICU) and by 2006 controlled most of southern Somalia. A brief period of calm followed, but beginning in late 2006, concerns over some of the international allegiances of the ICU—and the TFG's alliance with Ethiopia—led to an invasion by Ethiopia, with the support of the U.S. While the invasion achieved the objective of chasing the ICU out of the capital, it also resulted in the most radicalized element of the ICU—the *al-Shabab* (youth) movement—taking on the role of main opposition to the newly re-installed Transitional Federal Government. Fierce fighting between *al-Shabab* and the TFG and Ethiopian (and eventually African Union) forces led to the large-scale flight of people from Mogadishu—most of whom took refuge around Afgooye, just northwest of the city. Conditions in Afgooye were so bad that it was dubbed the "world's worst humanitarian crisis" in early 2008 (Reuters 2009). By 2008, *al-Shabab* controlled most of the countryside in southern Somalia and most of the towns, except for Baidoa (the seat of the TFG) and parts of Mogadishu. By the end of 2008, *al-Shabab* had made substantial inroads in the central region, having taken Dusamareb and Galgadud. The food security situation worsened steadily during this period—both as a result of climatic factors and the conflict. Table 7.1 depicts the growth in numbers of displaced people from 2005 to 2009. The *deyr* rains in south-central Somalia were relatively heavy in late 2009, leading to a good harvest and improved food availability—at least in the short term.

| Year | 2005 | 2006 | 2007 | 2008 | 2009 |
|---|---|---|---|---|---|
| **IDPs (000)** | 377 | 400 | 300 | 980 | 1,390 |
| **In need of food assistance (000)** | 875 | 2,100 | 990 | 1,830 | 3,200 |

**Table 7.2. IDPs and people in need of food assistance: 2005–2009**

Source: FSNAU 2010

## The role of food aid

Throughout this period, there were three separate food aid operations in Somalia, one led by the WFP, one by CARE, and one by the International Committee of the Red Cross (ICRC). By 2008, USAID was funding both the WFP and CARE pipelines, which between them covered nearly two million people, the vast majority of whom were in central and south central Somalia—the same area where, by this point, *al-Shabab* was presenting a major threat to the internationally supported, but internally weak, Transitional Federal Government. Food aid has always been a valuable commodity in Somalia. Food aid transporters were required to pay a deposit equal to the value of the particular food shipment in order to ensure its arrival at the intended destination. But given the context, there was inevitably some loss of food, and always large "fees" paid by transporters to local militias to permit vehicles to pass through territory they controlled (Jaspars and Maxwell 2008).

A special unit was set up to monitor food security in Somalia—the Food Security and Nutrition Assessment Unit (FSNAU). In the mid-2000s, in part because of pressures from competing warlords, FSNAU invented the Integrated Food Security and Humanitarian Phase Classification Map (known in shorthand as the IPC) (FAO 2008). Its purpose was technical—to ensure an accurate assessment of need to allow the impartial allocation of limited resources—but its rationale was political—to reduce intense political competition among warlords for food aid as a resource. To protect impartiality, extremely transparent and understandable indicators and processes were needed, and the IPC was the tool that provided them—in a violent and politicized context. By 2008, IPC analysis was including IDPs and urban populations at risk, as well as the more traditional rural food-insecure groups.

## Corruption, counter-terrorism, and "winning hearts and minds"

With the rise of *al-Shabab* and fears that Somalia would become a haven for anti-Western terrorists, external involvement was stepped up. Ethiopian troops on the ground clearly were there both to prevent the spread of radical Islam into eastern Ethiopia and to contain the spread of terrorism throughout the greater Horn of Africa. A U.S. counter-terrorism task force, set up in Djibouti, engaged in both military and "civilian" activities across the Horn, intending to contain radical elements in Somalia and to "win hearts and minds" elsewhere (Bradbury and Kleinman 2010).

Under the U.S. Patriot Act (specifically the Office of Foreign Assets Control or OFAC), it is illegal for any U.S. entity to aid or do business with anyone associated with a terrorist group. In late February 2008, the U.S. Government added *al-Shabab* to the list of terrorist organizations under the Patriot Act. This led to complications on the ground in Somalia, with its history of food aid diversion, corruption, and the regular raising of local revenues by militias and warlords through charging fees at checkpoints along roads within territory they controlled—practices subscribed to by *al-Shabab*, as well as by many of the groups *al-Shabab* was fighting against.

In late 2008, CARE pulled out of all its food aid operations in Somalia due to specific threats from *al-Shabab*—stemming at least partially from the perception that U.S. agencies were associated with U.S. military actions, a charge that CARE was quick to note was false. But even the hint by the U.S. that it wanted to enroll humanitarian agencies in implementing its security agenda in a place like Somalia elicits this kind of interpretation. WFP picked up most of the areas in which CARE was working, so CARE's withdrawal did not, in the short term, cut people off from needed aid.

But all deliveries of U.S. food aid to Somalia were cut off in late 2009 because of concerns over OFAC rules and fears that some U.S. food aid could benefit *al-Shabab*. Given the near impossibility of monitoring the end-use of food aid in Somalia, it was quite possible that some food or money might be falling into *al-Shabab* hands. However, it was not clear why OFAC was invoked when it was—two years after *al-Shabab* was listed as a terrorist organization, and after nearly twenty years of evidence of food aid diversion in Somalia. Some sources indicated that it was simply a legal concern over OFAC rules and a rather narrow concern that

American aid officials could be held liable for its diversion; others suggested that a broader strategic concern existed over funneling external assistance in a way that bolstered the legitimacy of the TFG.[7] WFP's pullout in December 2009 happened to coincide with the best harvest in south-central Somalia for several years, somewhat mitigating the effect of the pullout, but humanitarian crisis conditions continued in Hiran, Galgadud, and Galkaayo regions (FSNAU 2010). At the time, WFP contacts said that the pullout from south-central Somalia was not linked to the cutoff in U.S. food aid. In February 2010, however, the UN accused the U.S. of deliberately politicizing food aid. U.S. officials at the time responded that they were simply following U.S. law against assistance benefiting a terrorist organization. At about the same time, *al-Shabab* announced that it was banning WFP and food aid, accusing the aid organization of having "covert" political motives (Voice of America [VOA] 2010).

The impact of this kind of political standoff on emergency-affected populations is precisely what humanitarian principles are intended to prevent—and it is the reason humanitarian organizations traditionally seek to be perceived as independent of the political objectives of belligerent parties. It was perfectly within both the letter and spirit of international humanitarian law for a donor to ask for guarantees that assistance not be diverted by or to a belligerent party in a conflict—but there was also a compromise in place that had been worked out over twenty years in Somalia. Precisely why the U.S. decided to turn off the food aid tap in late 2009 remains unclear. The one thing that U.S. and *al-Shabab* policy makers could apparently agree on in early 2010 was that food aid should not go to southern Somalia. The views of food-insecure populations in those areas were not the subject of either party's calculus.

## Conclusions

Beginning in the aftermath of the embassy bombings in Nairobi and Dar es Salaam in August 1998, and particularly after the September 11, 2001 attacks, the U.S. began paying increased attention to the broader Horn of Africa, with a particular interest in preventing Somalia from being used as a base for terrorism. Outside of Somalia proper (i.e., among Somali-speaking populations in neighboring countries), the objective of the U.S. is to "win hearts and minds through the delivery of humanitarian and developmental aid" as part of a broader counter-insurgency and counter-terrorism strategy (Bradbury and Kleinman 2010). A 2010 study found that these efforts have been relatively small and that drawing major conclusions about impact was difficult—in terms of developmental, humanitarian, or security concerns (Bradbury and Kleinman 2010).

Several observations are worth noting. First, few outsiders have had access to south-central Somalia since early 2010. As all external analysis is done by remote control, judging the impact of the United States' actions is difficult. Second, several observers of Somalia in 2010 noted that in comparison to the millions of dollars falling into *al-Shabab's* coffers from port revenues, the diaspora, and other revenue-generation activities, the proceeds from food aid diversion are small, and many parties are competing for these proceeds. Third, based on the analysis that has been done by FSNAU and others, humanitarian conditions in much of south-central Somalia were not as bad as expected in 2010 due to above-average rainfall. But conditions in and around Mogadishu were worse than ever, and prolonged drought has deteriorated humanitarian conditions elsewhere. Many observers note that, under these circumstances, cutting off food aid may have had a perverse effect. Far from undermining *al-Shabab* or strengthening the TFG, it played right into *al-Shabab's* hands, in part because it got rid of influences that *al-Shabab* didn't want on the ground and in part because it provided them with a very handy excuse when widespread food insecurity reoccurred in 2011. Irrespective of organizational views of humanitarian principles or International Humanitarian Law, the subjugation of assistance to strategic or security aims may well be losing hearts and minds under these circumstances, rather than winning them.

## Ethiopia: Food—the Continuation of Politics by Another Means

### Introduction

Ethiopia has a long history of using food as a means of influencing both war and politics. Whatever the merits of the BBC story mentioned in the introduction, little doubt exists that the government at the time (the 1984 war) manipulated food as both a carrot and a stick in that war.[8] In the run-up to the famine, food was clearly being diverted from areas of rebel control or influence (the stick) and being used to coerce hungry peasants into accepting resettlement or conscription (the carrot) (Vaux 2003).[9]

Ethiopia is the biggest single recipient of food aid in Africa. Table 7.1 depicts the amount of international food aid going to Ethiopia over recent years.[10] There were significant food security crises in 2000, 2003, and 2005; and 2008–09 saw the combined impact of drought and high food price inflation. Though not a major humanitarian emergency, levels of food assistance increased significantly.

Stories of using food aid to influence political behavior began to emerge from Ethiopia again in the mid-2000s, in the run-up to national elections in 2005, and in the context of an on-going counter-insurgency conflict in Somali Region. Like the BBC story during the war against the Derg, these more recent stories have been documented, but only through scattered pieces of evidence. Making individual stories add up to a larger picture is difficult. At one level, accounts of abuse have been clearly documented, but viewed as a percentage of the total amount of food aid being delivered in Ethiopia, the documented cases of abuse add up to only a tiny proportion of the total. We will review two historical strands—that of electoral politics and the counter-insurgency conflict.

## Conflict

In 1984, resettlement was part of the Government's counter-insurgency strategy—moving people out of rebel-influenced areas to deny rebel movements a popular base. The use of food in the counter-insurgency effort was not the major cause of famine, but it was certainly a confounding factor. It was also the bait for enticing a reluctant populace into the army to fight an unpopular war. De Waal noted that while little food aid was going to the rural poor, a full ration was offered to those who joined the army or pro-government militias (de Waal 1997). This shored up short-term support for the Derg regime, but prolonged the war and was a double-edged sword—in the longer term, it increased support for the Tigray People's Liberation Front (TPLF) (Africa Watch 1991). The war against the Derg ended in 1991 when, nearly simultaneously, the Eritrean People's Liberation Front (EPLF) captured Asmara, and the TPLF—which had broadened its support base by merging with an Amhara-region-based rebel movement to become the Ethiopian People's Revolutionary Democratic Front (EPRDF)—captured Addis Ababa.

For several decades, a low-level anti-government insurgency has existed in the Somali Region of eastern Ethiopia, led by the Ogaden National Liberation Front (ONLF). The U.S. State Department's annual report on human rights in 2007 notes that both "the government and rebel forces restricted delivery of necessary food aid from donor organizations into the five zones in which military activity was the most intense. Flow of commercial traffic into these zones was also prevented, thereby creating food and supply shortages (U.S. Bureau of Democracy, Human Rights, and Labor 2008)." The 2008 report similarly notes "continued allegations of human rights abuses by all parties, *particularly diversion of food aid* from intended beneficiaries suffering from a severe drought."

## Elections

Ethiopia held elections in 1995, 2000, and 2005. Nascent opposition parties chose to boycott the 1995 elections. Though the 2000 elections were contested by other parties, in the context of the recent war against Eritrea, the EPRDF won the elections easily. The 2005 elections, however, were a much more fraught affair. While contested openly by a number of parties, violent incidents occurred, and accusations of voter intimidation, electoral fraud, and the use of food aid to sway the behavior of the electorate were voiced. The government imposed a ban on political protests throughout the period running up to the elections in May. The results were contested—the opposition claimed that they had swept Addis Ababa and were well on their way to winning a majority of seats in Parliament, when the government announced that the incumbent party had won the election and declared a state of emergency.

Given all the ways in which the 2005 elections were subjected to extraordinary political pressures, the misuse of food aid was relatively minor—except that food aid constitutes a constant form of interaction between the government and the rural populace in four of its most heavily populated regions. In the aftermath of the 2003 food crisis, the government of Ethiopia, international donors, and humanitarian agencies were determined to deal separately with chronic food-insecurity and acute crises and set up the Productive Safety Net Programme (PSNP) to meet the relatively predictable needs of the chronically food-insecure population on a multi-year funding basis. The PSNP, however, also reinforced a powerful tool in the hands of local leaders.

In the run-up to the 2005 elections, the Ethiopian Human Rights Council (EHRC) reported incidents of extra-judicial killing, torture, eviction from farmland, prohibition of public services, etc., in addition to the denial of food aid to opposition supporters (IRIN 2004). The U.S. State Department, in its annual report on the human rights situation prior to the elections, noted credible reports of threats by local officials to redistribute land or withhold access to food aid in order to encourage voters to support the ruling party (IRIN 2004). However, it is very difficult to estimate how widespread these reports were, or what their impact was. The number of reported incidents is small, but control over the PSNP gave the government a powerful tool.

## Conclusions

In Ethiopia, unlike many other countries, the government itself is directly involved in nearly all aspects of the delivery of humanitarian food assistance, which gives the government additional power over the use of food and makes independent monitoring difficult. Incidents of both voter "persuasion" and the diversion of food aid in the Somali Region have continued to be noted in the annual State Department reports since 2005, but nothing much ever comes of these allegations. These reports are little more than a minor embarrassment. Several dozen similar accusations turned up in an extensive review of available documentation. But in a country where, in a bad year, 15 million people require food assistance, it is very difficult to judge the significance of reported abuses. While some aid was suspended over the contested results of the 2005 election, this suspension was in response to the killing of civilians—it had little to do with food aid diversion. In brief, impact of these alleged abuses on the humanitarian situation, the election results, or the security situation in the Ogaden is difficult to judge. Clearly the diversion of aid in Somali Region has worsened humanitarian conditions there. But how much this influences the course of the conflict is difficult to judge given the dearth of hard information, the remoteness of affected areas, and the apparent willingness of donors to underplay such reports. The World Bank investigated allegations of manipulation related to the PSNP and found "no widespread patterns of aid misuse (IRIN 2010)." The U.S., which provided nearly a billion dollars' worth of aid to Ethiopia in 2009, similarly found "no evidence that food aid is being denied to supporters of the opposition (IRIN 2010)."[11] Hence, while there is a long history of using food to influence both conflicts and elections, there is little conclusive evidence about the impact of either.

# Zimbabwe: Food Power and Elections

## Background

Following a long and bitter struggle for independence and majority rule, Zimbabwe had several decades of growth and progress in the 1980s and 1990s. Land lay at the heart of the struggle for independence, and a land reform and redistribution plan was supported by international donors. The economy grew and, despite a *de facto* one-party state, relative political calm ensued for much of this period. A region-wide drought in the early 1990s affected production in Zimbabwe, but this crisis was well managed and no significant humanitarian crisis resulted. A decade later, a second region-wide drought occurred in the context of a deteriorating political consensus in Zimbabwe and had much more wide-ranging impacts. But these impacts played into the hands of the ruling party, providing a rationale for cracking down on dissent as well as the means of enforcing the crackdown—through controlling access to food. Control was much more all-inclusive in Zimbabwe than in some neighboring countries, allowing the state considerably more leverage.

## The 2000 crisis and the 2000 elections

Parliamentary and presidential elections in Zimbabwe used to be separate affairs—with parliamentary elections taking place every five years and presidential elections every six, beginning from 1990 when the constitution was changed to make an executive president rather than a prime minister head of government. The Zimbabwe African National Union–Patriotic Front (ZANU-PF) party led by Robert Mugabe easily won all the parliamentary elections in the 1980s and 1990s, and the presidential elections of 1990 and 1996. With a changing political climate, however, a coalition of urban and labor groups came together under the umbrella of the Movement for Democratic Change (MDC) and, for the first time, presented a serious electoral challenge to ZANU-PF in 2000.

In the context of a deteriorating economic situation and a serious political challenge, ZANU-PF abandoned the paced progress of the land reform program and began encouraging land invasions on large-scale, commercial, white-owned farms. "Fast-track land reform" displaced not only the landowners but also the sizable population of farm workers. Hurried redistribution of the confiscated land was often used to reward supporters of the party (Ndlela and Robinson 2007; Hellum and Derman 2004). Though portrayed in the press as the main cause of the ensuing national crisis, the land invasions were only one of several factors, including the HIV crisis, economic mismanagement, and an inability to control spending (Deutsche Presse-Agentur 1999). And there was a regional drought; though not as serious as previous droughts had been, the breakdown in the agricultural sector meant that much irrigated land was out of production—hence the land invasions and uncertainty in the commercial agricultural sector generally aggravated the impact of the drought. Furthermore, in many cases the new landowners lacked access to credit—and therefore to machinery and inputs to make their newfound land wealth productive. The commercial agricultural sector in Zimbabwe went into a period of decline from which it has yet to recover.

This situation became a self-perpetuating cycle of crippled food production, hyperinflation, and declining ability, particularly for urban Zimbabweans, to access adequate food—and increased political discontent and support for the opposition MDC. While the prevalence of acute malnutrition never rose to levels that would have constituted a humanitarian emergency in other parts of the region, requirements for humanitarian food aid sharply increased. In this context of growing economic and political crisis, control over food, including access to food aid, became a powerful tool in the hands of the ruling ZANU-PF, and it was used in a variety of ways to ensure ZANU-PF's hold on power

## Elections and the manipulation of food aid

The main staple food in Zimbabwe is maize meal, or "mealie meal." It could be accessed in five main ways: two market mechanisms, two safety net mechanisms, and humanitarian food aid. The two market mechanisms were the highly regulated commercial market and the (unregulated) parallel or "black" market. Government-operated drought-relief programs provided two safety-net means of access: subsidized purchases that were restricted to "needy" people, and wages in "self-targeting" food-for-work programs. The final means of access, international humanitarian food aid, was managed in large part by international NGOs. The system was plagued by unequal access (Edwards 2004). The food-for-work and the subsidized food distributions were run by the government and access was predicated on political affiliations (Itano 2002; Physicians for Human Rights 2002; Thornycroft 2002); access became more controlled as the crisis progressed. The parallel or "black" market was the most reliable source of food, but prices made food inaccessible to a large proportion of the population. The formal commercial market was largely undermined by price controls and supply-side failures.

Zimbabwe had long had a centralized Grain Marketing Board (GMB) that managed national stockpiles of various food commodities including maize meal. A June 2001 decision made buying or selling maize or wheat independently of the GMB illegal, handing it a virtual monopoly in grain trading. While some analysts justified this in terms of strategic management of a critical resource, others suggest it was simply the consolidation of power (Butcher 2008; Makaye and C. Munhande 2008). The major impact was to force more commercial grain trading onto the parallel market at much higher prices (Makaye and Munhande 2008). But this did centralize control of three primary means of access to food in the hands of the government, giving it power not only over who had access to food on the basis of "need" but even over who had access to "commercial food supplies." Local officials subsequently maintained three lists: for Grain Marketing Board sales, for subsidized sales, and for food-for-work programs.

In the context of increasing political competition and a protracted economic crisis, food aid became a tool to influence elections. The rhetoric and actions of ruling party officials became increasingly blunt: A senior government minister warned recalcitrant voters in Matabeleland in July 2002, in the run-up to presidential elections, "As long as you value the government of the day you will not starve, but we do not want people who vote for colonialists and then come to us when they want food. You cannot vote for the MDC and expect ZANU-PF to help you (*The Standard* 2002)." The Catholic Commission for Justice and Peace was prevented from distributing food to children in Binga for over a month in 2002 as party leaders claimed the organization was promoting anti-government sentiment (Butcher 2002; Physicians for Human Rights 2002). Hungry villagers were required to show ZANU-PF party membership cards as a condition for inclusion in the subsidized distribution programs or food-for-work programs, and local leaders created food aid rolls, with known MDC supporters conspicuously omitted from the list (Edwards 2002; Shaw 2003).

International food aid programming was not controlled in the same way that government-sponsored distributions and programs were. International agencies had to toe a very fine line: NGO managers feared that they could be shut down or forced out of the country, leaving the recipients of food under their programs considerably worse off. This made for muted criticism and, in many cases, accepting distorted distribution lists from local authorities (Human Rights Watch 2004). However, a coalition of fifty-four local NGOs found evidence of food aid manipulation in thirty-three of the fifty-four districts of the country (Itano 2002). They also reported greater quantities going to ruling party strongholds with grain distribution depots patrolled and run by the ZANU-PF youth wing.

A more sinister turn in the manipulation of food aid took place later in 2002, as by-elections neared in Insiza district in the southwest of the country. A relatively minor amount of WFP food aid was seized from a WFP-implementing partner by ZANU-PF officials and promptly redistributed to party supporters, triggering an immediate suspension of WFP distributions (IRIN 2002; Physicians for Human Rights 2002; Swarns 2002b). But the suspension of internationally managed aid played into ZANU-PF's hands, as they subsequently controlled the only food distribution mechanism in the constituency—indeed ZANU-PF officials likely predicted and deliberately sought WFP's reaction. Only months earlier WFP had warned of suspending distributions following a similar incident. It had become clear that international agencies could be intimidated to gain greater control over the food supply *(Financial Gazette* 2002). Needless to say, the Insiza by-election—a critical constituency—was won by the ZANU-PF candidate *(The Herald* 2002).

With greater control over food, government officials subsequently began scheduling distributions that coincided with opposition campaign rallies, resulting in the cancellation of numerous MDC campaign events. Hotly contested areas were infused with government food aid in the run-up to the election. Bags of food aid were prominently displayed at polling stations just days before elections—sending a clear and blatant message that food was conditional on support for ZANU-PF candidates. Allegations of explicit food-for-votes exchanges surfaced at polling stations (Swarns 2002a). The strategy of consolidating control of food aid in government hands was further entrenched in 2004 when the government expelled several international NGOs involved in food aid programming, saying that Zimbabweans chose not to "choke" on food aid from the international community (Saul and Saunders 2005). The cat and mouse game between the government and international agencies continued through the 2008 presidential election and beyond.

## Impacts

ZANU-PF maintained power in Zimbabwe from independence in 1980 until a power-sharing agreement was negotiated with the MDC following the contested 2008 presidential election. The MDC candidate, Morgan Tsvangirai, won more votes in initial polling than President Mugabe but, in a scheduled run-off, pulled out of the vote after post-election violence killed over one hundred MDC supporters. Under heavy international pressure, a government of national unity was formed, but as of this writing ZANU-PF still controls the bulk of state machinery.

In this case, much of the manipulation of food assistance was by the government of the recipient country, and while the humanitarian consequences were less grave in Zimbabwe, the political consequences were perhaps more pronounced. Although the declining access to food was no doubt one of many factors leading to disillusionment with the ruling party, the manipulation of this access appears to have been one of several factors that actually did succeed in preserving ZANU-PF's grip on power. Despite apparently losing the 2008 elections and being forced into a power-sharing arrangement, ZANU-PF still controls the "commanding heights" of the Zimbabwean state. Control over food aid and other means of access to food proved to be a powerful tool with which to manipulate electoral processes and retain power.

## Conclusions

Several brief observations can be drawn from these cases. First, in the context of conflict and competitive politics, access to food—whether through commercial channels or via humanitarian food assistance—is a means to an end that neither belligerents nor politicians can leave alone. Food aid has clearly been manipulated away from its food security objectives in both kinds of cases (and in many, many more than the few detailed here).

Second, the humanitarian impact of this manipulation has been variable: it was deadly in the Bahr al-Ghazal famine, but neither the manipulation of assistance nor the crisis underlying the need for food assistance in Zimbabwe led to a widespread humanitarian crisis—though *both* did lead to a protracted food-access crisis. The food security crisis in Ethiopia is ongoing, resulting from a combination of factors. But little hard evidence exists that any diversion of food aid substantially affects the overall humanitarian situation in Ethiopia. Prior to 2011, the limited evidence available suggested that individual communities have been hard hit by this phenomenon. In Somalia, the harvests in 2009 and early 2010 were significantly better than in other recent years, relieving some of the pressure from the shutoff of international assistance. But the situation turned dramatically worse in 2011. External humanitarian actors often have had little access to the areas affected by the 2011 famine. Where food aid is diverted from those who genuinely require it, whether for political reasons or simply to capture the economic value of the food, the consequences for humanitarian outcomes will be serious, though the degree of severity is contingent on many factors.

Third, to some degree, nearly all parties involved have misused food aid to one degree or another. Clearly the governments of recipient states have used their power to influence the provision of aid towards their supporters and away from their opponents—as the Zimbabwe, Sudan, and Ethiopia cases all suggest. Non-state actors have also been implicated: rebel factions in Ethiopia, militias in Sudan, and war-lords and *al-Shabab* in Somalia have all exerted influence over food aid towards their own political ends. Despite having signed onto the Good Humanitarian Donorship Principles, donor governments increasingly have made it clear that food aid is primarily intended to serve foreign-policy objectives and only secondarily to meet humanitarian needs (indeed, some argue that without the security and foreign policy leverage of food aid, there would be less political support in donor countries for humanitarian assistance). Even humanitarian actors have used food as a means of protecting themselves or recipient communities, to the detriment of humanitarian values.

Fourth, despite the fact that all of the actors (except non-state) just named have formally agreed to the normative guidelines intended to govern humanitarian assistance, little regard has been shown for these instruments when important political or strategic interests lie elsewhere. Little doubt exists that recurrent cycles of the kind of misuse detailed here have undermined the principles intended to insulate humanitarian assistance from politics; in other words, the more it happens, the more likely it is to continue happening. If one belligerent in a conflict abuses humanitarian principles, it appears likely that others will do so as well. This increases the danger to and operational complexities for humanitarian actors. But above all, it puts at higher risk the very people that such assistance is intended to serve. The normative instruments outlined at the beginning of this chapter are—and always have been—a compromise between humanitarian and security demands. They are weak, self-enforcing instruments. Humanitarian agencies, major donors and many recipient country governments have signed onto some or all of these instruments, but implementation is very mixed, and enforcement mechanisms don't exist.

Lastly, the political impact of manipulation is a question to be further explored. Paarlberg (1985) argued that the exercise of "food power" rarely achieves its political objectives. Wilder and Gordon argue that attempts to "win hearts and minds" using aid have rarely had the intended effect and run the risk in some contexts of having the opposite effect (Wilder and Gordon 2009). The evidence from these four cases tends to bear out Paarlberg's observations (with one important qualification). Little evidence exists that attempts to manipulate food aid during the Sudan civil war significantly affected the military situation on the ground—though they had devastating effects on the humanitarian situation. Equally little evidence exists that suddenly subjecting U.S. food assistance in Somalia to counter-terrorism objectives in 2009 increased on-the-ground support for the TFG or resistance to *al-Shabab*. In spite of repeated anecdotal evidence about the use of food aid to buy voter loyalties in Ethiopia, little consensus exists on the role that food aid plays in Ethiopian elections—the results of the most recent elections notwithstanding.

However, some basis exists for suggesting that the uses of "food power" generally—and the manipulation of humanitarian food assistance and social safety nets specifically—were an important tool in the arsenal of ZANU-PF in retaining power in Zimbabwe. But in many ways, this reinforces one of the observations made 25 years ago by Paarlberg. He suggested that the reason "food power" often fails is that there are too many alternative options—that no one country or party can control enough of these options to achieve political objectives. In Zimbabwe, the state directly controlled three of five mechanisms and was able to manipulate the other two (international food aid through intimidation, and the black market through hyperinflation). Here the ruling party appears to have been able to apply enough pressure to retain its hold on power, despite a prolonged crisis of increasing magnitude and despite apparently losing the popular support of the electorate. Further in-depth research will be required to verify this observation.

Thus food aid has on occasion been used for short-term advantage but has rarely proven very useful in achieving strategic political goals. The politicization of humanitarian food aid is generally in violation of international norms to which most of the parties reviewed in these case studies subscribe. And the undermining of these norms has led to diminished access in some of the worst food crises, dramatically worsening the humanitarian outcomes of those crises. The famine in Somalia is only the most recent of many such examples. These observations lead to two possible conclusions, a pessimistic one and a somewhat more optimistic one.

The pessimistic conclusion is that political concerns will always trump humanitarian concerns; food aid will always be a valuable resource in a resource-constrained environment; humanitarian access is increasingly difficult and therefore monitoring is more difficult; and any attempt to insulate humanitarian assistance from political concerns is swimming against the tide of current approaches that emphasize "coherent" responses or counter-insurgency efforts to "win hearts and minds." Thus the conclusion is that little can be done to depoliticize humanitarian assistance, and the end result will be not only the further erosion of humanitarian values, but also the increasing vulnerability of the most marginalized (i.e., least powerful) groups for whom the assistance is intended.

However, a more optimistic conclusion can also be drawn from these results: given that humanitarian goals (it has been shown) are directly undermined by this kind of manipulation, and given that political or security goals are not really served (as Paarlberg suggested 25 years ago), it seems rational to prioritize the norms that were intended to protect humanitarian assistance from manipulation in the first place. This is, roughly speaking, the kind of compromise that International Humanitarian Law and humanitarian principles were intended to be. The IPC is a pragmatic example of what can be done—it helped depoliticize the macro-level allocation of assistance in Somalia for several years at least. The evidence on both sides of this debate is somewhat limited, and further exploration of these questions will be necessary.

*The author would like to acknowledge the research assistance of Cynthia Sobieski, Eric Anderson, and Steven Allen, and feedback on earlier drafts from Robert Paarlberg, Chris Barrett, Jeffrey Gettleman, Mark Bradbury, Nick Crawford, Antonio Donini, Helen Young, Andrew Wilder and Peter Walker. Responsibility for any errors is mine.*

## Notes

[1] See, for example, USAID's Food Insecurity Response to Urban Populations (FIRUP) program. The program documentation contains explicit counter insurgency objectives incorporated into a program otherwise based on food security goals.
[2] It could be argued that this policy is not new—but what is new is the extent to which it is explicitly a formal policy.
[3] Overall levels of food aid have declined in recent years, but the proportion devoted to humanitarian assistance, and the total amounts of humanitarian food aid, have increased steadily since about 1980. For further information, see WFP/FAIS. http://www.wfp.org/fais/
[4] See the 1949 Geneva Conventions and additional protocols of the International Committee of the Red Cross, first published in 1974.
[5] http://en.wikipedia.org/wiki/Sphere_Project
[6] Subcommittee on Africa, U.S. House of Representatives, *America's Sudan Policy: A New Direction,* joint hearing between the Subcommittee on Africa and the Subcommittee on International Operations and Human Rights (107th Congress, March 28, 2001) Serial No. 107–8.
[7] This included an attempt by both the U.S. and the UN to recruit the services of external agencies—humanitarian and otherwise—to follow on an offensive by TFG and AU forces by concentrating services in areas held of regained by TFG forces in early 2010 (See J. Gettleman op.cit.). This is clearly a state-building agenda, and while no one doubts the need for the Somali state to be rebuilt, making humanitarian assistance contingent on rebuilding the state for one party in the conflict obviously violates humanitarian principles
[8] Actually, while the BBC followed generally accepted principles of investigative journalism (having more than one witness corroborate the story, looking for documentary evidence confirming the story line at the time, etc.), the evidence that forms the basis of the BBC report (and for that matter, the denials of the report) is fairly slim: several disgruntled former TPLF cadres, some recollections from a retired aid official, and an old CIA report that includes a few lines about suspicions of diversion of famine aid by the rebels. For better or worse, this is the story with much of the evidence about the diversion or manipulation of aid in Ethiopia.
[9] T. Vaux, *The Selfish Altruist: Relief Work in Famine and War* (London: Earthscan, 2003).

[10] This does not include significant amounts of food assistance purchased by the government of Ethiopia and distributed internally.
[11] Note, however, that this report does not comment on the situation in Somali Region.

## References

Africa Watch. 1996. *Evil Days: 30 Years of War and Famine in Ethiopia.* New York: Human Rights Watch, 206.

Agence France Presse. 1999. "Sudan Criticizes Clinton Green Light to Distribute Food to SPLA." Retrieved from ReliefWeb database.

BBC News. 2007. "Bob Geldof Demands Proof of BBC Ethiopia Aid Report." March 7. http://news.bbc.co.uk/2/hi/8554048.stm.

Bradbury, M., and M. Kleinman. 2010. *Winning Hearts and Minds? Examining the Relationship between Aid and Security in Kenya.* Feinstein International Center Report. Medford: Tufts University.

Bradbury, M., N. Leader, and K. MacIntosh. 2000. *The 'Agreement on Ground Rules' in South Sudan.* HPG Report No. 4. London: Overseas Development Institute.

Brigety, R. 2008. *Humanity as a Weapon of War: Sustainable Security and the Role of the U.S. Military.* Washington: Center for American Progress.

Butcher, T. 2002. "President Starves Political Opponents: Mugabe Using Food Shortages to Cling to Power." *National Post.* Ontario, Canada: Don Mills.

Club du Sahel. 1990. Food Aid Charter. Bissau: CILSS/Club du Sahel.

de Waal, A. 1997. Famine Crimes: Politics and the Disaster Relief Industry in Africa. Bloomington: Indiana University Press.

Deng, L. 1999. *Famine in the Sudan: Causes, Preparedness and Response: A Political, Social and Economic Analysis of the 1998 Bahr el Ghazal Famine.* Brighton, England: University of Sussex, Institute of Development Studies.

Deng, L. 2002. "The Sudan Famine of 1998." *IDS Bulletin* 33 no. 4: 28–38, 66.

Deutsche Presse-Agentur. 1999. "Zimbabwean Inflation Soars to Record 70 Percent." Hamburg, Germany.

Donini, A. 2008. *The State of the Humanitarian Enterprise. Humanitarian Agenda 2015: Final Report.* Feinstein International Center. Medford: Tufts University.

Drumtra, J. 1998. *The Political Roots of Famine in Southern Sudan.* Middle East Report 208. U.S. Foreign Policy in the Middle East: Critical Assessments, 5–6.

Edwards, S. 2002. "Mugabe Withholding Food Aid: Given to Supporters Only; Half of Zimbabwe's Population Facing Starvation." *National Post.* Ontario, Canada: Don Mills.

Euronaid. 1995. "Code of Conduct for Food Aid." Brussels: Euronaid.

European Commission. 2010. *Humanitarian Food Assistance Policy.* ECHO SEC 374. Brussels: ECHO.

FAO. 2008. *The Integrated Phase Classification Tool.* Rome: FAO.

*Financial Gazette.* 2002. "Zimbabwe: Violence Threatens Food Aid." *Africa News.*

Food Crisis Prevention Network (FCPN). 2007. "Charter for Food Crisis Prevention and Management." Paris: FCPN and OECD.

FSNAU. 2010. *Food Security and Nutrition Special Brief –Post Deyr '09/10 Analysis.* Nairobi: Somalia Food Security and Nutrition Assessment Unit.

Gettleman, J. 2010a. "U.N. to End Some Deals for Food to Somalia." *New York Times,* March 12.

—. 2010b. "Somalia's President Assails U.N. Report on Corruption," *New York Times,* March 17.

GHD Initiative. 2008. "Principles and Good Practice of Humanitarian Donorship." 2003, last updated April 2008.

Griekspoor, A., and S. Collins. 2001. "Raising Standards in Emergency Relief: How Useful are Sphere Minimum Standards for Humanitarian Assistance?" *British Medical Journal* 323 no. 7315: 740–42.

*Guardian, The.* 2010. "Protests as UK Security Put at Heart of Government's Aid Policy." August 29.

Hellum, A., and B. Derman. 2001. "Land Reform and Human Rights in Contemporary Zimbabwe: Balancing Individual and Social Justice through an Integrated Human Rights Framework." *World Development* 32 no. 10.

*Herald, The.* 2002. "Zimbabwe: ZANU-PF Routs MDC." *Africa News.*

Howe, P. 2010. "Archetypes of Famine and Response." *Disasters* 34 no. 1: 30–54.

Human Rights Watch. 1999. "Food Aid to Sudanese Rebels Opposed," contents of letter to Secretary of State Madeleine Albright. December 13. http://www.hrw.org/en/news/1999/12/12/food-aid-sudanese-rebels-opposed.

—. 2004. *The Politics of Food Assistance in Zimbabwe,* Briefing Paper, New York, 8–10.

IFRC. 1994. *The Code of Conduct. Principles of Conduct for the International Red Cross and Red Crescent Movement and NGOs in Disaster*

*Response Programmes.* http://www.globalhumanitarianassistance.org/analyses-and-reports/gha-reports/gha-report-2009.

IRIN. 1999. *IRIN Africa | SUDAN: WFP concern over US food for rebels.*

—. 2002. "Zimbabwe: By-election Marred by Allegations of Foul Play." Nairobi.

—. 2004. "Ethiopia: Government Acting to Prevent Any Abuses of Opposition Supporters – Spokesman." Addis Ababa. http://www.irinnews.org/Report.aspx?ReportId=52268.

—. 2004. "Ethiopia: U.S. Says Government Is Oppressing the Opposition." Addis Ababa. http://www.irinnews.org/Report.aspx?reportid=48770.

—. 2010. "Ethiopia: Government Denies Food Aid 'Manipulated' for Political Gain." (Addis Ababa. http://www.irinnews.org/report.aspx?ReportId=89382.

Itano, N. 2002. "Zimbabwe's Political Tool: Food," *Christian Science Monitor.* August, Boston, 6.

Jaspars, S., and D. Maxwell. 2008. *Targeting in Complex Emergencies: Somalia Case Study.* Feinstein International Center Report. Medford: Tufts University.

Macrae, J., and A. Zwi. 1991. "Food as an Instrument of War in Contemporary African Famine – A Review of the Evidence." *Disasters* 16 no. 4: 299–321.

Makaye, P., and C. Munhande. 2008. "The Contribution of Informal Food Trading to Urban Food Security in Zimbabwe: The Case Gweru 2000–2007." *Journal of Sustainable Development in Africa* 10 no. 2: 312–32.

Maren, M. 1997. *The Road to Hell: The Ravaging Effects of Foreign Aid and International Charity.* New York: The Free Press.

Marshal, R. 2009. "A Tentative Assessment of the Somali Hirakata Al-Shabab." *Journal of Eastern African Studies* 3 no. 3: 381–404.

Mourey, A. 1991. "Famine and War." *International Review of the Red Cross* 285: 549–57.

Ndlela, D., and P. Robinson. 2007. *Distortions to Agricultural Incentives in Zimbabwe.* Agricultural Distortions Working Paper 39. Harare: World Bank's Development Research Group.

Paarlberg, R. 1985. *Food Trade and Foreign Policy.* Ithaca: Cornell University Press.

—. 2010. *Food Politics: What Everyone Needs to Know.* Oxford: Oxford University Press.

Physicians for Human Rights. 2002. *Voting ZANU for Food: Rural District Council and Insiza Elections PHR-Denmark.* Risskov, Denmark: Physicians for Human Rights.

Reuters. 2009. "World's Worst Humanitarian Crisis." http://www.alertnet.org/db/crisisprofiles/SO_PEA.htm.

Rhodes, T. 2002. *Famine Politics and the Cycle of Relief Failure in Sudan's Civil War: A Case Study of the OLS Relief Operation in the Bahr el-Ghazal Famine, 1998.* Global Politics Network.

Saul, J. S., and R. Saunders. 2005. "Mugabe, Gramsci, and Zimbabwe at 25." *International Journal* 60 no. 4. (Africa: Towards Durable Peace.): 953–75. Retrieved from http://www.jstor.org/stable/40204093.

Shaw, A. 2003. "Zimbabwe Faces Food Riots after Five-fold Rise in Price of Maize." *The Independent* 15.

Sphere Project. 2004. *Humanitarian Charter and Minimum Standards in Disaster Response.* Geneva: The Sphere Project, 156.

*Standard, The.* 2002. "Zimbabwe: Minister Says People Will Starve Unless They Dump the Opposition." Harare, Zimbabwe.

Swarns, R. L. 2002a. "Food: ZANU PF's Newfound Weapon." *Zimbabwe Standard*, Africa News.

—. 2002b. "Zimbabwe Uses Food as a Political Tool, Aid Groups Say." *New York Times*, December 12.

Thornycroft, P. 2002. "Mugabe 'Refuses to Let Starving Rivals Buy Food.'" *The Daily Telegraph.* London, July 26. http://www.telegraph.co.uk/news/worldnews/africaandindianocean/zimbabwe/1402650/Mugabe-refuses-to-let-starving-rivals-buy-food.html.

U.S. Bureau of Democracy, Human Rights and Labor. 2008. *2007 Country Reports on Human Rights Practices: Africa: Ethiopia.* Washington DC: U.S. Department of State. http://www.state.gov/g/drl/rls/hrrpt/2007/100481.htm.

U.S. House of Representatives Sub-Committee on Africa. 2001.

Vaux, T. 2003. *The Selfish Altruist: Relief Work in Famine and War.* London: Earthscan.

Voice of America. 2010. "Somali Rebel Group Bans UN World Food Program." February 28. http://www1.voanews.com/english/news/Somali-Rebel-Group-Bans-UN-World-Food-Program-85766227.html.

Wilder, A., and S. Gordon. 2009. "Money Can't Buy America Love." *Foreign Policy,* December 1.

Young, H., and D. Maxwell. 2009. *Targeting in Complex Emergencies: Darfur Case Study,* part of a larger study commissioned by WFP. Feinstein International Center Report. Medford: Tufts University.

# CHAPTER EIGHT

# THE SEARCH FOR DOMESTIC ACCOUNTABILITY IN DEVELOPMENT AID: WHAT ROLE FOR THE APRM IN RESHAPING GOVERNANCE IN AFRICA?

KOJO BUSIA

## Introduction: Context and Concepts

For too long, donor agencies assumed that the impact of their aid policies, programs, and projects was essentially technical, with a neutral influence on the domestic politics of recipient countries. However, revisions to aid policies and practices over the past decade or so have led to the belated recognition that aid is not politically neutral and that it could have a debilitating impact on the institutions of domestic accountability in the recipient country. This realization was in part precipitated by the failure of structural adjustment programs of the 1990s, leading to the World Bank's revisionist approach—the Comprehensive Development Framework (CDF)—and the emergence of the Poverty Reduction Papers (PRSPs) in response to the lack of country ownership of governance strategies in developing countries (World Bank/IMF 2005, World Bank 2006). The PRSPs were intended not only to increase country ownership, but also to enhance donor alignment and harmonization with nationally determined priorities for donor support (Barbone and Sharkey 2006; Stiglitz 2002; World Bank 2002). Indeed, it is arguable that the entire aid effectiveness agenda—reflecting the recent shifts in thinking of aid modalities, planning, and delivery that have occurred since the Paris Declaration—is underpinned by the search for domestic accountability in development assistance.

To be sure, the aid effectiveness agenda was in part aimed at addressing the "vicious cycle" of preexisting weak governance institutions in developing countries and ineffective aid delivery, in which fragmentation of different aid projects runs parallel to recipient countries' budgets and priorities. This situation actually tended to undermine the recipient state's capacity to drive development forward, and consequently skewed government accountability outward toward donors rather than inward toward citizens (Foster 2000; de Renzio 2006; Williamson et al. 2008). There is no gain in saying that the principle of country ownership which stands at the pinnacle of the Paris Declaration emerged out of this paradoxical effect of the aid regime.

In addition to the aid effectiveness agenda, poor management of aid by recipient country governments—stemming from weak institutions, patronage politics, and corruption—limited the extent of country ownership over development priorities. This dilemma gave impetus to donors' making good governance a priority in parallel to efforts at improving country ownership of the development process. The simultaneous preoccupation with good governance in aid recipient countries on the one hand and the issue of country ownership on the other is embodied in the last principle of the Paris Declaration, known as mutual accountability. The Paris Declaration defines mutual accountability to encompass accountability relationship between donors and partner countries in terms of the effective use and management of aid budgets within the context of Public Financial Management (OECD 2005b).

The nexus between good governance and aid effectiveness was deemed important by the Paris Declaration for a number of reasons: first, democratic institutions and processes were not only good in themselves, but were also the best means of ensuring that executives manage aid budgets effectively (DfID 2007). For example, by signing the Paris Declaration, developing countries commit first to implementing development strategies through "broad consultative process," and secondly, to encouraging "participation of civil society and the private sector" (OECD 2005b, Article 14). However, while the Paris Declaration emphasizes increased country ownership, it does not explicitly use the language of democracy in the context of mutual accountability in the aid relationship. At the Accra High Level Forum (HLF) in September 2008, mutual accountability for aid was expanded to include democratic institutions in recipient countries. The Accra Agenda for Action (AAA) included significantly stronger language and commitments regarding both domestic accountability and mutual accountability for aid, thus moving the aid effectiveness agenda one step further. It emphasized the importance of transparency and ownership and linked transparency to development results (OECD 2008a). It stressed core accountability principles and focused on some of the key domestic accountability actors beyond the executive branch of government, namely parliaments, civil society, the private sector, the media and to some extent independent audit institutions of the state. It also included greater detail on mutual assessment reviews for mutual accountability and emphasized the need to draw on emerging good practices with stronger parliamentary scrutiny and citizen engagement. The key message of AAA is that domestic accountability is a *sine quo non* of mutual accountability of aid.

## The Search for Domestic Accountability

The Paris Declaration and the Accra Agenda for Action on aid effectiveness are by far the clearest acknowledgements by the international aid community that domestic accountability is a necessary precondition for increasing development effectiveness in donor-dependent countries. This is evidenced by the OECD/GOVNET work stream on the different dimensions of domestic accountability following the AAA conference in 2008. The primary focus of this work stream has been on how aid and its mechanisms for delivery can constrain or undermine domestic accountability systems and contribute to the externalization of accountability to donors rather than to domestic constituencies (OECD 2008b; Hudson 2009).

Thus, in the aftermath of the AAA, not only "country ownership" but also ensuring domestic accountability has been pushed to the center-stage of the aid architecture. There are several reasons why domestic accountability has assumed center stage in the aid effectiveness debate: first, there are concerns about what the Paris Principles really mean in practice, with a tendency for donors to narrowly interpret country ownership as belonging to the executive branches of government rather than to the broader population. Second, mutual accountability is often interpreted as accountability between donors and partner countries rather between the recipient country and its citizens. Third, the democratic ownership approach to aid is not explicitly included in the aid effectiveness agenda as it is often seen as complex and cumbersome to implement. Lastly, the aid effectiveness agenda, often preoccupied with management and delivery issues, may have unduly increased donor micro-management of partner country accountability and financial systems, thereby limiting the space for domestic accountability (de Renzio 2006).

The basic premise of this chapter is that if the core principles of the Paris Declaration and the Accra Agenda for Action are to be meaningful and have a positive impact on development practice and outcomes, then indigenously initiated and designed self-assessment and monitoring mechanisms such as the African Peer Review Mechanism (APRM) should be given priority by the donor community as an alternative to promoting both ownership and domestic accountability to achieve development effectiveness. The chapter's core argument is that the APRM represents an African governance initiative at the highest level of institutions and processes, aimed at mobilizing and transforming the voices of the hundreds of millions of citizens across the continent into a meaningful and relevant agenda for governance reforms. The mechanism provides an unprecedented opportunity to strengthen accountability systems and spur a cross-learning process across the continent.

There are several reasons why the APRM should be analyzed within the context of current debates on aid and domestic accountability in the development effectiveness agenda. First, the issue of reforming ownership is eminently important, not only on its own merits, but for two fundamental reasons given the current international emphasis on democratic ownership. After all, the emphasis on the need for ownership of policy reform is based on the recognition that externally imposed conditionality was insufficient and a defective means of achieving reforms (Killick 1997). Also, the concept of ownership undergirds the Paris Declaration and constitutes the most critical criterion of its success, the extent to which developing countries are allowed and given more scope to pursue and shape their own priorities, especially institutional reforms (Whitfield 2009; Welsh and Woods 2007; Unsworth 2007). Second, the ownership and mutual accountability principles of the Paris Declaration have greater implications for power relations between states and societies in Africa. In brief, domestic accountability is strengthened through enhanced ownership of democratic and institutional reforms and can shape the relationships between the state and its citizens (OECD 2008b; Whitfield 2009; Browne 2006). Third, the APRM provided a good basis for transforming the aid effectiveness agenda in the Paris Declaration to a development effectiveness agenda in the High Level Forum on aid held in Busan in November, 2011.

The basic proposition of this chapter, therefore, is that the APRM, born out of the NEPAD vision of African solutions to African problems, has the best potential to contribute towards strengthening governance institutions in Africa, through the enhancement of domestic accountability in African governance. Anticipating the core argument of this chapter, the APRM process is an exercise in strengthening domestic accountability that is sorely missing in externally driven (donor) accountability mechanisms that have so far proven to be ineffective in fostering governance reforms in Africa. The chapter supports recent important insights by many observers, donors included, that externally driven accountability mechanisms in Africa have achieved limited results and that there is a need for a new approach that emphasizes the demand-side accountability of addressing governance reforms in developing countries (OECD 2008a; Unsworth 2007; Stymer 2009).

The chapter is organized according to the following sections: section two provides a brief overview of what the APRM is all about and some of the initial debates that greeted the initiative at its very inception. This will help put into context the different perspectives that have emerged about the prospects of the initiative in the context of the New Partnership for Africa's Development (NEPAD) and the institutional history underlying the creation of NEPAD and the APRM as Africa's direct response to the international development debate on aid effectiveness. Section three summarizes the evolution and the trajectory of Africa's development strategies and the shifts that have occurred over time from state-led development approaches to a focus on popular participation in development. In section four the chapter attempts to demonstrate how the APRM is reshaping and transforming state and society relations in Africa in a manner that could lead to government accountability to citizens rather than to external donors. Finally, the chapter draws some general conclusions about donor approaches to strengthening governance institutions and about how the APRM is informing a perspective of domestic accountability.

## What Is the APRM? Where Did it Come From?

APRM is a key program of NEPAD, Africa's common vision and framework to lift its people and citizens out of poverty and underdevelopment. NEPAD provides a vision and a framework for development and progress and is a departure from the past in that it was conceived and promoted by African leaders and countries with little or no participation from international agencies. Among its programmatic pillars, NEPAD clearly identifies poor governance as an impediment to progress throughout much of the continent (NEPAD 2002). The APRM, largely recognized as the crown jewel of the NEPAD initiative, is an attempt by Africans to improve the status of good governance proactively by identifying weaknesses, setting benchmarks, and monitoring progress in meeting them. It has so much captured the imagination of the world that it has been referred to as "Africa's innovative thinking on governance" (German Chancellor Angela Merkel, cited in APRM 2008b). Officially speaking, the "purpose of the APRM is to foster the adoption of policies, standards, and practices that lead to political stability, high economic growth, sustainable development, and accelerated sub-regional and economic integration" (NEPAD 2003a).The APRM's self-assessment involves governments and all stakeholders including civil society actors and the private sector as well as external independent assessors and is intended to promote a national dialogue and build consensus about governance. The mechanism is designed in a way that involves a host of complex structures and lengthy processes that facilitate dialogue on governance issues among a whole range of stakeholders (Jinadu 2008; Herbert and Gruzd 2008; Masterson 2004). The designers of the APRM deliberately made it a non-punitive instrument to encourage adherence and commitment, perhaps out of the wisdom and lessons learned that reforms enforced through mandatory sanctions usually receive little adherence, or countries only pay lip service to reforms.

The voluntary accession to the process is intended to encourage participating African countries to learn from each other by recognizing and disseminating best governance practices. Contrary to popular belief, the concept of peer learning embedded in the APRM framework is aimed at encouraging and building responsible leadership through the self-assessment process, constructive peer dialogue at the summit level, and the sharing of information and common experiences in order to reinforce successful and exemplary practices among Africans (NEPAD 2002). Ultimately, the goal of the APRM is to advance the basic values of democratization and good governance in Africa, an issue that NEPAD explicitly recognizes as the key missing ingredient for sustainable development (APRM 2008a). Since its first mention in the NEPAD official documents in 2001 and the subsequent adoption of the accession of the Memorandum of Understanding (MOU) in 2003, the APRM has made considerable progress in terms of the number of countries acceding and the rolling-out of structures, institutions, and organization of the review process, as well as in the degree of active participation and engagement of stakeholders, both nationally and continentally. Participation in the APRM process rate has been growing steadily since 2003. By August 2011, thirty countries had officially voluntarily acceded to the APRM.

The pace of country reviews has also increased since the early days of implementation in the three pioneer countries of Ghana, Rwanda and Kenya. As of August 2011, fourteen countries had been "peer reviewed": Algeria, Benin, Burkina Faso, Ethiopia, Ghana, Kenya, Lesotho, Mali, Mauritius, Mozambique, Nigeria, Rwanda, South Africa, and Uganda.

The completion of the peer review exercise marks the final stages of the assessment process, whereby APRM country reports are submitted to the Heads of States Forum for peer review. The fourteen countries are at different stages of implementing their APRM National Plans of Action (NPoA), and there are about sixteen more countries at different stages of the process, which implies that more African countries will be reviewed within the next year or two. Collectively, the membership of the APRM represents more than 50 percent of the African Union (AU) member states and an equivalent of 74 percent of the total population of Africa (652.7 million). Thus, the APRM is a significant engagement within Africa and perhaps the most talked-about governance reform agenda currently exercising the minds and hearts of Africans throughout the continent (APRM 2008b).

| **Status as of August 2011** | **Countries** |
|---|---|
| Waiting to conduct second Country Self-Assessment | Ghana |
| Went through second Country Self-Assessment | Kenya |
| Countries implementing first NPoA | Algeria, Benin, Burkina Faso, Ethiopia, Ghana, Kenya, Lesotho, Mali, Mauritius, Mozambique, Nigeria, Rwanda, South Africa and Uganda (14) |
| Countries that have received first Country Support Mission and have thereby commenced the Self-Assessment process | Tanzania, Zambia and Sierra Leone |
| Countries that have acceded but are yet to receive first Country Support Mission | Angola, Cameroon, Republic of Congo, Djibouti, Egypt, Gabon, Liberia, Malawi, Mauritania, Sao Tome & Principe, Senegal, Sierra Leone, Sudan, Togo (14) |
| Countries yet to accede to APRM | Botswana, Burundi, Cape Verde, Central African Republic, Chad, Cameroon, Cote d'Ivoire, Dem. Rep. of Congo, Equatorial Guinea, Eritrea, Gambia, Guinea, Guinea Bissau, Liberia, Libya, Madagascar, Namibia, Niger, SADR, Seychelles, Somalia, Swaziland, Tunisia and Zimbabwe Morocco has suspended its membership in AU. |

**Table 8.1. Status of Countries with APRM**

Source: UNECA 2011

## Initial Reactions to and Critique of the APRM Initiative

The APRM naturally elicited a variety of reactions, ranging from an enthusiastic embrace of the novelty of the idea and the vision behind it as marking a new dawn in African governance, to a skeptical reception as yet another African initiative soon to be marred by the behavior of collective indulgence among African leaders who had so often ignored each other's governance shortcomings under the Organization of African Unity (Nyerere 1966). This critique stems from the history of mutual indulgence among African states where leaders have, in the past, "scratched each other's backs" in the name of preserving African solidarity. There was also a vociferous rejection of the APRM by civil society because APRM's framework was considered to lack domestic buy-in from the grassroots, and the approach to formulating NEPAD and the APRM was considered essentially a top-down development strategy.

At the core of this debate is the lack of sanctions or coercive measures contemplated to use against a reviewed state whose governance system falls below the APRM codes and standards. The common criticism is that the APRM process lacked teeth and would not make any difference in reforming African governance systems, particularly in the area of political governance. The absence of explicit punitive measures against governments violating the APRM principles gives the impression of a velvet mechanism (Gottschalk and Schmidt 2004; Bekoe 2002). However, Anglin (2006, 239) suggests that although "peer monitoring" did not lack precedence in terms of African leaders passing judgments on state behavior, usually in response to specific events like coups d'état, general elections and other lapses from constitutional rule, "peer review" was a significant advance in promoting good governance.

Another stream of critics challenges the value of a peer review without an institutionalized mechanism for tackling dissenters on the grounds that the voluntary nature of peer review means it is "too soft" to reform governance practices, and that therefore the credibility and independence of the review process is in doubt (Kanbur 2004; Venter 2003; Bekoe 2002). Indeed, the perception that the APRM lacked teeth was originally reinforced by another debate between NEPAD leaders and leading donor countries regarding the mechanism's design, which included a review of performance in political governance.

The pronouncements by then-South African president Thabo Mbeki that issues of political governance would not come under the purview of the APRM but rather would be handled by AU structures had a dampening effect on donor interest in the process. In contrast to the African leaders' perspective that the APRM would be non-adversarial and a process for constructive dialogue among Africans, the donors initially perceived the mechanism as an instrument for reinforcing traditional donor conditionality of good governance in exchange for development aid. The fact that NEPAD/APRM initially derived its external support from the G-8 made it appear that the APRM review had an element of donor conditionality. Indeed, the expected punitive approach adopted by the donor community is probably one reason African leaders did not see the necessity of applying sanctions in case of a negative review outcome.

This debate, however, has since been resolved: the APRM reviews now cover all four areas of the APRM, including democracy and political governance dimensions; and the APRM is not being used explicitly as a form of donor conditionality, even if donor behavior or engagement is inevitably being shaped by the outcomes of reviews in each of the participating countries.

Another criticism since the inception of the APRM process has come from the civil society sector. Because the initial promotion of NEPAD and the APRM was directed at the international community (i.e. the G-8), a perception was created that the mechanism's primary purpose was to appease the International Monetary Fund, the World Bank, and Western donors, and that it was largely unconcerned with achieving buy-in from African civil society (Verwey 2005; Deve 2006; Deng 2006). In response to this perception, civil society adopted two approaches: 1) to reject the APRM as a legitimate exercise; and 2) to examine methods that promote greater civil society participation and advocate for these methods to be adopted.

The harshest critique from civil society rejected the APRM's stated purpose, criticizing its design and operations, and most importantly, condemning the mechanism's architect for lack of broad and meaningful consultations prior to finalizing the APRM design (Verwey 2005; Deng 2006). While some of these criticisms were valid, they delayed civil society from participating in the APRM process, as much of the opportunity for early engagement in promoting and understanding the larger implications of the APRM were initially missed (Maloka 2004). In part, the lack of meaningful engagement from civil society was due to a lack of access to information on the APRM (Verwey 2005).

The debate about legitimacy and the lack of adequate participation was anticipated by African regional organizations, including the United Nations Economic Commission for Africa (UNECA). In a parliamentary paper presented at the biennial meeting of the Committee of Human Development and Civil Society, the governing body of its Governance Division, UNECA strongly advocated for strategies to enhance civil society participation in the APRM process (UNECA 2005b). The UNECA paper argued that the participation of civil society would present great opportunities to enhance the process that far outweighed any negative effects such participation might bring. For UNECA, the APRM presented an unprecedented opportunity to operationalize its long advocated position on the importance of popular participation in development (UNECA 1990). This point of view is also shared by other analysts who stress the important role of civil society participation in the APRM and the contribution that it can make to enhancing the legitimacy of the APRM and building confidence in its findings (Herbert 2003; Kajee 2004a; Landsberg 2002). Nevertheless, the initial pessimism that greeted the inauguration of the APRM has now given way to a healthy embrace by African civil society, which now fully participates in the APRM both at the national and continental levels. Indeed, the APRM may yet confound its initial critics, as the process has started in earnest and the interim results appear to be encouraging.

Nonetheless, vociferous critiques have been leveled against NEPAD, and also by implication against the APRM, that NEPAD is really a tool designed to negotiate the terms of aid with Africa's development partners, as epitomized by the G-8 summits (Bond 2005; Adejumobi 2009). A corollary of that charge is that NEPAD's prescriptions do not really differ from the neo-liberalism of the World Bank's policies of yesteryear in Africa. Although somewhat overstated, the criticism was not entirely unfounded, given the timing of announcing the APRM as the central plank of NEPAD. In fact, the notion of peer review did not appear anywhere in the various foundation documents that were merged to form NEPAD except for the UNECA operational document titled "A Compact for African Recovery" (Anglin 2006). The speed with which African leaders adopted the APRM foundational document—the Declaration on Political, Economic, Corporate Governance and Socioeconomic Development—at the 2002 AU summit in Durban to establish "an independent, effective, professional, and credible" African peer review mechanism (which was duly presented to the G-8 summit at the Kannanaskis in June 2002) led to speculation that "NEPAD emerged as Africa's external engagement strategy with the G-8 … and other developed countries" (Adedeji 2008, 251). Therein lies the paradox that has bedeviled NEPAD and its brainchild the APRM. As Adedeji succinctly puts it: "The presentation of NEPAD to the G-8 as a continental initiative is both its strength with the donor community and its greatest potential weakness in Africa" (Adedeji 2008, 251).

## The Evolution and Trajectory of African Development Thinking that Led to the Creation of the APRM

Two main strands of thinking lie behind the paradox that seems to have engulfed the creation of NEPAD and its brainchild the APRM. This chapter will argue that it is precisely this paradox that makes the APRM "potentially revolutionary, with reference to Africa's historical non-interference culture in the context of post-independence sub-regional and international cooperation" (Adedeji 2008).

First, at the end of the twentieth century, Africa's marginalization in a globalized world economy was total and complete. This situation precipitated a period of intense soul-searching among some African leaders, and also CSOs, leading to a desire to take charge of the destiny of the continent. At the heart of this sentiment, given the history of dissatisfaction with an externally driven development agenda, was the determination of African leaders to take complete ownership of and responsibility for the continent's development agenda and recovery. As Nigeria's former president Olusegun Obasanjo, one of the architects of NEPAD, once remarked:

> *In education and in industrialization, we have used borrowed ideas, utilized borrowed experiences and engaged borrowed hands. In our development programs and strategies, not much, if anything, is ours (Lancaster, 1999).*

This profound statement encapsulated the essence of African elite and popular sentiment on the eve of launching NEPAD. It captured Africa's sense of disempowerment and lack of ownership of its own development agenda in the midst of an increasingly globalized world that continued to marginalize the continent and its citizens. Indeed, globalization, with its integration of domestic economies into the world economy, had led to the increased dependence of some developing countries, especially in Africa (Stiglitz 2002). Africa faced daunting challenges; it was grappling with squalor, disease, violent conflicts, environmental degradation, unemployment, and a brain drain. Hence African leadership felt the urgency to rise to these challenges by reversing poverty and turning around the declining fortunes of the continent. Africans bemoaned the fact that over the years, the governance concepts of various donor agencies were showing contradictory elements and expectations, and African governments and civil society had increasing difficulty presenting their own views and experiences on good governance (Ndegwa and Green 1994; Mkandawire and Soludu 1999).

In this ominous context, the most pressing issue on African leaders' minds in formulating NEPAD/APRM was Africa's long and painful experience with the donor community, both in terms of economic and political conditionalities, as expressed in two decades of structural adjustment and stabilization policies, and in its more subtle successor program of poverty reduction strategies (Mkandawire and Soludu 1999; Kamkwenda 2004). The impact of structural adjustment—its failure to regenerate African economies as well as its debilitating effects on the state in terms of antagonistic relations with civil society—were fully discussed before NEPAD was conceived. There was no lack of consensus that reforms undertaken on the basis of structural adjustment conditionalities had led to pervasive economic, social and economic instabilities, the breakdown of public services and goods, and the collapse of African states' legitimacy due to reforms that were not owned or led by African states and their citizens (Mkandawire and Olukoshi 1995; Easterly 2006; Killick 1997).

Africans realized that these strategies, mostly dictated by the Bretton Woods institutions, had not been able to lift the continent significantly from its abject poverty. NEPAD was a clear signal to the international community that the days when policies and programs were externally determined without due cognizance of the peculiarities of the continent's situation was to give way to policies and programs which were mainly home-grown, that is, initiated by Africans, implemented by Africans, and owned by Africans. This thinking and attitude did not in any way imply that Africa was to extricate itself completely from the global economy or cease cooperation with the bilateral and multilateral international institutions; rather it was "anchored in the determination of Africans to extricate themselves and the continent from the malaise of underdevelopment in a rapidly globalizing world" (Nkuhlu 2002).

In fact, NEPAD reflected a consensus and a common determination among African leaders and peoples to change the destiny of the continent and redefine the paradigms of their relationships with the outside world in a positive and mutually beneficial way (Mbeki 2002; NEPAD 2001, paragraphs 148–149). Thus the initiative was perceived as an affirmation of Africa's determination to participate in globalization as an equal partner and to engage in a development partnership with the donors under the principles of the new international cooperation paradigm.

The second major strand of thinking behind NEPAD/APRM was the incipient consolidation and institutionalization of popular participation and democratic governance into the AU's official lexicon and normative code of conduct for member states. The silence of the OAU on good governance was bolstered in the 1960s by the emergence of an ideology of development which was associated with the thinking that economic development should be the highest goal of government (Adejumobi 2009). NEPAD, for the first time in post-colonial Africa's experimentation with numerous development strategies, explicitly reversed the priorities of African development strategies by categorically stating that "development is impossible in the absence of true democracy, respect for human rights, peace and good governance" (NEPAD 2001, paragraph 79). With this declaration, the AU and its development paradigm was decidedly premised on good governance, now officially recognized as a precondition for development. And to encourage compliance with these norms, NEPAD created a peer review mechanism by which African states could exercise a form of surveillance on each other in a bid to ensure adherence to good governance. The adoption of the APRM marked an unprecedented turnaround from normative principles to the actual monitoring of implementation of good governance in all its dimensions—political, economic, corporate, social, and peace and security.

A cursory review of African development strategies prior to NEPAD would easily demonstrate that although the momentum had been gathering through the various documents and declarations in the 1980s, the concepts of democracy and governance had not quite made their way to official African development strategy documents. The Lagos Plan of Action, the first major landmark African-initiated development strategy, reflected the development thought of its time and focused on collective self-reliance and state-led development with emphasis on the economy (Tawfik 2005; Anglin 2006). The relevance of democracy, governance and corruption to African development was not discussed in the document because it "was taboo to dwell on the non-economic factors essential for structural transformation without which rapid economic and social development itself was virtually impossible. Democracy and governance were among these taboo subjects" (Adedeji 2008, 245).

However, by the end of the 1980s, in part due to the extreme social cost of adjustment programs in Africa, it was becoming apparent that issues of democratic governance and human rights were emerging in continental African positions and conference declarations. One of the earliest such documents was the Khartoum Declaration: "Towards a Human-Focused Approach to Socio-Economic Recovery and Development in Africa," adopted by a UN-sponsored conference in the context of the UN Programme of Action for African Recovery and Development 1986–1990, and the Africa Priority Programme for Economic Recovery 1986–1990 (UNECA 1988). These last two documents were to be the framework for

Africa's development strategy during the so-called lost decade of Africa in the 1980s.

The Khartoum Declaration, for the first time, publicly acknowledged the need to change the political context of African development in order to promote human development, restore freedom and human rights, overcome political instability, and abolish over-centralization of the African state (UNECA 1988). Indeed, it could be argued that the Khartoum Declaration was the first official document to broach a discussion on reforming the African state and changing the governing style in Africa preceding the World Bank's 1989 much trumpeted report, "From Crisis to Sustainable Growth," often cited as the first publication to discuss "good governance" as the missing link in African development (World Bank 1989). Viewed in this context, then, the Khartoum Declaration was a dire critique of the authoritarianism engendered by structural adjustment policies both in design and implementation (Adejumobi and Olukoshi 2009). It is the argument of this chapter that the African discussion on governance preceded in many areas the global discussion on how to reform the state in Africa.

At the end of the 1980s, again owing to the devastating impact of structural adjustment programs on the fabric of African societies, UNECA mobilized its intellectual resources to design and respond to the World Bank with the publication of the African Alternative Framework to Structural Adjustment Programmes (AAF-SAP). Besides berating the macroeconomic policies of structural adjustment programs, the core message of the AAF-SAP was to advocate a more broad-based approach towards participatory structural adjustment programs so as to formulate an alternative framework to externally imposed adjustment programs, which are designed by international financial institutions rather than being owned and internalized by African countries (UNECA 1988). Emphasizing first the human dimensions of adjustments; second, paying attention to social sectors and vulnerable groups; third, focusing on manpower development and its utilization in the long run; and fourth, discussing ways of strengthening regional, international, and non-governmental organizations (NGOs) in African development, the African alternative framework sought to launch a new style of governing Africa. The effort of elaborating on the African alternative framework was complemented by the 1990 Arusha Conference on Popular Participation in Development, which subsequently adopted the African Charter on Popular Participation in Development and Transformation (UNECA 1990). Reflecting on the significance of the Arusha Declaration, this is how Adedeji puts it:

> *The output of the conference was the African Charter of Popular Participation in Development and Transformation—the 'African Magna Carta'....*

*The Charter, therefore, was the voice of the people. It well and truly led the drive for democracy in Africa (Adedeji 2004, 302).*

The charter unequivocally called for the role of popular participation in African development and linked its intrinsic value to better governance, "in which democracy, accountability, economic justice, and development for transformation become internalized, and the empowerment of the people, initiative and enterprise, and the democratization of the development process are the order of the day in every country" (UNECA 1990, 1). The charter also introduced a new mode of partnership between the state and civil society for promoting development based on popular participation on the continent. Civil society was also expected to mobilize the African masses to effectively participate in negotiating and debating development policies, with these organizations also serving in an oversight role that would review the extent to which the state was committed to implementing its development policies (UNECA 1990, Article 9).

Viewed retrospectively with the benefit of hindsight, one can now clearly see that the charter was conceived, at that time, as a bold African attempt to regain control and ownership of its development agenda in the years to come. In many ways, the African Charter was perceived as a means to operationalize an alternative—based on a transformation of how the state in Africa related to society in pursuit of developmental goals—to structural adjustment programs. The charter marked the genesis of a new theory of governance grounded on a "partnership or social contract" between state and society that was to foreshadow the APRM, initiated more than a decade later (Jinadu 2008). It is also worth recalling that organizationally, the charter urged the "imperative necessity" of establishing a monitoring mechanism for civil society in every African country to institutionalize this partnership (UNECA 1990, Article 23; Nyang'o et al. 2002).

Although it lacked a precise implementation mechanism, the charter was the first African development document to raise the issue of monitoring progress in popular participation on the basis of mutually agreed upon indicators—some of which were measureable—including the literacy rate, the number and scope of grassroots civil organizations, representation of the people in the national assembly; freedom of association, press, and media; political accountability of leadership; and decentralization of decision-making. More than ten years later, the fundamental principles of the African Charter would become the cornerstone of NEPAD and its crown jewel program, the APRM. According to Moyo, the charter has been influential in the way the AU and its structures have crafted their treaties, rules of procedure, and strategic plans. These have, in theory, given primacy to the participation of civil society (Moyo 2006, 165). Assessing the APRM's relevance to the right to development, Manby observes that the APRM "process and methodology provide an unprecedented level of popular participation in development that is closest to the ideals of the UN Declaration on the Right to Development" (Manby 2007).

To sum up, one cannot understand the ideological orientation of NEPAD and its singular agenda of regaining control of Africa's development and reshaping the relationship between the state and its citizens without reviewing the trajectory of African development strategies and frameworks of the 1980s and 1990s, especially the debate between the World Bank and African regional institutions on the need for ownership of policy reform and the general recognition by the development community that externally imposed conditionality was fundamentally flawed and ineffective (DfID 2005; OECD 2005 and 2008; Killick 1997; Collier 1997). The remainder of this chapter, therefore, argues that the overriding logic and strategic agenda of the APRM is to transform Africa's governance systems from being accountable to its external partners, to being accountable to its primary constituents—its citizens, a situation that would ensure true ownership of its development destiny.

## The APRM and the Re-shaping of Domestic Accountability in Governance

As argued above, the central message of NEPAD is that Africans must take control of their own development destiny in the context of marginalization of the continent in an increasingly globalized world. Governance reform ownership, as demonstrated by a review of African development documents, has been the rallying cry for Africans for at least a decade or more. Yet reform ownership implies that an externally imposed conditionality ought to cease and be replaced with an internally driven reform. However, reform "ownership" is viewed with skepticism by donors, simply because there was little or only partial commitment to policy reform in Africa during the structural adjustment period or even during the era of poverty reduction strategies. Still, the cry for policy ownership does reflect a genuine desire to create a specifically African vision of the developmental state grounded in domestic forces for change, not just as a response to external stimuli. The APRM was essentially invented to get Africa out of the dilemma of external pressure for change while still taking greater ownership of and control over Africa's reform agenda. The normative value of the mechanism is to defend a particular vision of ownership—one that involves African citizens and governments taking back control of their development policies and priorities. It does have "radical and progressive implications" if properly and faithfully implemented (Jinadu 2008).

The basic premise of the APRM, therefore, is that an externally imposed reform agenda has failed to achieve results for African governance, and that there is a need for a new approach to re-shaping African governance reform in the long term. This is achievable in three major ways: reforming African governance systems through restructuring the relations between state and society; strengthening the capacity of civil society to impact policy reforms; and creating a domestic-driven accountability system of governance, which is long overdue in Africa. This chapter argues that an African-led accountability mechanism has better potential to foster domestically-driven governance reforms than perhaps any previous, externally-driven approach, including the poverty reduction strategy papers (PRSP). Although the PRSP approach initiated by international financial institutions is advocated as an instrument to engage civil society development and poverty reduction, the process has not institutionalized popular participation as yet (Elberlie 2001; Cheru 2002).

The APRM, an inward-looking governance self-monitoring tool sponsored by the AU /NEPAD agenda, provides a home-grown domestic accountability mechanism as a resolution to this African dilemma. The APRM process is based on self-evaluation by the participating countries, validation by a group of eminent Africans, and a review of conclusions and findings by African peers. This is followed by a national plan of action that has the interest of domestic stakeholders attached to it in terms of implementation. The stakeholders for implementation, however, are not just domestic, but also regional neighbors and continental peers who are legitimate stakeholders in African development. This unique mechanism is an inverse of the externally driven accountability approaches that have dominated the African development landscape over the past fifty years since independence.

Whatever the shortcomings in countries conforming to the APRM standard review processes, peer review is shaping up to be the most open and inclusive form of national dialogue we have seen yet, and it is building support for a culture of domestic accountability that has been missing in many previous attempts to create governmental accountability in Africa. The mechanism is beginning to strengthen the voices of citizens and civil society by increasing demand-side pressures on government that would lead to a gradual increase in rules-based governance, transparency, and accountability within largely executive-dominant political systems.

The following section analyzes the empirical experience of how the APRM is reshaping and strengthening domestic accountability in a few countries that have gone through the process. The analysis is done at three main levels: 1) at the level of process and the methodology of the APRM; 2) at the level of the content of the APRM Questionnaire and review report; and 3) at the level of the mechanism's potential impact, both nationally and continentally. At each of these levels, the challenges confronting the mechanism are highlighted and suggestions provided for improving its effectiveness.

## Process and Methodology of Review

The APRM foundation documents are purposefully clear that the process and procedures of the country assessment are just as important as the findings, conclusions and recommendations of the review for a participating state (APRM. 2002) if Africa is to adopt a new approach to public policy, reform and development. Given that the APRM is based on a theory of African governance which aims to connect citizen to the state 'to enlarge the public space for the nurture of and consolidation of popular democracy and good governance', the process required inclusivity of all stakeholders at the level of government, civil society, the private sector, and African and international actors as well, including development partners (Jinadu. 2008).

## Engaging Civil Society and other Stakeholders

The process of establishing the structures and institutions needed to conduct the national self-assessment reports was important in providing opportunities for countries to make the APRM relevant to ordinary people by building trust between citizens and governments for a national dialogue on governance (Herbert and Gruzd 2008). Although each country took a different approach to suit the context of political development and maturity, there appears to be a consensus in the scant literature on the early experiences of the APRM that civil society is highly engaged in the APRM process across the board in a range of participating member states (Herbert and Gruzd 2008; Jinadu 2008; Bing-Pappoe 2007; Ouma Akoth 2007). In Ghana, the government saw the need to win the confidence of the citizenry by appointing a completely civil-society-led National Governing Council (NGC). The government took active steps to demonstrate openness, political maturity, and flexibility by consulting with opposition parties about individuals to be short-listed on the NGC, eventually selecting only those seen to be non-partisan representatives to this body. In addition, the government established an independent administrative secretariat outside of any ministry staffed by professionals who were not part of the public service; employed well respected and independent think tanks to conduct the self-assessment research; and developed a multi-pronged, robust research methodology to capture popular and elite opinion on the state of governance in the country. All these measures helped to persuade the public that the APRM was a serious national dialogue on matters affecting the welfare of ordinary people.

Critics of the Ghana process argue that although the process was open and participatory, there was no way to verify how the inputs from civil society and the general public were finally used in the APRM report (Bing-Pappoe 2008). Kenya established a task force of both government and NGO representatives to design and refine its peer review plans and allowed civil society to elect its own representatives to sit on the NGC. Although the process was acrimonious, reflecting the contentious nature of state-society relations in Kenya, it has opened up a space for civil society to dialogue with the state and has laid a firm foundation for eventually monitoring the implementation of the NPoA (Ouma Akoth 2007).

The process in Rwanda posed two major challenges: how to make the process participatory and inclusive without opening up opportunities for the "divisive ethnic-based politics" that has characterized the history of Rwanda, and how to make up for the massive depletion of research capacity in both government and civil society sectors as a result of the 1994 genocide. A third main challenge was the compression of time for conducting the national self-assessment, which made it difficult to allow sufficient time for consultation across all sections of society. Thus, in Rwanda, the tendency was to carry out the APRM self-assessment without seeking the contribution of civil society, though civil society did have to be included somewhat at a later point (Ouma Akoth 2007).

A number of problems have been identified across the various APRM-participating countries. First is the concern that the selection process for membership in the APRM National Governing Councils—the main bodies mandated to oversee the integrity of the country assessment process—has not been consistent with the principles and guidelines suggested by APRM background documents. Second, membership composition in the governing bodies has been controversial and in some cases not openly and transparently debated among the public. Lastly, due to the politics involved in the selection process, appointments of some governing councils were delayed for several months, undermining the time frame for completion of the process. These problems were attributed to the "conflicting formulations in various APRM doctrinaire statements" and to the "broad discretion which these documents seem to grant the governments of the member states in the APR processes" (Jinadu 2008).

While these concerns are valid, they overlook the fundamental lesson that meaningful popular participation in public policy processes has been the missing link in African development efforts, whether by externally imposed strategies or internally initiated approaches. In addition, popular participation always takes time, expertise, and resources to achieve minimum standards of expectations. Most of the first tier of APRM-participating countries also happen to be countries that were already engaged in PRSP processes, and yet, despite the fact that PRSP preceded APRM in many countries by at least five years, these governments were still struggling with how to effectively mobilize civil society participation. This is a clear indication of how little impact the PRSP has had on governance systems. It highlights the fact that despite much hoopla about PRSP institutionalizing consultative processes around development strategies, many countries in Africa still do not have the experience nor the will to foster a thorough, ongoing popular participation process. As observed by NEPAD officials, the PRSP process has had limited scope and legitimacy in institutionalizing participatory processes in development in Africa:

> *Through NEPAD, African leaders have fundamentally changed the development paradigm. The narrow approach of the Poverty Reduction Strategy Papers (PRSPs) has been replaced by a comprehensive and holistic approach to development. Through these interventions, the African people have, themselves, determined a development path for their countries and their continent (Nkuhlu 2005).*

In countries where democratic space exists and civil society is fairly strong, the APRM offered another opportunity for a legitimate home-grown public engagement in the development process. But in countries where for various reasons, civil society was relatively weaker—Rwanda, for example—the government took the lead in managing the review process. In countries where relations with civil society are fairly contentious—Kenya and South Africa—the APRM process mirrored the character of existing tensions and was not necessarily due to government manipulation. The APRM experience, so far, demonstrates that even when political will exists at the highest level—evidenced by the countries' accession to participate in the APRM process—the fostering of civil society consultation in development programs and policy reforms is not easy and country organizational capacities in a complex process like the APRM cannot be taken for granted. The process offers opportunity to all parties to increase their capacities to form partnerships for a new development approach on the continent.

## The APRM methodology enhances civil society engagement

In order to ensure the credibility and integrity of the APRM, the methodology of the APRM process calls for a number of institutional set-ups to undertake the countries' national assessments. A technical research institution (TRI in APRM parlance) is appointed by the NGC or national council to collate and analyze data and to present the views of the general population. The final report undergoes validation to ensure that the views of the public are not misrepresented. In general, following the example of Ghana as the first APRM-participating country to undertake the review, most countries have appointed independent civil-society-based think tanks or research institutions to undertake this role. Given the multiple and multidisciplinary thematic areas of the review, some countries had a combination of independent think tanks and universities or national councils of economic and social policy to undertake the country self-assessment research. The first four countries to undertake the review set the pattern for the others to follow. Ghana, Kenya and South Africa each appointed reputable independent research institutions and assigned them the task of assembling information for each of the four thematic areas. Rwanda, given its capacity shortfalls due to the genocide, turned to South African independent think tanks to assist with the assessments (Herbert and Gruzd 2008). The subsequent set of countries—Algeria, Nigeria, Benin, Uganda and Burkina Faso—all pretty much followed the same approach by using independent think tanks or quasi-public research institutions as TRIs.

A major focus of the entire APRM exercise is to improve the capacity of both the process and outputs of public policy in the African governance context, and as such, the use of TRIs clearly fulfills this function. It is noteworthy that the selected policy and research think tanks that ended up undertaking the APRM analytical assessment work were sophisticated African institutions that had track records of governance assessment or advocacy work in their countries or on the continent. These include CSOs that contributed to African democratic development during the 1990s, played crucial roles in the democratic transition period, and continue to work towards their consolidation (Gyimah-Boadi 2004). A few examples include the Institute for Democracy in South Africa, the Centre for Democratic Development in Ghana, the Centre for Democratic Development of Nigeria, Gerddes-Afrique in Benin, the Institute for Economic Growth in Kenya, and the South Africa Institute for International Affairs. These were issues-oriented institutions with a track record of policy advocacy and a reform agenda. Gyimah-Boadi makes the poignant observation that in those African countries "where the transition to democracy has reached an advanced stage or consolidation has begun, civil society [is] moving away from the crudely confrontational style of the early years in favor of a focus on consensus, moderation, more thoughtful policy debate, and other modes of constructive engagement" with the state (Gyimah-Boadi 2004, 101).

The APRM has provided a perfect framework through which civil society interaction with the state can contribute to policy dialogue and the building of domestic constituencies for reforms. Indeed, the partnership opportunities offered by the APRM process require the "reconstruction and reorientation of social relations in cooperative ways that will enable the three sectors—state, private sector, and civil society—to play a reinforcing, symbiotic role in strengthening democracy, securing the public interest, and improving governance in line with the APRM objectives" (Jinadu 2008). Interestingly, African CSOs and think tanks are forming regional and continental networks, comparing and sharing notes and best practices on the country review process, and undertaking studies such as the AfriMap post-review series with the aim of collectively strengthening the sector as a countervailing force that ultimately will move the reform agenda forward in Africa.

The rationale for using local research institutions in national self-assessment has wider implications for domestic accountability in policy reforms than merely enhancing the inclusive participation of civil society in the process. Besides the obvious effect of strengthening local research institutions' capacity to participate effectively in national governance processes, it is also an essential innovation of the APRM methodology to anchor knowledge production on governance in the domestic public sphere. This rationale is grounded in the NEPAD principle of African leadership in formulating development strategies and holding at bay the role of donor diagnostic tools and policy prescriptions that have generally been used to inform the design of reform.

The use of donor assessment templates—often conducted by "experts" with their blueprint policy prescriptions—has been a part of the debate as to whether African countries should commit to policy conditionalities imposed from outside without their participation in diagnosis of the problem (Mkandawire and Olukoshi 1995). That the APRM consciously and systematically grounds governance assessment in the domestic public sphere, where it makes sense to its citizens and policy elite, is a major departure from the donor-driven governance assessment methodologies often conducted by expatriate experts, sometimes with the collaboration of one or two local professionals. Consequently, the APRM methodology can be viewed as a deliberative alternative to external assessments—conducted by donors for internal corporate use—with little or no relevance for recipient partner countries in terms of deepening democratization or accountability between the state and its citizens.

Another important role played by civil society in the APRM process is at the stage of the country review undertaken by the APRM panel member and team of technical experts responsible for the country. The APRM guidelines require that the visiting team consult widely with all stakeholders—civil society, businesses, trade unions, academics, professional associations, and groups representing marginalized populations including women and children, etc.—in order to ascertain the integrity of the process and validate the national report and NPoA. So far, based on the experiences from the first cohort of countries, this stage of the APRM has proven to be a vital link in the process. This author has participated in at least four of the first cohort country reviews and can testify to the degree of vigilance the local CSOs, academics, and other stakeholders have brought to the process, providing invaluable information that fills important gaps in the original APRM country self-assessment. It is not an exaggeration to suggest that the country review reports have benefited tremendously from the inputs of local stakeholders during the visits of the external technical review team. The evidence from the pioneer countries points to the fact that within the complex APRM systems of checks and balances, political leaders cannot hide information from the independent external technical review teams. Besides being armed with their own "issues papers" for validating the draft country reports, the APRM panel and its team of experts have unfettered access to all stakeholders ready to provide additional sensitive information that could not be voiced openly. The reports of eight countries so far, from Ghana to the latest review of Burkina Faso, all raised sensitive governance issues.

## Implementation of the National Programme of Action

Notwithstanding these initial achievements, the real basis for assessing the impact of APRM on state-society relations and domestic governance reforms is the role of civil society and other stakeholders in seeing to the implementation of the NPoA as the final outcome of the process. In exercising this function, civil society confronts more than the usual constraints of inadequate capacity and lack of resources. They face two fundamental but interconnected problems: first, the apparent lack of information on the post-review stage has caused a lack of inertia within CSOs to monitor the implementation of the NPoA proactively; and second, the fact that initiatives not included in a government's medium-term national budgetary framework have very little chance of being funded has affected the rate of implementation of the NPoA. The roots of the second problem are the weak links that the APRM has with the existing national poverty reduction strategies in many countries (UNECA, forthcoming).

In most of the APRM countries, civil society seems to be waiting on cues from governments or institutional structures such as the national focal point or the NGC and are reluctant to own either the reports or the NPoA. Instead of viewing the NPoA as a reference document around which civil society can canvass and create demand for various reforms called for during the national self-assessment process, it appears that most organizations expect the government to invite them to participate in the plan's implementation. It is important that civil society see the APRM process as a continuum and mobilize in a proactive manner to foster debate and build broad coalitions within the ranks, encouraging and engaging the citizenry to demand accountability around the key reform issues initiated in the NPoA.

The related issue of integrating the NPoA into existing national development strategies stems from the fact that in most of the earlier APRM countries, the NPoA resulting from the process was not adequately costed and not reflected in the medium-term expenditure framework—the main budgeting instrument of countries undergoing the PRSPs. Understandably, the concern of the APRM framework with upstream participatory issues tended to undermine the attention to budgeting the NPoA systematically and integrating costs into the existing budgetary framework. This affects the monitoring and evaluation of the NPoA as it is difficult to identify specific government resources devoted to policy issues included in the PoA. Strategic partners like UNECA have embarked on a study of how to harmonize the NPoA and existing national development strategies like PRSPs into a common medium-term expenditure framework.

In the meantime, pioneer countries like Ghana, Rwanda and Uganda are already in the process of integrating and harmonizing their NPoAs into their national budgets. In Ghana, for example, the APRM's NPoA has been mapped onto Ghana's development plans, a budget prioritization committee has been established, and there is even an office in the Finance Ministry to track NPoA expenditures. In the area of monitoring, the Ghanaian government has decentralized by creating district-level oversight committees countrywide for monitoring the implementation of the APRM through linkage with national civic education centers (Appiah 2008). Rwanda has fully integrated its NPoA and economic development and poverty reduction strategies following a joint governance assessment using the APRM as the main point of departure. Uganda is in the process of integrating the NPoA into its national development strategy. The legitimacy of the APRM process as a participatory approach to governance rests on integrating its recommendations into the medium-term expenditure framework, to be monitored by all stakeholders. Thus, it is critical that late-comers to the APRM process be able to integrate their NPoAs effectively as lessons and best practices become available.

## National conversations on governance have been initiated

The APRM is expected to foster public debate over key policies that help to forge and preserve a "social contract"—in which the state is held accountable for meeting basic needs and providing basic services essential for life and livelihood—between the state and its citizens,. The nature of the debate that ensued in the first three cohorts of countries completing the APRM process—Ghana, Rwanda, Kenya, South Africa, Algeria, Nigeria, Benin, Uganda and Burkina Faso—demonstrates a fair reflection of the state of good governance in these countries and shows a level of maturity in civil society as it engages with public policy debates and other reform issues. Indeed, the APRM process opened up space for discussion of all aspects of governance, including the political, economic, and corporate, as well as the socio-economic realm. Compared to the spontaneous protests and upheavals led by CSOs against authoritarian regimes on the continent in the 1990s, Africa is witnessing a more sober, reflective and sanguine civil society approach to public policy reform in the framework of the APRM. Indeed, these changes in approach represent a significant departure from patterns and processes that have characterized the internationally sponsored PRSP. Numerous studies on the PRSP process point to the superficial engagement of CSOs in formulating strategic plans (Booth 2008). The evidence shows that PRSPs have not been institutionalized in many countries and therefore have been unable to respond to the need for greater domestic accountability of government to its own citizens. A sustained demand for policy reform is lacking in the PRS process, as observed by the critics cited above as well as by noted observers such as Francis Fukuyama: institutional reform does not take place without domestic demand (Fukuyama 2007).

Nevertheless, the space opened up by the APRM is a valuable opportunity to establish a sustainable culture of dialogue between civil society and government—an opportunity that should not be shunned. Whatever the shortcomings in countries' conforming to the standardized APRM review process as stated in the APRM documents and guidelines, it can be safely argued that the process is shaping up to be the most consultative national "development dialogue" on the continent, and the process is beginning to support a culture of domestic accountability that has often been missing from Africa's economic and political reforms. The real challenge for African countries undergoing the process is how to institutionalize the national dialogue and consultation processes around key governance issues, thereby creating a demand for accountability.

## Content of the APRM Country Reviews

In addition to process and methodology, the APRM framework allows for a new systematic and contextual approach to reviewing substantive governance issues that otherwise would have been very difficult to tackle within the domestic public sphere. The APRM Questionnaire, developed over protracted discussion and debate by all relevant stakeholders, agreed upon robust objectives, criteria and indicators that have "significant diagnostic potential for African governance issues" (Herbert and Gruzd 2009, 11). Across thematic areas of the APRM Questionnaire, from political governance to socio-economic development, challenging governance issues were framed in the context of a government that is responsible, responsive and accountable to citizen needs and aspirations. As Gruzd puts it: The nine participating states "have subjected virtually all facets of governance to scrutiny by their own citizens, African experts and ultimately heads of state; come up with frank assessments of real problems; and developed programs of action … to plug the governance gaps" (Herbert & Grudz. 2009).

The country review reports published by the APRM Secretariat so far have clearly established the professionalism, technical rigor, and integrity of the peer review process as led by the APR Panel. The Panel has shown competence and credibility as well as a willingness to criticize states undergoing the review and has therefore been a critical factor in establishing the usefulness and legitimacy of the process to an audience wider than Heads of State (Manby 2008; Herbert and Gruzd 2008). While criticism of the slow pace of the reviews may be valid, the perceived validity and credibility of the reports' content far outweigh the delays experienced in producing the reports. African needs governance assessment tools that speak to the heart of its governance challenges.

As one of the most innovative components of the peer review, the final reports of the countries reviewed so far have come up with a list of cross-cutting or overarching issues whose resolution is considered fundamental to ensuring good governance. These issues require the immediate attention of leaders and policy-makers. Among these structural issues are notably the management of diversity; land as a both a resource and a source of conflict; the management of elections; and corruption. In almost every African country, any one or a combination of these issues is a challenge to the governance system and must be overcome in order for governance to be effective. Both the post-election violence in Kenya and the xenophobic incidents that occurred in South Africa were accurately predicted by the APRM national reports (Manby 2008).

The APR Forum, the political body governing the continental process, is determined to deepen the discussions on the APRM cross-cutting issues which are common among most African countries. This was the impetus behind the extraordinary summit convened in October 2008 in the Republic of Benin, an APRM member state, to provide the opportunities for leaders to discuss how collectively these salient issues can be tackled with the benefit of learning from continental best practices. That African states openly embrace these issues as formidable governance challenges is, in itself, a major breakthrough in the change of attitudes toward governance assessment. In addition, it speaks to the increasing legitimacy of the APRM as a truly African-owned tool for governance assessment.

## National and Continental Impacts of Peer Review

One of the most misunderstood concepts of the APRM is the notion of peer review and peer learning as stated in the basic background documents of the process. From the perspectives of the participating heads of state and government in the APRM process, peer review remains at the summit level. Official documents refer to the participating heads of state and government comprising the APR Forum as the supreme governing body of the APRM and as the "peers" who will be involved in the review process. However, experiences from the first few countries show that peer review and learning are evident at all levels and stages of the process: not only among governance institutions at the domestic level, but also among emerging networks of CSOs, private sector institutions, research institutions and think tanks, governing councils, national focal points, and among ordinary citizens across the continent. It is this notion of peer review that constitutes the core of the APRM mechanism.

At the domestic level, the national self-assessment process provides a unique opportunity for governance institutions to interact, interrogate, and evaluate each other's functions and performances, in terms of both horizontal and vertical accountability. The APRM is essentially aimed at strengthening domestic accountability systems between state and society and among regional and continental peers, which is a unique feature emerging on Africa's governance landscape. The mechanism's guidelines stipulate that the governments must develop a road map for their national process 'in collaboration with key stakeholders . . . which should be widely publicized and provide information about national coordinating structures, the stages of the APRM and the roles and responsibilities of stakeholders from government, non-governmental organizations, private sector and international development partners" (NEPAD 2003c). These guidelines further stress that "the organization of public participation in the APRM process is in itself a central aspect of enhancing the state of governance and socio-economic development in the participating country." Such interactions can build trust as well as establish and clarify mechanisms for ongoing engagement and the empowerment of stakeholders.

Experiences from the eleven countries have shown that the self-assessment process is designed to evaluate the performance of institutions that make up the systems of governance in those countries. It is not a scorecard or rating of certain individuals in government or of political parties in past or present regimes. The APRM looks at both the systems of governance and the individual institutional functions in terms of performance in good governance. For example, the government's executive branch, parliament, and judiciary, as well as political parties, civil society, and the private sector all have to come to a consensus about the pressing governance issues affecting the nation and agree on the best way forward in addressing them. The APRM presents an alternative channel of accountability, albeit informally, within and between government institutions and non-governmental actors. Thus, the process creates opportunities for public demand for accountability (through representative institutions or organized civil society), which is said to be very low between elections in Africa (Logan and Bratton 2008).

At the regional and continental levels, the peer review offers a different kind of accountability pressure that can have an indirect positive impact on national governance systems. The networks of regional CSOs and research think tanks, government focal points, and NGCs have helped to reinforce the process of stakeholders' learning from each other and have deepened African solidarity. By raising sensitive cross-cutting and inter-state issues such as conflicts, land management, managing diversity, and corruption, the APRM provides an early warning system to avert political and economic crises in Africa. Likewise, accepting outsiders to examine national findings and express a view on how a country is governed is a fundamental shift in pan-African thought and a modification of sovereignty from the principle of non-interference under the OAU to the principle of non-indifference under the AU. By harmonizing reform efforts, tackling difficult inter-African issues and sharing best practices, the peer review is laying a critical foundation for a united states of Africa.

## Towards the Strengthening of Domestic Accountability: Implications for International Development Partners

One of the most topical issues in development partnership today is donor interest in assessing country governance in recipient countries and the degree to which countries can assume leadership of their assessment efforts. There is an increasing realization that donor-led assessments and assistance programs as well as modalities for implementation have all contributed to the lack of domestic accountability in recipient countries by instead strengthening external accountability to donors.

Domestic accountability is fundamentally different from externally driven (push) accountability mechanisms, which have proven to be ineffective. There is now a consensus that institutional reform does not take place unless there is a strong domestic demand, either bottom-up in terms of civil society or top-down in terms of elite demand-driven reform (Fukuyama 2007).

In the final analysis, the APRM seeks to address the following fundamental issues in development partnership for strengthening governance institutions in Africa:

- how to avoid interference in domestic accountability when governments are so dependent on aid (50 percent of the national budget in some cases) and ensure that governments are accountable to their citizens;
- how to avoid the "aid-institutions paradox" for aid-dependent countries, i.e., how to develop local institutions of the state and society that make politicians (leaders) more accountable to citizens rather than to external partners;
- how to create space for local institutional development—encouraging, exploration of processes, peer learning and sharing, learning by doing—that can help build pressure for reform from within and not from without.

The APRM is an inward-looking mechanism, designed to encourage the culture of domestic accountability in Africa based on self-imposed standards of good governance. It highlights the fundamental problem that institutional development designed by outsiders cannot be effective. Its ultimate value would be that the "software for institutions"—rules, habits, norms—that support growth and development are apparently a result of a long process, during which societies experiment and continually fine-tune to suit their needs, constraints, and opportunities. The mechanism can and should be perceived as Africa's hope that domestic accountability will be institutionalized so that external partners may eventually abandon their own monitoring process and accept the outcome of the APR as the basis for supporting democratic governance institutions in Africa (de Waal 2002).

## Conclusions

This chapter has traced the trajectory of Africa's development initiatives within the context of the continent's quest to identify a truly African-owned development strategy with programs that it can own and seriously commit to implementing. It has demonstrated that the absence of ownership, perceived or real, of development paradigms is one of the major reasons for lopsided success in implementing development policies and strategies that would lead to institutional reforms. The inauguration of NEPAD coincided with major shifts in international thinking about the need for development effectiveness: Africa's development partners were at this time searching for popular participation and democratic ownership of reforms and accountability to domestic constituents. The APRM appears to have provided a mutually agreeable approach that could satisfy both external partners' concerns with improving the quality and depth of development ownership by recipient countries and the need for government accountability to citizens of developing countries.

The APRM is beginning to have an impact and is charting a new course for improving governance systems across Africa. Several years into implementation, the APRM is shaping up to be an important milestone in Africa's move towards institutionalizing domestic accountability practices across the continent. While it is still too early to discern its sustainability and definitive impact on Africa's development, the current results call for cautious optimism about the APRM's future and potential in transforming African governance systems.

*The views and perspectives expressed in this chapter are those of the author alone and should not in any way be attributed to the United Nations Economic Commission for Africa (UNECA). The author acknowledges the research assistance provided by Ms. Saba Kassa in finalizing the references for this paper.*

## References


Adedeji, A. 2004. "The UNECA: Forging a Future for Africa." In *Unity and Diversity in Development Ideas,* ed. Yves Berhelot. Bloomington: Indiana University Press.

—. 2008. "NEPAD's African Peer Review Mechanism: Progress and Prospects." In *The African Union and Its Institutions,* eds. J. Akokpari, A. Ndinga-Muvumba, and T. Murithi. Sunnyside: Fanele.

Adejumobi, S. 2009. "The African Experience of Popular Participation in Development." In The *African Union and New Strategies for Development in Africa*, eds. S. Adejumobi and A. Olukoshi. Dakar: Codesria Books.

Anglin, D. 2006. "The African Peer Review of Political Governance: Precedents, Problematics and Prospects." In *Democratic Reform in Africa: Its Impact on Governance and Poverty Alleviation,* ed. Muna Ndulo. Athens, Ohio: James Curry Press.

Appiah, F. 2007. Presentation, UNECA Workshop on "APRM Ad-Hoc Expert Group Meeting on Deepening APRM Best Practices and Lessons Learned." May 28, Addis Ababa, Ethiopia. Mimeograph.

APRM. 2008a. African Peer Review Mechanism Annual Report. Midrand, South Africa.

—. 2008b. The Report for the African Partnership Forum. Midrand, South Africa: African Partnership Forum.

Barbone, L., and K. Sharkey. 2006. "Strengthening Governance through Engaged Societies: lessons from the implementation of povery reduction strategies." World Bank Policy Research Working Paper 3898.

Bekoe, D. 2002. "NEPAD and its Achilles Heels." *Alternatives: Turkish Journal of International Relations* 1(4), Winter.

Bing-Pappoe, A. 2007. "Ghana and the APRM: A Critical Assessment." Osiwa and Afrimap.

Bond, P. 2009. "Removing Neocolonialism's APRM Mask: A Critique of the African Peer Review Mechanism." *Review of African Political Economy* 36: 122, 595–603.

Booth, D. 2008. "Aid Effectiveness after Accra: How to Reform the 'Paris Agenda.'" ODI Briefing Paper. http://www.odi.org.uk/PPPG/politics and governance/publications/GAPODIBP39july08 aideffectiveness.pdf

Bräutigam, D. 2000. "Aid Dependence and Governance." Expert Group on Development Issues.

Browne, G. 2006. *Aid and Influence: Do Donors Help or Hinder?* London: Earthscan Publications.

Bunwaree, S. 2008. "NEPAD and its Discontents." In *The African Union and Its Institutions,* eds. J. Akokpari, A. Ndinga-Muvumba, and T. Murithi. Sunnyside: Fanele.

Cabral, A. 1973. "National Liberation and Culture." In *Return to the Source: Selected Speeches of Amilcar Cabral,* ed. A. Cabral. Africa Information Service, *New York Review Monthly.*

Cheru, F. 2002. "The PRPS Process in Ghana." Report of Second Meeting of the African Peer Learning Group on PRPS (PRSP-LG). 18-21 November, Brussels, Belgium.

Collier, P. 1997. "The failure of Conditionality." In *Perspectives on Aid and Development* 22, eds. C. Gwin and J. Nelson. ODC. Washington, DC: John Hopkins University Press

de Renzio, P. 2006. "Aid, Budget and Accountability: A Survey Article." *Development Policy Review* 24: 6, 627–645.

de Renzio, P., and J. Schultz. 2008. "Budget Work and Democracy-Building: The case of IBASE in Brazil." In *Budgeting for the Poor,* M. Robinson, ed. Palgrave Macmillan: UK.

de Waal, A. 2002. "What's new in the New Partnership for Africa's Development?" *International Affairs.* 78: 3.

Deng, B. K. 2006. "The African Peer Review Mechanism and its Participatory Process." *Inside AISA* 2, April/May. African Institute of South Africa.

Deve, T. 2006. "Taking a Firm Stance against NEPAD." Presented at the African civil society meeting on the occasion of the second conference of the Heads of State and Government of the Africa Union, Maputo, Mozambique, 27 June–July 2, Pambazuka. Accessed at: http://www.pambazuka.org/en/category/development/16447.

DfID. 2006. "Eliminating World Poverty: Making Governance Work for the Poor." UK.

—. 2007. "Governance, Development and Democratic Politics" DfID's Work in Building More Effective States." Available at: http://www.dfid.gov.uk/Documents/publications/evaluation/voice-accountability-synthesis.pdf

Diamond, L. 1994. "Rethinking Civil Society: Towards Democratic Consolidation." *Journal of Democracy* 5: 3.

Droop, J., P. Isenman, and B. Mlalazi. 2008. "The Paris Declaration on Aid Effectiveness: Study of existing mechanisms to promote mutual accountability between donors and partner countries at the international level." Oxford Policy Management Paper.

Droop, J., P. Isenman, and B. Mlalazi. 2008. *The Spirit of Democracy: The Struggle to Build Free Societies throughout the World.* New York: Times Books/Henry Holt and Co.

Easterly, W. 2006. *The White Man's Burden: Why the West's Efforts to Aid the Rest have Done So Much Ill and So Little Good.* London: Penguin.

Eberlie, W. 2001. "Accountability in Poverty Reduction Strategies: The role of empowerment and participation." Washington DC: World Bank, Participation and Civic Engagement. Social Development Paper 104/2007.

Fanon, F. 1968. *The Wretched of the Earth.* New York: Grove Press.

Foster, M. 2000. "New Approaches to Development Cooperation: What Can We Learn from Experiences with Implementing Sector Wide Approaches?" ODI Working Paper No. 140. London: ODI.

Fukuyama, F. 2007. "Civil Society and Improved Governance in Developing Countries." Keynote address at the Transparency and Accountability Program conference, Brookings Institute, March 20.

Gottschalk, K., and S. Schmidt. 2004. "The African Union and the New Partnership for Africa's Development: Strong Institutions for Weak States?" *IPG* 4.

Gyimah-Boadi, E. 2004. "Civil Society and Democratic Development." In *Democratic Reform in Africa: The Quality of Progress,* ed. Gyimah-Boadi. Boulder, Colorado: Lynne Reinner Publishers.

Herbert, R. 2003. "Becoming my Brother's Keeper." *e-Africa Newsletter* October 1. Johannesburg: SAIIA.

Herbert, R., and S. Gruzd. 2008. *The African Peer Review Mechanism: Lessons from the Pioneers.* Johannesburg: SAIIA.

Hope, K. 2005. "Towards Good Governance and Sustainable Development: The African Peer Review Mechanism." *Governance: An International Journal of Policy, Administration and Institution* 18: 2, April.

Horner, L., and Power, G. 2009. "The Democratic Dimension of Aid: Prospects for Democracy-Building within the Contemporary International Architecture of Development Cooperation." *Literature Review for International IDEA,* Global Partners and Associates: London.

Hubli, S., and A. Mandaville. 2004. "Parliaments and the PRSP Process." World Bank Institute Working Paper.

Hudson, A. 2007. "Parliaments and Development." ODI Briefing Paper. http://www.odi.org.uk/resources/odi-publications/briefing-papers/18-parliaments-development.pdf.

—. 2009. "Background Paper for the Launch of the Workstream on Aid and Domestic Accountability." OECD DAC Network on Governance (GOVNET).

Hudson, A., and A. Tsekpo. 2009. "Parliamentary Strengthening and the Paris Principles: Synthesis Report." ODI/Parliamentary Centre.

Hyden, G. 1992. "Governance and the Study of Politics." In *Governance and Politics in Africa,* eds. G. Hydén and M. Bratton. Boulder, Colorado: Lynne Rienner Publishers.

Jindau, A. 2008. The African Peer Review Process in Nigeria. Dakar, Senegal: Osiwa/AfriMAP.

Joseph, R., and A. Giles (eds). 2009. *Smart Aid for African Development.* Boulder: Lynne Rienner Publishers.

Kajee, A. 2004a. "The African Peer Review Mechanism: A Progress Report. Practical Limitations and Challenges." In *South African Yearbook of International Affairs 2003/04.* Johannesburg: SAIIA. Accessed at: http://www.foundationdevelopmentafrica.org/nepad/nepad_general/nepad_aprm_progress_report.htm.

Kajee, A. 2004b. "The African Union and the African Peer Review Mechanism: Implications for Regional Integration in the Context of Continental Structures." Unpublished paper.

Kamkwenda, M. 2004. "Forty Years of Development Illusions: Revisiting Development Policies and Practices in Africa." In *African Development and Governance Strategies for the 21st Century: Looking Back to Move Forward. Essays in Honour of Adebayo Adedeji at Seventy,* ed. Bade Onimode. London: Zed Books.

Kanbur, R. 2004. "The African Peer Review Mechanism: An Assessment of Process and Design." Mimeo. Ithaca, New York: Cornell University.

Keet, D. 2002. "The New Partnership for Africa's Development and the African Union: Unity and Integration within Africa or Integration into the Global Economy." Reprinted. Cape Town: Alternative Information and Development Centre.

Killick, T. 1997. "Principles, Agents and the Failings of Conditionality." *Journal of World Development,* 9: 4, 483–95.

Kreigler, Johann. 2006. "Democratic Reform in Africa." In *Democratic Reform in Africa: Its Impact on Governance and Poverty Alleviation,* ed. M. Ndulo.. Athens, Ohio: James Curry Press.

Lancaster, C. 1999. *Aid to Africa: So Much to Do, So Little Done.* Chicago: University of Chicago Press.

—. 2002. "Democratic Governance Pivotal for Africa's Future." *Global Dialogue* 73, November. Institute for Global Dialogue.

Landsberg, C. 2008. "The Birth and Evolution of NEPAD." In *The African Union and Its Institutions,* eds. J. Akokpari, A. Ndinga-Muvumba, and T Murithi. Sunnyside: Fanele.

Ligue des Droits de la Personne dans la Region des Grands Lacs. 2007. "Critical Review of the APRM Process in Rwanda." Kigali: AfriMAP.

Logan, C., and M. Bratton. 2008. "Voters, but Not Yet Citizens? Democratization and Development Aid." In *Smart Aid for African Development*, eds. R. Joseph and A. Gillies. Boulder, Colorado: Lynne Rienner Publishers, 181–206.

Malachia, M. 2003. "An African Peer Review Mechanism: A Panacea for Africa's Governance Challenges?" Policy Brief 29, August. Johannesburg: Centre for Policy Studies.

Maloka, E. 2004. "NEPAD and its Critics." *Africa Insight* 34: 4. December.

Manby, B. 2007. "The APRM and the UNECA and OECD Mutual Review of Development Effectiveness: A Report for the Human Rights Council 8 Session of the Working Group on the Right to Development." Geneva, 7–15, January.

—. 2008. "Was the APRM process in Kenya a Waste of Time? Lessons that Should Be Learned for the Future." In The APRM Monitor 5, April.

Masterson, G. 2004. "Governance Quality and Governance Commitment to the NEPAD African Peer Review Mechanism." EISA Research Report 5. Johannesburg: EISA.

Matlosa, K. 2005. "Governance Research Agenda: Towards a Democracy Assessment Framework for Southern Africa." EISA Occasional Paper No. 35. Johannesburg: EISA.

—. 2008. "The Feasibility of a Union Government and a United States of Africa: Dilemmas of Political Integration and Democratisation." In *African Politics: Beyond the Third Wave of Democratization*, ed. J. Pretorius. Cape Town: Juta.

Mbeki, T. 2002. "Letter of Thabo Mbeki to Canadian Prime Minister Jean Chretien as Reproduced in *Business Day"* (Johannesburg). November 18. Accessed November 19, 2002, at: http://allafrica.com/stories/printable/200211180348.html.

Meyer, S., and N. Schulz. 2008. "Ownership with Adjectives. FRIDE Synthesis report – Donor Harmonization: Between Effectiveness and Democratization." http://www.fride.org/publication/435/ownership-with-adjectives

Mkandawire, T., and C. Soludu. 1999. *Our Continent, Our Future.* IDRC and Codesria Publication. Trenton, NJ: Africa World Press.

Mkandawire, T., and O. Olukoshi (eds). 1995. *Between Liberalisation and Repression: The Politics of Adjustment in Africa.* Dakar: Codesria.
Mkandawire, T., and O. Olukoshi (eds). 1996. "Economic Policy Making and the Consolidation of Democratic Institutions." In *Domination or Dialogue: Experiences and Prospects for African Development Co-operation*, eds. K. Havnevik and B. Van Arkadie. Upsalla, Sweden: Nordiska Afrikainstitet.
Mkandawire, T., and O. Olukoshi (eds). 2005. "An analysis of the Implementation of the African Peer Review Mechanism in Ghana, Kenya and Mauritius." EISA Occasional Paper No. 29. Johannesburg: EISA.
Mkandawire, T., O. Olukoshi, and C. Soludo (eds). 1999. *Our Continent, Our Future.* International Development Research Centre and Codesria. Trenton, NJ: Africa World Press.
Mohiddin, A. 2009. "The National Process of the African Peer Review Mechanism: Challenges and Opportunities." In *The African Union and New Strategies for Development in Africa,* eds. S. Adejumobi and A. Olukoshi. Codesria Books: Dakar.
Moss, T., G. Petterson, and N. van de Walle. 2006. An Aid-institutions Paradox? A Review Essay on Aid Dependency and State Building in Sub-Saharan Africa." Working Paper 74, Centre for Global Development, January.
Moyo, S. 2006. "Opening up Democratic Space for Citizen Participation in Inter-governmental Institutions in Africa." In *The State, Democracy and Poverty Eradication in Africa,* eds. K. Matlosa, K. Prah, B .Chirro, and L. Toulou. EISA Books.
Ndegwa, P., and R. H. Green. 1994. *Africa to 2000 and Beyond: Imperative Political and Economic Agenda.* Nairobi: East African Edition Publishers.
NEPAD. 2001. New Partnership for Africa's Development. Lusaka, Zambia.
—. 2002. NEPAD Action Plans. Mimeo. July. Midrand, South Africa.
—. 2003a. African Peer Review Mechanism (APRM). Mimeo. Midrand, South Africa.
—. 2003b. APRM Country Self-Assessment Questionnaire. Mimeo. Midrand, South Africa.
—. 2003c. Memorandum of Understanding on the African Peer Review Mechanism. Mimeo. Midrand, South Africa.
NEPAD/APRM. 2002. The African Peer Review Mechanism. Base Document. NEPAD/HSGIC/03-2003/APRM/MOU/ANNEX II.
—. 2003a. The African Peer Review Mechanism. Organisation and Processes. (NEPAD/HSGIC/03-2003/APRM/GUIDELINES/OandP)

—. 2003b. The African Peer Review Mechanism. Objectives, Standards, Criteria and Indicators. NEPAD/HSGIC/03-2003/APRM/GUIDE LINES/OSCI.

Nkuhlu, W. L. 2005. "The New Partnership for Africa's Development: The Journey so Far." Address on the state of NEPAD implementation. NEPAD Secretariat. Midrand, South Africa.

Nnadozie, E. 2009. "NEPAD, APRM and Institutional Change in Africa." In *The Elusive Prince of Denmark: Structural Adjustment and the Crisis of Governance in Africa,* eds. S. Adejumobi and A. Olukoshi. Conference proceedings on African perspective on structural adjustment. Abidjan, Cote d'Ivoire: Codesria.

Nnadozie, E., and S. Adejumobi (eds). *The African Union and New Strategies for Development in Africa.* Dakar: Codesria Books.

Nyerere, J. 1966. *Freedom and Unity.* Dar es Salaam, Tanzania: Oxford University Press:

Nyong'o, A., P. A. Ghirmazion, and D. Lamba (eds). 2002. *New Partnership for Africa's Development (NEPAD): A New Path?* Nairobi: Heinrich Boll Foundation.

OAU. 1990. "African Charter for Popular Participation in Development." Addis Ababa. Adopted in Arusha Conference on Popular Participation.

—. 2005. "Strategies for Enhancing Civil Society Participation in the APRM Process." Parliamentary paper for servicing the biennial meeting of the Committee of Human Development and Civil Society. DMD/O5/2005.

Obasanjo, O. 1999. Cited in Lancaster, C., 1999. *Aid in Africa: So Much to Do, So Little Done.* University of Chicago Press.

OECD DACa. 2005a. "Security System Reform and Governance –DAC Guidelines." Reference Document. OECD: Paris. http://www.oecd.org/dataoecd/8/39/31785288.pdf.

—. 2005b. "Lessons Learned on the use of Power and Drivers of Change Analysis in Development Cooperation." Review commissioned by the OECD DAC Network on Governance (GOVNET). http://www.gsdrc.org/docs/open/DOC82.pdf.

—. 2008. "Governance, Taxation and Accountability: Issues and Practice." DAC Guidelines and Reference Series, OECD: Paris. http://www.oecd.org/dataoecd/52/35/40210055.pdf

—. 2009. "Draft Workplan for the Aid and Accountability Workstream." 2009/10.

OECD. 2005a. "Development Cooperation Report." 7 (1).

—. 2005b. "Paris Declaration and Aid Effectiveness: Ownership, Harmonization, Alignment, Results and Mutual Accountability." Second High Level Forum, February 28–March 2, 2005. http://www.oecd.org/dataoecd/11/41/34428351.pdf.

—. 2006. "Aid Effectiveness: Three good reasons Why the Paris Declaration Will Make a Difference."

—. 2008a. "Accra Agenda for Action." Third High Level Forum on Aid Effectiveness. September 2–4, 2008. http://www.oecd.org/dataoecd/58/16/41202012.pdf.

—. 2008b. "Aid Effectiveness: A Progress Report on Implementing the Paris Declaration." OECD: Paris.

—. 2008c. "Aid Effectiveness: Compendium of Donor Reports on Disseminating the Paris Declaration. OECD: Paris.

—. 2008d. "Survey on Monitoring the Paris Declaration: Effective Aid by 2010? What It Will Take. OECD: Paris.

Ouma-Akoth, S. 2007. "The APRM Process in Kenya: A pathway to a new state." Osiea/AfriMAP.

Stiglitz, J. 2002. "Globalization and Its Discontents." WW Norton and Company: New York.

Stymer, S. 2009. "Governance Assessment and Domestic Accountability: Feeding Domestic Debate and Changing Aid Practices." FRIDE, Working Paper No. 86, June 2009.

Stymer, S., and N.S. Schulz. 2008. "Ownership with Adjectives: Donor Harmonization. Between Effectiveness and Democratization: Synthesis Report." FRIDE, Working Paper No. 59, March.

Tawfik, R. 2005. "NEPAD and African Development: Towards a New Partnership Between Development Actors in Africa." Paper presented at Eleventh General Assembly of the Council for the Development of Social Science Research in Africa. Dakar: Codesria.

Third High Level Forum on Aid Effectiveness. 2007. "Mutual Accountability: The Key Driver for Better Results." Third International Roundtable on Managing for Development Results 2007. Presented at Hanoi, Vietnam, February 2007.

Third High Level Forum on Aid Effectiveness. 2008. September 2–4, 2008. http://www.oecd.org/dataoecd/56/52/41572502.pdf

UNDP. 1990. "Human Development Report 1990." Oxford: Oxford University Press.

—. 2002. "Human Development Report 2002." Oxford: Oxford University Press.

—. 2006. "Implementing the African Peer Review Mechanism: Challenges and Opportunities." Report of the VI African Governance Forum at Kigali, May 9–11. http://www.undp.org/agf/

UNECA. 1988. "The African Alternative Framework for Structural Adjustment Programmes for Socio-economic Recovery and Transformation." Addis Ababa: UNECA.

—. 1990. "African Charter for Popular Participation in Development." Arusha, Tanzania.

—. 2005a. "African Governance Report." Addis Ababa: UNECA.

—. 2005b. "Strategies for Enhancing Civil Society Participation in the APRM Process." Parliamentary paper for servicing the biennial meeting of the Committee of Human Development and Civil Society, DMD/O5/2005.

—. 2009a. "African Governance Report." Oxford: Oxford University Press.

—. 2009b. "African Governance Report II." Addis Ababa: UNECA.

—. 2011. "Progress Report on the Implementation of the African Peer Review Mechanism." Addis Ababa: UNECA.

Unsworth, S. 2007. "Focusing Aid on Good Governance: Can it Work?" In *Exporting Good Governance: Temptations and Challenges in Canada's AID Program,* eds. J. Welsh and N. Woods. Waterloo, Ontario: Center for International Governance Innovation and Wilfred Laurier University Press.

Venter, D. 2003 "Democracy, Governance and Leadership: Towards an African Renewal." Otto Krause Memorial Fund: Occasional Paper Series, 1/2003. Johannesburg: Rand Afrikaans University.

Verwey, L. 2005. "NEPAD and Civil Society Participation in the APRM." Occasional Paper. Idasa – Budget Information Service, Africa Budget Project. www.un-ngls.org/cso/cso8/nepad.pdf.

Welsh, J., and N. Woods (eds). 2007. *Exporting Good Governance: Temptations and Challenges in Canada's AID Program.* Waterloo, Ontario: Center for International Governance Innovation and Wilfred Laurier University Press.

Whilhem, V., and P. Krause. 2007. "Minding the Gaps: Integrating Poverty Reduction Strategies and Budgets for Domestic Accountability." World Bank and GTZ.

Whitfield, L. (ed). 2009. *The Politics of Aid: African Strategies for Dealing with Donors.* Oxford: Oxford University Press.

Williamson, T., and Z. Kizilbash-Agha, with L. Bjornstad, G. Twijukje, Y. Mahwago, and G. Kabelwa. 2008. "Building Blocks or Stumbling Blocks? The Effectiveness of New Approaches to Aid Delivery at the

Sector Level." ABIA Project Working Paper 6, The Advisory Board for Irish Aid.
Wood, B., D. Kabell, N. Muwanga, and F. Sagasti. 2008. "Evaluation of the Paris Declaration." Prepared for the Accra High Level Forum on Aid Effectiveness.
World Bank. 1989. "Sub-Saharan Africa: From Crisis to Sustainable Growth: A Long-term Perspective Study." Washington, DC: World Bank.
—. 2002. "Source Book for Poverty Reduction Strategies." Washington, DC: World Bank.
—. 2006. "Good Practice Principles for the Application of Conditionality: A Progress Report." http://siteresources.worldbanl.org/PROJECTS/Resources/40940114615847789/Conditionalitypaperfinal.pdf.
World Bank/IMF. 2005. "Poverty Reduction Strategy Papers: Progress in Implementation." 2005 PRS Review. http://.siteresources.worldbank.org/INTPRS1/Resources/PRSPReview/2005prsreviewconceptnote.pdf.

# CHAPTER NINE

# PEACE DIVIDENDS AND PEACE IMPLEMENTATION IN AFRICA'S RECENT PAST

NIKOLAS G. EMMANUEL

## Introduction

While donor assistance can clearly be used in a variety of manners and achieve a wide range of outcomes, economic aid can be especially beneficial when offered to bolster post-conflict peace. War is devastating and can create a high risk of recurring violence over an extended period of time, even after peace has been achieved (Collier et. al 2003). To counter this risk, external assistance promised to combatants in exchange for overcoming their differences and agreeing to solve their problems through bargaining and negotiation may represent a potential peace dividend. Simply put, these funds can be used "to persuade formerly warring parties to resolve conflicts peacefully" and end violence indefinitely (Forman and Patrick 2000). In such cases, the cessation of combat may bring widespread hope to the exhausted rivals and citizens that a windfall of aid will follow an agreement, facilitating the transition to more peaceful relations in the future. Economic assistance offered to post-conflict societies in this manner can be an important tool for peace. The goal of this chapter is to advance a better understanding of the peace dividend dynamic.

When aid providers back negotiated settlements with financial resources, there is a significantly higher likelihood that such agreements will "stick" or last longer than those that do not receive such funding (Rothchild 2001, Rothchild and Emmanuel 2006, Emmanuel and Rothchild 2007). This is important because, as Collier and Hoeffler argue, after a negotiated settlement "there is a considerable risk that conflict will resume, and aid might directly reduce this risk (Collier and Hoeffler 2002)." While providing evidence in support of this assertion, the research presented in this chapter asks: to what extent does donor economic assistance 1) facilitate the successful achievement of peace agreements and 2) help reduce the probability of the reemergence of conflict once peace has been achieved? To date, the incentives provided from economic assistance during the negotiation and implementation periods of peace accords have been largely ignored. This study aims to fill a gap in the literature on the durability of negotiated settlements by adding the element of economic aid to the equation.

Aid after conflict has deep implications for donors and recipients alike. On the donor side, large amounts of foreign economic and humanitarian assistance have historically been directed to help facilitate peace and stabilize post-conflict situations once peace has been achieved. Donors clearly desire to have a positive impact in these instances. They gain from the resulting goodwill and from a strengthening of the international state system, the enhancement of international norms, and the extension of a zone of peace in which they can engage in commerce and investment. For the war-ravaged recipients, donor assistance should provide a strong incentive for peace. Extensive aid packages promised after the conclusion of a civil war can increase the size of the pie available for division among former warring factions. Such societies find themselves in desperate need of resources to rebuild out of the ashes of war. External economic aid can clearly help meet these needs.

Part of the logic behind providing a peace dividend (i.e., an extensive post-conflict economic development assistance package) during a peace process is that by holding out the prospect of aid, the external actor or actors may be able to promote a successful settlement of the conflict by making the former combatants stakeholders in the new and hopefully more prosperous post-conflict order. It seems apparent that states and non-state rebel groups alike should be greatly influenced by such offers of development assistance. Central to this plan is the idea that a peace dividend can assist in alleviating the initial grievances that led to the conflict. Former combatants can convince their respective constituencies to pursue peace by touting the benefits of economic aid, including humanitarian assistance, reintegration of combatants, economic recovery, and the rebuilding of physical infrastructure, among other activities. As Cortright argues, aid should make the prospect of peaceful relations generally more attractive (Cortright 1997). Properly targeted economic aid does appear to matter in achieving lasting peace.

The research in this paper is broken down into four sections. First, economic development assistance is framed as an incentive offered during the negotiation and implementation phases of peace agreements. It is offered as a carrot to induce compliance. Second, the three primary economic aid patterns provided by donors at the end of—and following the end of—intrastate conflicts are discussed. These patterns are illustrated with brief case studies that focus on how economic aid packages have (or have not) impacted the peace process in each instance. Third, the recent theoretical and empirical literature is examined for alternative explanations of increased or diminished success and endurance of negotiated settlements. Finally, a statistical analysis of the impact of donor economic aid on the success rate of recent peace agreements in Africa is presented, along with the competing factors outlined in part three. The analysis includes a survey of sixty-five negotiated settlements in Africa during the fifteen years immediately following the fall of the Berlin Wall (i.e., 1989–2004). These dates are examined because of the dramatic increase in the use of peace agreements to settle intrastate wars during this period, as well as the increased availability of data on the subject.

## Aid as an Incentive in Negotiated Settlements in Africa

According to my hypothesis, donor economic assistance should act as a strong incentive for peace when offered during settlement negotiations and for the implementation period. Clearly, the timing of external intervention should matter in determining the type of aid necessary, and in helping to provide the strongest incentive possible. On the one hand, donor aid given during the negotiation phase should facilitate capacity building. On the other hand, economic development assistance may be more necessary for reconstruction in the implementation period once the country begins to function in a more post-war setting. Both types of aid (capacity building and reconstruction) provide important incentives and need to be offered in a well-orchestrated manner as part of a comprehensive peace dividend.

These types of incentives emerge when outside third parties (i.e., donors) offer material benefits to draw warring parties "sufficiently dissatisfied with their present costs … or future prospects" into a bargaining process (Zartman 2001). The adversaries should desire to agree to peace in order to gain the benefits that follow from ending the uncertainty of protracted conflict and creating new possibilities for economic development. In this context, incentives consist of distributive rewards that encourage the government and insurgents to shift their priorities and agree to a compromise on the major issues in contention (Rothchild 1997). For all parties involved, the incentives provided by the external peace dividend represent a significant investment in peace. Furthermore, and perhaps more centrally to the argument presented in this research, peace dividends encourage commitment to established political institutions and norms and raise the costs of breaking the new social contract and returning to war.

Negotiated settlements consist of peace agreements reached by at least two opposing belligerents in a conflict. According to Wallensteen and Sollenberg (1997), such accords are fundamentally an understanding of how the parties will "explicitly regulate or resolve their basic incompatibility (Wallensteen and Sollenberg 1997)." In addressing these problems, negotiated settlements spell out how the "warring parties contract to halt organized violence and redress outstanding political, social, and/or economic grievances (Toft 2010)." In the five decades following the Second World War, the vast majority of civil wars were decided by outright victory of either the state or the rebels (Pillar 1983; Stedman 1991). This changed as the global system shifted after the end of the Cold War. Since then, many intrastate conflicts have been ended through the achievement of peace agreements (H artzell and Hoddie 2007; Toft 2010). Especially in Africa, there has been a dramatic increase over the past two decades in the use of bargaining and negotiated settlements to end civil war. Recently, a number of well-known conflicts, such as those in the Democratic Republic of the Congo (DRC) or the Sudan's North-South war, among others, have ended with negotiated peace agreements (Harbom, Hogbladh, and Wallensteen 2006).

However, peace is not easily achieved through negotiation and bargaining. This is because the stakes are extremely high in war, especially in internal conflicts. As Roy Licklider points out, a key assumption is that civil wars are "difficult to resolve by negotiation" because the rival parties have to share the same state institutions and resources and live next to each other as neighbors once the fighting subsides (Licklider 1995). This leads to an exceptionally high risk of recurring violence and the frequent failure of negotiated settlements. This is true in Africa, as elsewhere. The implementation period is a perilous time for former combatants. Fundamentally, it is hard to judge whether the other side's commitment to peace is genuine. It is extremely difficult to obtain accurate and reliable information about an adversary's intentions. Are they using the peace process to stall and re-arm? Once an agreement is reached, will the other side abide by the agreement in the future? These are among the many questions that plague peace processes. It has been argued that this period is so difficult that most agreements do not hold even long enough to attain the implementation period (Stedman, Rothchild, and Cousens 2002). Licklider adds empirical support for the fact that peace agreements break down into renewed fighting much more often than do outright military victories by state or rebel groups (Licklider 1995). Yet among the sixty-five African peace accords scrutinized in this research, twenty-two (or 34 percent) lasted beyond five years. This demonstrates how difficult it is to achieve a negotiated settlement, though it is possible. However, in this group of African cases, when an extensive economic aid package was offered by donors during the peace process, almost half (47 percent) of negotiated settlements were successful beyond five years. Economic aid does appear to have an impact on the possibility of achieving sustainable peace.

## Three Patterns in Post-conflict Economic Aid Distributions

Three noticeable patterns can be distinguished in the economic aid trajectories of post-conflict countries: 1) sustained increases, 2) unsustained spikes, and 3) no increase (including decline). Each of these donor aid distributions has a distinct impact on the success or failure of negotiated peace settlements.

### Pattern 1: Sustained increase in economic assistance

Years of protracted warfare can leave a country devastated, with its infrastructure destroyed and its economic capacity in ruins. Rebuilding from the debris of war can prove extremely costly. In many cases, reconstruction depends upon the generosity of the international community. Furthermore, donor promises to contribute assistance can play a large part in moving negotiations between warring parties forward at critical junctures, and maintaining them once they are reached. In these cases, the Organization for Economic Cooperation and Development (OECD) donors use economic aid as an incentive to encourage the negotiating parties to reach a compromise and end their devastating conflict. Although outside the time range (1989–2004) for the quantitative element of this research, Zimbabwe presents a fascinating illustrative case for the phenomenon examined here.

Certainly aid donors can exert a considerable influence on the behavior of various actors negotiating peace accords, and Zimbabwe's transition to majority rule is striking in this manner. In 1979, the British government convened a conference at Lancaster House in London. In the ensuing negotiations the U.K. orchestrated a settlement to end the war and transfer power to majority rule, while providing some safeguards for the white minority. While the British played the central role in the negotiating process, the U.S. closely supported their efforts by providing important economic aid incentives at critical junctures. Reflecting on the role of these incentives in the negotiations, former U.S. President Jimmy Carter pointed out that "there's no doubt that to some degree financial promises played a role" in inducing the warring factions to accept the Lancaster House Agreement (Rothchild 1997).

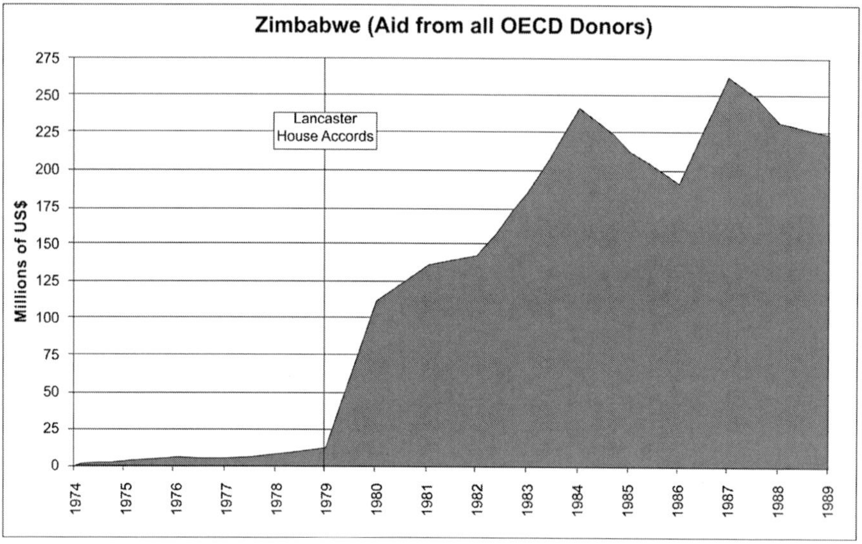


Figure 9.1. Zimbabwe (Aid from OECD Donors)

Land was the core issue for the Patriotic Front, and it came close to undoing the peace process. To overcome the impasse, President Carter pledged to contribute considerable aid once the negotiations reached a successful outcome. U.S. officials insisted that the money was not designed to buy out white-owned farms, but to be used for broader development purposes such as increasing agricultural production or boosting educational and job opportunities for the majority (Rothchild 1997). This incentive encouraged Patriotic Front leaders Robert Mugabe and Joshua Nkomo to sign on to participate in the Lancaster House peace process (Rothchild 1997). In return, the new majority government would provide certain guarantees to the white-minority community. It was stipulated that for a ten-year period land ownership in Zimbabwe could only be transferred on a "willing seller, willing buyer" basis, which was opposed by some as effectively limiting the extent of land reform. Furthermore, to reassure the European community, a parliamentary quota of twenty seats out of a total of one hundred elected on a communal roll basis— far exceeding the community's actual percentage of the population—was allotted for at least seven years. The economic aid incentives provided by the donors helped move the peace process forward.

As in other Pattern 1 cases, the peace dividend proved substantial for Zimbabwe. Donors committed to providing more than $2 billion dollars in economic reconstruction and development aid for Zimbabwe over ten years as part of an effort to facilitate the bargain reached at Lancaster House in 1979. The offer was enticing enough to harden "the political resolve of internal actors to maintain the momentum of the peace process (Boyce 1996)." While the peace dividends offered in this pattern represent positive donor incentives capable of facilitating bargaining, Patterns 2 and 3 fail to provide such hope.

## Pattern 2: Unsustained Spike in Economic Assistance

Two related but somewhat different issues come together when peace dividends are offered. On the one hand, economic aid is presented by an outside third party or parties as an incentive to help move peace negotiations and implementation forward. On the other hand, this same package of donor aid is offered to consolidate a negotiated settlement by addressing major obstacles to peace through, for example, reconstruction of physical infrastructure, institution building, employment generation, etc. In Pattern 1 cases, this economic aid is used for the consolidation of peace while being offered as an incentive during the negotiations. That is to say, consolidation aid is waved in front of the combatants as a carrot to facilitate successful negotiations. However, in Pattern 2 cases, primarily humanitarian aid is given during negotiations and is not used as an incentive to facilitate a peace process. This type of assistance is a band-aid, not an incentive.

In Pattern 2 the recipient experiences a sharp, but unsustained, spike in donor assistance given in an effort to facilitate peace. This type of donor response is similar to that elicited by natural disasters, in which large amounts of humanitarian relief are provided over a somewhat short period of time. The objective in these instances is to get targeted emergency aid to at-risk populations as quickly as possible and to stabilize an urgent situation. However, this is expected to have little impact on the calculus of former combatants in concluding and maintaining peace agreements, primarily because of the short-lived nature of the aid. Somalia in the early 1990s presents an excellent example of this outcome.

In these instances, aid pours into the recipient country swiftly after a catastrophic event (i.e. famine, earthquake, hurricane, etc.) as donors attempt to alleviate immediate needs. In most cases this influx of aid quickly falls back to pre-disaster levels and can be recognized as an aid spike, as seen in Figure 2 below. Foreign aid donors frequently respond to conflict situations in this manner as well. These man-made disasters cause an enormous amount of human suffering and insecurity that require urgent attention. Food production and distribution is disrupted in most cases. State services are frequently nonexistent, leaving civilians in extremely precarious situations. This often leads international donors to provide food aid and emergency medical assistance. Yet, as with natural catastrophes, once the immediate short-term crisis appears to be over, donors tend to shy away from costly longer-term programs of reconstruction and development. The resulting aid spike does not represent a peace dividend, and in turn "this pattern does little to consolidate peace (Emmanuel and Rothchild 2007)."

Although all cases are unique, Somalia represents one of the clearest examples of this "aid spike" distribution pattern. Massive amounts of humanitarian aid surged into Somalia from 1992–1994 as the international community tried to alleviate widespread famine. This emergency food and medical assistance poured into the country at the same time that an international military intervention, led by U.S. and UN forces, was put into place—initially to protect aid distribution from the insecurity that reigned in the country. Shortly after this humanitarian-military intervention began, however, it became clear that, in addition to ending the food emergency, a political solution to Somalia's problems was needed.

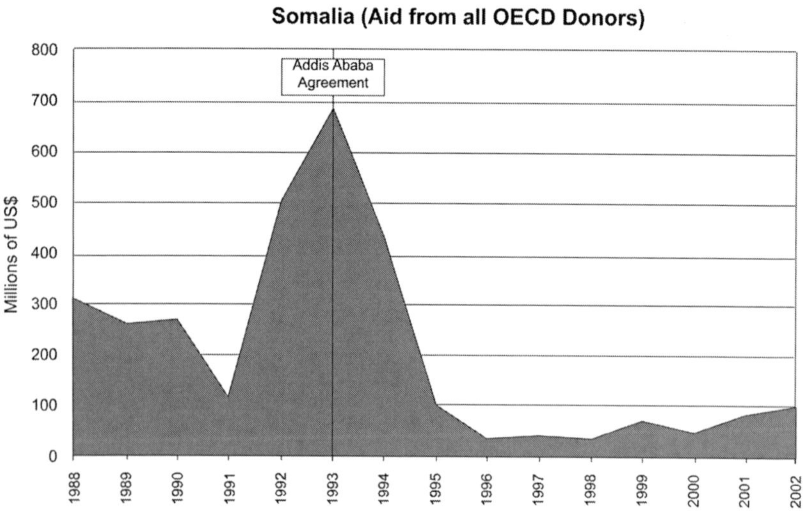


Figure 9.2. Somalia (Aid from all OECD Donors)

Shortly after the landing of U.S. marines on the shores of Somalia in December, 1992, UN officials began efforts to bring together the various militias and political factions. Early in 1993, the main Somali groups met as part of the Conference on National Reconciliation in Somalia under the auspices of the UN. This resulted in the Addis Ababa Agreement, made among the primary fifteen factions on March 27, 1993, in an effort to find a political solution to the mounting insecurity in the country. The attempted peace process clearly failed to end the violence, which spun out of control in the following months.

In Somalia, as with other Pattern 2 cases, although the need was tremendous, economic assistance was not offered to push the peace process forward. Large amounts of short-term emergency aid were provided, but this was not linked in any way to a political solution or to negotiated settlement. Here, economic aid was not an incentive for peace.

## Pattern 3: No Increase in Post-conflict Aid

Pattern 3 cases see no increase in aid allocations after reaching a negotiated settlement. Frequently, economic assistance may even decline after the conclusion of warfare. Here donors have little faith in the peace process and decide not to fund reconstruction. This can have an obvious negative impact on the likelihood that warring parties will reach a lasting peace. Interestingly, such donor responses are relatively commonplace. For over half of the African negotiated settlements explored in this research, the countries involved experienced either a decrease or no increase in assistance during their respective peace processes. This group includes: Algeria, the Central African Republic, Chad, Comoros, the Republic of Congo (Brazzaville), Côte d'Ivoire, Djibouti, Ethiopia, Guinea-Bissau, Mali, and Mozambique.

Ethiopia is an excellent example of this type of donor response. There was no instance of a peace dividend to share among exhausted combatants. External efforts to facilitate reconciliation in such a manner were nonexistent. In early 1991, after a long, bitter civil war, the regime of Mengistu Haile Mariam was on the verge of collapse. An assortment of rebel groups began seizing towns across the country, while the main rebel umbrella organization, the Ethiopian People's Revolutionary Democratic Front (EPRDF), was poised to take over the capital, Addis Ababa. No longer being able to count on support from the Soviet Union for assistance, and encircled by EPRDF forces on all sides, Mengistu was forced to flee into exile in Zimbabwe. The U.S. coordinated Mengistu's departure with the help of Zimbabwean President Robert Mugabe. When asked why Mengistu went into exile, a senior American official in Washington simply stated: "That's what we told him to do."[1] As the rebels prepared their assault on the Ethiopian capital, the U.S., fearing that a battle would destroy the city and cause countless casualties, brokered a ceasefire agreement in London in May 1991, asking the insurgent groups to pause at the outskirts of the capital city (Emmanuel and Rothchild 2007). In subsequent negotiations, U.S. Assistant Secretary of State for African Affairs Herman Cohen recommended that the Tigrean People's Liberation Front (TPLF), the dominant wing of the EPRDF, enter and take control of Addis Ababa to restore order (Cohen 1991). Two months later, in July 1991, the EPRDF, the Oromo Liberation Front (OLF), and other major former-rebel factions agreed to a transitional constitution establishing a Transitional Government of Ethiopia (Emmanuel and Rothchild 2007).

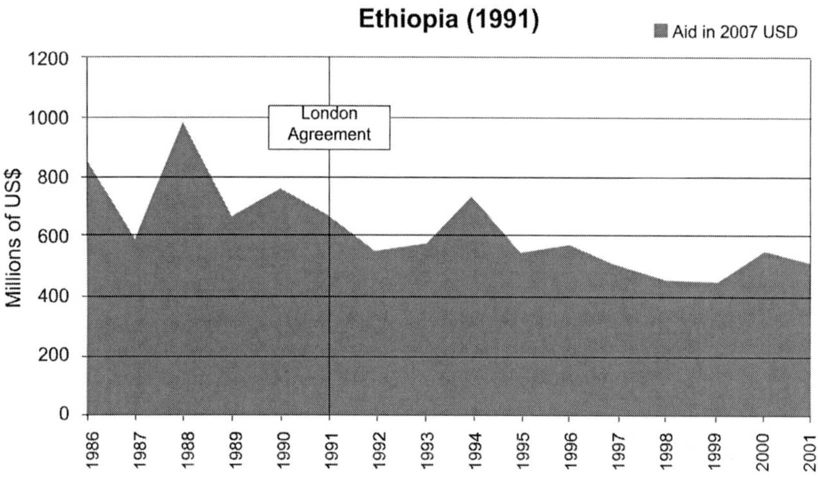


Figure 9.3. OECD/DAC Aid to Ethiopia

However, although the United States did back the peace process diplomatically, a peace dividend did not follow the negotiated settlement in Ethiopia. Unlike the Pattern 1 and 2 cases, where aid levels rise, Ethiopia did not experience an increase in assistance after the American-orchestrated conclusion of its civil war. As seen in Figure 3 above, outlays from OECD/DAC (Development Cooperation Directorate) donors to Ethiopia actually declined in the first two years after the agreement, then increased somewhat for one year, and finally fell abruptly back to levels below that seen during the war. Alex de Waal points out that this might perhaps have been because donors were not reassured by the democratic and human rights credentials of the new regime in Addis Ababa (de Waal 1992). However, it should be noted that economic aid from the U.S. rose sharply in the 2000s. Today Ethiopia is receiving something in the neighborhood of $3 billion in aid.

## Assessing the Impact of Peace Dividends in African Negotiated Settlements

Going beyond descriptive illustrations of the impact of these aid patterns on peace processes with brief case studies, it is desirable to search for generalizations about the relationship between peace dividends and negotiated agreements in Africa's recent past. In this section, the chapter's hypothesis [donor economic assistance should act as a strong incentive for peace when offered during settlement negotiations and for the implementation period] is analyzed statistically to provide a more detailed assessment of the overall relationship. Before going on to the statistical analysis, however, I would like to discuss the data, the dependent variable, and the explanatory variables operationalized in this study.

**Table 9.1: African Cases with Attempted Negotiated Settlements, 1989–2004**

| | |
|---|---|
| Algeria | Liberia |
| Angola | Mali |
| Burundi | Mozambique |
| Central African Repuplic | Niger |
| Chad | Rwanda |
| Comoros | Senegal |
| Congo Republic | Sierra Leone |
| DR Congo | Somalia |
| Djibouti | South Africa |
| Côte d'Ivoire | Sudan |
| Ethiopia | Uganda |
| Guinea-Bissau | |

The quantitative approach used here includes sixty-five negotiated peace settlements from intrastate conflicts across twenty-three Africa countries between 1989 and 2004 (see Appendix 1).[2] Low-intensity conflicts are also included in the dataset (i.e., where there have been at least twenty-five battle deaths in a given year). This takes account of conflicts in Casamance (Senegal) and Northern Niger, even though they do not meet the one thousand battle deaths-threshold used in datasets such as the Correlates of War. Table 9.1 provides a list of the countries involved in the analysis.

Information on these cases was obtained from the Uppsala Conflict Data Program's (UCDP) Armed Conflict and Peace Agreements dataset (UCDP 2006). The UCDP database begins providing information on its cases in 1989, the same year used as a starting point for the analysis in this study. As indicated earlier, there is also a theoretical reason for this start date, beyond the availability of data. Primarily, since the end of the Cold War, there has been an upsurge in the amount of intrastate conflict in which negotiated settlements have been attempted, especially in Africa. I have chosen to end the analysis with cases from 2004 in order to allow for the availability of five years of economic assistance data following each peace accord. This allows me to examine the immediate aid trajectory after the attainment of an agreement and compare this post-conflict assistance pattern with that from the five years before the accord. In all, ten years of data are analyzed. As of March, 2010, aid data from the OECD's Development Assistance Committee, used in this study, ended in 2008.[3]

My dataset, therefore, examines five years of Official Development Assistance figures (i.e., ODA net, excluding any debt relief, using 2007 constant U.S. dollars) from all OECD/DAC donors, starting with the accord year and continuing four years beyond it. The data is examined to judge the immediate post-conflict aid pattern, looking for what is referred to in this study as the peace dividend. The percent increase in ODA from the five years after the accord (including the accord year), compared with the ODA provided in the five years before the accord, represents the critical independent variable used in this study. This allows my study to judge whether a peace dividend is present in a given case, and if so, what impact it had on the dependent variable. For example, South Africa saw an aid increase of over 900 percent between these two periods, while Rwanda experienced a rise of 50 percent, and Ethiopia's economic assistance actually decreased about 20 percent, comparing the periods before and after their negotiated settlement.

As pointed out earlier, a significant aid package distributed along the lines of the Pattern 1 cases should help former belligerents achieve a negotiated settlement lasting beyond the five-year threshold established in the literature (Licklider 1995; Hartzell 1999; Walter 1997, 2002; Hoddie and Hartzell 2003). Accordingly, the dependent variable used in this study codes negotiated settlements as being successful (1) if peace is maintained for at least five years (i.e., no new outbreak of intrastate conflict) after the accord. Those cases in which a peace agreement does not succeed are coded with a zero (0). This variable is drawn from two sources that indicate the dates of a given conflict. The data are from the International Peace Research Institute, Oslo (PRIO) on armed conflict and the Center for Systemic Peace's "Major Episodes of Political Violence: 1946-2009 (Gleditsch et al. 2002; Marshall 2010)."

From the data used in this study, twenty-two of the sixty-five (or 34 percent) negotiated settlements in Africa from 1989 to 2004 resulted in peaceful interactions for at least five years. Inversely, this means that about two-thirds of all African negotiated settlements over this fifteen-year period failed, leading to renewed bouts of violence after the conclusion of an agreement. The success rate among recent African peace accords appears to be lower than what has been seen in previous studies. Licklider indicates that about half of all negotiated settlements break down in their first five years (although he uses a different time period and group of cases) (Licklider 1995).

## Independent Variables and Hypothesized Relationships

The next step in this study is to explore the data for some generalizable relationships between the dependent variable (i.e., the success or failure of a negotiated settlement to lead to lasting peace), post-conflict aid distributions, and five control variables found throughout the literature on the topic, including: the presence of peacekeeping operations after an agreement, Gross National Income (GNI)/capita at purchasing power parity (PPP) at the time of the agreement, the inclusion of power-sharing mechanisms in the negotiated settlement, total battle deaths during the conflict, and the duration of the conflict in years. The objective is to test the strength of the argument that aid matters when controlling for these other factors. However, before directly going on to the statistical analysis, over the following pages I would like to provide some additional information concerning the explanatory variables used in this study and their operationalization. To begin with, the table below points out the hypothesized interactions between the independent variables used in this study and the likelihood of the success or failure of negotiated settlements.

| Independent Variables | INCREASE Likelihood of a Successful Negotiated Settlement | DECREASE or NO IMPACT on the Likelihood of a Successful Negotiated Settlement |
|---|---|---|
| Substantial Aid Increase | X | |
| Aid Spike | | X |
| Peacekeeping | X | |
| Low GNI/capita at PPP | | X |
| Political Power-sharing | | X |
| High Intensity Conflict | X | X |

**Table 9.2: Hypothesized relationships**[4]

*Post-conflict economic assistance patterns*

This study argues that a substantial and sustained increase in economic assistance after an agreement (i.e., a peace dividend) should have a positive impact on the longevity of a negotiated settlement.

Hypothesis 1: A significant increase in aid after a negotiated settlement should increase the probability of peace beyond five years.

To capture this dynamic, as discussed in the previous section, I operationalize the critical aid variable by comparing the overall economic assistance from all OECD/DAC donors for five years before the accord with the total of ODA from five years following the agreement (starting with the accord year). This study uses OECD data concerning total ODA net, measured in constant 2007 US dollars, excluding debt forgiveness from all DAC donors. The example of the ODA flows from before and after the 2002 Machakos Protocol between the Sudanese government in Khartoum and the Sudanese People's Liberation Army/Movement (SPLA/M) illustrates this.

| Millions of US$ (constant 2007) | **1997** | **1998** | **1999** | **2000** | **2001** | **2002** | **2003** | **2004** | **2005** | **2006** |
|---|---|---|---|---|---|---|---|---|---|---|
| **Sudan** | 130 | 230 | 224 | 149 | 176 | **317** | 409 | 978 | 1610 | 1618 |

**Table 9.3: The Machakos Protocol (2002) and Total ODA net to Sudan**

In the five years before the Machakos Protocol in 2002, Sudan received a total of $909 million in economic assistance from DAC donors. This is compared with a monumental $4.924 billion in the five years following the negotiated settlement (2002–2006). This represents a phenomenal 442 percent increase in economic assistance from the DAC donors for the five years following the accord, compared with total ODA net before the accord. This type of aid pattern should increase the likelihood that peace will last.

Additionally, this study posits that a dramatic, unsustained increase in donor assistance, along the lines of a response to a natural disaster, does little to help cement a peace agreement.

Hypothesis 2: An unsustained spike in economic aid is not expected to increase the likelihood that a negotiated settlement will be successful beyond five years.

This hypothesis is operationalized as a dichotomous variable, with one (1) being used to indicate a brief spike in aid.

*Peacekeeping operations*

The intervention of peacekeeping forces (i.e., the United Nations, major powers, regional bodies, sub-regional actors, etc.) should help maintain a negotiated settlement once it has been achieved because outside third parties can help the former belligerents maintain peaceful relations. Peacekeeping operations are put into place to separate belligerents, monitor ceasefires, maintain buffer zones, and to enhance the general security situation in post-conflict situations (Heldt 2008). Clearly, the impact of peacekeeping should be positive on agreement duration and has been discussed in the literature for quite some time now (Touval 1982). Barbara Walter provides the clearest reasons for this (Walter 1997). She states that external third parties, such as the United Nations, help raise the likelihood of success of a negotiated settlement because the interveners help provide credible commitments to support and enforce the terms of an agreement.

Peacekeeping forces facilitate the settlement by reducing fear among former combatants that the other side will cheat on the agreement and use the negotiating process to rearm and potentially take the upper-hand. Doyle and Sambanis (2000, p.795) go even further and conclude that "peacemaking aimed at facilitating a peace treaty is potentially life-saving" and can "help secure longer-term peace (Doyle and Sambanis 2000)." Fortna (2003, 111) in her analysis also supports this hypothesis, indicating that "peace lasts longer when peacekeepers are present than when belligerents are left to their own devices. In other words, peacekeeping works."

Hypothesis 3: The presence of peacekeeping operations should increase the likelihood of a successful settlement.

Since the end of the Cold War, third parties have intervened widely following African conflicts. Thirty-four of the sixty-five agreements (52.3 percent) in Africa between 1989 and 2004 were supported by a variety of third-party peacekeeping forces. Some of the largest operations were undertaken by the UN. These include MONUC, with over twenty thousand UN peacekeepers in the Democratic Republic of the Congo (DRC), and UNMIL, with over fifteen thousand military personnel deployed in Liberia. Additionally, the hybrid African Union and UN mission to Darfur (Sudan), referred to as UNAMID, has over twenty thousand armed personnel in place. These peacekeeping operations on the African continent represent the most extensive deployment of troops under UN command anywhere on the planet, and throughout the organization's history. The data for this variable is drawn from Heldt (2008) and is coded as a dichotomous variable, that is, (1) represents a peacekeeping operation present after the accord; (0) indicates no peacekeeping operation is present (Heldt 2008).

*Economic conditions*

Poor economic conditions should decrease the likelihood that a negotiated settlement will be successful. Collier and Hoeffler indicate that factors such as GDP per capita can provide good indicators of the opportunity costs for individuals to participate in politically-motivated violence (Collier and Hoeffler 2004, 1998). When potential income levels are low, the payoff for joining a rebellion can exceed the earnings from more legitimate economic activities. Barbara Walter also explores these micro-level economic motivations for the breakdown of peace agreements and the recurrence of civil wars (Walter 2004). From previous research, it appears that the unavailability of jobs and the presence of low wages can act as an incentive for individuals to join (or return to) a rebel group. If the job supply is adequate and wages are relatively high, alternative options exist and taking part in a rebellion looks less attractive. This makes recruitment more difficult and undermines the potential of various groups to mount an insurgency.

Hypothesis 4: Low incomes should decrease the success of a peace agreement.

In this study's sample of cases, GNI per capita at purchasing power parity (PPP) averages only US$895 (at current international US dollars) according to the World Bank's World Development Indicators (World Bank 2010). This puts almost all of the African cases in this study into the World Bank's low-income group. This should generally have a negative impact on the possibility of ending conflict through negotiated settlement. To assess this factor, I use the GNI/capita at PPP variable (at current international US dollars) from the WDI and log the results.

*Political power-sharing mechanisms*

It seems to make sense that the inclusion of political power-sharing mechanisms in a peace agreement should enhance the settlement's likelihood of success. Not only the environment of the peace agreement matters, but the content of the accord itself should have a consequence on its success or failure. However, the existing literature on the impact of political power-sharing provisions in negotiated settlements appears to indicate that these types of institutions do little to facilitate lasting peace.[5]

Hypothesis 5: The presence of political power-sharing arrangements in peace agreements should have little impact on the likelihood of success of negotiated settlements over time.

I constructed this independent variable using the Peace Research Institute Oslo/ Uppsala Conflict Data Program (PRIO/UCDP) data (Harbom, Högbladh, and Wallensteen 2006). The resulting indicator creates a dichotomous variable that codes (1) for those accords with elements of political power-sharing, and (0) for those without such mechanisms.

*Conflict intensity (battle deaths and conflict duration)*

There is a contradiction in the literature on the success of peace agreements after particularly brutal and long civil conflicts. On the one hand, does wariness set in and push tired combatants toward an agreement (Mooradian and Druckman 1999)? Perhaps a mutually hurting stalemate

can help bring exhausted warring parties to the bargaining table, as for example in places like Sudan (North-South conflict). On the other hand, is it possible that sunken costs and bitter memories propel a conflict onward? Along these lines, Walter argues that "wars that inflict high costs on combatants and supporters could exacerbate animosity between them and create a strong desire for retribution even if the war ends (Walter 2004)." Therefore, intense violence should decrease the probability of reaching a lasting peace. Recent quantitative research points to this second hypothesis. In their studies, Doyle et al. (2000), Hartzel et al. (2001), and Quinn et al. (2007) agree with Walter and find that peace is harder to achieve in situations where the conflict costs are high (Doyle et al. 2000; Hartzel et al. 2001; and Quinn et al. 2007).
Hypothesis 6a: High intensity conflicts should increase the success of peace-building processes.

Hypothesis 6b: High intensity conflict should decrease the success of peace-building processes.

To test these two opposing hypotheses, I operationalize two additional control variables. First, this study examines the impact of annual battle deaths (logged) from PRIO/UCDP (Lacina and Gleditsch 2005). Second, the overall duration of a given conflict in years (logged) is deployed. Both explanatory factors are used to approximate the costs and intensity of a given conflict.

## Statistical Results

Can the provision of a peace dividend increase the likelihood that a negotiated settlement will endure beyond the five-year threshold established in the literature? In addressing this question, this study uses a logistic regression technique to compare the impact of the varying patterns of economic assistance with several control variables on a base of sixty-five recent peace agreements in Africa. However, before continuing, it must be pointed out that the statistical conclusions in this study must be tempered due to problems related to determining the direction of causation. That is to say, although case-based information leads me to believe that in most instances economic aid contributions are acting as an incentive that leads former warring factions to sign on to negotiated peace settlements, some may find it possible to argue the opposite—that successful peace agreements are attracting large sums of donor aid. This is not an easy problem to address. Yet, I must add again that based on information drawn from the numerous country-cases used in this study, it appears that peace dividends are being used as incentives by donors and that in some situations this aid is having a positive impact on peace processes, not the opposite.

In testing for basic statistical correlations between variables, before conducting the logistic regression, it became obvious that the proxies used for conflict intensity (i.e., overall conflict battle deaths and total conflict duration) inter-correlate at a rather high level (0.63). As a result, the logistic regression using these control variables will have to be divided into two models, one with the battle deaths variable and the other using the indicator for conflict duration. An additional model, only including the aid variables, has been used in order to examine these factors in relationship with the dependent variable without the presence of the controls. The statistical results of this can be seen in Table 9.4 below.

| Independent Variables: | Model 1 Coef. (S.E.) | sig. | Model 2 Coef. (S.E.) | sig. | Model 3 Coef. (S.E.) | sig. |
|---|---|---|---|---|---|---|
| Peace Dividend | 1.087 (0.395) | ** | 1.199 (0.507) | ** | 1.271 (0.525) | ** |
| Aid Spike | -0.889 (0.858) | | -0.834 (0.876) | | -0.916 (0.893) | |
| Peacekeeping | | | 0.291 (0.719) | | 0.324 (0.712) | |
| GNI/Capita@PPP (logged) | | | 0.302 (1.069) | | 0.267 (1.086) | |
| Political Power-Sharing | | | -0.888 (0.744) | | -0.904 (0.748) | |
| Battle Deaths (logged) | | | 0.151 (0.341) | | | |
| Conflict Duration (logged) | | | | | -0.141 (0.686) | |
| N=65 | Pseudo R2 = 0.203 | | Pseudo R2 = 0.227 | | Pseudo R2 = 0.225 | |

Note: * = p < .1, **= p < .05, *** = p < .01

**Table 9.4: Logistic Regression Analysis Results**

Several interesting observations can be made from these statistical results. First and foremost, it is important to note that the critical variable used to determine the impact of the peace dividend is consistently positive and is statistically significant (at a level of $p < .05$) across all three models. This suggests that external aid donors can and do play a critical role in helping peace processes to be successful. The willingness of assistance providers to back negotiated settlements with financial resources appears to increase the likelihood that peace will endure beyond the five-year threshold discussed in the literature. This gives credence to the argument that a peace dividend can support former belligerents in getting through the critical implementation period of a peace process. The promise of a peace dividend gives them something to hope for, while significantly raising the costs of returning to war. None of the control variables is statistically significant, although for the most part they lead in the expected directions. Relative to the peace dividend variable, these additional factors do not appear to have much of an influence on the success of an accord among African cases. This may have important ramifications for aid donors and recipients alike. Based on these results, post-conflict economic assistance seems to be a critical element in achieving lasting peace.

## Conclusion

This research sheds light on the importance of economic assistance in sustaining peace after the signing of a negotiated settlement. Among recent African cases, I find that when donors provide significant and sustained post-conflict aid, peace agreements are much more likely to endure. That is to say, peace dividends reduce the likelihood of civil war recurrence beyond the five-year threshold established in the literature. For the results presented here, it appears obvious that a significant increase in donor aid can raise the probability of a lasting peace in two ways. First, peace dividends help alleviate some of the grievances that led to the conflict initially. Second, substantial development assistance after an intrastate conflict can provide a strong incentive for the state and rebels alike to successfully implement a negotiated settlement. This can work to convince former combatants and their constituencies of the fruits of ending conflict. If lasting peace is to be achieved, donors must realize how truly important their efforts are. Aid matters much more than anticipated.

# Appendix 1: Peace Accords, Agreement Stability, and Aid Change (1989-2004)

| Country | Agreement Name | Accord Year | DV Stable Agreement? (5 years) | Aid Change |
|---|---|---|---|---|
| Algeria | Concorde Nationale | 1997 | NO | -0.481 |
| Angola | Gbadolite Declaration | 1989 | NO | 0.299 |
| Angola | Bicesse Agreement | 1991 | NO | 0.363 |
| Angola | Lusaka Protocol | 1994 | NO | 0.403 |
| Angola | Memorandum of Intent | 2002 | YES | -0.085 |
| Burundi | Arusha Peace and Reconciliation Agreement | 2000 | NO | 0.394 |
| Burundi | Accord du Cessez-le-feu entre le Gouvernement de Transition du Burundi et le CNDD-FDD | 2002 | NO | 1.331 |
| Burundi | The Global Ceasefire agreement between Transitional Government and the Forces pour la defence de la democratie (CNDD-FDD) of Mr. Nkúrunziza | 2003 | NO | 1.183 |
| CAR | National Reconciliation Pact | 1998 | NO | -0.446 |
| Chad | El Geneina agreement | 1992 | NO | -0.289 |
| Chad | Tripoli 1 Agreement | 1993 | NO | -0.33 |
| Chad | Abeche agreement | 1994 | NO | -0.396 |
| Chad | The Dougia Accord | 1995 | NO | -0.388 |
| Chad | National reconciliation agreement | 1997 | NO | -0.365 |
| Chad | Donya agreement | 1998 | NO | -0.376 |
| Chad | Reconciliation agreement | 1999 | NO | -0.279 |
| Chad | Tripoli 2 agreement | 2002 | NO | 0.356 |
| Comoros | Antananarivo Peace Agreement | 1999 | NO | -0.314 |
| Comoros | The Famboni Declaration | 2000 | NO | -0.31 |
| Comoros | The Famboni II Agreement | 2001 | NO | -0.273 |

| | | | | |
|---|---|---|---|---|
| Comoros | Agreement on the transitional arrangements in the Comoros | 2003 | NO | -0.065 |
| Congo Rep. | Accord de Cessez-le-feu et de Cessation des Hostilités | 1999 | NO | -0.797 |
| Cote d'Ivoire | Linas-Marcoussis Peace Accords | 2003 | NO | -0.359 |
| Cote d'Ivoire | Accra III | 2004 | YES | -0.246 |
| Djibouti | Accord de paix et de la réconciliation nationale | 1994 | NO | -0.251 |
| Djibouti | Accord Cadre de Reforme et de Concorde Civile | 2000 | YES | -0.396 |
| Djibouti | Accord de reforme et concorde civile | 2001 | YES | -0.395 |
| DR Congo | Lusaka Accord | 1999 | NO | 0.657 |
| DR Congo | Declaration of Fundamental Principles for the Inter-Congolese dialogue | 2001 | YES | 1.657 |
| DR Congo | Global and Inclusive Agreement on the Transition in the Democratic Republic of Congo | 2002 | YES | 1.884 |
| DR Congo | Inter-Congolese Political Negotiations: The Final Act | 2003 | YES | 1.773 |
| Ethiopia | Communique Commun des Groupes Rebelles Ethiopiens | 1991 | YES | -0.197 |
| Guinea-Bissau | Abuja Peace Agreement | 1998 | YES | -0.471 |
| Liberia | Banjul III Agreement | 1990 | NO | -0.503 |
| Liberia | Yamoussoukro IV Peace Agreement | 1991 | NO | -0.393 |
| Liberia | Cotonou Peace Agreement | 1993 | NO | 0.013 |
| Liberia | Akosombo Peace Agreement | 1994 | NO | 0.204 |
| Liberia | Abuja Peace Agreement | 1995 | YES | 0.269 |
| Liberia | Abuja II Peace Agreement | 1996 | NO | 0.324 |
| Liberia | Accra Peace Agreement | 2003 | YES | 3.442 |
| Mali | Tamanrasset Accord | 1991 | NO | -0.259 |
| Mali | Pacte Nationale | 1992 | NO | -0.283 |

| | | | | |
|---|---|---|---|---|
| Mozambique | The Protocol on the Agreed Agenda | 1991 | YES | 0.025 |
| Mozambique | Acordo Genral de Paz (AGP) | 1992 | YES | -0.079 |
| Niger | Paris Accord | 1993 | NO | -0.262 |
| Niger | Ouagadougou Accord | 1994 | NO | -0.333 |
| Niger | Accord d'etablissant une paix définitive entre le gouvernement de la republique du Niger et l'organisation de la résistance armée | 1995 | NO | -0.408 |
| Niger | Protocole d'accord additionnel entre le Gouvernement de la Republique du Niger et l'Union des Forces de la Resistance Armee (FPLS, MUR, FAR) et les Forces Armees Revolutionnaires du Sahara | 1997 | YES | -0.335 |
| Rwanda | N'Sele Ceasefire Agreement | 1991 | NO | 0.638 |
| Rwanda | The Protocol of Agreement between the Government of the Republic of Rwanda and the Rwandese Patriotic Front on the Rule of Law | 1992 | NO | 0.53 |
| Rwanda | Arusha Accords | 1993 | NO | 0.539 |
| Senegal | Accord général de paix entre le gouvernement de la République du Sénégal el le Mouvement des forces democratique de la Casamance (MFDC) | 2004 | YES | 0.297 |
| Sierra Leone | Abidjan Peace Agreement | 1996 | NO | 0.446 |
| Sierra Leone | Lomé Peace Agreement | 1999 | NO | 2.026 |
| Sierra Leone | Abuja Ceasefire Agreement | 2000 | YES | 2.079 |
| Sierra Leone | Peace Agreement Between the Revolutionary United Front (RUF) | 2001 | YES | 1.273 |
| Somalia | Addis Ababa Agreement | 1993 | NO | -0.165 |
| Somalia | Nairobi Declaration on National Reconciliation | 1994 | NO | -0.645 |
| Somalia | The Cairo Declaration on Somalia | 1997 | NO | -0.803 |

| | | | | |
|---|---|---|---|---|
| South Africa | Interim Constitution | 1994 | YES | 9.379 |
| Sudan | Khartoum Agreement | 1997 | NO | -0.143 |
| Sudan | Machakos Protocol | 2002 | YES | 4.426 |
| Sudan | Agreement on Security Arrangements During the Interim Period | 2003 | YES | 4.726 |
| Sudan | Protocol Between the GOS and SPLM on Power Sharing | 2004 | YES | 4.982 |
| Uganda | Yumbe Peace Agreement | 2002 | YES | 0.367 |

## Notes

[1] "Ethiopia: Mengistu Resigns," *Africa Research Bulletin*, 1–30 May 1991, p.10130.

[2] A number of countries had more than one peace accord during the time period examined in this study. Also, if more than one agreement was made in a single year for a given case, the most comprehensive accord was included in the dataset.

[3] OECD/DAC, "ODA Distributions by Recipient," March 2010. http://stats.oecd.org/Index.aspx?DatasetCode=ODA_RECIP.

[4] It should be pointed out that two of the variables related to intensity of warfare (battle deaths and conflict duration), are associated with conflicting views in the literature concerning their impact on the longevity of negotiated settlements.

[5] See Hartzell, Hoddie, and Rothchild 2001, 183–208; Hartzell and Hoddie 2003, 318–332; Walter, 2002; Hoddie and Hartzell 2005; Mukherjee 2006, 479–504; and Jarstad and Nilsson 2008, 206–223.

## References

Boyce, J. K. 1996. "External Resource Mobilization." In *Economic Policy for Building Peace: The Lessons of El Salvador,* ed. J. K. Boyce, 129–154. Boulder, CO: Lynne Rienner Publishers.

Cohen, H. J. 1991. *Intervening in Africa: Superpower Peacemaking in a Troubled Continent.* New York: St. Martin's Press, ARB, 1–30 May 1991, 10134.

Collier, P., and A. Hoeffler. 1998. "On Economic Causes of Civil War." *Oxford Economic Papers*, Oxford University Press, 50, 4, October, 563–573.

Collier, P., and A. Hoeffler. 2002. "Aid, Policy, and Growth in Post-conflict Societies." Washington, DC: World Bank, Policy Research Working Paper 2902, October, 5.

Collier, P., and A. Hoeffler. 2004. "Greed and Grievance in Civil War," *Oxford Economic Papers.* Oxford, UK: Oxford University Press, 56, 4, October, 563–595.

Collier, P., V. L. Elliott, H. Hegre, A. Hoeffler, M. Reynal-Querol, and N. Sambanis. 2003. "Breaking the Conflict Trap: Civil War and Development Policy." Washington, DC: World Bank.

Cortright, D. 1997. "Incentive Strategies for Preventing Conflict." In *The Price of Peace: Incentives and International Conflict Prevention,* ed. David Cortright, 273. Lanham, MD: Rowman and Littlefield.

de Waal, Alex. 1992. "Ethiopia: Transition to What?" *World Policy Journal* 9:4, Fall/Winter, 719–737.

Doyle, M., and N. Sambanis. 2000. "International Peacebuilding: A Theoretical and Quantitative Analysis." *American Political Science Review* 94: 4, 795.

Emmanuel, N., and D. Rothchild. 2007. "Economic Aid and Peace Implementation: The African Experience." *Journal of Intervention and State-building,* 1(2), June, 176–178.

Ethiopia: Mengistu Resigns. 1991. *Africa Research Bulletin,* 1–30 May, 10130.

Forman, S., and S. Patrick, eds. 2000. *Good Intentions: Pledges of Aid for Postconflict Recovery.* Boulder, CO: Lynne Rienner Publishers.

Fortna, V. P. 2003. "Inside and Out: Peacekeeping and the Duration of Peace after Civil and Interstate Wars." *International Studies Review* 5, 111.

Gleditsch, N. P., P. Wallensteen, M. Eriksson, M. Sollenberg, and H. Strand. 2002. "Armed Conflict 1946–2001: A New Dataset." *Journal of Peace Research* 39, 5, 615–637.

Harbom, L., S. Hogbladh, and P. Wallensteen. 2006. "Armed Conflict and Peace Agreements." *Journal of Peace Research* 43: 5, 617–631.

Hartzell, C. 1999. "Explaining the Stability of Negotiated Settlements to Intrastate Wars." *Journal of Conflict Resolution,* 43, 12.

Hartzell, C., M. Hoddie, and D. Rothchild. 2001. "Stabilizing the Peace after Civil War: An Investigation of Some Key Variables." *International Organization,* 55, Winter, 183–208.

Hartzell, C., and M. Hoddie. 2003. "Institutionalizing Peace: Power Sharing and Post-Civil War Conflict Management." *American Journal of Political Science* 47, April, 318–332.

Hartzell, C. and M. Hoddie. 2007. *Crafting Peace: Power Sharing Institutions and the Negotiated Settlement of Civil Wars*. University Park, PA: Pennsylvania State University Press, 10.

Heldt, Birger. 2008. "UN and Non-UN Peacekeeping Operations, 1948–2005." Appendix to "Trends from 1948 to 2005: How to View the Relation between the United Nations and Non-UN Entities." In *Peace Operations: Trends, Progress, and Prospects,* ed. D. C. Daniel, P. Taft, and S. Wiharta. Washington, DC: Georgetown University Press.
Hoddie, M., and C. Hartzell. 2003. "Civil War Settlements and the Implementation of Military Power-sharing Arrangements." *Journal of Peace Research* 40, May, 303–320.
Hoddie, M., and C. Hartzell. 2005. "Power Sharing in Peace Settlements: Initiating the Transition from Civil War." In *Sustainable Peace: Power and Democracy after Civil Wars,* eds. P. G. Roeder and D. Rothchild. Ithaca, NY: Cornell University Press.
Jarstad, A. K. and D. Nilsson. 2008. "From Words to Deeds: The Implementation of Power-Sharing Pacts in Peace Accords." *Conflict Management and Peace Science,* 25, 3, July, 206–223.
Lacina, B., and N. P. Gleditsch. 2005. "Monitoring Trends in Global Combat: A New Dataset of Battle Deaths." *European Journal of Population,* 21: 2–3, 145–166.
Licklider, R. 1995. "The Consequences of Negotiated Settlements in Civil Wars, 1945–1993." *American Political Science Review,* 89, 3, September, 681, 683, 685.
Marshall, M, 2010. "Major Episodes of Political Violence: 1946–2009." *Center for Systemic Peace*, http://www.systemicpeace.org/warlist.htm.
Mooradian, M., and D. Druckman. 1999. "Hurting Stalemate or Mediation? The Conflict over Nagorno-Karabakh, 1990–1995." *Journal of Peace Research,* 36, 709–728.
Mukherjee, B. 2006. "Why Political Power-Sharing Agreements Lead to Enduring Peaceful Resolution of Some Civil Wars, But Not Others." *International Studies Quarterly,* 50, 2, 479–504.
OECD/DAC. 2010. "ODA Distributions by Recipient." March 2010, http://stats.oecd.org/Index.aspx?DatasetCode=ODA_RECIP.
Pillar, P. R. 1983. *Negotiating Peace: War Termination as a Bargaining Process.* Princeton: Princeton University Press.\
Quinn, J. M., T. D. Mason, and M. Gurses. 2007. "Sustaining the Peace: Determinants of Civil War Recurrence." *International Interactions* 33: 167–193.
Rothchild, D. 1997. *Managing Ethnic Conflict in Africa: Pressures and Incentives for Cooperation.* Washington, DC: Brookings Institution, 178, 259.
—. 2001. "The US Foreign Policy Trajectory on Africa." *SAIS Review* 21.1, 179–211.

Rothchild, D. and N. Emmanuel. 2006. "The Impact of Economic Assistance in Africa's Peace Processes." *Africa Contemporary Record: 2001–2002,* (28).

Stedman, S. J. 1991. *Peacemaking in Civil War: International Mediation in Zimbabwe, 1974–1980.* Boulder, CO: Lynne Rienner.

Stedman, S. J., D. S. Rothchild, and E. M. Cousens. 2002. *Ending Civil Wars: The Implementation of Peace Agreements.* Boulder, CO: Lynne Reinner, 663.

Toft, M. D. 2010. *Securing the Peace: The Durable Settlement of Civil Wars.* Princeton, NJ: Princeton University Press, 7, 150.

Touval, S. 1982. *The Peace Brokers.* Princeton, NJ: Princeton University Press.

UCDP. 2006. UCDP Peace Agreement Dataset v. 1.0, 1989–2005, http://www.pcr.uu.se/research/UCDP/data_and_publications/datasets.htm. SEE: Harbom, Lotta, Stina Högbladh and Peter Wallensteen, "Armed Conflict and Peace Agreements," *Journal of Peace Research,* 43,5, 617–631.

Wallensteen, P., and M. Sollenberg. 1997. "Armed Conflicts, Conflict Termination, and Peace Agreements, 1989–1996." *Journal of Peace Research,* 34, 3, August, 342.

Walter, B. 1997. "The Critical Barrier to Civil War Settlement." *International Organization* 51, 3, Summer.

—. 2002. *Committing to Peace: The Successful Settlement of Civil Wars.* Princeton, NJ: Princeton University Press.

—. 2004. "Does Conflict Beget Conflict? Explaining Recurring Civil War." *Journal of Peace Research* 41, 3, May, 372, 373.

World Bank. 2010. World Development Indicators, March.

Zartman, I. W. 2001. "Negotiating Internal Conflict: Incentives and Intractability." *International Negotiation,* 6, 3, 301.

# CHAPTER TEN

# ASSESSING THE PROMISES OF BUDGET SUPPORT: CASE STUDY EVIDENCE FROM RWANDA

HALEY J. SWEDLUND

Since the early 2000s, budget support—a direct resource transfer into the recipient country's treasury—has become a dominant aid modality. In 2001, 13 percent of lending from the International Development Association came in the form of budget support. Only four years later, the percentage of lending as budget support more than quadrupled to 50 percent (Barkan 2009). Proponents of budget support argue that the aid modality lowers transaction costs, provides more predictable funding, and improves coordination, harmonization, domestic accountability, and public expenditure efficiency. However, given that this aid modality is relatively new, we know very little about its actual impact in aid-dependent states. In this chapter, I examine whether or not budget support has fulfilled some of its key promises in post-genocide and civil war Rwanda. In particular, I focus on whether or not budget support has led to higher levels of *donor coordination*, increased *alignment* with the national government's priorities, and improved *government capacity*.

My analysis of the Rwandan case is based on fieldwork I conducted in Kigali, Rwanda, during 2009 and 2010.[1] Data sources include: 1) interviews with donor agencies and Government of Rwanda (GoR) officials; 2) primary documents such as meeting minutes and official government policy documents; and 3) previously published reports on budget support and aid to Rwanda.[2] In addition, I was able to attend a joint review of budget support while in Kigali.

In this chapter, I suggest that on the surface budget support has done marginally well in fulfilling the aforementioned promises (donor coordination, alignment, and government capacity). However, if one scratches the surface, important qualifications about the capacity of budget support to fulfill these promises become visible. In particular, I find that budget support probably only increases coordination among budget-support donors and may actually lead to the exclusion of non-budget support donors. I also concluded that there is no way of knowing whether or not budget support actually encourages the funding of national priorities, because donors and the GoR are so intertwined. While budget support may be a promising new aid modality, my research suggests that its implementation is anything but straightforward and faces a number of challenges.

## Budget Support as Effective Aid

### From aid pessimism to aid effectiveness

Budget support emerged in response to growing pessimism about foreign aid and is part and parcel of what many call the aid effectiveness agenda. Over the course of the '90s, voices critiquing the record of foreign assistance, particularly to sub-Saharan Africa, grew dramatically —and with good reason. Although more than $500 billion dollars (the equivalent of four Marshall Plans) was dispersed to sub-Saharan Africa between 1960 and 1997, per capita GDP actually *declined* throughout much of this period (Ayodele et al. 2005). By the early 2000s, rising pessimism about the ability of foreign aid to promote substantial economic growth and/or social transformation had given way to three categories of responses: stop aid, increase aid, and make aid more effective.

First, some, such as Moyo (2009), have called on donors and recipient countries to abandon foreign aid altogether. While popular in certain circles, this is unlikely to happen anytime soon, as both donors and recipient countries are deeply invested in the current aid structure. Second, there has been a global push, led by the likes of Jeffery Sachs and other academic and real life superstars, to increase aggregate aid flows, particularly to Africa. As part of its push to reach the Millennium Development Goals by 2015, the United Nations is once again urging developed countries to contribute at least .7 percent of their gross national product (GNP) to official development aid (ODA). At the G-8 summit in Gleneagles in 2005, rich countries pledged to dramatically increase their contributions to development assistance, and a host of new initiatives, such as Tony Blair's Commission for Africa and George W. Bush's President's Emergency Plan for Aids Relief (PEPFAR) and the Millennium Challenge Corporation

(MCC), have sprung up. Each promises billions more in aid, particularly to sub-Saharan Africa.

Third, practitioners and academics are increasingly focusing on improving the *effectiveness* of aid. That is, instead of a) abandoning aid or b) increasing aid, the focus of the so-called "aid effectiveness agenda" is to improve the quality of the aid. In the mid-2000s, the *Paris Declaration on Aid Effectiveness* and the *Accra Agenda for Action* (OECD 2005, 2008) institutionalized a focus on aid effectiveness. Attempting to go beyond questions about whether or not aid is working, scholars and practitioners in the aid effectiveness camp use evidence-based research to explain why aid has not produced better results and to propose potential solutions. As part of this agenda, a host of edited volumes and policy papers have emerged that draw on the lessons of ineffective aid to produce policy recommendations on how to "reform," "improve" or make aid "smarter" (see, for example, Devarajan et al. 2001; Joseph and Gillies 2009; Carlsson et al. 1997; van de Walle and Johnston 1996).

To these debates, academics such as Nicolas van de Walle, Mick Moore, and Deborah Bräutigam have contributed a better understanding of how aid changes the incentive structure and political dynamics of recipient states. Van de Walle (2001) argues that the aid system prolonged many African neo-patrimonial regimes by providing a huge influx of resources and technical capacity. In a similar vein, Bräutigam's work suggests that the aid system makes it more difficult to build a capable state, because it "provides incentives and informal rules that reinforce the political constraints faced by reformers in aid dependent countries and in donor agencies" (2000, 7). Lastly, Moore (1998) argues that there are more incentives for governments to listen to donors than to citizens in aid-dependent states, because governments are dependent on donors, not taxpayers, for revenue. Collectively, these scholars drive home the point that foreign aid is not just an influx of resources into a needy country; it fundamentally changes the political environment of the recipient country.

## The Emergence of budget support

It is within the focus on aid effectiveness that budget support emerged as a prominent aid modality, and proponents often paint this modality as a way to overcome the shortcomings of earlier approaches to foreign assistance (Hammond 2006). Budget support is not necessarily a completely new type of aid modality.[3] However, what is sometimes called "new" or "partnership" budget support is generally considered to have emerged in the late 90s and early 2000s at the World Bank. "New" budget support places an emphasis on poverty reduction and on partnerships between donors and the recipient government, and it is tied to the Poverty Reduction Strategy (PRS) program of the Bretton Wood Institutions (Purcell et al. 2006). Under the PRS, which began in 1999, countries develop their own medium-term development goals and strategies and in return receive significant debt reduction.

Budget support defines itself in contrast to older aid modalities, such as structural adjustment programs and project approaches, which are top-down, donor-driven, and blind to country particularities (Cheru 2006). Alternatively, budget support (a type of program aid) transfers development aid directly into the budget of the receiving country and allows the recipient country to use its own allocation, procurement, and accounting structures. Although sector budget support is earmarked for a particular sector, such as education or health, it is not earmarked for a specific project.[4] General budget support (GBS) is a completely un-earmarked transfer into the recipient country's treasury (Beasley et al. 2005).

## Promises of budget support

Budget support is argued by proponents to have a variety of benefits, including lower transaction costs, more predictable funding, and increased domestic accountability.[5] Additionally, budget support is often seen as a way for donors to scale-up their aid commitments quickly without increasing country staff (Barkan 2009). In this chapter, I concentrate on three of the core promises of budget support—government capacity, donor coordination, and alignment. These three promises encapsulate why budget support has become the preferred aid modality of so many prominent bilateral and multilateral donors.

First, budget support is argued to build *government capacity* by channeling aid through government structures. In low-income and aid-dependent environments, national systems and budgets are often subsidiary to donor structures. Without a strong tax base, governments lack a consistent source of funding, and the provision of basic services (i.e. health and education) often falls to donors. When these services are provided in the form of project funding, execution falls to donors and their implementing partners (i.e., NGOs). Consequently, government systems and capacity do not improve, because there is little incentive to strengthen them.

The result is a vicious circle. Government systems are not utilized, because capacity is low; yet capacity remains low, because government systems are not utilized. By channeling development aid through national budgets, this cycle is thought to be broken. Additionally, given that donors want to decrease fiduciary risks, budget support packages often include significant funding for technical assistance, and frequently the continuation of budget support relies on the government making improvements in the country's public financial management (PMF) systems. Due to these additional funds and incentives, budget support is thought to foster capacity building in ways traditional project aid does not.

Second, proponents of budget support argue that the aid modality will increase *donor coordination* by establishing common frameworks and pooling donor resources. As a result, the transaction costs (both immediate and insidious) of recipient and donor countries are thought to decrease (Knack and Rahman 2008).[6] Acharya and his colleagues (2006) find that recipient countries, on average, must work with twenty-six different donor agencies. The presence of multiple donor agencies places a heavy burden on recipient governments, as each agency has its own procedures, priorities, planning cycles, and reporting requirements, each of which must be met to receive funding (van de Walle and Johnston 1996; Woods 2005). The demands of donors on recipient countries are often so great that recipient governments have begun to institute "quiet periods" or periods were requests from foreign agencies and delegations are highly limited. Furthermore, as donors proliferate, gaps or overlaps in services are frequent (Directorate General for Development 2006; van de Walle and Johnston 1996). Needs may not be met or donors may be wasting money on similar projects in the same areas. Budget support will not prevent donor *proliferation,* but the hope is that it will decrease donor *fragmentation* by coordinating and aggregating the activities of donors. Instead of donors making individual decisions about where to build a school or implement an HIV/AIDS program, budget support pools funds in support of the national education budget or a country-wide HIV/AIDS prevention program.

Third, the modality is thought to increase the *alignment* of donor activities with national priorities, because budget support allows recipient governments to allocate aid as they wish. As Cheru argues, "external aid is likely to be more effective in reducing poverty if donor policies, procedures and practices are aligned with government-led poverty reduction-related processes" (2006, 370). To ensure that donors' funds are being spent wisely, budget support is tied to the country's Poverty Reduction Strategy (PRS). The country's PRS provides a contract of sorts between the recipient government and the donors; donors agree to fund the state, if the state fulfills its own self-assigned poverty reduction strategy. As Knoll writes, by using the PRSP, donors seek to avoid "imposing conditionality and demanding policy alignment from recipient countries" and instead "draw their conditionality from a comprehensive, nationally elaborated strategy on development and poverty reduction" (Knoll 2008, 2).

Table 10.1 lists each of the promises outlined above and a summary of the rationale for each promise. Additionally, the last column lists potential indicators for each promise. These indicators will be used in the subsequent assessment.

| Promise | Rationale | Indicators |
|---|---|---|
| **Government Capacity** | Budget support funds and encourages the use of national systems. | PMF systems improve and there are fewer parallel implementation units. |
| **Donor Coordination** | Budget support pools donor resources and decreases donor fragmentation. | Donors work together more often and transaction costs decrease. |
| **Alignment** | Budget support allows recipient countries to decide where foreign aid is allocated. | Donors use national systems more often and fund the priorities identified in the country's PRSP. |

**Table 10.1: The Promises of Budget Support**

## The "politics" problem

Despite the many promises of budget support, its actual impact in aid-dependent countries is relatively unknown, and the evidence that does exist suggests that budget support, like other aid modalities, often results in unintended outcomes. In this section, I discuss potential limitations of the modality, and why further analysis on the actually impact of budget support in aid-dependent countries is needed.

When discussing the shortcomings of budget support, two concerns are often raised. First, budget support, like all foreign aid, is unpredictable. This can be devastating for national governments who calculate their budgets based on donor commitments (Beasley et al. 2005; Celasun and Walliser 2006; Eifert and Gelb 2006). To limit the effects of this problem, a variety of solutions, including variable trenches and discounting donor predictions in budget preparations, have been implemented (Directorate General for Development 2006; Norwegian Agency for Development Co-operation 2006).[7]

Second, budget support, like most foreign aid, is fungible, i.e. is capable of mutual substitution (Koeberle and Stavreski 2006).[8] Once the money has been disbursed to the national budget, how it is spent is at the discretion of the national government. Consequently, the funds can be used for a variety of unsavory purposes, such as arms or bribes. Of course, if the money is spent unwisely, donors can suspend future support. Additionally, budget support is only provided to states that meet certain criteria (e.g., low levels of corruption and a commitment to improving Public Financial Management (PFM) systems). However, indicators for such criteria are often based on relatively subjective measures.

The first case study of budget support was conducted by Lawson and his colleagues in Tanzania. They found an association between increased government discretionary spending and an expansion in health and education services. However, they also found: a) few signs of improvements to public spending efficiency or the limiting of long-term obstacles to services quality, b) that the "challenge function" of the budget process remained weak, and c) that intra-government incentives and democratic accountability failed to improve as expected (Lawson et al. 2006). A five-country case study conducted by USAID also found that: a) donor harmonization is proceeding more slowly that predicted; b) transaction costs have likely increased, not decreased, due to GBS; and c) GBS does not always appear to strengthen democracy or public accountability (Beasley et al. 2005). Lastly, a more comprehensive cross-country evaluation of GBS suggests that the impact of budget support is highly variable (IDD and Associates 2006).

Answers to why the introduction of budget support has resulted in these unforeseen effects may be found in an emerging literature that focuses on the "politics" of new aid modalities. Recently, a plethora of scholarship has emerged that critiques contemporary aid practices, such as PRSPs and budget support. This work highlights a variety of intervening political-economic and contextual variables that are argued to cause the new aid modalities to fail (see, for example, de Renzio et al. 2008; Gould 2005; de Renzio 2006; Craig and Porter 2003; Unwin 2004; Whitfield 2009; de Renzio 2009). Much of this work concentrates on debunking the idea that new modalities increase country ownership, suggesting a more complicated outcome that Harrison calls post-conditionality or "a sort of mutual dependence between donors and state elites" (2001, 22).

Such scholarship has a long way to go in terms of offering precise variables and mechanisms. However, collectively, this growing body of literature suggests that analysis on new aid modalities cannot just consist of simplistic measures. Instead, it needs to dig deep, paying attention to the broader political implications of the aid modality. In this chapter, I use data collected during fieldwork in Kigali, Rwanda to examine the Rwandan experience with budget support. I problematize each of the aforementioned promises, digging below the surface to highlight the larger consequences of the aid modality.

## Numbers and Figures

### Budget support worldwide

Accurate figures on budget support are hard to come by, as aid is often not disaggregated by type. However, it is clear that the prevalence of budget support is increasing, and several major donors have indicated their intention to scale-up their aid programs through further increases in general budget support. This is particularly so in sub-Saharan Africa, where, since 2000, approximately 60–70 percent of GBS has been disbursed (Knoll 2008). In many African countries, GBS now accounts for 20–40 percent of the government's budget (Lawson et al. 2006).

The push towards budget support is certainly not universal (for example, there is little indication that the U.S. will increase budget support in the near future). However, particular donors, such as the UK and the European Commission, are clearly moving away from project approaches. Instead of funding new, stand-alone projects, these donors clearly prefer to increase budget support totals. One of my interviewees estimated that 75–80 percent of foreign aid provided by the UK and the European Commission to Rwandan now comes in the form of GBS (Interviews, Kigali: 11.04.09).

According to surveys by the Strategic Partnership for Africa, from 2004 to 2008 Rwanda received the highest proportional amount of general budget support in sub-Saharan Africa.[9] As Table 10.2 indicates, the largest recipient of GBS in Africa during this time period was Tanzania. However, when the relative size of each country's economy is taken into account, we see that GBS actually made up a larger percentage of Rwanda's GDP than it did in Tanzania—or any other country included in the survey for that matter—during this period. If budget support does not have a measurable impact on donor coordination, alignment, or government capacity in Rwanda, there is little reason to assume it will have an impact elsewhere.

| | 2004 Survey | | 2006 Survey | | 2008 Survey | | 2004–2008 |
|---|---|---|---|---|---|---|---|
| | GBS Disbursed (US$m) | GBS as %of GDP | GBS Disbursed (US$m) | GBS as %of GDP | GBS Disbursed( US$m) | GBS as %of GDP | Average GBS as %of GDP[10] |
| **Benin** | 10.92 | 0.53% | 72.06 | 1.61% | 112.27 | 0.76% | 1.06% |
| **Burkina Faso** | 131.55 | 2.65% | 186.44 | 3.10% | 236.31 | 3.50% | 3.12% |
| **Ethiopia** | 193.48 | 2.41% | 264.66 | 0.12% | | | 2.06% |
| **Ghana** | 301.69 | 3.69% | 331.54 | 3.44% | 306.71 | 2.04% | 3.24% |
| **Kenya** | | | 60.83 | 0.70% | | | 0.35% |
| **Madagascar** | 103.72 | 1.73% | 113.41 | 2.62% | | | 2.25% |
| **Malawi** | 103.08 | 3.12% | 120.82 | 4.14% | 99.73 | 2.32% | 3.08% |
| **Mali** | 255.98 | 4.34% | 110.51 | 2.00% | 108.65 | 1.44% | 2.26% |
| **Mozambique** | 230.88 | 4.57% | 317.33 | 4.88% | 294.97 | 3.71% | 4.84% |
| **Rwanda** | **86.17** | **2.37%** | **155.09** | **6.47%** | **186.1** | **5.55%** | **5.80%** |
| **Sierra Leone** | 52.26 | 5.18% | 64.08 | 6.97% | 28.93 | 0.66% | 4.93% |
| **Tanzania** | 580.38 | 3.47% | 548.13 | 3.82% | 653.4 | 3.76% | 3.78% |
| **Uganda** | 404.07 | 4.93% | 346.65 | 2.73% | | | 3.75% |
| **Zambia** | | | 86.42 | 1.41% | 194.13 | 1.58% | 2.56% |

**Table 10.2: General Budget Support Disbursal Rates by Country**

Source: Strategic Partnership with Africa, Budget Support Survey Database

## Budget support in Rwanda

New or partnership budget support began in Rwanda after the first PSRP was finalized in the early 2000s. Currently, there are four major budget support donors: the UK's Department for International Development (DfID), the European Commission (EC), the World Bank, and the African Development Bank (AfDB). Historically, Sweden also provided budget support to Rwanda, but Swedish budget support was suspended in 2008 after a UN report accused the GoR of supporting armed rebellion in the neighboring Democratic Republic of the Congo (Swedish Government Offices 2008). Three additional bilaterals—Germany, Belgium, and the Netherlands—provide smaller levels of budget support, with the latter two providing sector budget support only.

Figure 1 provides an overview of GBS to Rwanda. As the chart shows, since 2005 over $150 million per year has been distributed to Rwanda in the form of GBS ($185.83 million in fiscal year 2007/2008). Additionally, GBS appears to have become more predictable, with almost 100 percent of committed funds being disbursed in 2007/2008. The new budget support package signed in December, 2009, increases pledges for the 2010/2011 fiscal year by 21 percent, to $335.4 million. The World Bank is set to contribute $91 million, the EC $80.5 million, the UK $63.1 million, the African Development Bank $27.6 million, Germany $15.2 million, the Netherlands $14.4 million, and Belgium $4.3 million (Kagire 2009).[11]

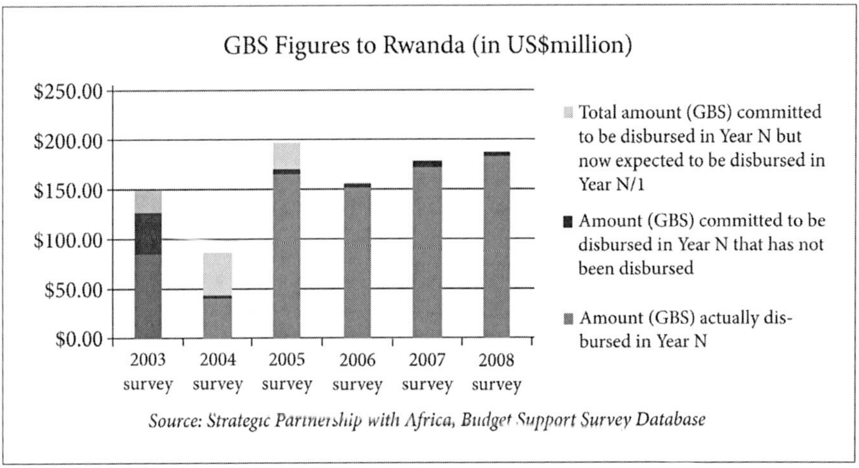


Figure 10.1. GBS Figures to Rwanda

Figures for sector budget support to Rwanda are incomplete and not worth repeating here. However, we do know that certain sectors are more supported by budget support than others. For example, currently all aid to education comes in the form of general or sector budget support (Chiche 2008), and significant sector budget support is provided to the justice, health, and agricultural sectors.

Budget support in Rwanda is currently overseen by the Budget Support Harmonization Group (BSHG), a working group of the Development Partners Coordination Group (DPCG). The DPCG is composed of GoR representatives (Secretaries General and Directors of Planning) and heads of bilateral and multilateral donors.[12] Members of the DPCG who provide more than $10 million each year in budget support are eligible to be members of the BSHG. The exception to this rule is the International Monetary Fund (IMF), which is considered a full member of the BSHG because of its role and mandate regarding macro-economic policy issues (BSHG 2008). Additionally, those giving less can participate in the group as observers.[13]

The BSHG was established by a partnership framework signed in November 2003 (BSHG 2003). For several years, the partnership framework guided budget support in Rwanda. However, after the adoption of Rwanda's second PRSP, a new memorandum of understanding was adopted and signed in September, 2008 by nine signatories: the Government of Rwanda, the African Development Bank, the UK's Department for International Development, the European Community, the IMF, Germany, the Netherlands, Sweden, and the World Bank (IMF 2009; BSHG 2008).

According to its terms of reference, the BSHG is a forum, not a technical working group (BSHG 2006c).[14] The objectives of the BSHG are "to create a common understanding of achievements by and performance changes for all budget support partners; to provide a forum for open discussion; and to reduce the transactions cost of budget support" (BSHG 2006, 1). The forum is chaired by the Secretary General and Secretary to the Treasury of the Ministry of Finance and Economic Planning, and donors alternate co-chairing. While the chair is responsible for convening and determining the agenda for the meetings, the co-chair is responsible for the day-to-day dialogue and communication between donors and the government. Twice a year the BSHG conducts a review of budget support. During these reviews the GoR reports to donors using the Common Performance Assessment Framework (CPAF), which tracks progress towards the PRSP. These reviews are multi-day events and assess Rwanda's overall progress, as well as progress in the economic, social and governance clusters. Following the review, a report is published and shared with all donors.

## Assessing the Promises of Budget Support

Proponents of budget support often claim that the aid modality can solve a variety of problems and challenges facing foreign assistance. In this chapter, I focus on three of these promises: government capacity, coordination, and alignment. In the following section, I outline my findings regarding the impact of budget support in these three areas. I argue that budget support does appear to have increased government capacity in

Rwanda. However, there is no way of knowing whether budget support has actually fostered better alignment with national priorities, because donors and the Rwandan government are so intertwined. It is therefore difficult to distinguish their priorities from one another. Lastly, I find that, in Rwanda, budget support appears to increase coordination only among budget support donors and may actually lead to the exclusion of non-budget support donors.

## Government Capacity

Budget support packages often include capacity-building components to: a) help the receiving country manage the funds and b) lower fiduciary risks. Therefore, after several years of budget support in Rwanda we should see improvements in the GoR's overall capacity to manage these funds. My analysis of budget support in Rwanda finds that budget support does appear to have improved government capacity, particularly PFM systems. However, at times, budget support has stretched the capacity of the GoR.

Since budget support began in the early 2000s, the GoR's overall capacity has readily improved, though many of these reforms are not directly attributable to budget support. However, there is reason to believe that budget support contributed to these improvements, particularly in regards to financial management. In 2006, the Organic Law on State Finance and Property was adopted. The law provides the legal grounds for "preparation, adoption, execution and monitoring" of the national budget. It decentralized certain powers to budget agencies and enacted more robust rules and procedures for budget reallocation and budget execution oversight. Additionally, in 2006, the government published consolidated national accounts for the first time (Chiche 2008; OECD-DAC 2008).

In 2007, Rwanda's PFM quality rating increased to 4.0 (higher than the worldwide average),[15] and the first public expenditure and financial accountability assessment took place (OECD-DAC 2008). Furthermore, the GoR made four major PFM reforms: 1) introducing a new chart of accounts and preparing an annual financial report for 2006 and 2007 (for the first time since 1989); 2) strengthening the financial decentralization framework; 3) moving toward a zero-sum single treasury account; and 4) strengthening the internal audit and procurement reforms (Chiche 2008, 13).

In regard to managing aid flows, the GoR has also made important improvements.[16] In 2005, the External Finance Unit was created to serve as the "key entry point for the oversight and management of external aid"

(GoR 2007a, 7). The External Finance Unit is also responsible for implementing a new aid policy and a Development Assistance Database.[17] The Aid Coordination Unit, a program of the UN Resident Coordinator's office, currently supports the External Finance Unit. However, the Aid Coordination Unit is gradually being phased out as the capacity of the External Finance Unit grows.

According to an evaluation of the budget process conducted in 2008, the GoR now has a structured budget process, with clear rules and key dates in its preparation (Chiche 2008).[18] Additionally, Rwanda received an "A" for both its revenue collection and budget preparation in the 2008 Survey on Monitoring the Paris Declaration (OECD-DAC 2008). While none of these results is directly attributable to budget support, budget support does appear to have created additional incentives for PFM reforms and resulted in more technical assistance to support these efforts.

The capacity of the GoR has improved greatly since it was all but destroyed in the 1994 genocide and civil war. However, significant challenges remain and there is evidence that budget support sometimes taxes the GoR's abilities. In my interviews with donor representatives, capacity challenges were often mentioned as an impediment (Interviews, Kigali: 10.23.09). Additionally, reviews of the budget process in Rwanda have concluded that low levels of capacity do affect the budgeting process, with the major problems being late delivery and lack of coverage in key government documentation (Chiche 2008; Highton 2009). During my observation of the November 2009 Joint Budget Support Review, I was told by one donor representative that although things had been going well overall, at times the meeting had been chaotic because the GoR wasn't prepared. This lack of preparedness was also apparent to me in the session on governance, as GoR officials often struggled to answer donors' questions.

Overall, it appears that budget support does well at fulfilling the promise of improved government capacity—at least of PMF systems relevant to the budgeting process. By channeling development aid through the state, the state is no longer on the sidelines but instead an active participant and encouraged to build its capacity. In that regard, budget support is likely better than project aid at improving government capacity.

Nevertheless, meaningful capacity-building is likely to take a great deal of time, and budget support is a relatively new aid modality. It will, therefore, remain important to continue to monitor budget support's impact over the long term. Additionally, as the next section argues, it is often unclear whether national preferences or donors are really driving the agenda. Therefore, even if technical capacity is improving, there is no evidence that the state is less dependent on donors.

## Donor coordination

Regarding donor coordination, my analysis of budget support in Rwanda finds that budget support has likely increased coordination among budget support donors. However, there is little compelling evidence to support the claim that transaction costs have decreased due to the introduction of budget support. Additionally, my research suggests an important qualification to the promise of donor coordination. While donor coordination appears to have increased among budget support donors, there is no evidence it has increased coordination among non-budget support donors. In fact, its introduction appears to have actually fostered hierarchical divisions between the two groups.

Since the early 2000s, the GoR and budget support donors have made great strides in harmonizing their activities (Strategic Partnership with Africa 2003). First, through the partnership framework and then the memorandum of understanding, budget support donors have coalesced around a shared set of principles. Additionally, budget support donors communicate frequently with each other and through the BSHG. The meeting minutes of the BSHG reflect that, through the forum, donors share their dispersal rates and provide updates on their organizations' activities (see for example BSHG 2006b, 2006a). Additionally, budget support donors are more than twice as likely to engage in joint missions (beyond budget support) according to a new Donor Performance Assessment Framework carried out by the Rwandan government in 2007 and 2008 (GoR 2009).[19]

Most importantly, through the BSHG, budget support donors have established joint reviews using the Common Performance Assessment Framework (CPAF). The CPAF is a set of fifty indicators based on Rwanda's second PRSP. These fifty indicators were agreed upon by donors and the GoR, and each donor chooses the indicators that trigger that donor's disbursement of budget support. The CPAF includes a wide variety of indicators from which donors can choose. At the same time, the CPAF provides the GoR with a consistent assessment rubric and limits donor-specific reporting requirements.

That being said, there is little evidence that transaction costs have decreased substantially as a result of budget support. The meetings of the Budget Support Harmonization Group (or any of the other donor-government forums) do not take the place of bilateral meetings, and country strategies are still agreed on bilaterally with the GoR. This is not likely to change anytime soon, as the BSHG's memorandum of understanding clearly articulates that it does not supersede bilateral agreements (BSHG 2008). While the hope is that such forums will decrease overlaps and ensure that services are more equitably distributed, there is no hard evidence that this is happening. Instead, what is apparent is that donors and the GoR spend much of their day running in between Kigali conference rooms.

Furthermore, there is little reason to believe that budget support has decreased donor coordination countrywide. Budget support donors represent a highly influential, but small, percentage of Rwandan donors. Budget support donors meet with one another and the GoR regularly; however, bilateral and multilateral non-budget support donors, not to mention NGOs, are less tied into the actions of other donors and the government. Since the introduction of the BSHG, the role of the larger Development Partners Coordination Group (DPCG) has been in question. The DPCG no longer meets on a frequent or regular basis, and the clarity of its goals has decreased overtime. Non-budget support donors are quick to point out that the body is an important forum because it includes all donors. However, its current purpose is highly ambiguous and its meetings irregular (Interviews, Kigali: 06.10.10; 06.18.10; 06.29.10).

Additionally, there is clear evidence that donors who provide GBS have more influence. A representative of the Netherlands told me that, as a GBS donor, you get access to everything, because there is a need to discuss everything (Interview: Kigali, 06.18.10). As a GBS donor representative explicitly put it, "we do what we want" (Interview: Kigali, 06.10.10). While big donors like the U.S. are not likely to lose their influence anytime soon, even they feel the effects of budget support. A representative of DfID noted that the U.S. is often left out and has less impact, particularly over the policy dialogue, because it is so tied to contracts (Interview, Kigali, 11.04.09). Recently, the U.S. has been included in meetings of the BSHG as an observer.[20] However, the impact of U.S. participation is still relatively unknown, and a host of other donors remain completely on the sidelines.

## Alignment

Regarding budget support's impact on alignment, my analysis of the Rwandan case finds that budget support donors have made significant efforts to align with national systems and the GoR's priorities. However, just as with donor coordination, there is an important qualification to this finding. First, donors and the GoR are so intertwined it is difficult to see where the priorities of one end and the others begin. Even "nationally owned" documents such as the PRSP are a product of intense donor/GoR collaboration, and there is a good deal of evidence that donors remain deeply involved. Second, budget support probably increases the participation of high-ranking GoR officials in the policy process. However, these officials are not necessarily representative of the larger national population, and their increased influence can alter domestic political dynamics in favor of those already in power.

Data from 2008 DPAF shows that budget support donors are much more likely to use national systems (see Table 10.3). On average, budget support donors utilized the GoR's budget execution, auditing procedures, financial reporting systems, and procurements systems 50 percent of the time. Alternatively, non-budget support donors utilized them 7 percent of the time.[21]

| **Percent of ODA disbursed in 2008:** | **Budget support donors** | **Non-budget support donors** |
|---|---|---|
| in the context of PBA | 41% | 5% |
| using GoR budget execution procedures | 49% | 1% |
| using GoR auditing procedures | 42% | 4% |
| using GoR financial reporting systems | 49% | 4% |
| using GoR procurements systems | 58% | 19% |
| Number of parrell PIUs | 36 | 12 |
| % of TC provided through coordinated programs | 70% | 80% |

**Table 10.3: Selections from Preliminary Results of 2009 DPAF Round of Monitoring**

However, it is important to remember that budget support donors use national systems inherently. In order to be classified as budget support, funds must go through national systems. Therefore, while the numbers do suggest that alignment with national systems occurs more often for budget support donors, this is not surprising, nor is it likely that budget support donors are using national systems much more than what is required to be classified as budget support.

More interesting is how well budget support is aligned with Rwanda's national priorities. Alignment in Rwanda, as in other aid-dependent countries, is often judged by how well donors are aligned with the PRSP. This is because the PRSP is arguably a "nationally owned" document, because it is drafted and approved by national stakeholders.

By most accounts, budget support is well-aligned with Rwanda's second poverty reduction strategy, the Economic Development and Poverty Reduction Strategy 2008–2012 (EDPRS).[22] Both the national budget and sector working groups are aligned with the PRSP, as is the Common Performance Assessment Framework that budget support donors use to trigger aid disbursements. However, as others have noted, donors are the impetus behind the PRSP and are often highly involved in drafting (Unwin 2004). This was clearly the case in Rwanda.

PSRPs are a requirement of the Heavily Indebted Poor Countries (HIPC) program. A program of the Bretton Woods Institutions, HIPC provides substantial debt relief to participating countries. To qualify for the HIPC program, a country's poverty reduction strategy must be endorsed by the boards of both the World Bank and the IMF. When Rwanda reached the HIPC completion point in 2005, the country became entitled to debt relief of $1.4 billion (nominal terms) (IMF 2005).[23] Therefore, producing a PSRP that will be approved by the boards of the IMF and World Bank is clearly advantageous to the GoR.

Additionally, donors were heavily involved in the drafting and implementation of the EDPRS. At a high-level meeting between donors and the GoR in 2007, the Secretary General of the Ministry of Finance and Economic Planning noted that "the EDPRS was developed through an extensive eighteen-month consultation, led at a high level by the GoR and involving all major stakeholders in ten sector working groups and cross-cutting issue groups" (GoR 2007b, 8). During my interviews, both GoR and donor representatives further clarified that although Rwanda's PRSP was "government-driven," it was produced by all stakeholders. One donor went as far as to tell me it was "signed off" by donors (Interviews: Kigali, 06.01.10; 06.10.10).

The drafting of the EDPRS was officially overseen by the EDPRS National Policy Steering Group, a body composed of GoR ministers (and chaired by the Minister of Finance). However, the Technical Steering Group, which was composed of GoR representatives and donor representatives from the World Bank, the UNDP, the EC, and DfID, actually monitored and oversaw the consultation process and drafting (GoR 2006a, 5).[24] Additionally, donors were highly active on the eleven sector working groups that designed the EDPRS policies and interventions, and international consultants heavily supported the drafting process.[25] The use of international consultants is largely justified by low ministry capacity, and consultants often lend a degree of creditability to the process. International consultants are not supposed to represent donors, but their paychecks and future jobs are dependent on donors. Regardless of their allegiance to donors, their active participation in the drafting of the EDPRS indicates that international ideas and notions about how best to foster economic development often guide national priorities.

Second, there is very little indication that domestic actors outside the central government have been involved in the budget support or EDPRS process. Power is relatively centralized in Rwanda, and there is little reason to believe that budget support changes this. The Ministry of Finance manages both budget support and the EDPRS. As budget support has grown more and more prevalent, the Ministry of Finance has grown more and more powerful. This has likely come at a cost to other actors. A 2006 report on budget support in Rwanda found that the aid modalities had resulted in "government empowerment," particularly of the Ministry of Finance, but had done little to foster domestic accountability. The report notes that "the feedback process is not very inclusive," and line ministers and other domestic stakeholders are not fully engaged (IDD and Associates 2006, 89).

Civil society organizations do not have representation in the BSHG, and when funds are channeled through budget support instead of through projects, their role as implementers is cut off. The executive director of the Rwandan Civil Society Platform worries about this, telling me that the government's push for budget support leaves civil society vulnerable (Interview: Kigali, 06.03.10). Key reports such as the CPAF are only presented to donors, not to parliament (Interview: Kigali, 06.18.10). Therefore, parliamentarians do not have the opportunity to comment on indicators used for the CPAF or its findings. On the 2010 Open Budget Index, Rwanda scored eleven out of a possible one hundred, indicating that it is "virtually impossible for citizens to hold the government accountable for its management of the public's money" (Open Budget Partnership 2010, 1).[26]

These two qualifications suggest that budget support has not necessarily resulted in alignment, as is commonly portrayed in the development literature. Rather, what we see developing is close collaboration between donors and the GoR. Donors remain invested in the process and work closely with a select group of domestic actors. Recent allegations against the current regime, such as a UN mapping report that links the current president, Paul Kagame, and his political party, the Rwandan Patriotic Front,[27] to atrocities in Eastern DRC[28] and a string of events preceding the 2010 presidential elections,[29] likely strain relationships between donors and the GoR. However, for now, donors (particularly those engaged in budget support) have been relatively hesitant to criticize the regime publicity.[30] Referring to the events surrounding the 2010 presidential elections, one of my interviewees noted that donors have been "remarkably silent" (Interview: Kigali, 07.02.10).

| **Predicted Outcome** | **Findings** | **Qualifications** |
|---|---|---|
| Government Capacity | Evidence that budget support increases the capacity of PMF systems | |
| Donor Coordination | Evidence of increased coordination among budget support donors but little evidence of decreased transaction costs | *Budget support likely only increases coordination among budget support donors and may actually lead to the exclusion of non-budget support donors.* |
| Alignment | Evidence that budget support increases use of national systems & that donors support PRSP | *Donors and the GoR are so intertwined that there is no way of knowing whether budget support actually fosters better alignment with national priorities.* |

**Table 10.4: Summary of Findings**

## Summary of findings and qualifications

Table 10.4 summarizes the findings and qualifications presented in section three. On the surface, budget support appears to have fulfilled many of its promises, particularly in regard to increased government capacity. However, just below the surface, my analysis of the Rwandan experience with budget support points to two important qualifications that simplistic, policy-oriented predictions about budget support miss. First, budget support likely only increases coordination among budget support donors and may actually lead to the exclusion of non-budget support donors. Two, donors and the GoR are so intertwined that there is no way of knowing whether budget support actually fosters better alignment with national priorities.

The implementation of budget support, like other aid modalities, is not likely to be straightforward and is most likely affected by a variety of political and contextual variables. When implementing aid modalities, scholars and practitioners alike need to be much more precise about the actual impact of the policies they are relying on to make important changes in aid-dependent countries.

## Concluding Remarks

My findings suggest that donors and recipient countries need to take more safeguards to ensure that budget support results in the intended outcomes. In particular, I suggest that: 1) aid harmonization groups meet frequently and include all donors (not just budget support donors); and 2) additional mechanisms to decipher national priorities should be added. If increased donor coordination is the goal, even those donors who do not participate in budget support need to be included, and donors and governments should be very wary of the potential to create an additional hierarchy among donors. Furthermore, there is a need to develop ways of gauging national priorities that are not linked to donor preferences. This is likely to be difficult, but presently donor preferences and national priorities are so intertwined it is impossible to gauge where one ends and the other begins.

Budget support is a new and important tool in the foreign assistance toolbox. However, it is not the only tool and is not a fix-all solution. Instead, the aid modality needs to be used with precision and accuracy for it to have the intend effect. Just like all other aid modalities, if it is not used carefully it may result in counter-intuitive and counter-productive outcomes.

*The author would like to thank the organizers of the Cornell Aid Symposium, Muna Ndulo and Nicolas van de Walle, and other participants in the conference for helpful comments and suggestions. Thanks also to Paolo de Renzio, Hans Peter Schmitz, Malte Lierl, and Hannah Allerdice for their comments on versions of the project.*

## Notes

[1] Fieldwork was conducted in the context of a larger dissertation project entitled *Donorship to Ownership? Evolving Donor-Government Relations in Rwanda.*

[2] Most of these documents are available at: http://www.devpartners.gov.rw.

[3] For a discussion on whether or not budget support is really "new" see Knoll (2008).

[4] For an analysis of sector budget support specifically, see Williamson and Dom (2010).

[5] See Hammond 2006, p. 96, for a large list of the outcomes promised by proponents of budget support.

[6] For an excellent discussion and critique of this assumption see Killick (2004).

[7] Typically the delay of funds is due to administrative and technical problems, not political reasons (although this certainly happens too), and there is evidence that

predictability is increasing (Norwegian Agency for Development Cooperation 2006; Strategic Partnership with Africa 2009).
[8] Morrisey (2006) argues the fungibility critique of budget support is largely misplaced.
[9] Since 2003, the Strategic Partnership with Africa Budget Support Working Group (SPA-BSWG) has conducted a yearly survey of African countries engaged in budget support. This dataset is not without its flaws; it is not comprehensive, commitment and disbursement rates are self-reported, and the number of countries in the survey fluctuates. However, it is currently the most extensive source of data on budget support available.
[10] Calculated using figures for GBS as a percentage of GDP for all the years between 2004 and 2008, not just the years shown in this chart. Values for other years were omitted due to space constraints.
[11] An additional $39.3 million will be provided through joint financing mechanisms accounts.
[12] Members of civil society and the private sector also have very minimal representation.
[13] The United Nations Resident Coordinator also has observer status.
[14] However, there can be up to two technical meetings each year (GoR 2006b)
[15] To score high on this rating system by the World Bank, a country has to meet several criteria including: linking budget to policy priorities, effective financial management systems, and timely and accurate accounting and fiscal reporting (OECD-DAC 2008).
[16] For a summary of the GoR's aid monitoring instruments see Chiche (2008, 13).
[17] The DAD (http://dad.synisys.com/dadrwanda) is an online tool for collecting, tracking, and analyzing development assistance in Rwanda.
[18] See Chiche (2008) for a graph of Rwanda's National Planning and Budgeting Framework (p. 4) and Rwanda's Annual Planning and Budget Preparation Calendar (p. 6).
[19] On average, budget support donors engaged in joint missions 24 percent of the time, while non-budget support donors did so 12 percent of the time.
[20] This is because the U.S. is considering providing sector budget support to agriculture in Rwanda (Interview II-VIII, 06.09.10). The U.S. would need to provide $10 million or more in budget support to be a full member of the BSHG.
[21] The only non-budget support donor to use the GoR systems to any significant degree was the United Nations, an observer member of the BSHG whose monetary contributions to the GoR are relatively low.
[22] The EDPRS can be found at:
http://siteresources.worldbank.org/INTRWANDA/Resources/EDPRS-English.pdf.
[23] "Nominal terms" refers to the actual dollar value of debt service forgiven over a period of time (IMF 2005).
[24] Civil society and the private sector also had very minimal representation.
[25] Two international consultants supported the Ministry of Finance and Economic Planning with drafting for approximately two years, and an international consultant supported each sector (Interview: Kigali, 06.15.10; GoR 2006b).

[26] A more user-friendly budget was recently created, and MINECOFIN (Rwanda's Ministry of Finance and Economic Planning) did present the last budget to civil society (Interviews, Kigali: 11.10.09 and 07.02.10).
[27] The RPF is a militia turned political party. In 1990, the RPF invaded Rwanda from the north, beginning a civil war. In 1994, they reached Kigali, assuming power and effectively ending the genocide that had begun approximately 100 days earlier.
[28] A recent UN mapping exercise of the atrocities committed in Eastern Zaire from 1993–2003 suggests that the Hutu population living in Zaire (not just persons responsible for the 1994 genocide against the Tutsis) were directly targeted. The report suggests that such atrocities constitute a potential genocide, and it documents RPF involvement in such campaigns (OHCHR 2010).
[29] In the months preceding the election, several high-profile candidates and political parties were prevented from registering, and newspapers critical of the regime were shut down. In addition, there were multiple cases of attempted and successful assassinations of opposition leaders and RPF defectors (Beaumont 2011).
[30] Following the presidential elections, the US expressed concern about the "disturbing events" surrounding the election, but there has been no visible effect on U.S. policy in Rwanda (Reuters 2010).

## References

Acharya, A., A. de Lima, and M. Moore. 2006. "Proliferation and Fragmentation: Transactions Costs and the Value of Aid." *The Journal of Development Studies* 42:1, 1–21.

African Development Bank. 2005. *Rwanda Reaches Completion Point in HIPC Initiative: Obtains Major Debt Relief from the AfDB.* July 6, 2005.

Ayodele, T., F. Cudjoe, T. Nolutshungu, and C. Sunwabe. 2005. "African Perspectives on Aid: Foreign Assistance Will Not Pull Africa Out of Poverty." *Economic Development Bulletin*, no. 2.

Barkan, J. 2009. "Rethinking Budget Support for Africa: A Political Economy Perspective." In *Smart Aid for African Development*, ed. R. A. Joseph and A. Gillies. Boulder: Lynne Rienner Publishers.

Beasley, A., D. Colin, J. Malick, A. Melnyk, M. Pitter-Lunn, D. Ray, B. Frantz, and J. Lieberson. 2005. *General Budget Support: Key Findings of Five USAID Studies.*

Beaumont, P. 2010. "Deadly Attacks on Rwandan Opposition Spark Warning by UN." *The Observer*. July 18. http://www.guardian.co.uk/world/2010/jul/18/attacks-rwandan-opposition-un-warning. Accessed July 20, 2011.

Bräutigam, Deborah. 2000. *Aid Dependence and Governance*. Stockholm: Almqvist & Wiksell International.

BSHG. 2003. "Partnership Framework for Harmonisation and Alignment of Budget Support Between the Government of Rwanda and its Development Partners." Kigali: Ministry of Finance and Economic Planning, Republic of Rwanda.

—. 2006a. "First Quarter 2006 Meeting Minutes." Budget Support Harmonization Group, March 1, 2006. Kigali: Ministry of Finance and Economic Planning, Republic of Rwanda.

—. 2006b. "Second Quarter 2006 Meeting Minutes." Budget Support Harmonization Group, June 15, 2006. Kigali: Ministry of Finance and Economic Planning, Republic of Rwanda.

—. 2006c. "Terms of Reference, Budget Support Harmonisation Group." Kigali: Ministry of Finance and Economic Planning, Republic of Rwanda.

—. 2008. "Memorandum of Understanding Governing the Provision of Direct Budget Support in the Implementation of Rwanda's Economic Development and Poverty Reduction Strategy." Kigali: Ministry of Finance and Economic Planning, Republic of Rwanda.

Carlsson, J., G. Somolekae, and N. van de Walle. 1997. *Foreign Aid in Africa: Learning from Country Experiences*. Uppsala: Nordiska Afrikainstitutet.

Celasun, O., and J. Walliser. 2006. "Predictability of Budget Aid: Recent Experiences." In *Budget Support as More Effective Aid? Recent Experiences and Emerging Lessons*, ed. S. Koeberle, Z. Stavreski, and J. Walliser. Washington, DC: The World Bank.

Cheru, F. 2006. "Building and Supporting PRSPs in Africa: What Has Worked Well so Far? What Needs Changing?" *Third World Quarterly* 27:2, 355–76.

Chiche, M. 2008. "Putting Aid on Budget: A Case Study Rwanda." In *A Study for the Collaboration Africa Budget Reform Initiative (CABRI) and the Strategic Partnership for Africa (SPA).* Oxford, England: Mokoro Ltd.

Craig, D., and D. Porter. 2003. "Poverty Reduction Strategy Papers: A New Convergence." *World Development* 31:1, 53–69.

de Renzio, Paolo. 2006. "Aid, Budgets, and Accountability: A Survey Article." *Development Policy Review* 24:6, 627–45.

—. 2009. "More Aid or Smarter Aid? Donors, Governance, and Accountability." In *Smart Aid for African Development*, ed. R. A. Joseph and A. Gillies. Boulder: Lynne Rienner Publishers.

de Renzio, P., L. Whitfield, and I. Bergamaschi. 2008. "Reforming Foreign Aid Practices: What Country Ownership is and what Donors can do to Support it." Briefing Paper by Global Economic Governance Programme. Oxford: University College, Oxford University.

Devarajan, S., D. Dollar, and T. Holmgren. 2001. *Aid and Reform in Africa: Lessons from Ten Case Studies*. Washington, DC: World Bank.

Directorate General for Development, European Commission. 2006. "European Commission Budget Support: An Innovative Approach to Conditionality." In *Budget Support as More Effective Aid? Recent Experiences and Emerging Lessons*, ed. S. Koeberle, Z. Stavreski, and J. Walliser. Washington DC: World Bank.

Eifert, B., and A. Gelb. 2006. "Improving the Dynamics of Aid: Towards More Predictable Budget Support." In *Budget Support as More Effective Aid? Recent Experiences and Emerging Lessons*, ed. S. Koeberle, Z. Stavreski, and J. Walliser. Washington, DC: The World Bank.

GoR. 2006a. "Cabinet Paper on Preparing a Five-year 'Economic Development and Poverty Reduction Strategy.'" Kigali: Republic of Rwanda.

—. 2006b. Draft Report. Paper read at launch of the Economic Development and Poverty Reduction Strategy (EDPRS) process, February 2–3, 2006, at Intercontinental Hotel, Kigali.

—. 2007a. *Development Cooperation and Aid Coordination in Rwanda, from 1990–2005*. Kigali: External Finance Unit, Ministry of Finance and Economic Planning, Republic of Rwanda.

—. 2007b. "Report on the Seventh Annual Government of Rwanda and Development Partners Meeting." Paper read at Stimulating Growth and Poverty Reduction through Strong Partnerships and Sound Economic Governance, Report on the Seventh Annual Government of Rwanda and Development Partners Meeting, November 25–26, 2007, at Serena Hotel, Kigali.

—. 2009. "Rwanda Donor Performance Assessment Framework, Preliminary Results from the 2009 Round of Monitoring." Kigali: Republic of Rwanda.

Gould, J., ed. 2005. *The New Conditionality: the Politics of Poverty Reduction Strategies*. London, New York: Zed Books.

Hammond, M. A. 2006. "A Framework for Evaluating General Budget Support." In *Budget Support as More Effective Aid? Recent Experiences and Emerging Lessons*, ed. S. Koeberle, Z. Stavreski, and J. Walliser. Washington, DC: World Bank.

Harrison, G. 2001. "Post-Conditionality Politics and Administrative Reform: Reflections on the Cases of Uganda and Tanzania." *Development and Change* 32:4, 657–79.

Hayman, R. 2009. "From Rome to Accra via Kigali: 'Aid Effectiveness' in Rwanda." *Development Policy Review* 27:5, 581–99.

Highton, N. 2009. "Mutual Accountability at the Country Level: Rwanda Country Case Study (Draft)." In *Joint Venture on Managing for Development Results*, ed. N. Highton: Overseas Development Institute.

IMF. 2005. "International Monetary Fund and World Bank Support US$1.4 billion in Debt Service Relief for Rwanda." Press Release No. 05/84. April 13. http://www.imf.org/external/np/sec/pr/2005/pr0584.htm. Accessed August 8, 2011.

—. 2009. "Rwanda: 2008 Article IV Consultation, Fifth Review Under the Three-Year Arrangement Under the Poverty Reduction and Growth Facility, and Request for Waiver of Non-observance of Performance Criterion. Staff Report; Staff Supplement and Statement; Public Information Notice and Press Release on the Executive Board Discussion; and Statement by the Executive Director for Rwanda." Washington, DC: International Monetary Fund.

IDD and Associates. 2006. "Evaluation of General Budget Support: Synthesis Report, Executive Summary." In *Joint Evaluation of General Budget Support, 1994–2004*. Birmingham, UK: International Development Department (IDD), School of Public Policy, University of Birmingham.

Joseph, R. A., and A. Gillies. 2009. *Smart Aid for African Development*. Boulder: Lynne Rienner Publishers.

Kagire, E. 2009. "Donor Budget Support Increases by 20 Percent." *The New Times*.

Killick, T. 2004. "Politics, Evidence and the New Aid Agenda." *Development Policy Review* 22:1, 5–29.

Knack, S., and A. Rahman. 2008. "Donor Fragmentation." In *Reinventing Foreign Aid*, ed. W. Easterly. Cambridge, MA: MIT Press.

Knoll, M. 2008. "Budget Support: A Reformed Approach or Old Wine in New Skins." In *UNCTAD Discussion Papers*. Geneva, Switzerland: United Nations Conference on Trade and Development.

Koeberle, S., and Z. Stavreski. 2006. "Budget Support: Concept and Issues." In *Budget Support as more Effective Aid? Recent Experiences and Emerging Lessons*, eds. S. Koeberle, Z. Stavreski, and J. Walliser. Washington, DC: World Bank

Lawson, A., D. Booth, M. Msuya, S. Wangwe, and T. Williamson. 2006. "Does General Budget Support Work? Evidence from Tanzania." In *Budget Support as More Effective Aid? Recent Experiences and Emerging Lessons*, eds. S. Koeberle, Z. Stavreski, and J. Walliser. Washington, DC: World Bank.

Moore, M. 1998. "Death without Taxes: Democracy, State Capacity, and Aid Dependence in the Fourth World." In *The Democratic Developmental State: Politics and Institutional Design*, ed. M. Robinson and G. White. New York: Oxford University Press.

Morrissey, O. 2006. "Fungibility, Prior Actions, and Eligibility for Budget Support." In *Budget Support as More Effective Aid? Recent Experiences and Emerging Lessons*, ed. S. Koeberle, Z. Stavreski and J. Walliser. Washington, DC: The World Bank.

Moyo, D. 2009. *Dead Aid: Why Aid is Not Working and How There is a Better Way for Africa.* New York: Farrar, Straus and Giroux.

Norwegian Agency for Development Cooperation. 2006. "Direct Budget Support, Disbursement Mechanisms, and Predictability." In *Budget Support as More Effective Aid? Recent Experiences and Emerging Lessons*, ed. S. Koeberle, Z. Stavreski and J. Walliser. Washington, DC: World Bank.

OECD-DAC. 2008. "Rwanda, 45." In *2008 Survey on Monitoring the Paris Declaration: Making Aid more Effective by 2010,* Volume 2 (Country Chapters).

OECD. 2005. "Paris Declaration on Aid Effectiveness." Paris, France: Paris High Level Forum on Aid Effectiveness, March 2, 2005.

—. 2008. "Accra Agenda for Action (AAA)." Accra, Ghana: Third High Level Forum on Aid Effectiveness (HLF-3), September 2–4, 2008.

OHCHR. 2010. United Nations Office of the High Commissioner Report 2010. United Nations.

Purcell, R., C. Dom, and G. Ahohamuteze. 2006. "Rwanda Country Report." *Joint Evaluation of General Budget Support, 1994–2004.* http://www.bmz.de/en/publications/type_of_publication/evaluation/international_joint_evaluations/GBS_Rwanda.pdf. Accessed June 28, 2011.

Reuters. 2010. "U.S. Expresses Concern about Rwanda Election." Reuters Africa. August 14. http://af.reuters.com/article/topNews/idAFJOE67D00N20100814. Accessed July 20, 2011.

Strategic Partnership with Africa, Budget Support Working Group. 2003. "Report of a Second Mission to Rwanda."

—. 2009. "Survey of Budget Support 2008, Volume 1: Main Findings."

Swedish Government Offices. 2008. "Sweden Stops Budget Support to Rwanda, Press Release." Stockholm: Ministry for Foreign Affairs, Government of Sweden. December 17. http://www.regeringen.se/sb/d/11214/a/117770. June 15, 2011.

Unwin, T. 2004. "Beyond Budgetary Support: Pro-Poor Development Agenda for Africa." *Third World Quarterly* 25:8, 1501–23.

van de Walle, N. 2001. *African Economies and the Politics of Permanent Crisis, 1979–1999*. Cambridge, New York: Cambridge University Press.

van de Walle, N., and T. A. Johnston. 1996. *Improving Aid to Africa*. Policy essay, no. 21. Washington, DC: Overseas Development Council.

Whitfield, L., ed. 2009. *The Politics of Aid: African Strategies for Dealing with Donors.* Oxford: Oxford University Press.

Williamson, T., and C. Dom. 2010. "Making Sector Budget Support Work for Service Delivery: An Overview." Oversees Development Institute, Project Briefing no. 36.

Woods, N. 2005. "The Shifting Politics of Foreign Aid." *International Affairs* 81: 2, 393–409.

# CHAPTER ELEVEN

# ETHICAL PARADOXES OF FAITH-BASED AID IN CAMEROON AND KENYA

CECELIA LYNCH

How do faith-based groups provide aid in Africa and what are the ethical paradoxes they confront in their work? Scholars and policy makers are increasingly coming to grips with the roles of faith-based organizations in providing humanitarian assistance, in terms of both emergency relief and development programs (Marshall 2007). In Africa, these groups are largely comprised of mainline Christian and Islamic denominations that have long provided clinics, schools, and hospitals as part of various colonial projects and postcolonial presences; faith-based transnational nongovernmental organizations (NGOs) such as World Vision, Caritas, and Catholic Charities, the Heifer Project, the Mennonite Central Committee, Islamic Relief, and many more; and in recent years, Pentecostal and charismatic Christian groups (Miller and Yamamori 2007; de Surgy 2001; Gifford 2009). A major argument in favor of faith-based aid is that religious groups already exist in difficult-to-reach areas, and/or that they are already trusted by their constituent members. A major argument against faith-based aid is that it is either tied to proselytizing or promotes religious exclusivism and potentially conflict.

This chapter first maps the array of faith-based aid groups operating in Cameroon and Kenya, where the author conducted interviews with several dozen representatives of humanitarian NGOs during three research trips beginning in late 2006 to early 2007. Kenya, as the sub-Saharan base of several UN agencies (Nairobi, along with Geneva, New York, and Paris, is the site of major UN offices), is also an African hub for transnational groups as well as for mainline denominational assistance. Despite assistance to Africa being "in vogue," Cameroon by comparison has fewer transnational aid organizations, relying instead on networks provided by Presbyterian, Catholic, and Baptist churches as well as numerous mosques, and buttressed by some international groups and an influx of small Pentecostal church programs. Both countries present a religiously plural array of faith-based aid, including Christian, Islamic, "traditional" religious and interfaith groups. Mapping the organizational trends in these two countries thus provides important information about the ways aid organizations, including faith-based ones, operate in Africa. The aid phenomenon in Africa should also be situated in the context of the end of the Cold War and the rapid expansion of nongovernmental organizations (NGOs) both transnationally and locally, and high-profile, including celebrity, attention to poverty, disease, and conflict on the continent, from Live Aid to Jubilee 2000 to the One Campaign (Lynch 2009).

The second part of the chapter examines several ethical synergies and paradoxes that result from these trends. Interfaith groups in both countries work together on many health issues (e.g. malaria, women's health, HIV/AIDS), as well as on human rights issues, famine prevention, and conflicts over land, indicating that religious exclusivism does not present a major obstacle to interfaith cooperation. Nevertheless, interfaith aid programs have been hindered by transnational pressures on Islamic groups imposed as part of the "war on terror." Moreover, religious groups, like secular NGOs, have found their work shaped by broader economic pressures, especially on the part of donors, to show quick results without creating "dependency." These pressures are more severe in Kenya than in Cameroon at this time. Finally, doctrinal issues tend to influence assistance for health-based issues related to sexuality. The chapter examines the degree to which domestic religious groups and transnational faith-based NGOs, both Christian and Muslim, are affected or not by trends in non-faith-based assistance, and the ethical paradoxes that can result. This section draws on research conducted in Cameroon in December 2006 to January 2007, and in Kenya in June–July, 2007 and August–September, 2008, as well as website materials and secondary sources.[1]

## Mapping Faith-Based Humanitarianism in Cameroon and Kenya

Faith-based aid, also called religious humanitarianism, is part and parcel of development and emergency assistance today, although tracking and "counting" it has only begun recently. For example, the UK's Charity Commission, which monitors numbers and types of nongovernmental groups operating from UK bases, has only begun to enumerate faith-based groups as a separate category in the past few years.[2] Scholars, however, are increasingly noting the importance of faith-based groups in providing humanitarian aid.[3] For the purposes of this paper, faith-based aid includes both emergency relief and development assistance, both of which are increasingly included under the rubric of "humanitarianism" (Barnett and Weiss 2008).[4]

Kenya and Cameroon, in East and Central Africa, respectively, provide very different examples of the impact of faith-based humanitarian assistance. Both countries' forms of NGO assistance are shaped by their religious histories, including the spread of Christianity through missions and colonialism, and the spread of Islam through trade and immigration. Both experienced Christian missionizing in the nineteenth and twentieth centuries as part of European colonization, although Cameroon was originally colonized by the Germans and later (as part of post-World War I settlements) divided, with the South-West province being given over to British control while the rest of the country was controlled by the French. Kenya experienced a bitter war of independence from the British, made famous by the Mau Mau rebellion.

Cameroon's major Christian denominations today include Presbyterian and especially Catholic, while the north is heavily populated by Muslims. Kenya has a strong Anglican presence, as well as Catholic, Presbyterian, and African Independent Churches. Kenya's Muslims live primarily in the northeast and the coastal region of the Indian Ocean, where there is also a smaller Hindu population. Evangelical and Pentecostal Christians have made significant inroads in both countries, and both have significant numbers of people who practice forms of African Traditional Religion (ATR). In Kenya, "syncretic" African Initiated (or Instituted) Churches (AICs), have for a century been an integral part of the religious landscape in the country. Quantifying religious adherence is a difficult task in either country due to the inability of most measures to account for religious syncretism.[5] For example, the Cameroonian population is said to be approximately 35 to over 50 percent Christian, approximately 18–30 percent Muslim, and from approximately 10 to over 50 percent African Traditional Religion. The statistics for Kenya are only slightly less confusing: 60–65 percent Christian (majority Catholic, also Protestant), from 6 to more than 10 percent Muslim, and from 10–34 percent "indigenous" or some form of African church religion.[6]

The nongovernmental organization presence in these two countries, however, is considerably different. Both countries began to regulate NGOs in the early 1990s in the aftermath of the Cold War, which triggered a new wave of democratization and expansion of neoliberal economic policies. Democratizing and privatizing trends each encouraged the growth of new local and transational NGOs to take over social welfare tasks that the state was unwilling or unable to undertake. This scenario contrasts with the role of NGOs during the Cold War, when NGOs were much more likely to be faith-based and were frequently tied to mainline religious communities because these denominations were better able to maneuver around requirements to affiliate with the ruling party in one-party systems of government. Faith-based schools, hospitals, and other affiliated aid organizations reached into rural areas throughout these two countries from the mission period onwards, and this expansive reach remains one of their primary strengths (in contrast to newer secular transnational groups) today.

Since the end of the Cold War, however, Kenya has become a hub for NGO activity, hosting numerous groups that operate within the country as well as others that work in neighboring countries such as Sudan and Somalia. Nairobi, as a major city in sub-Saharan Africa, hosts the regional offices of many UN agencies. As a result, a number of additional regional and Africa-wide organizations have headquarters or major offices in that city. Far fewer transnational NGOs operate in Cameroon, and these are located primarily in the capital, Yaoundé.

NGO assistance is also heavily influenced by the presence or relative absence of conflict in each country and surrounding areas. For example, aid workers and scholars report many areas of Liberia and Sierra Leone in West Africa, and Northern Uganda and Sudan in East Africa, to be overrun with NGOs. Other states such as Ghana and Nigeria are NGO magnets either because of the relative ease of conducting operations in them (Ghana) or their size and regional importance (Nigeria). In East Africa, Somalia, while embroiled in conflict, has had fewer NGOs than Sudan or Uganda, because many of the faith-based Christian and secular groups that would otherwise work in the country have not had channels of access.[7] At this time it is unclear to what degree the DRC has become a magnet for NGO activity, but the number of aid organizations operating in the country appears to have increased in recent years.

Cameroon occupies a unique position in the composite picture of aid to Africa. While not in the midst of or recovering from civil war, its population remains extremely poor, corruption is rife, and other indices of development remain low. The UN Development Agency's Human Development Index ranks Cameroon at 131 out of 169 countries on both its multidimensional poverty index and its Human Development Index (for comparative purposes, Kenya ranks slightly better at 128).[8] Transparency International ranks Cameroon only slightly better than Kenya on indices of corruption, although rankings are difficult to construct for either country.[9] According to many measures, therefore, Cameroon is an ideal place for relief and development projects. However, religious (church and mosque-based) aid appears to be the primary form of health, education, and other aid present in the country. Some organizations such as the Heifer Project, CARE, parts of Oxfam, Caritas, Catholic Relief, and the development office of ACT (Action by Churches Together) operate in both Cameroon and Kenya. However, others, including Save the Children, World Vision, Médecins Sans Frontières (Doctors without Borders), NetsforLife, the ACT emergency program, Church World Service, the American Friends Service Committee, Samaritan's Purse, World Relief, Adventist Development and Relief Agency (ADRA), and Islamic Relief, have programs in Kenya but not in Cameroon. Muslim Aid, like Islamic Relief (a UK-based transnational NGO), currently has no programs in Cameroon (although its website indicates that it worked there previously), but in 2008 it established a field office in Kenya.[10]

Possible reasons for the relative lack of transnational NGOs in Cameroon as compared to Kenya include the relationship between corruption and the Cameroonian government, which has been ruled as a virtual dictatorship by President Paul Biya since 1982. Biya's rule has kept a tight lid on potential dissent resulting from regional and linguistic differences (for example, the complaint by Anglophones that the government has long favored the majority Francophone population). As a result, Cameroon's poverty does not receive much public or media attention outside the country, especially when compared to the overt violence in nearby countries such as the DRC, Nigeria, Chad, or Ivory Coast. (I frequently heard Cameroonians express pride that their country was unlikely, even in the absence of a dictator, to disintegrate into violent conflict like many of its neighbors.) Second, the centralization of governmental corruption may affect aid distribution in countries like Cameroon in ways that encourage NGOs to work in other places instead. On my trip to Cameroon I accompanied the West/Central African representative of a medical assistance NGO, who found that some of the medicines sent to clinics had expired at the port due to lack of or insufficient bribes to port officials. On a different occasion, a Cameroonian colleague reported seeing an ad from the German Embassy in Yaoundé inviting NGOs to come to the Embassy to collect aid funds, indicating attempts to bypass the central government. This is not to say that corruption is nonexistent in Kenya or other countries that host large numbers of transnational NGOS, or that corruption is not a problem in donor countries, as the recent financial and mortgage crises have reminded us. Yet in countries like Cameroon, the centralization of power can allow little room for NGOs to maneuver in attempting to provide aid. Given the need to improve Cameroon's reputation, it is no wonder that one of President Biya's two major accomplishments for 2006, as reported by the state-controlled newspaper, was obtaining HIPC (Heavily-Indebted Poor Country, or PPTE [pays pauvres très endéttes]) status.[11] This status, conferred by an initiative begun by the World Bank and IMF in the mid-1990s, allows the possibility of considerable debt relief for recipient states. The Cameroonian government had lobbied for HIPC status to assist the economy and signal publicly that its international profile had improved, opening the possibility of access to additional multilateral and bilateral sources of aid. It is unclear, however, whether the result has been tighter control of assistance or more transparency. In sum, NGOs appear to congregate either where access is easier or where the public nature of disaster and conflict make it appear more imperative to act.

It is also interesting that transnational Islamic NGOs such as Islamic Relief and Muslim Aid (both based in the UK but with offices in many parts of the world) have bases of operation in Kenya but not in Cameroon. Nairobi offices make sense as a regional East African hub of operations, but Kenya has a particular, problematic history with Muslim NGOs. Between 1998, when the U.S. embassy was bombed, and September 11, 2001, Kenya, with the support of the U.S. government, severely restricted the movement of many Muslim nongovernmental groups, creating considerable consternation among many in the aid community.[12] Several people I interviewed in 2007 and 2008 related instances of Muslim aid groups that operated in areas such as Kibera, the large slum on the edge of Nairobi, or in the Coastal region, having been forced out of the country. The fact that Muslim Aid was given a temporary license to open a field office in February 2008, with the expectation of a permanent license to come, indicates that even with Kenya's participation in restricting groups using the discourse of the "war on terror," transnational, Western-based Islamic humanitarian aid groups have recently made inroads in Kenya. Again, Cameroon, with a larger percentage of Muslims in the population, is not a focal point for these aid groups, despite the relatively amicable relations among religious entities in that country.

Thus transnational faith-based NGOs, both Christian and Muslim, have a much greater presence in Kenya than in Cameroon. It is unclear what percentage of aid faith-based (as opposed to "secular") groups provide (although, for example, Gifford cites one estimate that "64 percent of all Kenya's educational institutions" are church-based[13]), but many nonreligious transnational groups (for example, Direct Relief International) contract with local faith-based partners in both countries, thus increasing the proportion of aid actually provided by religiously-affiliated organizations. Large Pentecostal groups that have regular open-air meetings in Kenya have not yet made Cameroon a strong base of operations, although storefront Pentecostal churches and Jehovah's Witness halls are common. Similarly, although transnational evangelical groups such as Samaritan's Purse (operated by Franklin Graham) or the Saddleback Church (run by Pastor Rick Warren) do not operate in Cameroon, evangelical offshoots of mainline churches have opened mega-church sites in the capital, Yaoundé.

These trends indicate that in Cameroon, faith-based aid is still strongly tied to the schools and hospitals as well as churches and mosques established by Catholic, Presbyterian, Baptist, and Muslim missionaries and immigrants. Even though the in-country leadership is largely "indigenized," Cameroon remains a site for mission work (based on technical expertise) by doctors and educators from Europe and North America affiliated with these religious sects. Evangelical churches tend to be offshoots of mainline Protestant denominations or charismatic Catholics, instead of independent Protestant churches or transnational evangelical movements. Transnational Islamic groups with bases in the global West/North tend not to have major programs in Cameroon, despite its considerable number of Muslims, high rates of poverty, and a proclivity toward famine. Kenya, in contrast, hosts offices of the two major transnational Islamic aid groups and many of the transnational Christian aid groups. While church denomination and mosque-based aid is also common, the transnational component of aid in Kenya is more bureaucratized and significant. Moreover, traditional religion occupies a different place in each country. In Cameroon, syncretic practices appear to be common but are not always discussed openly. Some interviewees told me that traditionalists, who are widespread throughout the country, are not well-organized, although the transnational organization of traditional healers known as PROMETRA (Promotion des Médecines Traditionelles, or Promotion of Traditional Medicine, based in Dakar, Senegal) has a well-known leader in Yaoundé. In Kenya, the establishment of African Independent/Initiated Churches (AICs) through the twentieth century indicates a considerable institutionalization of a particular blend of traditional and missionary forms of religion, and hence potentially of aid. While not comprehensive, these two countries provide an idea of the range of faith-based aid taking place on the continent.

Nevertheless, humanitarian assistance and various forms of aid, while taking different forms, are critical to both countries. Much of this assistance is provided by religious organizations: one study estimates that between 30 and 70 percent of healthcare in Africa is provided by faith-based groups.[14] As a result, the Anglican Health Network praised the World Health Organization (WHO) for beginning to map faith-based health facilities in November of 2009. "Given the claims that faith-based health facilities can equal if not exceed the number of state health facilities in a number of developing countries, it is essential for any national health planning exercise to include all service providers."[15] In Cameroon, the Catholic and Presbyterian churches have major networks of hospitals and clinics that provide a significant amount of medical care (along with state-run and independent clinics and hospitals). For example, the Catholic Church at the end of 2007 operated 28 hospitals and 235 clinics in the country.[16] For comparative purposes, the Cameroonian state runs three central and 136 district hospitals.[17]

Interfaith networks, active in both countries, sometimes carry out aid projects as well. Those that do not are connected to many of the faith-based humanitarian organizations operating in various parts of the continent. Nairobi houses the offices of the Programme for Christian-Muslim Relations in Africa (PROCMURA), the Inter-Faith Action for Peace in Africa (IFAPA), and the All Africa Conference of Churches (ACC). Moreover, both countries are represented in the global interfaith organization World Conference of Religions for Peace, which works on issues such as women's rights and HIV and AIDS prevention and care, as well as interfaith understanding.

## Ethical Synergies and Paradoxes of Faith-Based Aid

### Aid and neoliberal pressures

The relatively greater importance of transnational forms of aid—faith-based and secular—in Kenya compared to Cameroon would lead to the expectation that transnational aid trends would affect aid to Kenya more than aid to Cameroon. In two respects, this appears to be the case. First, donor pressures to show quick results and enumerate the successes of assistance provided were frequently described by interviewees in Kenya, but less so in Cameroon. (It should be noted that while faith-based organizations have a base of funding in their congregations, they also rely to differing degrees on the typical donor communities, including USAID, the EU, other European and Canadian state aid agencies, and major foundations such as Gates and Clinton.) In other work I describe these pressures as conforming to neoliberal forms of governance, or "governmentality" (Lynch 2009; Sending and Neumann 2006). In my interviews, faith-based NGO representatives in Kenya (more than in Cameroon) tended to describe their work in "NGO-speak," using terms such as "capacity-building," "training," "partnerships," and "sustainability." In Cameroon, NGO representatives expressed a great deal of gratitude for the interest in their work. In Kenya, NGO representatives were knowledgeable about networks of aid and donor contacts, while in Cameroon people asked more questions about how to obtain assistance. In Kenya, moreover, other people I encountered who were not being interviewed (guest house personnel, waiters, cab drivers, etc.) often asked about the availability of NGO assistance for their needs, whereas in Cameroon (again, late 2006/early 2007), this type of question did not arise. In other words, the NGO presence and impact were considerable in the parts of Kenya where I conducted interviews (Nairobi, Mombasa, and the coast, and parts of Masai Mara), but much less so in the parts of Cameroon where I travelled (Douala, Yaoundé, and towns and villages in the Southwest Province). The NGO world had saturated society in Kenya, and people either asked about how to obtain NGO assistance, expressed suspicion of "briefcase" NGOs, or sometimes both.[18]

What is the effect of the ubiquity of NGO activity on faith-based groups in parts of Africa like Kenya? I have argued elsewhere that it is a mistake to view the ethical results simply as a process of "secularizing" faith-based groups.[19] In interviews, Christian groups in both countries were usually very willing to explore the faith "bases" of what they do and why they embark on some methods over others. Muslim groups with transnational connections (or aspirations, including some who were looking for funding by Western donors), tended to present themselves as more secular than either the more localized, mosque-based Muslim groups or Christian groups. Donor pressures, therefore, do appear to move groups towards particular forms of rationalization and create a potential homogenization of aid procedures, particularly in Kenya. Should such rationalization continue to spread to states such as Cameroon, similar results could obtain. At the time of my interviews in Cameroon, the local Anglophone Presbyterian church leadership was looking for partners in U.S. churches, following a process of "twinning" that has been in place elsewhere, including Kenya, for some time (Gifford 2009). The channels of access to transnational donors in Cameroon likely remain at best indirect, as they appeal first to European or U.S. churches, who themselves have access to a broader array of national and multilateral aid agencies.

One example of the way rationalization resulting from donor pressure influences the religious ethics of aid concerns the move by many Christian organizations away from "charity" toward more rights-based objectives. While charity remains a pillar of Islamic ethics, preliminary research indicates that the interpretation of its meaning in humanitarian aid is expanding and possibly changing as well. The conceptions of charity and rights both have advantages and disadvantages. One of the major problems with notions of charity in Christian understanding is its connotation of *noblesse oblige* strategies of aid. As a way of moving beyond this connotation, many Christians and some transnational Muslim groups now emphasize that aid must be "sustainable," which means that it can enable self-help and result in projects that will eventually need no external funding. Sustainability's opposite, "dependency," is a term that has become extremely negative in NGO and donor literature. At least two ethical questions are at stake in this debate. First, does the move away from charity in some Christian thought result in reconceptualizing human dignity as based in individualistic notions of rights, and to what degree do Christian (especially) aid organizations participate in trends that measure success by questionable but obtainable metrics? Such ethics and methods could push into the background notions of "common good," communal rights, and holistic understandings of personhood. Second, to what degree does the need to measure results, for either Islamic or Christian aid groups, have the effect of tying strings to aid that move it further away from the notion of selfless giving without the expectation of return connoted by earlier religious understandings of the term?

## Interfaith religious activity on aid

Some of the literature on religion assumes a competitive market-based relationship between faith traditions as they vie for adherents. Studies of Christianity and the growth of evangelicalism and Pentecostalism in Latin America, in particular, promote the concept of religion as commodity that pits the offerings of prosperity and/or apolitical notions of new forms of Protestantism against both the conservative and liberationist wings of Catholicism. To a degree, this view receives confirmation in Cameroon and Kenya, but nuance and social context are necessary (as David Martin points out for Latin America) to understand the appeal of Pentecostal and evangelical forms of worship (Martin 2002). For example, a Presbyterian Church official acknowledged that some parishioners had moved to Pentecostal churches in the South-West Province of Cameroon, but also remarked that many return to their roots in the Presbyterian Church when their expectations, which may include healing or prosperity, are not fulfilled. In Kenya, African Initiated/Independent Churches have long made inroads into mainline Christian denominations, yet today there are also moves from AICs to Pentecostalism, and moves that incorporate Pentecostal or charismatic ideas and forms of worship into mainline churches. In each of these cases, adherents experiment to some degree, but their participation in these forms of Christianity also indicate that recombinations of traditional commitments with newer forms of worship continue (on these recombinations, see Martey 1996 and Meyer 2004).

In both countries, faith-based aid groups frequently work together in both formally-organized and informally-organized settings. For example, both countries are represented in World Religions for Peace, a transnational organization that tries to create interfaith religious councils in all countries of the globe to foster dialogue on both spiritual issues and "temporal" ones of conflict, poverty, and epidemics. Regional interfaith organizations of different kinds are also common in Africa, and several are based in Nairobi. PROCMURA, mentioned earlier, was founded by Christians in the period just before decolonization to promote Christian-Muslim understanding, while IFAPA, also mentioned earlier, is a more recently created organization founded to promote peace and human rights by working through the seven major faith traditions found on the continent, including African Traditional Religions, the Baha'i faith, Christianity, Islam, Hinduism, Traditionalism, Buddhism, and Judaism. Finally, local interfaith organizations have also been organized in both countries, some on an *ad hoc* basis and others more permanently. For example, in the district of Mamfe, Cameroon, a priest gave me typed documents concerning a council including local Catholic, Protestant, and Muslim leaders as well as chiefs and town officials who had been called to discuss the problem of an accusation of witchcraft. This type of *ad hoc* consultation by different faith groups, chiefs, and government officials is typical for areas of common concern.

Interfaith interaction on humanitarian aid, however, is especially interesting in the context of Christian-Muslim collaborations. The discourse of the "war on terror" has hindered interfaith collaboration in Kenya and heightened suspicions of Muslims in both countries. African Muslim women, for example, stated in conversations with Christians in 2004 that the media breeds suspicion of "Muslims as terrorists" all over the world.[20] In Cameroon, this suspicion was alluded to informally by some as the government's hidden watchfulness over Muslims, while others asserted that religious pluralism was widely respected in the country. Kenya, however, went even further in hindering collaboration by ejecting many non-domestic Islamic groups from the country between 1998 and 2001 and, in cooperation with the U.S. government, setting up the East African Counter-terrorism Initiative in 2003 (Hammer 2007; Hirsch 2006; Lynch 2011b). As Gifford points out, debates over a new Kenyan constitution prior to the referendum of summer 2010 also frequently inhibited constructive interfaith interactions, as some government officials assisted in pitting groups against each other by, for example, raising suspicion among Christians of Muslim efforts to institutionalize Islamic family law courts (Gifford 2009; see also Lynch 2011b on the Khadis courts debate).

Nevertheless, Kenyan government pressures and collaboration with the U.S. in the "war on terror" have also, paradoxically, encouraged new interfaith collaboration in some areas, as for example in the Indian Ocean Coastal area of Kenya. During both of my visits to the coast, Muslim as well as Christian activists and both religious and lay leaders narrated the story of the interfaith coastal council's work on human rights, against the deportation of Muslims, and for conflict resolution in land disputes. While this interfaith interaction did not prevent, for example, some Christians from praying for the conversion of their Muslim brethren during Ramadan,[21] the ties between Muslim and Christian denominations were consistent and strong, and stories of government injustice and interfaith collaboration were frequently repeated to me in interviews with Muslim and Christian leaders separately and together.

### Faith-based aid and traditional practices

Traditional religions and practices remain strong in both countries, although differences appear to obtain as well. For example, while African Independent/Initiated Churches (AICs) are well established in Kenya (and also in Ghana, Nigeria, and Congo), I have not found evidence of similar strength within Cameroon. Yet traditional religion is extremely strong in Cameroon, and most (though not all) of my Christian interviewees said they negotiated on an almost quotidian basis the mixture of Christian and traditional rites.

However, traditional practices such as female genital circumcision/mutilation (FGC/M) are widely disparaged by religious leaders in both countries.[22] A number of faith-based aid groups, including World Vision, a Cameroonian women's network, various churches, and Islamic rights groups all work separately (and sometimes together) to eradicate female circumcision/mutilation. In doing so, they align with outside donors, who are increasingly prioritizing programs to address women's rights and redress women's poverty. Despite the inclusion of traditionalists in a number of interfaith forums, these anti-FGM programs are generally couched in a desire to differentiate "modern" forms of accepted development from what Christians, Muslims, and donors argue are harmful traditional rites.

## Conclusions

Faith-based assistance to Africa is a well-established and still growing phenomenon. Transnational nongovernmental organizations may be either faith-based or secular. Faith-based groups may be tied to a particular religious denomination (like Caritas, Episcopal Relief and Development, or the Mennonite Central Committee) or be independent of any particular church or mosque (World Vision, Islamic Relief), although both types provide aid regardless of the religious affiliation of the recipients.[23] Individual churches and mosques (and synagogues) frequently have "projects" in various parts of Africa, and to an increasing degree, the African offices of aid organizations have become "indigenized" with the hiring of local staff.

Nevertheless, faith-based aid in some parts of Africa is much more internationalized than in others, as illustrated by the cases of Kenya and Cameroon. Faith-based assistance provides a significant amount of aid in both countries, but it is much more organized at the local parish, mosque, and individual church levels, as well as at the level of nationally-based denominations, in Cameroon. Kenya, by contrast, is a hub for transnational NGO organizations operating within the country as well as in surrounding states. Even with the active collaboration between the Kenyan and U.S. governments in the East African Counter-Terrorism Initiative, including U.S. funding of the Kenyan Anti-Terrorist police (Hammer 2007; Lynch 2011), and the complaints regarding continuing deportation of Muslims, transnational Islamic groups have a greater presence in Kenya than in Cameroon.

One result of the burgeoning "humanitarian international" movement (de Waal, 1997) is that the ethical stances of faith-based organizations in Kenya are in general more aligned with donor imperatives that press for results, for example "sustainability" over "dependency," and these organizations are more likely to work in partnership with state and NGO donors. As Cameroonian organizations (and the Cameroonian government) seek more assistance from abroad, we should analyze whether the discourse of faith-based assistance in that country also becomes more "neoliberal" in nature. In particular, traditional religious ethics of aid, including "charity" and "dignity," might be transformed in the process.

Finally, the relationships among Christian and Islamic, on one hand, and traditionalist groups, on the other, also deserve additional scrutiny. Traditionalist groups—including both organized networks such as PROMETRA and localized gatherings of traditional healers and religious leaders, such as is found on the Kenyan coast—are included in many (though not all) of the interfaith organizations operating on the continent. Yet some of the issues promoted by transnational donors and transnational religious communities, especially concerning women (such as eradicating female circumcision) create a hierarchy among "modern" faith-based groups and "backward" ones. There is some evidence that this type of hierarchy is being resisted with the creation of traditionalist NGOs, although this trend needs to be explored in future research.

## Notes

[1] I thank the Andrew W. Mellon Foundation New Directions Fellowship for support. This paper represents part of a larger project on "Islamic and Interfaith Religious Ethics in World Crises," funded by the Mellon New Directions fellowship.
[2] The Charity Commission of England and Wales continues to try to categorize and count faith-based groups. A 2008 Working Paper notes that faith-based charities operating from the UK totaled 29,495, or 17 percent of the total number of charities accounted for in the UK. This number is expected to change as congregation-based charities continue to be counted. Dr. Sarah Brennan, Working Paper —Faith Based Charities, Sept. 2008, p. 2. www.ncvo-vol.org.uk/uploadedFiles/NCVO/Events/Events_Archive/2008/Brennan.pdf, accessed September 4, 2011.
[3] The University of California Santa Barbara's Orfalea Center, for example, conducted a three-year series of conferences on religious nongovernmental organizations funded by the Luce Foundation.
[4] In fact, some governmental reports criticize programming that separates the two. According to an April 2011 overview of the Humanitarian Emergency Response Review commissioned by the British government, "Despite its mandate to look only at rapid-onset disasters, the HERR recognizes that separating humanitarian and development assistance is fundamentally incoherent." Humanitarian Policy Group at ODI, "The UK's review of humanitarian aid: an agenda for radical change?" Overseas Development Institute, London, April 2011, www.odi.org.uk/50years, accessed June 2011.
[5] Although admittedly a problematic term, I use "syncretism" here to capture the pluralism and sometimes fluidity of religious adherence, a characteristic that I argue needs more recognition in studies of politics and religion generally.
[6] Adherents.com compiles statistics by location (country), source, and year compiled, and thus provides a very useful resource. For both Cameroon and Kenya, the site lists different ways of breaking down religious adherents according to different research reports, including various encyclopedias (Britannia, Larousse, etc.), the CIA World Factbook, the reports of various religious groups themselves, etc. www.adherents.com, accessed 4/9/10.
[7] This situation may be changing as of this writing, because of the 2011 famine in Somalia and the increased role of the UN and partner NGOs in providing food aid to parts of the country.
[8] The report does note some improvement in Cameroon's situation, stating that "between 1980 and 2010 Cameroon's HDI rose by 0.9 percent annually." UNDP, Human Development Index, Nov. 4, 2010, Cameroon country profile, www.hdrstats.undp.org/en/countries/profiles/CMR.html; and International Human Development Indicators, www.hdrstats.undp.org/en/indicators/38406.html; accessed 9/1/11.

[9] Transparency International, www.transparency.org/policy_research/surveys_indices/cpi, accessed 9/1/11.
[10] www.muslimaid.org, accessed 4/9/10.
[11] *Cameroon Tribune,* 5 January 2007, pp.3–4.
[12] Cecelia Lynch, "Local and Global Influences on Islamic NGOs in Kenya," *Journal of Peacebuilding and Development,* 6,1 Summer 2011.
[13] *National Mirror,* July 2006, p.10, cited in Gifford, p.46.
[14] "Faith-based organizations provide up to 70 percent of healthcare in some African communities," *Africanpress,* July 31, 2010, Nairobi.
[15] The report continues, "This might sound obvious, but there is still resistance to seeing religious service providers as intrinsic components in a publicly defined health system." "Snapshots," *Anglican Health Network,* Autumn 2009, http://ahn.anglicancommunion.org/index.cfm, accessed April 10, 2010.
[16] Catholic News Agency, Mar. 3, 2009, "New statistics on Angola and Cameroon published ahead of Pope's trip," accessed April 9, 2010.
[17] Source: researchafrica.rti.org:Sub-Saharan Africa – Cameroon, accessed April 10, 2010.
[18] Paul Gifford's study of Christianity in Kenya confirms these findings. Gifford, 2009, pp.159–160.
[19] In this respect I differ somewhat from Gifford's analysis of the impact of NGOs on churches. See Cecelia Lynch, "Religious Humanitarianism and the Global Politics of Secularism," in Craig Calhoun, Mark Juergensmeyer, and Jonathan VanAntwerpen, eds., *Rethinking Secularism,* Oxford and New York: Oxford University Press, 2011.
[20] Elizabeth Odhiambo, "What we can do together, let us not do it differently from each other – Christian and Muslim Women Speak Out," PROCMURA/SRICA newsletter, Nos. 61 and 62, July–December 2004, p. 21, also cited in Lynch, "Religion, Identity, and the 'War on Terror': Insights from Religious Humanitarianism," in Patrick James, ed., *Religion, Identity, and Global Governance,* Toronto: University of Toronto Press, 2010.
[21] This was part of the prayer pamphlet in pews in a Protestant church I attended.
[22] I use both the terms "circumcision" and "mutilation" to indicate the fraught nature of the debate: while "circumcision" can connote an acceptable cultural practice, "mutilation" generally connotes unacceptable violence that must be stopped.
[23] The question of whether aid can be legitimate if accompanied by proselytizing, however, remains an extremely divisive question that I do not address in this paper, although I have done so in other work.

## References

Adherents.com. 2010. www.adherents.com, "Cameroon," and "Kenya."

*Africanpress.* 2010. "Faith-based organizations provide up to 70 percent of healthcare in some African communities." 31 July, Nairobi.

*Anglican Health Network.* 2009. "Snapshots." http://ahn.anglicancommunion.org/index.cfm, Autumn.

Barnett, M., and T. Weiss, eds. 2008. *Humanitarianism in Question: Politics, Power, Ethics.* Ithaca and London: Cornell University Press.
Brennan, S. 2008. Working Paper: Faith Based Charities. September, www.ncvo-vol.org.uk/uploadedFiles/NCVO/Events/Events_Archive/2008/Brennan.pdf: 1–16.
*Cameroon Tribune.* 2007. 5 January, 3–4.
Catholic News Agency. 2009. "New statistics on Angola and Cameroon published ahead of Pope's trip." March 3.
De Surgy, A. 2001. *Le Phénomène Pentecôtiste en Afrique Noire: le cas béninois.* Paris, Budapest, Torino: l'Harmattan.
deWaal, A. 1997. *Famine Crimes: Politics & the Disaster Relief Industry in Africa.* Oxford, UK, and Bloomington, IN: African Rights & The International African Institute, in association with James Currey and Indiana University Press.
Ela, J-M. 1986. *African Cry.* Maryknoll, New York: Orbis.
Gifford, P. 2009. *Christianity, Politics and Public Life in Kenya.* New York: Columbia University Press.
Hammer, J. 2007. "The African Front: Have aggressive post-9/11 policies fomented the very sectarianism they were meant to fight?" *New York Times Magazine,* December 23.
Hirsch, S. F. 2006. *In the Moment of Greatest Calamity: Terrorism, Grief, and a Victim's Quest for Justice.* Princeton and Oxford: Princeton University Press.
Humanitarian Policy Group at ODI. 2011. "The UK's review of humanitarian aid: an agenda for radical change?" April. Overseas Development Institute, London, www.odi.org.uk/50years, accessed June 2011.
Lynch, C. 2009. "Liberalism and the Contradictions of Global Civil Society," in *The Ethics of Global Governance,* ed. A. Franceschet. Boulder, CO: Lynne Rienner.
—. 2010. "Religion, Identity, and the 'War on Terror': Insights from Religious Humanitarianism." In *Religion, Ethics, and Global Governance,* ed. P. James. Toronto: University of Toronto Press.
—. 2011a. "Religious Humanitarianism and the Global Politics of Secularism." In *Rethinking Secularism,* eds. C. Calhoun, M. Juergensmeyer, and J. VanAntwerpen. Oxford and New York: Oxford University Press, 204–224.
—. 2011b. "Local and Global Influences on Islamic NGOs in Kenya." *Journal of Peacebuilding and Developmen,* 6:1, 21–34.
Marshall, K., and R. Marsh, eds. 2003. *Millenium Challenges for Development and Faith Institutions.* Washington, DC: The International Bank for Reconstruction and Development / The World Bank.

Martey, E. 1996. *African Theology: Inculturation and Liberation.* Maryknoll, NY: Orbis.
Martin, D. 2002. *Pentecostalism: The World Their Parish.* Oxford: Blackwell.
Meyer, B. 2004. "Christianity in Africa: From African Independent to Pentecostal-Charismatic Churches." *Annual Review of Anthroplogy* 33: 447–74.
Miller, D., and Te Yamamori, 2007. *Global Pentecostalism: the new face of Christian social engagement.* Berkeley and Los Angeles: University of California Press.
Muslim Aid website. 2010. www.muslimaid.org.
Odhiambo, E. 2004. "What we can do together, let us not do it differently from each other – Christian and Muslim Women Speak Out." PROCMURA/SRICA newsletter, Nos. 61 and 62, July–December, 21, Nairobi.
Research Africa website. 2010. researchafrica.rti.org:Sub-Saharan Africa – Cameroon.
Sending, O. J., and I. Neumann. 2006. "Governance to Governmentality: Analyzing NGOs, States, and Power." *International Studies Quarterly* 50: 3, 651–672.
Transparency International, www.transparency.org/policy_research/surveys_indices/cpi.
United Nations Development Programme. 2010. "Human Development Index, Cameroon country profile." November 4. www.hdrstats.undp.org/en/countries/profiles/CMR.html; and "International Human Development Indicators," www.hdrstats.undp.org/en/indicators/38406.html.

# CHAPTER TWELVE

# CANADIAN AND CHINESE AID TO AFRICA: PROPOSAL FOR INTERNATIONAL STRATEGIC ALLIANCES

MOSES N. KIGGUNDU

*If you want to go fast, travel alone, if you want to go far, travel with others.*
—Old Chinese proverb

## Introduction

Whether from the West or from South-South "brothers" like China, aid to Africa is always controversial. Supporters and critics alike agree that the results are at best mixed, and that new approaches are needed. Both Canada and China have deep historical and institutional roots as major donors of aid and development assistance to Africa, but they operate separately. Although initial reactions to China's growing engagements with Africa were hostile, recent reflections are more balanced, and the international community (e.g. the World Bank) is beginning to forge partnerships with the Chinese in Africa. As part of a broader initiative seeking innovative and more beneficial ways of engaging the Chinese in Africa, this chapter proposes the formation of a mutually beneficial strategic alliance between Canadian and Chinese aid programs in Africa for Africans. After providing a brief overview of Canadian and Chinese aid programs to Africa, the chapter presents the concepts and applications of international strategic alliances, value chain analysis including hybrid value chains, and organizational cluster development as these apply to Africa's aid and development. In spite of apparent differences between Canada and China (e.g. ideology, delivery mechanisms, aid constituencies, etc.), emerging new realities (e.g. China rising, Canadian apparent retreat, changing demographics) speak to the need for such an alliance. The chapter concludes by discussing the prospects and challenges of making such alliances work, and the possibility of other players such as the Development Assistance Committee (DAC) members or investors using this model as a template for future collaboration with the Chinese in Africa.

The Canadian foreign aid story starts in Europe with the Marshall Plan and in Asia with the Colombo Plan before going on to Africa. Faith-based organizations such as the Unitarian Service Committee (USC) and the Mennonite Central Committee (MCC) as well as secular non-government organizations (NGOs) were set up soon after World War II to provide humanitarian assistance to the "poor European cousins." In 1950, a few months after the People's Republic of China came into being in Beijing, Commonwealth foreign ministers met in Colombo Ceylon (now Sri Lanka), to establish the Colombo Plan to attack the poverty upon which Communist political movements in East and Southeast Asia were thought to feed.[1] Canada was represented at the meeting by then foreign minister Lester B. Pearson, who a decade later was invited by Robert McNamara, then President of the World Bank, to chair the commission on foreign aid. Through his work at the United Nations and as Canada's Prime Minister, Pearson built the foundation for Canada's philosophy, values, principles, understanding, and institutions for the country's foreign aid. These values include the belief that aid can and does make a difference and that there is a collective duty and obligation to help the needy and most vulnerable in the world, especially children and women. Given the increasingly interdependent world and the complex nature of the context within which aid is given and received, Canadians also believe that aid is best managed in partnership with others, both domestically and internationally. For most ordinary Canadians, *humanitarianism,* not economic development, is the *la raison d'etre* (or essence) of foreign aid.

Unlike Canada, China's foreign aid to Africa was not informed by either the Marshall plan or the Colombo Plan. Rather, it developed out of resistance and revolutionary opposition to colonialism and imperialism and the need to protect and preserve the independence and sovereignty of vulnerable newly independent states in Asia and Africa, and to support ongoing struggles for independence. According to Professor Li Anshan of Peking University, China first provided military and civilian aid to Egypt in 1956 because of the Suez Canal Crisis, just as it provided assistance to Tanzania and Zambia to build the Tanzara railway in 1964, after the West had declined to help.

Undoubtedly, the world has changed since Pearson and the Suez Canal Crisis. It has become more globalized, more complex, dynamic, uncertain, and above all more interdependent and multi-polar. At the same time, Africa's development challenges continue to pose a serious challenge, not only to the Africans themselves but to the entire international community. In the words of the former British Prime Minister, Tony Blair, "Africa is a scar on the world's conscience." Addressing Africa's development challenges and effectively implementing sustainable solutions to its apparently intractable problems requires the international community to work collaboratively. No single donor country has a monopoly on solving Africa's development problems. A recent World Bank report on the future of Africa (2011) recommends that the best way to deal with the pervasive fragility of the African state is by forming partnerships with regional and international development partners, including China. Indeed, one of the challenges to aid effectiveness, in Africa and elsewhere, is the failure of donor countries to work together consistently and effectively. This is the constant message one gets from the Pearson report in the 1950s, from the Paris Declaration on Aid Effectiveness in 2005, from the Accra Action Plan in 2008 (AAA), and from the more recent UN Millennium Development Goals (MDGs) Summit in 2010 (UN 2010). It is because of this realization that I propose the development of an international strategic alliance between development actors in Canada and in China to work together in Africa so as to advance the development interests for all Africans.

## Canadian Aid to Africa

For most Canadians, the country's foreign aid philosophy, strategy, institutions and operations are rooted in the work of the former Prime Minister Lester B. Pearson, who at the invitation of then-President of the World Bank Robert S. McNamara chaired the Commission on International Development and on September 15, 1969, produced the *Partners in Development* Commission Report.[2] The Commission was charged with developing a strategy for renewing international aid and addressing the crisis of declining aid commitments by rich donor countries. Twenty-five years after the introduction of the Marshall Plan, the Pearson Commission was aimed at reassuring Canadians and the rest of the world of the critical role foreign aid plays in international development, and to uphold the values of multilateralism, humanitarianism, and the standards of international human rights. Although the Report includes the word *partners* in its title, Pearson did not include China or other Communist countries. For this, the Report offered both an excuse and hope, when Pearson wrote:

> *The Commission is conscious of the fact that it has not had the benefit of contact with, and information from, Communist countries. This omission, together with the absence of detailed published information from those countries, means that their programs of development cooperation and*

*aid—nearly all of which are bilateral—are not dealt with in this Report. It would, of course, be most helpful to the cause of international development if Communist and non-Communist countries could work together more closely in this field. The Commission ventures to hope, therefore, that this will increasingly be the case... The political and economic future of Mainland China will clearly have a very great impact on all the countries under consideration" (Pearson 1969, ix, Annex 1, 330).*

Here we see Pearson regretting the exclusion of China and other Communist countries from the Report's deliberations, but also recognizing the important role non-Western partners can play in international development. Specifically, he hoped and called for Communist and non-communist countries to work together to enhance aid effectiveness. Yet, more than half a century after Pearson, the world is still debating the proper role for, and possible partnership with, China in providing foreign aid to Africa and other parts of the world (Bergsten et al. 2009; Brautigam 2009; Davies 2007; Kragelund 2008; Lancaster 2007, the World Bank 2008b).

Aid coordination, or lack thereof, among donors and between donors and recipient countries is one of the most persistent causes of aid ineffectiveness. Indeed, both the Paris Declaration on Aid Effectiveness and the Accra Action Plan speak to the complex challenges of aid coordination. Canadians understand this because Pearson called for better aid coordination among different types of aid partners and was very clear when he wrote:

*The international aid system today, with its profusion of bilateral and multilateral agencies, lacks direction and coherence. A serious effort is necessary to coordinate the efforts of multilateral and bilateral aid-givers and those of aid-receivers. There is a need for consistent reviews of performance and for authoritative assessments of aid requirements. We recommend that the President of the World Bank should, in the course of 1970, invite the heads of the appropriate organs of the United Nations and other multilateral agencies as well as representatives of bilateral aid-givers and of developing countries, to a conference to consider the creation of machinery to the efficiency and coordination of the international aid system" (Pearson 1969, 22).*

Table 12.1 provides a summary of the ten recommendations contained in the Pearson Commission Report, which were all intended to strengthen international cooperation for development. It is interesting to note that the first two recommendations do not deal with foreign aid. Rather, Pearson's first two recommendations deal with the development of a global framework for free and equitable international trade (similar to today's World

Trade Organization), and the promotion of mutually beneficial flows of foreign direct investment (FDI) from developed to developing countries.

**The principle objectives are to:**

1. Create a framework for free and equitable international trade
2. Promote mutually beneficial flows of foreign direct investment
3. Establish a better partnership, a clearer purpose, and greater coherence in development aid
4. Increase the volume of aid (0.7% of GDP for aid, 1.0% of GDP for ODA by 1975).
5. Meet the problems of mounting debt
6. Make aid administration more effective
7. Redirect technical assistance, e.g. to support recipient national and local systems, institutions
8. Slow the growth of population
9. Revitalize aid to education and research
10. Strengthen the multilateral aid system.

**Table 12.1: Summary of the Recommendations of the Pearson Commission Report for Strengthening International Cooperation**

Source: L.B. Pearson. *Partners in Development*. (1969, 14–22).

In addition to recommending the establishment of a better partnership, clearer purpose and greater coherence in development aid, the Report also speaks to the need to make aid administration more effective, support recipient countries' state and non-state capacity building, deal with problems of mounting debt, slow population growth, revitalize aid for education and research, and strengthen the multilateral aid system. Table 12.1 also reminds us of the origins of the perennial calls for rich countries to increase the volume of aid to 0.75 percent of GDP for aid, and one percent of GDP for official development assistance (ODA), with 1975 as the original target date. These are all issues Canadians and the Chinese understand and associate with aid in Africa.

## From Pearson to Harper: Progress, Criticism and Disappointment

From Pearson (1969) to Harper (present administration), Canadians have gone through various policy and operational foreign aid changes, including decentralization-centralization, different country/geographic-sectoral areas of focus, bilateral-multilateral swings, results-based management (RBM), Sector-wide approaches (SWAps), program based approaches (PBA), tied-untied aid, women in development (WID), and direct budget support. Detailed discussion of all these changes and their effects on African aid and development is beyond the scope of this chapter; suffice it to say that Canadians have grown increasingly critical and sceptical about their country's aid policy and performance, especially in Africa (Brown and Jackson 2009; Canadian International Council 2009; Canadian Council on Africa 2009). While Canada's ODA organizations such as the Canadian International Development Agency (CIDA) and the International Development Research Centre (IDRC) like to highlight the progress and contributions Canada has made to international development, especially in Africa, critics point to wide-ranging policy, funding, programming, operational, and partnership problems with Canadian aid. For example, in 2007 The Standing Committee on Foreign Affairs and International Trade of the Canadian Senate published a scathing report on Canada's aid in Africa. Drawing on evidence from 400 witnesses in Africa, Europe and North America, the Committee concluded that all players in sub-Saharan Africa have failed the region. It blamed the failure on three main causes:

1. the crippling subsidies and market protectionism of the international trade regime, including Canada;
2. slow, unacceptable, and poorly-designed development assistance and ineffective aid institutions both in Africa and Canada, including (CIDA), and
3. poor governance, limited capacity and pernicious leadership both in government, business and not-for profit sectors in Africa.

Wishing to change Canada's foreign aid focus from social welfare to economic and business development, the Committee recommended that "Canada should orient its foreign policy to assist only those African countries that are making a *real* effort to strengthen their political and economic governance, to build healthy private-sector economies, to improve their economic infrastructure, and to generate employment opportunities for their citizens" (Canadian Standing Senate Committee on Foreign Affairs and International Trade 2007, 14).

Responding to concerns of aid dependency, the Committee observed that vibrant economies and good governance—not international development—are the long-term answers for Africa. Most importantly for the evolution of Canadian aid, the Committee called on the government to develop a statutory mandate for Canada's foreign aid, with clear and measurable objectives that can be monitored and scrutinized by Parliament. The Committee also made the controversial recommendation that CIDA should either be reformed or abolished.

Table 12.2 provides a summary of the key recommendations of the Senate Committee Report separately for Africans, the international community and Canada. Although the Report does not call for the development of a strategic alliance with China, it makes it clear that all partners in international development in Africa have failed the test of aid effectiveness, and that the African aid enterprise is in trouble and in urgent need of rethinking, redesigning and rebuilding. However, much as the Committee's recommendations appealed to a significant cross-section of the Canadian public, most of the recommendations appear to have been ignored by the government. Only one was implemented. These recommendations provide a foundation for building domestic and international strategic alliances for improving aid and aid effectiveness in Africa.

| **What Africa Needs to Do** | **What the International Community Needs to Do** | **What Canada Needs to Do** |
|---|---|---|
| 1. Develop a private sector.<br>2. Improve the overall state of governance.<br>3. Aggressively tackle corruption.<br>4. Improve infrastructure and access to energy.<br>5. Make agriculture a priority.<br>6. Raise agricultural performance.<br>7. Improve ability to trade.<br>8. Enhance regional integration.<br>9. Take fight against HIV:AIDS and malaria seriously.<br>10. Invest in all levels of education. | 1. Finish the Doha Development Agreement (DDA).<br>2. Make Structural Adjustment policies of the World Bank and IMF more flexible, less onerous.<br>3. Change development assistance radically.<br>4. Redirect development assistance that is given to fewer countries and towards economic development.<br>5. Focus aid on microfinance. | 1. Support peace and security efforts in Africa.<br>2. Develop a clearer, comprehensive and coherent policy on Africa.<br>3. Decide the future of CIDA.<br>4. Shift all Canadian development work in Africa into an Africa Office.<br>5. Dramatically change approach to ODA.<br>6. Seek out Canadian commercial opportunities in Africa.<br>7. Resolve visa issues for African business and political leaders. |

| | | |
|---|---|---|
| 11. Make strides towards gender equality.<br>12. Practice good governance and prevent conflict.<br>13. Strengthen African peace and security architecture. | 6. Improve the delivery of aid.<br>7. Help African countries build better institutions and battle corruption.<br>8. Help Africa with medical crises.<br>9. Take African conflicts seriously and aggressively help to resolve them.<br>10. Deal aggressively with the conflict in the Democratic Republic of the Congo.<br>11. Harmonize policies, regulations and definitions regarding conflict resolutions | 8. Adjust Canadian trade policy on Africa.<br>9. Deal effectively with HIV/AIDS and malaria. |

**Table 12.2: Summary Recommendations of the Canadian Senate Report on Aid to Africa**

Source: Overcoming Forty Years of Failure: A New Road Map for sub-Saharan Africa. The Canadian Standing Senate Committee on Foreign Affairs and International Trade, 2007.

**Box 12.1: Summary of the Purpose and Major Provisions of the Canadian Development Assistance Accountability Act, 2006**

**Background**:
Following the UK example of the International Development Act (IDA 2002), and responding to domestic pressures for a more rational approach to the financing and management of foreign aid, the Canadian Parliament passed the Development Assistance Accountability Act (aka Bill C-293), an Act respecting the provision of development assistance abroad.

**Purpose**
The purpose of the Act is to establish a legislative mandate for Canada's official development assistance with a clear purpose for aid spending that focuses on poverty reduction, improves transparency and accountability, and establishes specific criteria for the disbursement of Canadian assistance, consistent with the Act.

The driving force behind the Act is the need to concentrate on reducing poverty and promoting Canadian values, foreign policy and international human rights standards. Clause 2(2) requires that all Canadian development assistance activities be carried out in accordance with the principles of sustainable development, defined as development that meets the needs of the present generation without compromising the ability of future generations to meet their own needs.

**Criteria for Disbursement**
Clause 4 of the bill sets out the criteria for the disbursement of Canadian development assistance. Before providing international assistance, the Minister must be satisfied that development assistance is consistent with the following criteria: 1) Contributes to poverty reduction; 2) Takes into account the perspectives of the poor, and 3) Is consistent with Canada's human rights obligations. The bill contains provision for the Minister to consult international and Canadian non-government organizations to ensure compliance with the Act.

**Definition of ODA**
The bill adopts the DAC definition of ODA as funding transferred to developing countries and multilateral institutions provided by official (government) agencies which meets the following criteria: 1) It is administered with the promotion of the economic development and welfare of developing countries as its main objective, and 2) It is concessional in character and conveys a grant element of at least 25 percent.

**CIDA**
The Canadian International Development Agency (CIDA) is the federal agency charged with planning and implementing the majority of Canada's ODA (over 80 percent of the aid budget). The authority of the Minister of Foreign Affairs over CIDA, the provision of international development assistance by Canada and the role of the Minister of International Cooperation, through whom CIDA reports to Parliament, are set out in the Department of Foreign Affairs and International Trade Act (DFAIT Act).

**Advisory Committee**
Clause 6 of the Act establishes a new Advisory Committee for International Development (the Advisory Committee) to advise the Minister on matters related to the exercise of ministerial powers under the Act. The Advisory Committee, whose mandate, qualifications and tenure are prescribed by the Act, may review any matter relating to development assistance, and may receive petitions from residents of a developing country who believe that Canadian development assistance may be inconsistent with the provisions of the Act.

**Reporting Requirements**
The Act provides for different levels of reporting requirements by the Advisory Committee, the Minister responsible for the administration of the Act, and the Minister of Finance. In addition to reporting on the annual activities of the Advisory Committee, the Minister of International Cooperation must include a summary of CIDA's (but not IDCR's) Departmental Performance Report, and the Minister of Finance must include a summary of representations made by Canadian representatives related to priorities and policies of the Bretton Woods institutions, and a summary of the manner in which Canada's activities under the *Bretton Woods and Related Agreements Act* have contributed to carrying out the purpose of the Act, and details of any operations that have directly affected Canada.

Source: Elizabeth Kuruvila (2006). Notes on Bill C-293: An Act Respecting the Provision of Development Assistance Abroad (Development Assistance Accountability Act). Library of Parliament, Law and Government Division, 20 September 2006. (PRB06-31E).

The one recommendation of the Senate Committee that the Harper government decided to implement was the development of a statutory mandate governing Canadian foreign aid. In 2006, Parliament passed Bill C-293, an Act Respecting the Provisions of Development Assistance Abroad (aka the Development Assistance Accountability Act), with the explicit purpose of establishing a legislative mandate for the management and oversight of Canada's foreign aid. Box 1 provides a summary of the objectives and major provisions of the Act. Specifically, the Act stipulated that Canadian aid spending must be focused on poverty reduction, improved transparency and accountability, and promoting Canadian values, foreign policy objectives, and international human rights standards.

## Canadian Aid and the Millennium Development Goals

According to the Harper government, since the Millennium Declaration was adopted in 2000, Canada has made significant and lasting contributions to the achievement of all the eight Millennium Development Goals (MDGs) in Africa and elsewhere, especially in the areas of maternal, newborn and child health, education, gender equality, and addressing hunger by supporting food security and agricultural development. As host to the 2010 G-8 and G-20 summits, the government championed the Muskoka Initiative on maternal, newborn, and child health, whereby the international community made commitments to address development challenges associated with MDG4 (child mortality and improving maternal health) and MDG5 (combating HIV/AIDS, malaria and other diseases). [3] The Muskoka Declaration estimates that by 2015 the international community, led by the G-8, will contribute over $10 billion, of which Canada pledged $2.85 billion over five years. The key goals for the Muskoka Initiative are to: 1) prevent the deaths of 1.3 million children; 2) prevent the deaths of 64 thousand mothers; and 3) provide access to modern methods of family planning to 12 million couples. For more details of how Canada contributes to each of the MDGs, see CIDA (2010; www.cida.gc.ca; Biggs 2010).

The government also claims to have taken steps to transform how it delivers aid by strengthening thematic and regional focus, efficiency, and accountability consistent with the Development Assistance Accountability Act as well as with the principles of the Paris Declaration on Aid Effectiveness. It has done this by:

1. Establishing five priority themes to guide Canadian international development assistance. These themes are: increasing food security, focusing on children and youth, stimulating economic growth, ensuring security and stability, and advancing democracy.
2. Moving more CIDA operations into the field (decentralization) to increase impact and responsiveness, and
3. Fully untying food aid in 2008 and the rest of Canadian aid by 2012–2013.

Apart from advancing democracy, all these are areas where creative collaboration with the Chinese is potentially possible. Canadian aid also has a number of cross-cutting themes such as sustainable development, climate change, poverty alleviation, gender equality, and addressing HIV/AIDS in Africa that are potentially appealing to the Chinese in Africa.

The share of Canadian bilateral aid going to the least developed countries, most of which are in Africa, has increased from 53 percent in 2005 to 69 percent in 2008. Of the more than $4.6 billion allocated to various developing regions, over $ 2.1 billion, or 46.6 percent, was allocated to Africa, compared to $1.2 Billion or 27.3 percent for Asia. Indeed, the Harper government does not accept the accusations by its foreign policy critics that it is abandoning Africa. It points to initiatives such as increasing the lending capacity of the African Development Bank, contributions to peace and security in the Sudan and Sierra Leone, debt forgiveness of about $ I billion to the poorest countries, and doubling aid by 2012.

However, in the area of developing a global partnership for development (MDG8), the government limits itself to confirming its commitment to work within the framework of the Organization for Economic Cooperation and Development (OECD) Development Assistance committee (DAC), including the Working Party on Aid Effectiveness and the multilateral system under the United Nations. Unfortunately, the government of Canada does not recognize the need to reach out and forge development partnerships with non-traditional, non-DAC/OECD, emerging donors like China and other South-South participants active in Africa. This is regrettable in part because it is not consistent with Pearson's earlier warning and advice, but more significantly, it does not seem to acknowledge the changing realities in Africa resulting from China's growing influence and engagements with Africa. As critics have quipped, when it comes to foreign relations, the Harper government "does not get it."

In recent years, the Harper government's foreign and aid policies in Africa have received growing criticism from both Africa and Canada, especially from the leadership of the Canadian civil society organizations involved in international development. The Canadian organizations most critical of the government's policies in Africa include the Canadian Council for International Cooperation (CCIC; www.ccic.ca), a coalition of Canadian voluntary sector organizations involved in international development; the Canadian Council on Africa (www.ccafrica.ca), and the Walter and Duncan Gordon Foundation, with historical roots in the Liberal Party of Canada (Walter Duncan was a Toronto Liberal Member of Parliament and Finance Minister in Pearson's government (see www.gordonfn.org; Gulrajani 2010). In the past few years, these organizations have organized conferences and commissioned studies all aimed at showing that the Harper government's aid policy in Africa is headed in the wrong direction. For example, while acknowledging that the Canadian ODA Accountability Act is a remarkable piece of legislation, a recent CCIC report calls its implementation disappointing because government reporting is "sketchy, incomplete and non-transparent" (Barr 2010, 9). In a series of papers, Gulrajani (2010) calls for a re-imagining of Canada's foreign aid in the areas of strategy, governance, policy making, and organization management. At a conference organized by the Canadian Council on Africa, participants expressed dissatisfaction with the Harper government's policy on Africa for:

- Ideologically biased foreign and aid policy that marginalizes Africa in favor of other regions such as Latin America and the Caribbean;
- Promoting commerce, trade, and investment at the expense of foreign aid and humanitarianism;
- Policy incoherence and inconsistencies, keeping CIDA and other development organizations in a state of ambiguity, confusion, and disorganization (Brown and Jackson 2009);
- Poor governance, leadership, management, structuring, and staffing of the Canadian foreign aid system, with too many unqualified junior ministers in charge of aid;
- Reducing Canadian presence and influence in Africa by reducing the number of core countries, diplomatic missions, trade representatives, and visa officers;
- Looking at Africa as a source of problems and challenges rather than opportunities for mutually beneficial, closer political, diplomatic and commercial ties;
- Frustrating people-to-people contacts by restricting visas to Africans wishing to visit Canada for business or other purposes.

The conference ended with two overarching concerns of coherence and commitment. Specifically, the conference report concluded that "An effective partnership with Africa requires a recalibration of Canada's priorities with Africa in a coherent way across a range of policies on aid, trade, investment, peace, and security. If we are serious about contributing to Africa's development for the benefit of all, we need a picture of development and partnership that takes all into account" (Bradet 2009, 8).

All this points to disappointment, disconnect and lack of trust and confidence between the Harper government and most Canadians involved in African and international development. Acknowledging the existence of this ideological gap, a retired senior CIDA staffer told me that the problem is lack of trust and confidence between the government and the Canadian aid community of professionals and volunteers. What is important here is the concern that if, as Canadians, those in government and those in the aid business cannot work out their differences and establish harmonious working relationships in the interests of Africa and the poor, how could they be expected to partner effectively with outsiders like the Chinese, who are very different in many respects? Yet complete achievement of MGD8—developing a global partnership for development—requires reaching out beyond traditional allies and forging creative collaborative arrangements with former adversaries and those very different from us.

## Chinese Aid to Africa: From Bandung to FOCAC 1V

China's economic engagement in general and aid to Africa in particular has always been unconventional, controversial, misunderstood, and detested by the West, which in turn makes the Chinese defensive. This part of the chapter provides brief accounts of China's aid to Africa, focusing on delivery mechanisms and institutions used, its underlying principles, common criticisms levelled against it, summary of a recent evaluation, and opportunities for collaboration and international strategic alliance with Canada and other aid providers. Under the current Forum on China-Africa Cooperation (FOCAC IV), China identified the following foreign aid priorities for Africa: debt relief, human resource development, education, poverty reduction, medical care and public health, disaster assistance and relief, and climate change and environmental protection (FOCAC 2009). Canadians identify with most of these priorities for Africa.

China's rationale and modes of aid delivery in Africa have not changed much since the 1950s. According to Hamrel and Widstrand (1964), the Chinese first came to Egypt in 1956, following the Non-Allied Movement's Bandung Conference of 1955, in response to what they perceived as aggressive moves by the Soviet Union. On April 21, 2011, the Information Office of the State Council of the People's Republic of China published China's first ever White Paper on Foreign Aid. The Paper claims that China's foreign aid started in 1950 when China provided material assistance to the Democratic People's Republic of Korea (DPRK) and Vietnam, two neighboring countries having friendly relationships with the newly established Communist regime in Beijing. The report also states that in 2009, Africa was the single largest recipient of Chinese aid, with 45.7 percent the of aid budget, seconded by Asia at 32.8 per cent (China Information Office of the State Council 2011). According to Rotberg (2008), during the Maoist regime (1950s–1970s), the Communists supported various anti-colonial liberation movements and left-leaning governments as part of the Cold War era. However, during the globalization period beginning in the 1980s, China's engagement in Africa promised to be much more *transformational*. Rotberg writes:

> *China's current thrust into sub-Saharan Africa promises to do more for economic growth and poverty alleviation there than anything attempted by Western colonialists or the massive initiatives of the international lending agencies and other donors (2006, viii).*

At the same time, it is accepted that China is no altruist. Rather, it can be extractive, opportunistic, and insensitive to local needs, as it seeks to meet its own national economic, commercial, and political strategic interests, including seeking support at the United Nations and against Taiwan. While strategic in its dealings with Africa, China is not always operationally tactful.

Muller (1964) gives four methods by which the Chinese give economic and technical aid to Africa:

1. Foreign Trade as the most important form of economic cooperation and aid;
2. Long-term credit and grants;
3. Scientific and technical cooperation, e.g. the building of factories and plants, work on planning and research, technical services, and sending out specialists; and
4. Cultural cooperation and education assistance.

These modes of delivery have not changed much over time and have been documented by others (Lancaster 2007, Davies 2007, Brautigam 2009). One of the important differences from Canada's aid is China's greater emphasis on trade, investment, and economic development, rather than on social welfare, humanitarianism, governance, and human rights. It is also the case that Canada's aid community is less interested in trade and investment in Africa than in traditional aid, focusing on human and social development.

In terms of governance and delivery, China's foreign aid is much more state controlled than Canada's; it is also organized differently and is more closely integrated with the country's foreign and domestic political, diplomatic, security, and economic interests. At the policy level is the State Council (federal cabinet), which is assisted by three key Ministries of Commerce (MOFCOM), Foreign Affairs (MFA), and Finance. Within MOFCOM, the lead ministry for foreign aid, the three departments responsible for aid are: Department of Aid to Foreign Countries, Department of Western Asia and Africa, and the Executive Bureau for International Cooperation, which reports to the regional department for Western Asia and Africa. At the operational level, the Chinese Embassy's Economic Councillor's office in the field takes the lead for project management and implementation. Traditionally, projects are simply assigned without competitive bidding either to line ministries such as health, education, or transport, state owned enterprises such as the China Road and Bridge Corporation (www.crbc.com), provincial government agencies, especially Town and Village Enterprises (TVEs) such as Anhui Foreign Economic Construction (Group) Corporation (which is connected to the Anhui provincial government and the Communist Party). However, as China moves toward a more market-driven economy and as its executing agencies begin to compete for international aid contracts, there is more competitive bidding using World Bank Contracting Guidelines. Financing of aid, which is kept secret, is coordinated by the two ministries of finance and commerce (MOFCOM), and implemented by the state development banks, notably the Chinese Bank for Exports and Imports (EXIM), which is the most active financier of China's activities in Africa, providing grants, commercial or concessional loans, credit, long-term loans, trade and contract financing (Hubbart 2008).

Reviewing fifty years of Sino-African relations, Liu and Yang (2009) argue that Chinese (and Asian) engagement with Africa goes beyond development cooperation and sets the stage for redefining development in Africa and reshaping relationships with Western countries including Canada.

Here we see some interesting similarities and differences between Canada and China. While both countries seek to align their foreign aid policies with their national values and interests, China appears to be much more *strategic, coherent, committed, and less detracted by temporary or short-term failures or setbacks.* This may explain at least in part why the Chinese are reluctant to provide data on aid disbursements and aid effectiveness. It is not so much how much they give that matters. Rather, it is how much they *change the rules of the game* in advancing national interests, no matter how much it may cost in the short run. Accordingly, concepts like results-based management take on different meanings. China does not have agencies equivalent to CIDA or IDRC, although, according to Lancaster (2007), they may be looking at structures similar to those used by the UK and Sweden. Unlike Canada, China does not have a well developed network of nongovernment organizations (NGOs) actively involved in foreign aid policy and delivery. While Canada's foreign aid community—NGO leaders and professionals, volunteers, academics, journalists—is diverse and includes faith-based organizations, in China interest in foreign aid is limited to a few government agencies, ministries and contractors, very few academics, and a budding NGO sector still under state control and influence. These differences provide opportunities for Canada and China to work together, learning from each other and adopting best practices. For example, critics have argued that Canada's foreign aid is inefficient because of the use of NGOs, which are too small to enjoy economies of scale or scope. Yet attempts to restructure Canada's NGO sector have been frustrated because most of the NGOs have strong local political connections. In addition, Canadian foreign aid would benefit from more active involvement of the private sector. While Canada's foreign aid policies and programs are always contested, in China decisions are relatively easy to make, implement and sustain.

## Aid Principles: China and the OECD Countries

China's aid is guided by a set of principles, which are supposed to inform policy, management and delivery of aid and establish a working relationship with recipient governments. These principles were first advanced by Premier Zhou Enlai when he visited Africa in December 1963 to January 1964. Table 3 provides a comparison of these principles with those of the OECD/DAC, predominantly made up of Western countries like Canada.

In 1982, Premier Zhao Ziyang visited eleven African states and announced the "Four Principles" on Sino-African Economic and Technical Cooperation of equality, bilateralism, effectiveness, and co-development or partnership with recipient countries. As Table 12.3 shows, taken together, these principles are very similar to the Paris Declaration commitments on aid effectiveness, which include ownership, alignment, harmonization, managing for results, and mutual accountability, as well as the more recent principles of the Accra Agenda for Action.

| China: Zhou Enlai's Aid Principles (1963–64) | OECD/DAC Principles |
|---|---|
| 1. Co-development, Partnership<br>2. Aid not unilateral, but of mutual benefit<br>3. Conditionality:<br>4. Neither condition nor privileges attached to aid<br>5. Debt Burden:<br>6. Reduce burden with no-interest/low interest, extended repayments<br>7. Local Ownership:<br>8. Purpose of aid is to help recipient countries to develop *independently*<br>9. Aid Effectiveness:<br>10. Increase recipient country's incomes by producing results faster with less investment<br>11. Appropriate Technology Transfer:<br>12. China will provide best equipment and materials; otherwise replace them.<br>13. Capacity Building:<br>14. Local technicians to master relevant technology<br>15. Equal Treatment:<br>16. Experts from China never to enjoy privileges not available to local experts | Paris Declaration (2005)<br>1. Ownership:<br>2. Partner countries take leadership of aid programs.<br>3. Alignment:<br>4. Aid programs must be aligned with country strategies, systems and procedures.<br>5. Harmonization:<br>6. Donors' actions must be coordinated.<br>7. Managing for Results:<br>8. Aid programs should focus on results for people, not processes.<br>9. Mutual Accountability:<br>10. Donors and recipients hold each other accountable for performance and results.<br><br>Accra Agenda for Action (2008)<br>1. Predictability<br>2. Ownership<br>3. Country Systems; Local Capacity<br>4. Conditionality<br>5. Untying Aid<br>6. Aid fragmentation<br>7. Transparency<br>8. Partnerships |

**Table 12.3: Comparison of China's Principles of Technical Aid and OECD Principles of Aid Effectiveness**

Sources: Zhou Enlai's Eight Principles, as translated by Li Anshan in Rotberg 2008, 26–27. For the Paris Declaration, see World Bank 2008a; also see Accra High Level Forum; www.accrahlf.net.

Indeed, there are more similarities than differences between the Chinese and OECD countries in terms of the guiding principles for aid in Africa. For example, they both emphasise the importance of aid effectiveness, local ownership, the need for capacity building, and the need to focus on results that matter for the recipient countries and their citizens. In addition, China also emphasizes the need for co-development (tied aid?), the right of recipient countries to develop *independently (alignment, ownership);* equal treatment of local experts and the giving of aid without conditions *(conditionality).* The similarities as well as the differences provide a foundation on which collaboration and a strategic alliance can be established between China and Canada or other OECD countries.

Both for the Chinese and for the OECD countries, including Canada, the need for the development of these guiding principles grew out of concerns for the challenges of aid effectiveness and sustainable human development. Canadians share the findings of the report of the Senate that talks about forty years of failure in Africa and are desperately looking for different ways of delivering aid to Africa. During my interviews with Chinese officials and academics in Beijing, I was told that the Chinese are also concerned about aid in Africa. In addition to concerns about the challenges and limitations of state and non-state capacities, Chinese officials are concerned about the dangers of *creating dependency* (not co-development), and *escalating commitments* (more is better). For example, almost fifty years since they helped to build the Tanzara railway, the Chinese are still expected to provide technical assistance to turn the project into an economically viable enterprise. As well, the FOCAC initiative runs the risk of turning into a race for more (not better), as the success for successive meetings is measured by how many more billions of dollars is thrown at the Africans, rather than how much contribution is made to African sustainable human and institutional development .[4] Visiting Beijing in the summer of 2010, I got the impression that China's foreign aid establishment is overworked and understaffed in part because the country's aid program is growing and changing too fast without corresponding personnel and organizational development. In order to address these and similar challenges, both China and OECD countries like Canada need to work together much more closely in a much better coordinated manner.

One area of common interest between China and Canada—and indeed the entire international community—is Africa's peace and security. As a recent report on China's growing role in Africa's peace and security points out, there is a wide array of external actors playing various roles in supporting African peace and security. The report points out that the "more these actors cooperate with one another, the more effective their actions will be" (Saferworld 2011, 61).

| |
|---|
| 1. Exploiting Africa's inherent weaknesses: vulnerabilities, institutional voids |
| 2. Substandard work |
| 3. Unfair labor, employment and business practices |
| 4. Ignoring human/social/cultural/community/land rights; not working closely with African civil society |
| 5. Dancing with/propping up African dictators |
| 6. Secrecy: lack of transparency/accountability; unwillingness to coordinate aid with DAC, Non-DAC donors, recipient countries |
| 7. Disregard for environmental concerns |
| 8. Militarization |
| 9. Failure to build African capacities where it matters most: infrastructure versus institutions/human/social capital |
| 10. Not working hard enough to transform the African economy; too much focused on own national interests |
| 11. Bullying: Taiwan, opposition parties, trade unions, local businesses, etc. |
| 12. Bilateral tied aid |
| 13. Lack of symmetry: China is too big, moves too fast, offers too much; overwhelms. |
| 14. International finance: debt management, contracting, trade, foreign direct investment, bartering, over/under-invoicing |
| 15. Illicit financial flows (in and out) |
| 16. Movements of People: illicit migration, visa restrictions, mistreatment of African immigrants in China |

**Table 12.4: Common Criticisms of Chinese Engagements in Africa**

Compiled from: Kiggundu 2010a; Brautigam 2009, and Lancaster 2007.

## Criticism and Assessment of Chinese Aid to Africa

There have been many justified and unjustified criticisms of China's aid and overall engagements with Africa. It is beyond the scope of this chapter to discuss them all. Here I provide a brief summary and discussion of some of the criticisms, especially those most relevant for aid effectiveness and possible collaboration and strategic alliance with Canada. Issues shown in Table 12.4 relating to China's apparent disregard for human rights, the environment, governance, and lack of transparency are important to Canadians and may impede collaboration. On the other hand, other issues such as tying of bilateral aid, financing of aid, and the challenges of building African state and non-state capacities for development more directly relate to challenges of development in Africa, and may serve as a basis for opening dialogue and finding areas of common interests between Chinese and Canadian aid actors. These are also the issues on which they are most likely to find common ground with African aid partners.

It is almost impossible to provide an evaluation or assessment of China's aid to Africa because all foreign aid data and information are kept secret. For example, estimates of how much aid China gives to Africa range from a low of half a billion to a high of $5 billion (Lancaster 2007). According to Professor Li Anshan of Peking University, between 1956 and 1977 China provided $ 2.476 billion in economic aid to thirty-six African countries. This amounted to about 58 percent of China's total foreign aid of $4.276 billion. One of the criticisms of China-Africa aid and cooperation is that China's commitments stand in stark contrast to the lack of any formal, coherent and united policy from Africa. African governments, with limited state capacity, find themselves in a constant *reactive mode* when dealing with the Chinese, who are known to be strategic and calculating, with a high long-term orientation. The general observation is that the Chinese are too big, offer too much, move too fast, and overwhelm their African partners, making win-win results almost impossible. For example, President Hu, addressing the 2006 FOCAC III Summit in Beijing, promised to double aid to Africa within three years (see www.china view.cn ).

In 2007, the Centre for Chinese Studies, University of Stellenbosch, South Africa, with funding from the Rockefeller Foundation, undertook a study of China's FOCAC commitments to eight African countries. The study found, among other things, that the EXIM Bank, one of China's three policy banks, was playing the lead role in financing China's economic engagements with Africa. As the sole provider of concessional loans, by 2007 it had financed over three hundred projects in Africa, constituting almost 40 percent of its total loan portfolio. The bank was designated to manage both the US$5 billion China-Africa Development Fund announced at the FOCAC III in 2006, and the US$10 billion pledged at the FOCAC IV Sharm el-Sheikh, Egypt Conference in November 2009. In addition to financing concessional loans, the bank finances the entry of Chinese firms in the African economy. It has signed several memorandums of understanding (MOUs) with the World Bank to undertake major development projects in Africa, including the Mohandas Nkuwa Dam in Mozambique. The report makes several recommendations, specifically directed at the

Africans, but equally relevant for donor countries like Canada. Specifically, the report points to the need to develop better understanding of the Chinese approach to aid: facilitating regional coordination; avoiding poor coordination leading to Chinese aid fatigue; strengthening the African voice; improving monitoring and reporting mechanisms; improving debt management; and avoiding divisions between Western (OECD) donors and the Chinese. These recommendations point to areas where China, working together with Canada and other donors, would improve aid effectiveness in Africa (Edinger 2007).

## International Strategic Alliances, Value Chain Analysis and Cluster Development

An *international strategic alliance* (ISA) is an agreement between two or more parties *from different countries* to cooperate in any value chain activities of their work. It can be formal, with legally binding requirements on the parties, or informal, with only shared understanding but no legally binding obligations. It is not a merger, acquisition, or joint venture. The parties maintain their separate identities and independence, but agree to collaborate on specified activities related to shared goals and objectives. It is strategic in the sense that it deals with long-term, system-wide and contextualized, not temporary or short-term interests, of the parties. Every international strategic alliance must have clearly articulated and mutually understood, accepted, and shared goals and objectives. Table 12.5 provides a list of goals and objectives, which an international strategic alliance between Canadian and Chinese aid partners working in Africa could strive for. Collaborating partners in an ISA bring competency, commitment, and complementarities to the aid value chains that contribute to sustainable human development. At the moment, however, there is very little trust or confidence between Canadian and Chinese aid organizations in Africa; they hardly talk to each other. The three-way confidence and mutual trust-building initiatives listed in Table 12.5 are designed to make sure that African aid participants are not excluded.

1. Building three-way confidence and mutual trust
2. Dealing with shared, immediate, concrete "pressure points," e.g. security in DRC, challenges of cross-border trade in eastern and southern Africa, piracy in the Bakassi Peninsula, Gulf of Guinea, where Chinese fishing boats have been attacked with deadly results, etc.
3. Developing "safe" platforms for dialogue, learning, sharing lessons of experience, practices, knowledge skills, and resources
4. Joint field experimentation in areas of common interest (e.g. green energy, public health, local ownership, science and technology, poverty reduction, etc.)
5. Pulling resources together (e.g. building human capital, funding, joint biddings, etc.)
6. Facilitating three-way sectoral dialogues and collaboration (e.g. energy, infrastructure, mining, public health, human resource development, trade, foreign direct investment, etc.)
7. Building state/local development capacities (e.g. strengthening African ministries of foreign affairs, independent NGOs, rural/farming communities, etc.)
8. B2B2B (business to business to business) dialogues and confidence-building with African indigenous firms
9. Experimenting with three-way Ministerial Dialogues (e.g. ministers for international cooperation, foreign ministers, finance ministers, agriculture, health, infrastructure, etc.)
10. Jointly seeking practical ways to institutionalize the strategic alliance.

NB: These proposals are based on the realization that it is better to start with areas of common interest rather than focus on issues where the parties fundamentally disagree.

**Table 12.5: Suggested Initial Goals and Sequencing of Alliance Activities for Confidence Building**

The next objective is for the parties to deal with issues of immediate shared concern or "pressure points" whose successful resolution is of immediate payoff for both. Here I give the examples of improving security in the Democratic Republic of the Congo, where both Canada and China have vital interests, and control of sea piracy in the Indian Ocean and the Gulf of Guinea, where Chinese fishermen have been attacked and lost lives. According to press reports, in March 2010, seven Chinese nationals were kidnapped off Bakassi Peninsula by a group calling itself the African Commandos opposed to the peace treaty between Nigeria and Cameroon giving control of the peninsula to Cameroon. Western nationals have also been kidnapped in the same area.

Under these circumstances, it is possible for the parties to construct *"safe" platforms* for sharing best/worst lessons of experiences. For the Chinese, "safe" platforms would be venues and deliberations where they are guaranteed not to lose face or experience public shame or condemnation. For Canadians, "safe" platforms would simply try to avoid embarrassing the Canadian government or their respective home institutions. Experimentations would cover areas such as green energy, agriculture and rural development (infrastructure, community development, institutions, climate change, etc.), where China and Canada have complementary resources and competencies and can both benefit from new knowledge. Safe platforms can also be established by removing long-standing irritants or obstacles to the advancement of bilateral relations. For example, in the summer of 2011, after winning a parliamentary majority, the Harper administration decided to improve bilateral relations with China in order to boost trade and investments. Before the Foreign Minister left for Beijing for an official visit, the government of Canada decided to return to China Mr. Lai Changxing, the notorious fugitive accused of running bribery and smuggling rings, who had successfully avoided extradition for over ten years (McGregor 2005). This pleased Chinese officials and created a safe platform for strengthening trade and investment relations between the two countries.

It is also important for these alliances to include private sector actors from China, Canada and Africa, because private or enterprise sector development remains one of the most neglected but critical factors in African development. China's recent announcement of the creation of the Africa Development Fund (ADF), with billions of dollars allocated to support Chinese foreign direct investments in Africa, provides opportunities for the development of indigenous African enterprises, as recommended by Pearson. An ISA with active participation of Chinese enterprises would not only boost trade, but would also create opportunities for trade diversification in Africa. Both Canada and China share corporate interests and capabilities in sectors such as oil and gas, mining, forestry and fisheries, agribusiness and services. On a wider scale, the Donor Committee for Enterprise Development (DCED) could be an ideal partner here. Finally, once there is a record of successful collaboration in different areas of the aid-value chain, preparatory work can begin for three-way ministerial dialogues, involving China, Canada and African governments. These ministerial meetings can then deal with a range of development issues at the policy, aid management, and project levels, aimed at improving aid effectiveness from different types of donors. This interests-based approach to building strategic alliances differs from the top-down FOCAC approach, which concentrates only on government-to-government cooperation.

It is important for the parties to identify significant and practical areas where trilateral (or bilateral) interests converge. For example, studies show that Africa suffers from illicit movements of finance and migration (inflows and outflows). Global Financial Integrity estimates that in 2009 alone, US$29 billion and US$6 billion were spirited out of Nigeria and Angola, respectively, thus depriving the people of badly needed resources for development (Kar and Cartwright-Smith 2010). These illegal transactions, which do not respect borders, are connected to international criminal groups with negative consequences for both Canada and China. Both Canada and China have experience with and a wide range of expertise in dealing with similar problems of illegal movements of money and people. This is an area where trilateral interests converge, and "safe" platforms can be developed bringing together public and private sector organizations from Canada, China, and Africa to address associated problems to mutual advantage.

In order to build a strong and enduring alliance, it is important to identify key attributes or characteristics of the parties, which act as the building blocks for the alliance. For example, there are significant structural, institutional, procedural and cultural differences and similarities between Canadian and Chinese aid systems and actors. These differences and similarities can be used to identify areas where the alliance could be advisable or not. For example, on delivery mechanisms, while China relies mostly on a highly centralized system of government ministries, state owned enterprises (SOEs), and private sector firms, Canada depends much more on a fragmented/decentralized delivery system dominated by non-government organizations, small to medium sized consulting/engineering firms, and local aid actors. This creates a potential area of collaboration, whereby Canadian NGOs can establish strategic alliances with China's SOEs and private sector firms in the delivery of more effective aid in Africa. Clearly, Canadian NGOs bring a different set of values, resources, and competencies to aid in Africa than China's line ministries, SOEs or private sector firms. As well, since China covers more African countries than Canada, there may be opportunities for Canadian presence in geographical areas or sectors of less focus by pooling resources with the Chinese. China and the African partners may also be able to persuade Canadian aid actors to provide direct support to local private firms. On the other hand, issues of tied aid, transparency, human rights, direct budget support, and conditionality may be so controversial, keeping the parties apart, that they may be best left alone until the alliance has matured and become mutually trusting enough to deal with politically, culturally and ideologically divisive issues. The "safe" platforms discussed above can be used as a testing ground for identifying issues ready for more open dialogue and collaboration. Threats, shaming, or public criticisms do not create a conducive environment for the development of safe platforms for dialogue and joint problem solving.

## Value Chain Concepts and Applications

According to Michael Porter (1985), value chain analysis (VCA) involves a careful study of all the activities and functions required to produce and support a product or provide a service in order to enhance organizational efficiency, effectiveness, and competitiveness, and to add value for the ultimate consumer or beneficiaries at lower costs. Technically, the value chain of an organization is made up of four types of interrelated activities: *upstream activities* such as research and development; *primary activities* such as operations, manufacturing, marketing and sales; *downstream activities* such as delivery, repair and maintenance; and *support activities* including human resource management, organization design and control, and technology development and application (see Cullen and Parboteeah 2011, 175, and Figure 1 below). The utility of the value chain is that it enables ISA-participating organizations to determine their respective and joint cost-benefit structures associated with different value chain activities. The results of the organizational benchmarking provide ISA-participating partners with the information they need to work together to create more value to human development by reducing costs and maximizing benefits to the aid beneficiaries. International strategic alliances are widely used in the private sector by multinational corporations because this allows them to leverage and complement their unique resources, competencies and capabilities. The collaborating parties do not need to be identical, only complementary or potentially complementary in different value chain activities, resources, capabilities, or competencies (Chen Zhiqi 2003).

More recently, value chain concepts, tools, and methods have been widely used to enhance domestic and international competitiveness in African agriculture. For example, Webber and Labaste (2010), and Kaplinsky and Morris (2002) have documented several case studies of value chain applications for the production, marketing, and export of African agricultural goods and services including cut flowers in Kenya, mango exports in Senegal, pineapples in Ghana, beef export in Botswana, and cashew nuts in Mozambique. The World Economic Forum (January 2009) has produced a report documenting a series of interventions that have proven effective at strengthening production and consumption of food value chains' activities in Africa and other poor regions of the world. The report emphasizes the need to better understand key constraints of food value chain activities—production and consumption—and how best to overcome them in ways that are economically viable and socially beneficial, especially to the "bottom billions. Some of the suggestions for improving food value chain activities in Africa include unleashing the potential of food producers and consumers, empowering agro-food entrepreneurs, creating creative collaborations and life-enhancing foods and services, building markets for sustainable trade, designing nutritious food for poor citizens, improving access, and overcoming infrastructure gaps and the relevant institutional voids.

Other international organizations applying VCA in their development work include UN organizations, Germany's agency for international development (GTZ), Canada's IDRC, America's Agency for International Development (USAID), and the World Bank (see Webber and Labaste 2010, 16). Common sectors of application include agro-business, horticulture, small and medium enterprise development, and export development. All these applications point to the potential usefulness of the applications of VCA for improving effectiveness and promoting dialogue and collaboration among alliance partners. Although we could not find in the literature value chain applications by Chinese organizations in Africa, the value chain concepts, tools, and methods can be instrumental in building strong alliances among Canadian, Chinese and African aid organizations. Agricultural development is a priority area both for Canada as part of the strategy for food security, and China by way of FOCAC IV.

## Hybrid Value Chains

Hybrid value chains are collaborative arrangements formed by firms or organizations across sectors to deal with major global social challenges such as housing, education, public health, or poverty with a view to bringing about significant lasting social change. They represent a new and systematic shift in the way private sector enterprises collaborate with civil society organizations in the pursuit of social change. This is particularly the case in those countries where civil society organizations and social entrepreneurs have developed leadership, management, entrepreneurial, and technical capabilities comparable with private sector firms with whom they seek collaboration along the human development value chain. Likewise, the leadership of the private firms is able and willing to collaborate with social entrepreneurs to address global challenges by leveraging resources and core competencies. Drayton and Budinich (2010) describe the applications of hybrid value chains between various business firms and civil society organizations in countries such as India, Brazil, Mexico, and Colombia, together providing life-changing products (e.g. eye glasses) and services (e.g. ambulance services) to previously underserviced citizens, thereby adding value to their human development and welfare. This is possible because the leadership of the participating hybrid value chains are team players ready to take risks and challenges because they believe strongly that what they are doing is not only about profits but also about human progress (Drayton and Budinich 2010, 64). Although all these conditions do not necessarily currently exist in Africa's civil society and enterprise sectors, they are essential for effectively addressing the continent's intractable development challenges and reaching the millions of underserviced citizens (Kiggundu 2009).

The hybrid value chain concepts and applications have the potential to contribute to African development by:

- Creating value along multiple dimensions to find new markets or to reach previously underserviced, hard to reach communities and citizens;
- Bringing together unique but complementary resources and competencies from the private sector (e.g. scale operations) and civil society organizations (e.g. social networks, local knowledge);
- Contributing to technical, organizational, governance, and social innovations in ways locally meaningful and sustaining, while at the same time taking advantage of modern technologies, management, and business models developed and tested elsewhere;
- Creating opportunities for local emergence and development of leadership, managerial and social entrepreneurship in participating African communities;
- Fostering a global mindset of responsible citizenship among Africans, especially the elite, youth, and emerging middle class.

## Cluster Development

There are several challenges associated with value chain applications in international development. These include maintaining trust and cooperation among alliance members; governance issues related to joint responsibilities; power differences due to differences in size, resources, technology, and power (the elephant versus the ant); and differences in the drive for innovation and consensus for determining interventions and points of focus. An effective way of overcoming these and similar challenges is by establishing clusters among alliance members. Clusters are highly collaborative collections of organizations, coordinated to focus on achieving objectives that are important for creating and adding sustainable value to the human development value chain. Clusters emphasize collaboration among participating organizations to achieve objectives beyond the capabilities of individual alliance members or value chains. Clusters and cluster development are key concepts in value chain analysis with significant implications for the effective management of development in Africa. For example, in the case of Kenya's horticultural industry of cut flowers and avocado production, Webber and Labaste (20010, 151–160) describe how collaborating organizations both in the public and private sectors created synergy along the various activities of the value chain. As shown in Figure 12.1 below, these clusters include government agencies (e.g. the Export Promotion Council of Kenya), trade and industry associations (e.g. Kenya Flower Council), education, research, extension, and training institutions (e.g. Kenya Agricultural Research Institute), quality and standards assurance organizations (e.g. Kenya Plant Health Inspectorate Services), production, marketing, and delivery organizations (e.g. farming, transport, post-harvesting firms), and donors (e.g. USAID). Drawing on these and similar African field experiences, it would appear that similar clusters can be developed from Canadian, Chinese, and African aid organizations in the pursuit of similar socioeconomic and human development goals in Africa.

## Framework for International Strategic Alliances, Value Chains and Clusters

Figure 12.1 brings together the key component parts of the proposed international strategic alliance (ISA), value chain analysis (VCA), including hybrid value chains, and cluster development organizations, with a view to creating socioeconomic value for sustainable human development. The Figure provides ten value chain activities considered important for a "typical" African aid program. They include commonly known activities such as policy analysis and development, program design and management, monitoring, and evaluation. More significantly, the value chain also includes development activities often neglected in aid value chain analyses. These include experimentation, social mobilization, citizen and community access and engagement, and contributions to sustainable development. It is particularly important to pay attention to the last two value chain activities of shared learning among alliance partners and beneficiaries, as well as the program's contributions to bringing about transformational change and institutionalization of the intended development interventions (see Figure 12.1). These are some of the areas where serious gaps still exist in Africa's aid effectiveness, and this framework is intended to provide a systematic way of addressing them.

Figure 12.1 also provides for international strategic alliances of the three participating countries and their contributions to human development through each of the listed value chain activities. Although only Canada, China, and Africa are listed, there is room for other countries to participate. For example, this framework could be used for the advancement of South-South aid to Africa by replacing Canada with non-traditional (non-DAC) emerging new donors such as Brazil, India, Kuwait, and Turkey. For a detailed discussion and classification of non-DAC (Development Assistance Committee of the OECD) donors to Africa, see Davies (2008) and Kragelund (2008).

Finally, the Figure provides examples of cluster organizations and hybrid value chain applications by sectors, including government as well as regional, international, and multilateral organizations, because these types of organizations play a very important role in the formulation and management of Africa's aid programs. The concepts associated with hybrid value chains are robust enough to extend beyond business and civil society organizations. Indeed, the real test of this framework is the extent to which it can foster better collaboration among aid organizations, local and foreign, improve effectiveness and add significant value in all value chain activities, and bring about sustainable human development for the greatest number of African citizens and communities. Africa's typical value chain constraints and limitations—caused by factors such as lack of infrastructure, poor governance, lack of producer and consumer capacity, lack of access to capital, lack of public sector capacity, and global isolation—can be overcome by careful and strategic applications of various aspects of this framework.

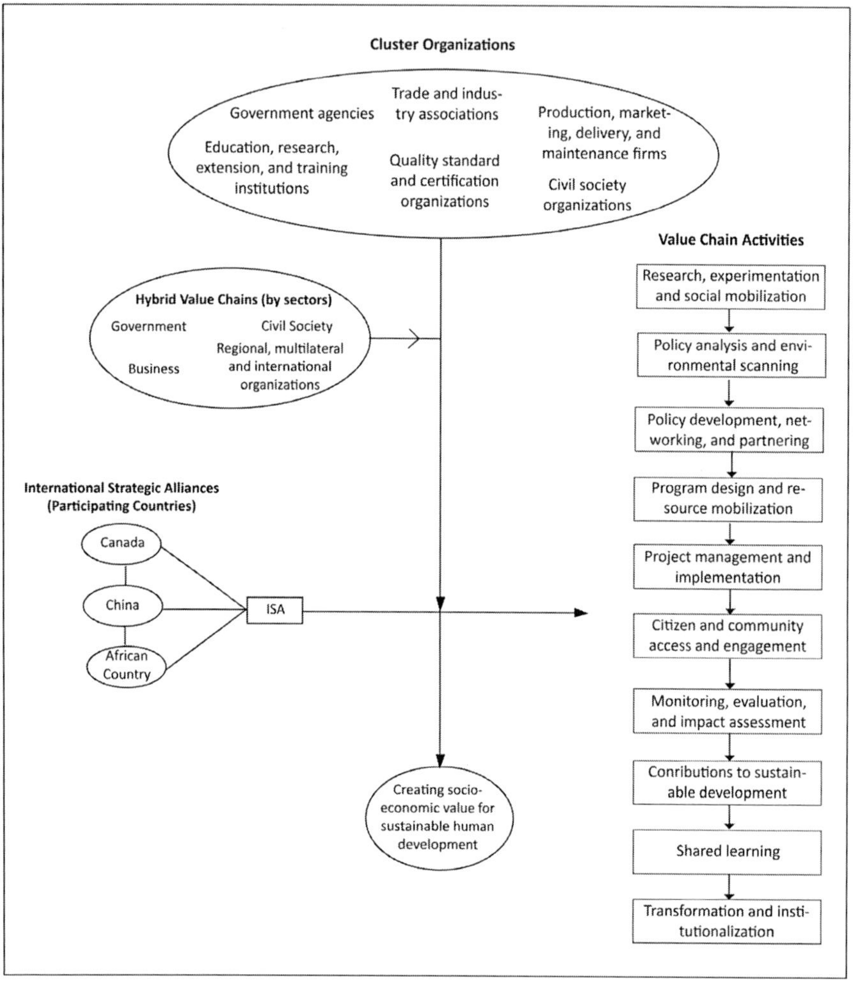


Figure 12.1: Framework for International Strategic Alliances, Value Chain Analyses and Cluster Development for Sustainable Human Development

A combination of international strategic alliances with China, one of the world's fastest growing and most dynamic economies, and Canada, a respected middle power in Africa and elsewhere; applications of proved business models (e.g. VCA) that enhance urban and rural productivity and consumption; creative collaborations and genuine and informed African participation in their development across sectors (e.g. by way of cluster organizations); and improved access and engagement of previously underserviced citizens and communities all make this framework particularly suitable for addressing Africa's most fundamental development challenges. These include problems of growth with equity (see the World Bank Growth Report 2008b); employment creation, especially among youth and women; cross-generation poverty alleviation; advances in human rights and social justice; and overcoming pervasive national fragility (World Bank 2011).This framework has the potential to reach and transform remote and fragile communities both in fragile and non-fragile states (Kiggundu 2010b). Africa's poor and misruled as well as the millions of underserviced citizens deserve better, and this unconventional ISA approach may well provide them with the way out of their predicament.

## Other Voices in Support of the Alliance Idea:

To Lester B. Pearson, who more than half a century ago called on the international community to collaborate with China in international development, more recently others have added their voices. The World Bank has taken practical steps to collaborate with China in the financing and implementation of infrastructure projects and the development of industrial zones in various African countries. The proposed industrial zones are to be located in Egypt, Mauritius, Mozambique, Tanzania/Kenya, and Zambia. In her study of the Chinese aid system, Lancaster added her voice, along with those speaking in defense of China's role in Africa (for example Harneit-Sievers et al. 2010). For example, in a report written to contribute to increased understanding of China's role in Africa from the Chinese perspective, and targeted at civil society organizations, Davies (2007) called for the establishment of *triangular dialogue approaches* between the Chinese and other aid participants. She explains the triangular approach as follows:

> *A triangular dialogue approach is needed between Chinese, African and traditional donors/Western governments, and between CSOs in China, Africa, and Western countries. These two triangles should in turn overlap so that dialogue is not just carried out between governments but also between governments and CSOs, who could contribute with important on-the-ground knowledge to inform policies (2007, 97).*

These triangular dialogues can be upgraded to the level of international strategic alliances. Canada is a very good candidate for facilitating the development, coordination, and organizing of these triangular arrangements because as Corin and Smith (2010) point out, Canada is not a threat and is perceived as an honest broker, separate from Europe and the U.S.

Canada has membership credentials in a wide range of multilateral organizations such as the G-20, the Commonwealth, *la Francophonie,* NATO, the Organization of American States, etc. China has repeatedly emphasized the significance of working through the UN system and is increasingly, although selectively, choosing the multilateral approach to addressing global issues. Corin and Smith express the hope that:

> *In the medium term, there may be scope for exploring potential synergies in working together in the development field. China will soon be one of the largest foreign aid donors and it is important to build a dialogue to address China's challenge to existing norms by ignoring the conditionality that has evolved in the donor community. One way to succeed is to champion the transformation of international donors' arrangements to include China as a full member (Corin and Smith 2010, 3).*

In a recent fact-finding study in China, Lancaster (2007) provides a summary of what we know and what we do not know about China's aid system. She also provides evidence pointing to a possible window of opportunity for developing strategic alliances with the Chinese. For example, she observed that the challenge for aid-giving governments in Europe, North America and Japan is to expand lines of communication and collaboration with the Chinese, who are clearly set to play a major role in aid-giving worldwide. She also reported that the Chinese have initiated contacts and consultations with Western aid agencies including Britain's Department for Foreign and International Development (DfID), the Swedish International Development Agency (SIDA) and the Canadian government, although I could not get any Canadian officials to confirm this. China has also signed MOUs with the International Finance Corp—the World Bank's commercial financing arm—to finance environmental sustainability projects in Africa. Chinese officials have indicated some willingness to become part of donor coordination groups in a select group of African countries.

African aid partners are also calling for closer collaboration with China. For example, in a recent study assessing China's FOCAC commitments in eight African countries, respondents from Uganda observed that while China has a preference for bilateral government-to-government engagement, Western donors like the EU pursue a multilateral engagement focusing also on Uganda's ordinary citizens rather than the elites. They suggested that it would be beneficial if China could engage to a greater extent with other donors active in Uganda to increase aid effectiveness and create synergies for Uganda's economic development (Centre for Chinese Studies and The Rockefeller Foundation 2010).

Both Europeans and Americans are seeking alliance opportunities with the Chinese on issues of international cooperation and development. According to Davies (undated), following the recommendations of the Accra Agenda for Action (AAA 2008), the European Commission decided to establish a three-way EU-China-Africa dialogue focusing on the issues of: 1) peace and security; 2) infrastructure development; 3) sustainable management of the environment and natural resources; and 4) agriculture and food security. In January, 2009, The China-DAC Study Group, together with the International Poverty Reduction Centre in China, was set up to facilitate sharing of experiences and promoting learning about growth and poverty reduction in China and Africa. In the United States, several private foundations have established collaborative arrangements with Chinese and African aid participants so as to make China's engagements in Africa more mutually beneficial. For example, The Rockefeller Foundation works with the Centre for Chinese Studies, University of Stellenbosch, South Africa, and Chinese scholars to improve understanding of China's aid and other FOCAC commitments to Africa. The Leon H. Sullivan Foundation works with the Council on Foreign Relations, the Brenthurst Foundation of South Africa, and the Chinese Academy of Social Science under the umbrella of the Africa-China-U.S. Trilateral Dialogue to organize conferences to "discuss how companies can contribute to economic and social development in Africa" and "to engage corporate leaders and analysts from Africa, China and the U.S. on lessons learned in corporate social responsibility and the best strategies to pursue accelerated economic development" (Sullivan 2009). At a conference held in Monrovia, Liberia, February 24–25, 2010, the Trilateral Dialogue produced a paper on corporate social responsibilities relevant for Africa. Drawing on previous global initiatives and new African thinking, the paper sets out an African perspective on corporate social responsibility built on six core principles—the Monrovia Principles—designed to: 1) promote stability and inclusive ownership, 2) encourage growth and entrepreneurship, and 3) ensure government and business act as good citizens (see The Brenthurst Foundation, www.brenthurstfoundation.org). These and similar collaborative arrangements can serve as models or templates for Chinese, Canadian and African aid participants to negotiate international strategic alliances appropriate for their value chain activities in the African aid system.

Public security and security of the person remain serious development challenges and a growing concern for the international community—including Canada and China—in many parts of Africa. While it may be premature for Canadian and Chinese defense, security, and intelligence organizations to form ISAs, there is no reason they cannot collaborate on matters of African security. As a result of many years of active engagements in Afghanistan, Haiti, DRC, North Africa, the Indian Ocean and the Horn of Africa, Canadian defense and security organizations—the Department of National Defence, the Royal Canadian Mounted Police (RCMP), the Canadian Security Intelligence Service (CSIS), and Canada Border Services—have acquired field experiences combining defense (security), development, diplomacy, democratization, and promoting respect for human rights. Such practical experiences can prove very useful for establishing collaborative arrangements with Chinese and African potential partners (Saferworld 2011).

## Challenges Ahead

Professor Li Anshan (2008) has identified five areas of conflict in China-Africa relations:

1. Competition between China and Africa in markets for goods, services, finance and labour;
2. China's national interests versus China's business interests;
3. China's interests versus Western interests;
4. China's needs for commodities and natural resources versus Africa's needs for equitable and sustainable development; and
5. Short term versus long term interests.

These are interest-based conflicts and challenges; strategic alliances between China and Canada at official (bilateral, multilateral) business, institutional, and people-to-people levels could help to address these challenges more effectively, taking into account Africa's interests and vulnerabilities. Canada is particularly suited for this task because it has a long history of successfully mediating public and private interests at international, federal, provincial, and local levels. Privately, Chinese diplomats in Ottawa admit that they have learned a lot from Canada.

In terms of international cooperation and development, from the Pearson Commission (1969) to the Development Assistance Accountability Act (Kuruvila 2006) and the recent Muskoka Initiative, Canada's foreign aid to Africa (and other parts of the world) has not lived up to expectations, especially in the areas of poverty alleviation. Canadians are understandably disappointed and looking for alternative approaches.[5] It is therefore appropriate that we begin the second decade of the twenty-first century prepared to *rethink*, *redesign,* and *rebuild* Canada's foreign aid in Africa. Yet it is not possible to think about the future of Africa without *thinking* about China in Africa (and the world). It is not possible to redesign new systems, structures, and practices without thinking about the systems, structures, and practices China has and will *design* for Africa. It is not possible to rebuild physical, digital, institutional, and community structures for Africa without taking into account the resources, structures, and systems China is *building* for Africa. All this needs carefully crafted strategic alliances with various actors, including Canada, China, and Africa. Individual African countries cannot go it alone—they are no match for the Chinese or the international community.

Up to now, China's phenomenal economic growth has been fueled by cheap labor, enormous waste, and environmental damage. Chinese companies operating at home and abroad (in Africa) will have to reduce consumption of raw materials; mitigate environmental impact of their operations; radically improve product quality, governance, and corporate social responsibility—including building sustainable communities; hone their management skills; help build sustainable national and local systems; and learn fairly quickly how to draw on local and indigenous knowledge in order to contribute effectively to African development. China cannot do it all alone, and yet the future of Africa depends on these things happening.

For the proposed alliance to work, it must receive the support of the Canadian NGO community and civil society in general, but the support of these constituencies is not guaranteed. On the positive side, these communities represent some of the most globally-minded and skilled Canadians, with experience in collaboration with both domestic and international partners, including foundations and private sector firms. Since the early 1980s, Canadian NGOs have responded to government budget cuts by forging creative strategic alliances and locating different sources of funding, including private foundations and multilateral organizations. Since China's financial contribution to Africa is likely to grow much more than Canada's, and since China appears to be willing to contribute more than cash to Africa's development, the hope is that Canadian NGOs might be equally creative in accessing these resources. It is also the case that the average Canadian NGO is small in size, unable to enjoy economies of scale. Developing strategic alliances with the bigger and more endowed Chinese partners might help Canadian NGOs to scale up in size, scope, and depth. On the negative side, however, Canada's NGO and development community in general is very concerned about issues of human rights and social justice, the environment, and democratic development. If they feel that China is not doing enough in these areas, they may refrain from doing business with Chinese aid workers in Africa.

Perhaps the biggest challenge to a Canadian-Chinese strategic alliance for Africa is the attitude of officials on all sides. Bodomo (2011) reminds us that it is wrong to assume, given their historically unfavorable experiences with aid coordination, that Africans are necessarily in favor of trilateral dialogues or ISAs with donors. Within government, Canadian response to China's engagement in Africa is quite hostile and even alarmist. One official told me that "the government of Canada's position on China in Africa is *agnostic*…there is no policy position." It is often stated that "China is a competitor for Canadian business/commercial interests in Africa, especially in the areas of infrastructure, engineering, mining, and other extractive industries." At a recent public lecture, a CIDA senior official, when asked about China in Africa had this to say,

> *There is a problem with how China is doing things. China does not want coordinating aid. China needs to become a member of the DAC like Korea has done.... We need to bring China into the conversation so as to talk about what and how to do development."*[6]

The implication here is that Canada and the West, through DAC, *should teach China how to do aid.* This is not a good way to start a collaborative conversation, because the Chinese believe they have better experience with development in areas such as rural development, poverty reduction, employment creation, industrial development, and population control; and therefore *China should teach Canada how to do aid.* The issue is not that China does not want to collaborate; rather the issue is that China does not necessarily want membership in established organizations like DAC as a precondition for collaboration. This position was made clear by a visiting Chinese scholar and advisor to government. Asked if China is ready to join DAC-type aid coordination, this is what he had to say:

> *I have had some discussion with the World Bank. But there is a need by the traditional donors (read Canada) to be a little bit more humble, not to treat other countries (read China) as subordinates.... [There should be] more flexibility to think about what is best for the local people (read Africa)...to avoid creating new monopolies (read OECD-DAC) for the aid industry...to treat others as equals."*[7]

Critics of collaborative approaches between Canada and China raise two important questions relating to the motivation for such collaboration and the practical ways of making it happen, especially since Canada belongs to the Western donor club, the DAC, while China is so far unwilling to join. In general, the issue of motivation is best addressed by examining the mandate, interests, and strategic objectives of the Canadian and Chinese participating organizations as well as the needs and interests of African development. While in the past Chinese engagements with Africa were predominantly of a government-to-government bilateral nature, today there is a wide range of actors including provincial governments, state-owned enterprises (SOEs), private sector business investors, and private Chinese citizens seeking for economic opportunities and personal freedoms.

The second question on how to implement such collaborative approaches has been discussed in this chapter with various concepts, frameworks, and illustrations. While there is no single "blueprint" for implementing ISAs, the frameworks discussed in this chapter provide a useful starting point and some diagnostic tools for identifying areas of common interest (e.g. VCA). Yet it is also the case that Western attitudes toward the growing engagement of the Chinese with Africa may be hardening. For example, in the summer of 2011, while NATO was bombing Libya, Western governments ratcheted up criticism of China's policy in Africa. While travelling in eastern and southern Africa, U.S. Secretary of State Hillary Clinton accused China of neo-colonialism in Africa; while visiting Nigeria, British Prime Minister David Cameron accused them of stealing business from British firms; and the Germans accused them of contributing to the drought and famine in eastern Africa. It is important to note that Canada did not join in this fray. Undoubtedly, implementation of the proposed collaborative approaches will require sagacious and transformational leadership from all participating partners.

Looking ahead, the challenge is how to get the parties out of their entrenched positions, create "safe" platforms, and begin substantive dialogue and negotiations leading to strategic alliances for the benefit of all. I think the international community puts too much emphasis on aid and not enough on the totality of African development. Multi-donor strategic alliances, including both traditional and South-South donors, could help shift the emphasis to focus on what matters most for Africa's overall development and transformation (UN 2009). Already the Europeans, and to a lesser extent the Americans, are making efforts to open dialogue with the Chinese, learn from and with them, and establish institutional arrangements for effective collaboration for development. For Canada and China, the Muskoka Initiative and FOCAC IV (2010–2013) priorities provide excellent starting points. My hope and expectation is that the model and ideas presented here can be extended beyond China and Canada. When it comes to their own development, Africans don't want to travel alone.

## Notes

[1] According to the *Canadian Encyclopaedia*, The Colombo Plan for Cooperative Economic Development in South and Southeast Asia was established following a January 1950 meeting of Commonwealth Foreign Ministers in Colombo, Ceylon, to attack the poverty upon which Communist political movements in Asia were thought to feed. Initially, Canadian involvement was cautious, with contributions of only $25 million in 1951–1952. Ottawa participation then grew and expanded, especially in India, Pakistan, Sri Lanka, and later Bangladesh and Indonesia, but not in China.

[2] See Pearson 1969. For a critical review of the Report, its exclusion of China and ideological biases, see Byres 1972.

[3] The eight Millennium Development Goals are: 1) eradicate extreme poverty and hunger; 2) achieve universal primary education; 3) promote gender equality and empower women; 4) reduce child mortality; 5) improve maternal health; 6) combat HIV/AIDS, malaria and other diseases; 7) ensure environmental sustainability; and 8) develop a global partnership for development. Goal 8 is confusing and misunderstood as different African countries use different measures to assess progress. See www.un.org/africarenewal.

[4] FOCAC = Forum on China-Africa Cooperation. These are High Level Ministerial Meetings between Chinese and top African government officials where China announces its commitments to Africa for the next three years. There have so far been four such meetings: FOCAC I, Beijing, 2000; FOCAC II, Addis Ababa, 2003; FOCAC III, Beijing, 2006; FOCAC IV, Sharm el-Sheikh, Egypt, November 2009. For each successive meeting, China has promised significantly more. For details see www.focac.org/eng.

[5] For example, as the country prepared to host both the G-8 and the G-20 in the summer of 2010, the Canadian International Council initiated a major foreign policy mapping initiative designed to generate fresh perspectives and ideas about Canada's priorities in international affairs. Under the theme of "recasting development for the twenty-first century," key discussion questions include: Why have the billions of dollars of development assistance not been effective at alleviating poverty? What is CIDA's role in the world where private contributions to development far outweigh national development agencies for on-the-ground impact? How can development assistance be made more effective and accountable? See www.canadianinternationalcouncil.org, accessed April 12, 2010.

[6] These quotes are from personal conversations with public officials who must be anonymous. I have observed that on a number of occasions, when African Foreign Ministers or other senior officials visit Ottawa, they are forced to explain to Canadian officials why their governments have close ties with China. I find this disturbing.

[7] China Engagement with Africa: Challenges or Opportunities? For Whom? Speakers of Renewal Series Lecture, given by Dr. Xue Lan, Monday, March, 2010, IDRC, Ottawa, Canada.

## References

Barr, Gerry. 2010. "ODA Accountability Act is a Remarkable Legislation, Disappointing Implementation." In *Time to Act: Implementing the ODA Accountability Act*. Canadian Council for International Cooperation. Accessed at www.ccic.ca.

Bergsten, F. C., C. Freeman, N.R. Lardy, and D.J. Mitchell. 2009. *China's Rise: Challenges and Opportunities*. Peterson Institute for International Economics, Washington, DC: Centre for Strategic and International Studies, October.

Biggs, M. 2010. "Development in a Changing World." Presentation made to the Society for Sustainable Development, Carleton University, February 11.

Bodomo, A. 2011. *The Globalization of Foreign Investment in Africa: Europe, China and India in Tandem.* University of Hong Kong.

Bradet, L. 2009. "The New Africa: Redrawing the Blueprint for Canada-Africa Partnership." Conference Report, Ottawa, October 2–3, 2009. Accessed at www.ccafrica.ca.

Brautigam, D. 2009. *The Dragon's Gift: The Real Story of China in Africa*. New York: Oxford University Press.

Brown, C., and E.T. Jackson. 2009. "Was the Senate Correct? Should CIDA be Abolished?" In *How Ottawa Spends, 2009–2010,* ed. A.M. Maslove. Montreal/Kingston: McGill-Queen's Press, 151–174.

Byres, T. J. 1972. *Foreign Resources and Economic Development: A Symposium on the Report of the Pearson Commission.* London: Frank Cass.

Canadian Council on Africa. 2009. *The New Africa: A Timely Opportunity to Build a New Canada-Africa Partnership*. Conference Report on Recommendations, October 2–3.

Canadian International Council. 2009. *Positioning Canada for the Africa of 2015: Why Africa Matters and Why Canada Doesn't Get it*. Report of the CIC-Ottawa Africa Study Group Seminar, November 18.

Canadian Standing Senate Committee on Foreign Affairs and International Trade. 2007. *Overcoming 40 Years of Failure: A New Road Map for Sub-Saharan Africa.* Accessed May 6, 2013 at http://www.parl.gc.ca/Content/SEN/Committee/391/fore/rep/repafrifeb07-e.htm.

Cartwright-Smith , K.D., and Cartwright-Smith, D. 2010. *Illicit Financial Flows from Africa: Hidden Resource for Development, 1970–2008.* March. Washington DC: Global Financial Integrity. www.gfip.org/storage/gfip/documents/repc.

Centre for Chinese Studies and the Rockefeller Foundation. 2010. "Evaluating China's FOCAC Commitments to Africa and Mapping the Way Ahead." A report by the Centre for Chinese Studies. University of Stellenbosch, prepared for the Rockefeller Foundation.
Chen, Z. 2003. "A Theory of International Strategic Alliance." *Review of International Economics* 11:5, 758–769.
China Information Office of the State Council. 2011. *China's Foreign Aid.* White Paper, April 21, Beijing.
CIDA. 2010. "Canada's Contributions to the Global Effort to Reach the Millennium Development Goals." Government of Canada. Gatineau, Quebec. Accessed September 22, 2010, at www.cida.gc.ca.
Corin, B., and G. Smith. 2010. "Working with China: Towards a New International Architecture: A Strategic Partnership with Canada on Global Issues of Mutual Interest." Canadian International Council CIC, January. Accessed March 2, 2010 at www.canadianinternationalcouncil.org.
Cullen, J.B., and K.P. Parboteeah. 2011. *Multinational Management: A Strategic Approach.* Fifth Edition. Mason, OH: Thomson.
Davies, P. 2007. *China and the End of Poverty in Africa: Towards Mutual Benefit*? The Swedish development aid organization Diakonia and the European Network on Debt and Development Eurodad, Sundbyberg, Sweden, August.
—. 2008. "Aid Effectiveness and Non-DAC Providers of Development Assistance." Background document to Round 9 of the Third High Level Forum on Aid Effectiveness HLF-3. Accra, Ghana, September 2–4.
—. n.d. "Think Piece on Aid And Development Cooperation Post-Accra and Beyond—Steps toward a Development Dialogue for the Twenty-first Century. The Examples of EU, China and Africa." Unpublished manuscript. Diakonia, Sweden.
Drayton, B., and V. Budinich. 2010. "A New Alliance for Global Change: Hybrid Value Chain." *Harvard Business Review* 88: 9, September, 56–65.
Edinger, H. 2007. "How China Delivers Aid to Africa." The Centre for Chinese Studies CCS, Faculty of Arts, University of Stellenbosch. Reported in *The Monitor*, April. Available at www.ccs.org.za.
FOCAC. 2009. Forum On China Africa Cooperation. Sharm El Sheikh Action Plan 2010–2012, dated November 12, 2009. Available at www.focac.org/eng.
Gulrajani, N. 2010. *Re-imagining Canadian Development Cooperation: A Comparative Examination of Norway and the UK.* Toronto, Ontario: Walter and Duncan Gordon Foundation, July.

Hamrel, S. and C.G. Widstrand, eds. 1964. *The Soviet Bloc, China and Africa*. The Scandinavian Institute of African Studies. Sweden: Uppsala.

Harneit-Sievers, A., S. Marks, and S. Naidu. 2010. *Chinese and African Perspectives on China in Africa*. Fahamu Books and Pambazuka Press.

Hubbart, P. 2008. "Chinese Concessional Loans." In *China into Africa: Trade, Aid, and Influence,* ed. R. Rotberg. Washington DC: Brookings Institution Press, 217–229.

Kaplinsky, R., and M. Morris. 2002. *A Handbook for Value Chain Research*. Ottawa, Ontario: IDRC.

Kar, D., & Cartwright-Smith, D. 2010." Illicit financial flows from Africa: Hidden resource for development." Washington DC: Global Financial Integrity.

Kiggundu, M.N. 2009. "BOP: A Business Partnership Strategy for Reaching Underserviced Poor Citizens." Paper presented at the International Association of Schools and Institutes of Administration Annual Conference, Rio de Janeiro, Brazil, August.

—. 2010a. "Anti-Poverty and Progressive Social Change in Brazil: Possible Lessons for other Emerging Economies." Paper presented at the International Association of Schools and Institutes of Administration, July. Bali, Indonesia.

—. 2010b. "Africa and China in the Teens: Growing Pains, Challenges and Opportunities." Paper presented at the Institute of African Studies, Carleton University, February 23.

Kragelund, P. 2008. "The Return of Non-DAC Donors to Africa: New Prospects for African Development." *Development Policy Review* 26:5, 555–584.

Kuruvila, Elizabeth. 2006. "Notes on Bill C-293: An Act Respecting the Provision of Development Assistance Abroad (Development Assistance Accountability Act)." Library of Parliament, Law and Government Division.

Lancaster, C. 2007. "The Chinese Aid System." June. http://www.cgdev.org. Accessed February 16, 2010.

Li, A. 2008. "China's New Policy toward Africa." In *China into Africa: Trade, Aid, and Influence,* ed. R. I. Rotberg. Cambridge: World Peace Foundation, 21–49.

Liu, H. and J. Yang, eds. 2009. *Fifty Years of Sino-African Cooperation: Background, Process, and Significance.* Yunnan University Press.

McGregor, J. 2005. *One Billion Customers: Lessons from the Front Lines of Doing Business in China.* New York: Wall Street Journal Books.

Muller, K. 1964. "Soviet and Chinese Programmes of Economic and Technical Assistance to African Countries." In *The Soviet Bloc, China and Africa*, eds. S. Hamrel and C. G. Widstrand. Uppsala: The Scandinavian Institute of African Studies, 101–130.

Pearson, L. B. 1969. *Partners in Development: Report of the Commission on International Development.* New York: Praeger Publishers.

Porter, M. E. 1985. *Competitive Advantage: Creating and Sustaining Superior Performance.* New York: Free Press.

Rotberg, R. I., ed. 2008. *China into Africa: Trade, Aid and Influence.* Washington, DC: Brookings Institution.

Saferworld. 2011. *China's Growing Role in African Peace and Security.* London: Saferworld. www.saferworld.org.uk.

Sullivan, L. H., Foundation. 2009. "Is Foreign Aid to Africa Still Worth it? A Constituency for Africa Forum." Ronald H. Brown African Affairs Series, September 23. http://www.thesullivanfoundation.org/foundation/news/index.asp. Accessed March 2, 2010.

UN. 2009. "Support to UN Development Assistance: South-South and Triangular Cooperation. Improving Information and Data." Office of ECOSOC Support and Coordination, Department of Economic and Social Affairs, November 4, New York.

—. 2010. "The Millennium Development Goals Report 2010." New York.

Webber, M. C., and P. Labaste. 2010. *Building Competitiveness in Africa's Agriculture: A Guide to Value Chain Concepts and Applications.* Washington, DC: World Bank.

World Bank. 2008a. "Building a New Aid Relationship: The Paris Declaration on Aid Effectiveness." Paper prepared with CIDA and OECD for the Third High Level Forum on Aid Effectiveness, September 2–4, Accra, Ghana.

—. 2008b. "The Growth Report: Strategies for Sustained Growth and Inclusive Development." Commission on Growth and Development, www.growthcommission.org.

—. 2011. "Africa's Future and the World Bank's Support to it." Washington DC: World Bank, March. www.worldbank.org/africastrategy.

World Economic Forum. 2009. *The Next Billions: Business Strategies to Enhance Food Value Chains and Empower the Poor.* Geneva, Switzerland, January. www.weforum.org.

# CHAPTER THIRTEEN

# JAPAN'S NATIONAL ECONOMIC IDENTITY AND FOREIGN AID: THE CASE OF GHANA

HOWARD P. LEHMAN

With the emergence of China's assertive foreign policy in Africa, earlier understandings of Japan's lengthier relationship to the continent have lapsed. For many observers and policymakers in Japan, China's active and extensive intervention in Africa has shifted the policy focus away from Japan's own "Asian" model; indeed, China has usurped Japan's distinctive approach toward foreign aid in Africa. Discussion of Japan's foreign policy is essential at this point in order to understand how Japan's approach to foreign aid differs from that of China as well as from the approaches of other major donors. At one level, Japan's renewed assertiveness in providing foreign aid to Africa is on par with the more active approaches of other donor countries. It might appear to some that Japan's motivation to lend capital and technical assistance to African countries is shared by all lending countries. However, I argue that Japan's Official Development Assistance policy makes important departures from the widely accepted ideology and policy objectives of the Washington Consensus. By taking a more distinctive path toward foreign aid policy in Africa, Japan seeks to demonstrate its own leadership position in the donor community. As one well regarded Japanese economist claimed recently, Japan has been "walking the splendid path of isolation" (Ishikawa 2005, 34).

Two traditional explanations of Japan's aid motivations have often been put forward. The first one typically focuses on the country's commercial and business coalitions (Inukai 1995). Japan decides its foreign aid policy simply based on its domestic commercial interests. The second explanation highlights the influence of Japan's domestic bureaucratic politics (Hook and Zhang 1998). This view closely observes the dominant political alliances and shifts in bureaucratic influence of the main foreign policy agencies: the Ministry of Foreign Affairs, the Ministry of Finance, and the Japan International Cooperation Agency, etc. Few studies of Japanese foreign aid to Africa have derived from the perspective of developmental strategy. Rather the focus has been on traditional analyses, which is understandable given that Japan's foreign policy toward Africa is not widely known or studied. Japan does not have a clear historical connection to Africa, nor has it been a colonial power on the continent. Yet the Japanese government has organized a series of important conferences; along with representatives from the United Nations, the World Bank, NGOs, and leaders from several dozens of African governments, Japan has hosted the Tokyo International Conference on African Development (Lehman 2005) every five years since 1993. Despite the budgetary constraints and cutbacks in Japan's ODA in the past several years, Japan has remained consistent in scheduling these conferences. Rather than turn its attention away from Africa during this economic slump, Japan has moved forward with its aid policies toward Africa. Japan has sought to portray its own developmentalist model as a series of lessons that African countries could adapt and modify according to their own constraints and development objectives. This view—that is, of what some African countries could learn from Japan—is the focus of this chapter. The chapter examines the complicated and revealing Japanese national development identity that explains its aid policy to Africa in general and to Ghana in particular.

The chapter frames the analysis of Japan's overall foreign aid policy to Africa by first highlighting the macro-level themes of Japanese national development and then examining the micro-level goals of its foreign aid policy to Ghana. Japan has focused its aid attention on Ghana, and its broad involvement in Ghana's development strategy offers an important examination of Japan's aid policy to Africa. Moreover, as world attention has shifted to China's aid policy, there have been very few recent studies of Japan's policy in a specific African country, much less on the underlying motivations that shape Japan's aid approach to the continent. In this chapter, I intend to highlight the strategic objectives and priorities of Ghana's growth and development strategy—as outlined in the Growth and Poverty Reduction Strategy II (GPRSII)—and its relation to the policies, directives and strategies of Japanese aid to Ghana. The research is based on the Growth and Poverty Reduction Strategy II of Ghana and Japan's Country Assistance Programme for Ghana (CAP-Ghana), both published in 2006, through the conclusion of the GPRS II in 2009.

The first section of the chapter examines the macro-level themes of Japan's national economic identity. These themes set the parameters of Japan's foreign aid policy and direct foreign aid, in particular to African countries. The second section presents the main priorities and objectives of the GPRS II. This section lays out the determinants, strategies, policies and comparative advantages of Japanese Official Development Assistance (ODA) to Ghana and its position of supporting the strategic objectives and priorities of the GPRS II. In the third section I outline the implementation of Japanese aid to Ghana in accordance with Japan's CAP-Ghana policies as well as in the context of Japanese ODA to Ghana vis-à-vis both Development Assistance Committee (DAC) and non-DAC donors. The fourth section is an analysis of the effectiveness of Japanese aid in terms of both Japan's ODA objectives and Ghana's own development strategy. In the concluding section, I will bring together both the macro- and micro-levels pertaining to Japan's foreign aid policy to Ghana.

Given that 2009 is the concluding year of the GPRS II, a review of Japanese aid effectiveness in achieving the objectives of this strategy, particularly the challenges, successes and lessons learned during this time period, would serve as an important and timely contribution to the study of Japanese development assistance in Ghana. A comprehensive review would increase understanding of how best to formulate future development strategies for Ghana, further refine the efficiency and comparative advantages of Japanese ODA in Ghana, and spotlight lessons that could be scaled to fit the objectives of Japanese ODA in Africa.

## Themes of Japan's National Economic Identity

A Japanese observer wrote that the distinctive Japanese approach toward development rests on three features. First, the government places the highest priority on the supply side of the economy, namely on production and employment. Second, the government focus is on a long-term perspective based on economic growth. And third, the market does not grow spontaneously without the help of the government (Kohama 1998, 58).

The pro-growth development policy embedded in Japanese policy at least since the Meiji period continued following the end of World War II. Vestal makes the argument that "perhaps the most valuable lessons concerning pro-growth industrial policy for developing economies today lie in Japan's utilization of competition as a tool to shape the direction of growth" (Vestal 1993, 163). Competition for a developmental state does not mean the same as for a liberal state. In Japan's case at this time, the meaning of competition arose out of a complex relationship among the large holding companies, the bureaucratic state, and a defensive posture that focused on domestic development. In the aftermath of the war's destruction, the government felt it had no alternative but to utilize government regulations including subsidies and trade barriers to promote economic growth.

## Historical Lessons

One underlying theme in Japanese foreign aid is its history of economic development both within Japan and within Asia. The historic importance of Japanese development patterns stems in part from the late nineteenth century adaptation of the development state. Many of the elements of contemporary development policy can be found in earlier periods of Japanese history. But as one scholar pointed out, the foundation for Japanese growth and development was in place at this earlier time. Adem writes that "the foundation which had been laid during the Edo period was thus solid when the country was fully opened to the outside world after the Meiji Restoration in 1868" (Adem 2005, 635). One of the key components from the Meiji period is the recognition of government engagement with the management of the national economy. Some observers point to the 1868 Meiji Restoration and the experiences of post-World War II development as lessons for successful economic strategies. In both cases, the push for growth derived from importation of foreign technology, high productivity, low consumption, and a dualistic structure of the economy (Okita 1980, 116). The initial principle of Japanese economic growth at that time was a production-oriented approach that led to rapid economic growth. As Okita describes the process, the government at that time focused on basic industries, then on the modernization of those industries, then the establishment of new industries, which led eventually to export-promotion policies (ibid 127).

Richard Grant (1998, 45) writes that "an emphasis on "self-help" runs through Japan's aid planning and implementation, a focus that derives from Japan's experience of postwar economic development, which depended relatively little on foreign aid." The idea of self-help, to a certain extent, also derived from the Meiji period. This period reflected the advantages of state-managed and state-directed development. The key trait was to modify existing institutions and values by incorporating more capitalist features. Meiji Japan borrowed foreign technology, imported Western models of development, and placed greater emphasis on education. But the overarching objective of this strategy was to maintain control over the national economy by emphasizing export expansion and import substitution (Nafziger 2005). The Meiji government's efforts to build upon Japan's cultural base as much as possible further reinforces the image of "self-help." In other words, according to Adem (2005, 657), "Japan's culture did not change to fit the putative requirements of modernity; instead it was modernity which was made to serve the dictates of Japan's culture." According to Nafziger (1995, 166), "the Japanese experience indicates the advantages of self-directed development to transform a country away from its peripheral position in the global economy."

Self-directed development hinges on the influential and accepted role of the government in creating and regulating economic institutions. The historical roots of this focus are clearly set in the Meiji period. As Preston writes, the government was the only mechanism that could pursue long-term industrial development, engage in the necessary social, political, and economic reforms, and develop a collaborative policy emphasizing growth and welfare (Preston 2000, 47–50).

## East Asian Experience

Japan's status as a major donor in Africa relies heavily on the image it attempts to disseminate to other countries. The Japanese government has sought for many years to portray its contemporary foreign aid policy to Africa as stemming from its post-World War II relationship with other Asian countries. Indeed, as the next section will discuss in greater detail, the Japanese effort to redefine its aid image has led to an alternative type of donor support. The creation of this image began immediately after World War II in Japan's relations with its neighbors. According to Inoguchi, Japan's national identity was based on debt, disdain, and detachment. By this, he means a general, deep connection to its Asian neighbors that continues to shape Japan's self-image as a major economic power as well as its ongoing relations with those neighbors. The debt that Japan owes to the surrounding countries is of course based on its history of colonialism, exploitation, and expansion. Each generation in Japan has sought to internalize this debt by continuously focusing the country's foreign policy, in general, and foreign aid, in particular, on the Asian region. As Ishikawa (2005, 2) has written, Japan's model of foreign assistance was formed on the basis of making reparations to its neighbors, but has now expanded to the African continent as well.

The second historical theme of Japan's relationship to East Asia centers on disdain. This emotive response derives from the historic isolation of Japan from the West, but in more recent terms it relates to the economic success of a nation that was not highly dependent on the West. Japan is the only non-Western nation that has developed into a rich, industrialized country in the twentieth century. Given Japan's success in this regard, its leaders have looked to its Asian heritage as a reason for its continued assertion of leadership in Asian foreign policy.

The third theme, according to Inoguchi (2004, 35), is detachment. He writes that "detachment derives from ambivalence." Japan tried, until recent years, to keep China at arms length and to remain strongly anti-militant. By doing so, it sought to be economically active in Asia yet to remain distant militarily from the rest of the world. That policy of relative isolationism and detachment has changed substantially in the past several years.

Since the early 1990s, these three themes have emerged as Japan's decision to mobilize its resources for more forceful foreign aid to the developing world. Japan no longer feels it is in debt to its Asian neighbors; rather, its self-identification is based more on its leadership role as a successful non-Western industrialized nation. Japan strongly believes that its economic development pattern offers profound lessons not only for its neighbors but also for other developing countries.

One of the more important aspects underlining Japan's ODA policy is its relationship to the "Asian economic model." Former Prime Minister Koizumi (2005a) said in a speech at the 2005 G8 summit that "Asia's post-war experiences in economic development are valuable assets for us in assisting African development." He went on to argue that "in view of Asian experiences, the key to African economic development is to foster the private sector through the promotion of trade and investment" (ibid, 3).

The East Asian economic miracle was a powerful force in linking African and Asian societies. According to Japanese economists, "a key lesson from East Asia is that if aid is to be effective in the long run, it would have to lead to private capital formation, both domestic and foreign" (Hino 2006, 16). Moreover, the East Asian experience has affected Japan's approach to development and aid in Africa. In particular, the main characteristics of Japan's ODA facilitate self-help and partnership through industrialization and trade. Experience has shown that Japan puts a high priority on economic infrastructure development, with a heavy emphasis on loans.

As one Japanese economist noted in regard to Japanese policy in Ghana, "based on its own and East Asian catch-up experiences, Japan considers it essential to address the structural problems of the Ghanaian economy and support its economic growth and attainment of self-reliant and sustainable economic development" (Ohno 2007: 18). Given its success in East Asia and its own economic history, Japan has increasingly shown assertiveness in the donor community. The organization and commitment to the TICAD process has been one important and visible affirmation of Japan's self-identity as a leading donor country.

Compared with the neoclassical orthodoxy that stresses macroeconomic stability and free markets, the emerging Japanese view is distinct in its primary pursuit of long-term real targets, recommendation of fundamentally dissimilar policies for different initial conditions and stages of development, emphasis on the active roles of government organizations as initiators of change, and—though not explicit in official documents but nonetheless real—the acceptance of authoritarian developmentalism in the early stages of development.

Japan's historical development during the Meiji period and since World War II has shaped its relationship with developing countries. Several themes have played a key role in forming Japan's foreign aid policy to the developing world, in general, and to African countries in particular. First, following upon Japan's adaptive response to the destruction of the war, Japan adheres to a self-help focus in which the recipient country assumes ownership over the aid. As is often said in Japanese foreign aid circles, aid is neither charity nor a moral obligation. Second, Japanese policy takes the view that government, at least in the early stages of development, should take an active role in creating an environment favorable to economic production and industrialization. One scholar strongly supports this view by writing, "perhaps the most profound impact of Japanese efforts in foreign aid is the emergence of Japan's own development philosophy, favoring a role for government in directing private sector growth versus what it terms the "excessive free-market reliance" of multilateral institutions" (Grant 1998, 59). Third, in congruence with Japan's emphasis on production and industrialization, the time frame is equally long-term. Foreign aid is not simply a quick fix, but an ingredient in a complicated recipe of long-term development.

Self-help refers to the ability of the recipient country to identify its priority development concerns and to marshal domestic and foreign resources toward those areas. In theory, this approach focuses on Japan's willingness to have a "policy dialogue in which the two parties participate with independence and on equal footing" (Ishikawa 2005, 24). In other words, the recipient country identifies its own financing needs and approaches Japan with an informed request. By allowing the receiving countries to initiate the dialogue over aid, Japan means to share "ownership" with those countries. Ownership implies accountability and responsibility over the use of foreign aid and thus responsibility over the payment of loans. Several reasons have been put forth to explain the use of self-help in Japan's foreign aid policy. Ishikawa suggests that the practice reflects "the Japanese sense of atonement inherited from reparations to East Asian countries" (22). The official statement in the ODA White Paper argues that "regarding the support it has provided to East Asia, Japan has provided support to the recipient countries on a request-basis, so as not to force Japan's views on them" (Ministry of Foreign Affairs 2006, 11). Akira and Yasutami (1999, 147) write that the "aid donor should not impose its plans on aid recipients but rather do its best to search out and discover nascent independent projects in a developing country and then lend a deft and experienced helping hand to ensure that these small seeds can grow to fruition. This is what self-help effort is all about." They go on to write that self-help emphasizes that "aid means helping those who help themselves, i.e., supporting the people of developing countries in their own efforts to improve their present circumstances, efforts that are their responsibility to work out for themselves" (ibid, 152–3).

Yet Japan also recognizes that self-help in and of itself is not sufficient as an effective aid policy. While ownership is crucial to the overall lending strategy, the content of that strategy needs to incorporate the mobilization of private capital. According to Hino and Iimi (2006, 16), "an objective of aid should be to assist the private sector development, and its effectiveness should be judged to a large extent by its impact on private investment." A leading foreign aid scholar writes that "what is clear from the lessons learned from the East Asia model is that mutual trust was established when Japan provided aid without conditionalities and by continuing serious policy dialogue based on equal partnership" (Ishikawa 2005, 28).

The Japanese emphasis on self-help, ownership, and the economic objective of production has emerged into a comprehensive policy embedded in TICAD. An earlier official statement co-sponsored by Japanese and African delegates offered the following objectives. First, the representatives agreed to poverty reduction through economic growth; that is, only through industrial development and production can there be sufficient growth to reduce the poverty rate. A high level Japanese diplomat said in 2005 that "while East Asia has made great strides over the last twenty-five years—particularly between 1990 and 2001—when there was an improvement in the economic situation of about 200 million people, Africa has not had such progress. Japan has been trying to replicate the 'East Asian miracle' in Africa" *(Japan Times* 2005). In recent years, Japan's ODA has moved toward social development, and the government has supported the Development Strategy of DAC and the Millennium Development Goals. However, according to one analyst, the continued reliance on economic infrastructure is a "recognition that even if resources are put into social development in an effort to reduce poverty—by building schools to improve education, for example—[poverty will not be reduced] unless there are jobs for educated people, and in order to create jobs, economic infrastructure needs to improve so that it will be easier to attract foreign investment" (Yamauchi 2003, 87). The Japanese government underscores this view in the 2006 ODA White Paper. Drawing on the economic success in East Asia, where Japan's foreign aid assisted in reducing the number of people living in absolute poverty, the government has recently argued that "an increase in direct investment received and trade resulting from economic stabilization" has played a role in poverty reduction (Ministry of Foreign Affairs 2006, 3).

The government's stance on poverty reduction was embedded in a 2005 document, Japan's Medium-Term Policy on Official Development Assistance. In it, the government catches up to other donors' positions on human security, yet it does so with a twist. Human security involves poverty reduction and sustainable growth as well as social development issues. The report states that "as the experience of development in East Asia demonstrates, sustained economic growth is a necessary condition for reducing poverty. Therefore, poverty reduction should be pursued comprehensively through actions that address both the economic and social dimensions" (Ministry of Foreign Affairs 2005, 5). Second, as taken from the East Asian strategy, African ownership is crucial for promoting growth that will lead to sustainable development. And third, development strategies need to utilize private capital resources within the context of appropriate government incentives (TICAD-NEPAD, 2004). TICAD's self-help initiative received widespread support, including from former Japanese Prime Minister Koizumi, who said in 2005 that "to achieve nation-building, the most critical thing is each nation's determination to bring about development through its own will and its own effort." Moreover, he went on to say that "Japan through public and private sectors will provide assistance in applying to Africa the knowledge garnered through Asia's movement towards higher productivity" (Koizumi 2005b).

Unlike Japan's relationship with its Asian neighbors, Japan's relationship with Africa is relatively unknown even within Japan. Yet a cornerstone of Japan's foreign aid policy in Africa is the recognition of clear and crucial interests in facilitating Africa's development. This view of strong connections was also supported by former Prime Minister Koizumi (2005b) when we said in a speech that "as we fortify the partnership between Asia and Africa, it will be critical to share our experiences and our knowledge through dialogues between civilizations, between cultures, and between individuals." The acknowledgment of shared concerns is, by definition, expressed by African officials. According to one report, "at the TICAD conference, a number of African participants pointed to the attraction of the Asian development model as one of the factors drawing them toward closer ties with that continent." At this conference, a Kenyan official said that "given our two continents, Africa and Asia, are faced with globalization in an era when pressures for liberalization are pretty strong, we in Africa have a lot to learn from the Asian experience" (Harsch 2004, 1).

Japan's foreign aid experience in East Asia has led to another set of lessons for its aid relationship to African countries. The combination of ownership, capital mobilization, and long-term development has led to an innovative yet controversial foreign aid strategy in Africa. First, according to the Japanese model, aid needs to complement sound macroeconomic policies and good governance. This objective does not waver from the traditional IMF financing approach. Japan's ODA White Paper explores this point by asserting that "because one key to sustainable economic growth is the private sector taking on a leading role, it is important to promote and stimulate the activities of the private sector, including trade and investment. However, there is a vast number of policy measures that governments of developing countries must carry out in order to develop an investment climate to attract the private sector" (Ministry of Foreign Affairs 2006, 1). Second, the focus on immediate social needs is understandable and appropriate given the dire living circumstances of so many Africans. However, according to one analysis, "the balance has shifted too far in that direction at the expense of long-term development objectives, including economic infrastructure" (Hino and Iimi 2006, 17). The government's Medium-Term Policy statement continues this stance: "Infrastructure is of fundamental importance in promoting private sector activities. Japan has actively supported the provision of economic and social infrastructure underpinning economic growth through such means as *yen* loans, and has played a particularly major role in providing the basis for economic growth mainly in the Asia region" (Ministry of Foreign Affairs 2005, 10). Third, in consideration of the self-help philosophy still embedded in Japanese aid policy, additional support of ownership is necessary. Aid projects that develop the social sector should complement long-term production goals, but all within the framework of ownership and accountability. What is being called for is greater accountability and full ownership. Thus, these authors argue that program aid should be given to "local communities to fund social projects they select and implement, instead of supporting the central government budget" (ibid, 18).

## The Japanese Model as Distinct from that of other Donors

Japan has tried to carve out its own separate path of ODA policy. Two historic factors distinguish Japan's aid and development vision from that of other donors. Japan is the only non-Western country with a history of successful industrialization, and Japan's postwar decision to abandon military forces implies that ODA plays a special role in Japanese diplomacy. Japanese officials moreover have at times distanced themselves from the dominant policy prescriptions embedded in the Washington Consensus. The Washington Consensus has been widely criticized in Japan as being ineffective and unfair in its application to African countries. The typical structural adjustment program may be effective in middle-income economies, but it is less effective in low-income economies with underdeveloped markets. An influential Japanese economist has suggested that in such economies there is a need to first build appropriate institutions. These country-specific institutions should be based on a "proper understanding of cultural values and social norms" (Hayami 2003, 56).

In this departure from the Washington Consensus framework, government officials in Japan have also advanced poverty reduction, not as an immediate objective of development assistance, but as a consequence of economic growth. What this entails for Japanese aid agencies is a justification of a "new paradigm which emphasizes strengthening the voice and power of poor people (empowerment) and maximizing the initiative of aid-recipient communities (ownership) in the design of development assistance" (ibid, 57). Japan's ODA White Paper asserts that poverty reduction should be carried out through economic growth. It highlights the experience of East Asia, where development was based on economic growth—which ultimately contributed to poverty reduction (Ministry of Foreign Affairs 2006, 13). Koizumi (2005a, 1) took the lead in this discussion in 2005 when he declared in a speech that "the Japanese government has been leading international discussion on African development by advocating the importance of ownership of Africa and partnership with the international community."

Japan's foreign aid strategy has developed into a distinctive path that is considered an alternative to the dominant lending positions of other donor countries. Japan's strategy draws extensively on ties to its own historical development and from its emergence as a non-Western economic power. Several observers have suggested that Japan's rise as an industrial power came about as a result of its own decisions, separate from the rest of the world, and moreover, its development became a uniquely Asian path. Japanese officials and observers frequently point to Japan's domestic economic progress and the success that Japan has obtained in assisting its Asian neighbors as examples of the Asian economic strategy.

An influential Japanese economist, Kenichi Ohno, has explored the distinctive vision of Japan's ODA strategy, presenting several important fissures between Japanese and other donor perspectives. First, according to Ohno, self-help efforts and ownership are important traits in foreign aid. Aid is neither charity nor a moral obligation; rather the results are what matters most and aid effectiveness is seen to be based on establishing a stake in the process for the recipient country. Second, the public-private sector tension should be resolved so that government intervention is permitted and encouraged during the early stages of development (Ohno 2007).

Japan has also tried to break away from the dominant Washington Consensus framework in order to examine what Japan believes to be the essential barrier to development, i.e., lack of economic productivity. The president of the Japan International Cooperation Agency (JICA), Sadako Ogata, said in a 2007 speech (Ogata 2007) that her agency would be paying more attention to African development. "Japan's assistance to Africa," she said, "has followed the international consensus to focus on poverty reduction through promoting projects, covering education, healthcare, water, and agriculture.... While remaining active in these fields, we are, however, beginning to look more and more to accelerating overall economic growth" (ibid, 2). Even with the adoption of the UN Millennium Development Goals, in which poverty reduction took center stage, the Japanese government's belief was only reinforced that "economic growth is a strong driving force for poverty reduction and betterment of people's lives" (Sunaga 2004, 18).

The fundamental principles of the Washington Consensus are well known. Some of them include fiscal discipline, competitive exchange rates, trade liberalization, openness to foreign direct investment, privatization, and deregulation (Williamson 1989). Japanese foreign aid policy clearly differentiates itself from many of these principles. Indeed, the Asian approach has been referred to as the Third Way, between neo-liberalism and bureaucratic interventionism. Jayasuriya and Rosser commented that the Third Way is based on three elements. The so-called new Washington Consensus is composed of governance, civil society, and expanded social safety nets. Whereas neo-liberalism posits the importance of reduced state activism, this new policy paradigm emphasizes an appropriate mixture of government and market functions (Jayasuriya and Rosser, 2001). Hayami, who refers to this new paradigm as the post-Washington

Consensus, equally argues for the acceptance of the critical role of institutions in developing countries (Hayami 2003, 57).

Second, the post-Washington Consensus offers a new identification of poverty reduction. The dominant Washington Consensus examines poverty reduction as a consequence of economic growth, while the post-Washington Consensus argues for poverty reduction as an immediate objective of foreign aid (ibid, 57). This is a crucial difference since "if poverty reduction is considered an overarching immediate objective, nonmarket instruments may have to be used to redistribute market-produced income in favor of the poor" (ibid, 57). Japan's policy fits directly into this updated version of the Washington Consensus. In the Medium-Term Policy on ODA, the government stated that poverty reduction should no longer be a tangent of growth, but an immediate consequence of a growth strategy (Ministry of Foreign Affairs 2005).

Third, the Japanese emphasis on self-help and ownership resonates within the post-Washington Consensus. As Hayami stated, this understanding of good governance and the proper role of public institutions is suggestive of the Japanese focus on self-help. Hayami (2003, 56) highlights this view by asserting the "need to incorporate country-specific institutions based on proper understanding of cultural values and social norms" of the recipient countries.

Japan has come under pressure from the donor community to abandon its somewhat isolationist donor strategy. A 2005 study reported that Japan remains set apart in terms of its self-help focus and its emphasis on infrastructural development as opposed to social sector investment to fight poverty (ODI 2005, 16). A Japanese development institute examination of Japan's ODA strategy highlights this pressure on the country to realign itself with the rest of the donor community. Donor countries are promoting aid harmonization, which is meant to rationalize and coordinate the use of aid resources "through focusing on shared goals and strategies and avoiding redundancies and duplications" (Sunaga 2004, 17). Japan doesn't oppose this harmonization mode, but it favors only strategies that "support ownership of the development process by recipient developing countries and [ensure] a diversity of aid modalities" (ibid, 17).

## Data on Japan's ODA to Africa

Historically, Japan has focused its foreign aid in Asia. However, in recent years, Japan has shifted its focus toward an increase in the volume of aid to Africa. Japan's promise to double aid to Africa in 2007 was met, however, primarily through high levels of debt relief. According to the

Development Assistance Committee, Japan has fulfilled many of its commitments during the past ten years, including grants to Africa arising from TICAD III in 2003 and additional grants issued at the 2005 Asia-Africa Summit (DAC 2010). At TICAD IV in 2008, Japan made another commitment to double its foreign aid to Africa, which has also largely been met.

| Region | Amount (million US) | Percentage of Total |
|---|---|---|
| Africa | $1,403.22 | 23.1 |
| Middle East | 500.67 | 8.2 |
| Asia | 2218.05 | 36.5 |
| Latin America | 142.58 | 2.3 |
| Oceania | 111.90 | 1.8 |
| Europe | 156.46 | 2.6 |
| Other (multiple regions) | 1548.12 | 25.5 |
| Total | 6081 | 100 |

**Table 13.1: Japan's Bilateral ODA by Region, 2009**

Source: Ministry of Foreign Affairs, 2011: Chart III-10.

Japan's preference is for bilateral aid, which in 2008 accounted for 84 percent of the country's total foreign aid to Africa. This preference reflects Japan's lending ideology, which emphasizes political leverage and accountability. Moreover, Japan uses loans to a far greater extent than grants or technical cooperation. The relatively high use of loans again reflects Japan's historical perspective of fiscal responsibility, accountability, and repayment as well as its emphasis on reinforcing self-reliance among the recipient countries (Lehman 2005).

Japan has been a significant donor of foreign aid to Africa for many years. While overall foreign aid amounts have fallen in the past ten years, Japan still remains an important donor to the African continent. In 2009, Japan's bilateral foreign aid to Africa amounted to $1.4 billion, or 23 percent of Japan's global foreign aid distribution. This percentage has fallen significantly since 2006, when it had reached 34 percent of global distribution, but has increased since 2008, when Africa's share of Japan's distribution amounted to 20 percent. Nevertheless, Africa still remains the second largest regional recipient of Japanese foreign aid (Ministry of Foreign Affairs 2011, Chart III–2).

Another indicator of Japan's unique status as a global donor is its distribution by economic sector. Two characteristics are most revealing. In

2008, Japan distributed 17 percent of its total foreign aid to social infrastructure, compared to 39 percent distributed by other DAC donors. And Japan provided over one-third of its total global foreign aid distribution to economic infrastructure projects, while the other DAC donors only provided 16 percent in this area (Ministry of Foreign Affairs, 2011: Chart IV-34). The DAC review of Japan's ODA policy states that "given Japan's long involvement in economic infrastructure, these departures from the DAC average are not surprising" (DAC 2010, 47).

## Ghana's Strategies for Development, the GPRS II

An examination of the macro-level forces behind Japanese national economic identity points to a distinctive Asian approach. This approach tends to emphasize a pro-growth and industrial infrastructure strategy. Moreover, the Japanese government emphasizes the responsibility of the recipient country to seek out aid from Japan and to maintain ownership of the loans. Finally, the East Asian model of development tends to be embedded in its growth strategy. The most recent DAC review of Japan's ODA underscores this argument. It states that Japan's policy is "distinctively Japanese," as demonstrated by its emphasis on economic growth instead of poverty reduction, on partner ownership, and on primarily state-to-state relations (DAC 2010, 30). Japan's approach to foreign aid in Africa has been highlighted in its particular policy toward Ghana. The underlying motivations of its foreign aid policy in general can be identified in an analysis of its aid policy in Ghana.

The previous section highlighted the key themes in Japanese foreign aid policy to Africa; these themes carry over in Japan's ODA strategy in Ghana. In particular, Ghana's current development plan, the Growth and Poverty Reduction Strategy II, embodies Japan's distinctive perspective on economic development. This section will demonstrate that the GPRS II mirrors the broad themes of Japanese foreign policy and, in particular, Japan's push to use the so-called "East Asian development model" in Ghana's development policies. The GPRS II highlights these themes, including an emphasis on long-term production and employment, long-term economic growth, self-help in terms of Ghana's input into foreign aid, and ownership as demonstrated by the Ghana Joint Assistance Strategy. The rest of this chapter will illustrate how Japan's broad historical reliance on its unique economic strategy has played out in its foreign aid policy in Ghana.

Ghana has long been an important recipient of Japanese foreign aid. In 2009, Ghana was the top recipient of Japan's bilateral aid (See Table 14.2). As a share of total foreign aid to Africa, Ghana was the seventh largest in terms of grant aid, the fifth largest in technical cooperation, and the fifth in overall foreign aid allocation from Japan (Ministry of Foreign Affairs 2011: Chart III-14). Moreover, Ghana is an excellent example of how Japan's development doctrines affected its ODA policy. Data in Table 3 underscore Japan's emphasis on self-help. In 2009, Ghana did not receive any loans from Japan; instead it received its ODA in the form of grants and technical assistance.

| Country | Amount (US Millions) |
|---|---|
| Tanzania | 120 |
| Sudan | 111 |
| Ethiopia | 98 |
| Democratic Republic of Congo | 66 |
| Ghana | 65 |
| Mozambique | 61 |
| Uganda | 54 |
| Burkina Faso | 50 |
| Senegal | 47 |
| Namibia | 40 |

**Table 13.2: Top Recipients of Japanese Bilateral Aid to Africa, 2009**

Source: Ministry of Foreign Affairs, 2011: Chart IV-15.

| Region | Grant Aid | Technical Assistance | Loan | Total |
|---|---|---|---|---|
| Ghana | 44.93 | 19.87 | 0 | 64.80 |
| Africa | 1012.13 | 331.11 | 59.98 | 1403.22 |

**Table 13.3: Japan's ODA to Ghana and to the African Region, 2009 (in US millions)**

Source: Ministry of Foreign Affairs, 2011: Chart III-14.

The Growth and Poverty Reduction Strategy II succeeded the Ghana Poverty Reduction Strategy I of 2003–2005 and shifted the strategic focus away from attaining the MDGs' anti-poverty objectives to outlining a strategy of growth in order to achieve a new overarching strategic goal. This new goal, to accelerate economic growth, is defined as raising the average per-capita income to US $1,000 per year by 2015 (Government of Ghana 2007a, 14). This change in income is significant because it would mean that Ghana has reached middle-income status while concurrently reducing by half the number of Ghanaians living in poverty (Government of Ghana 2005, preface i).

The hallmark of the GPRS II is its emphasis on prioritizing and implementing programs and policies that will not only induce current economic growth but will also foster sustainable development and wealth creation while reducing overall poverty. The priorities of the GPRS II, which point to this end, focus on a continuation of macroeconomic stability, acceleration of growth in the private sector, continued development in human resources, and a continued commitment to civic responsibility and good governance (ibid, xxi).

The GPRS II outlines current constraints on growth within each of these five priorities and proposed policy interventions in order to transform and mitigate the effect of these structural constraints. Furthermore, strategic support services are outlined to facilitate policy implementation and increase the effectiveness of proposed policies. While the focus on the GPRS II is to increase the per capita income of the Ghanaians to middle-income status by 2015, policy directives are also geared toward creating "quality of life" improvements and sustainable growth measures as represented in the policy objectives of human resource development and accelerated growth of the private sector.

Embedded in the GPRS II is a monitoring and evaluations program that tracks the progress of the policies and monitors their effectiveness. The findings are published in the Annual Progress Report to identify bottlenecks and ineffective or underutilized policies (Government of Ghana 2005, xxix). The estimated cost of implementing the three-year strategy is US$8.06 billion (ibid).

While the GPRS II outlines the central strategic goals and development priorities of the state, the role of overseas development assistance is mainly defined in two documents: the Ghana Joint Assistance Strategy (G-JAS) and the Ghana Partnership Strategy (GPS) . The G-JAS, developed in consultation with Ghana's development partners, builds on commitments by Ghana's development partners to implement assistance that is in line with the goals and objectives of the GPRS II. The Ghana Partnership Strategy provides a framework to monitor the effectiveness of development assistance that supports GPRS II objectives. The GPS accounts for funded activities to GPRS II policy priorities, monitors the harmonization of action plans, and creates an overview of external assistance. Nearly 95 percent of all official development assistance flows to Ghana come from development partners who are involved in the G-JAS (Government of Ghana 2007a, 1).

The G-JAS is supported by the Ghana Partnership Strategy, which details commitments by Ghana's development partners to harmonize supportive efforts to implement the GPRS II directives. The G-JAS also attempts to improve harmonization of aid with the objectives of the GPRS II and increase the transparency and effectiveness of the aid through ensuring little overlap between the commitments of the development partners. To this end, the G-JAS' assessment of the current country conditions and the major challenges facing Ghana and its pursuit of the MDGs and middle-income status is assessed jointly with the development partners.[1] Furthermore, the G-JAS mandates that development partners agree to a statement on the principles and commitments of how G-JAS countries will work together, with the government, civil society, and private stakeholders. The G-JAS details the priorities for the joint Development Partners' response to the GPRS II goals as well as arrangements for monitoring and risk mitigation (Government of Ghana 2007a, 1).

The G-JAS also includes the expectations of the Ghana Partnership Strategy, which constitute Ghana's measures of success in harmonizing and coordinating development partners' responses to GPRS II goals and priorities. The measures are as listed below.

- higher quality dialogue between the donors and the government;
- improved aid delivery through a better division of labor;
- greater harmonization in the way development assistance is delivered;
- increased reliance on program-based modalities and coordinated technical assistance programs that support government priorities;
- improved predictability in resource flows and reduced transactions costs for government; and
- better alignment of donor country strategies and resource allocations with GPRS II goals and priorities. (ibid, 2).

The success of the Ghanaian Joint Assistance Strategy hinges on how well it is able to foster development assistance in line with the GPRS II development agenda, coordinate the development assistance priorities of both DAC and non-DAC donor nations, and coordinate the interests of the NGO and private sectors.

## The Role of Japanese ODA in Ghanaian Development Strategies

For many years, Japan has targeted Ghana as a primary recipient of Japanese development cooperation and technical support. Japan has watched as Ghana outlined a coherent development strategy that emphasizes growth factors, poverty reduction strategies, and attempts to increase transparency, aid effectiveness and harmonization. Furthermore, Japan views Ghana's growth and poverty reduction strategies as being supported by increasingly stable and legitimate political and social systems that have taken ownership of Ghana's development agenda (Ohno 2007, 27). Ghana also has also taken a leading role in West Africa, as evidenced by its efforts as chair of the Economic Community of West African States and architect of pan-African diplomacy. Japan has described Ghana as playing a pioneering role in West Africa and a "test of whether a democratic and stable management of the economy and politics can lead to the improvement of the livelihoods of the majority of the population" (Government of Japan 2006, 3).

In addition, Japan has targeted Ghana for development assistance because of Japan's belief that its unique approaches and comparative advantages in foreign aid support Ghanaian development strategy objectives. As a non-Western, industrialized country with a "latecomer perspective to current debates and aid practices," Japan offers a different perspective on development, along with expertise in production and rural infrastructure development (Ohno 2007, 27; Government of Japan 2006, ii). Furthermore, Japan's emphasis on a country's self-help development strategies and country ownership match well with Ghana's approach to development as outlined in the GPRS II.

As a signatory to the Ghana Joint Assistance Strategy, Japan's Country Assistance Program-Ghana places particular weight on supporting the Growth and Poverty Reduction Strategy II development priorities in its own overall development assistance strategy. However, along with the United States, Japan has chosen to be an observer of Ghana's Multi-Donor Budget Support program at its inception rather than a signatory. This means that Japan planned to continue favoring traditional project-based aid modalities rather than non-project aid in the form of budgetary support (Government of Ghana 2007b, 1). CAP-Ghana does, however, leave room for budget support as a means to scale up the outcome of a given project (Government of Japan 2006, Appendix iii). The basic policy for Japan's ODA to Ghana is constructed on a framework of three policies that support the strategic objectives of the GPRS II. The three goals are: 1) to formulate aid policies in line with Ghana's own development policy, based on its ownership thereof; 2) to implement aid on the premise of Ghana's self-help efforts; and 3) to implement results-based assistance with a long-term perspective (ibid, 18). In order to support the GPRS II and its objectives, Japan has established two pillars of development that harmonize with some of the pillars of the GPRS II. These two pillars of CAP-Ghana are: 1) accelerating rural development, and 2) promoting industrial development.

The first pillar of support focuses on aspects of human security and aims to reduce poverty in rural regions to combat increasing regional disparity. This kind of targeted poverty reduction leads to an environment that promotes economic development. The goal is to increase the incomes of smallholder farmers by improving agricultural productivity, processing, and marketing, in combination with rural infrastructure development (ibid, Annex i). This pillar also supports basic social services, i.e. health and education, and encourages proactive participation by rural populations in social and economic development.

The second pillar of development support focuses more on the medium- and long-term economic development of Ghana. Its goals are to achieve sustainable poverty reduction by creating employment and increasing income through promotion of potentially viable industries while strengthening the competitiveness of domestic and international markets. To support these two pillars, Japan also supports action to strengthen institutional development and public administration to ensure self-sustained development. Although strong institutions and public administration are not in themselves pillars of development, they are a seen as requisite to ensuring sustainability beyond the effective duration of CAP-Ghana (ibid, Annex i).

In order to increase aid effectiveness, Japan has also created four strategic objectives to focus its assistance within these two broad pillars. These objectives guide and prioritize aid inputs and instruments in accordance with the two pillars through mapping "focal cooperation areas" where Japanese assistance can be directed in order to achieve the strategic objectives (ibid, Annex i.). The four objectives are: the promotion of agricultural development, the improvement of basic social services in deprived areas, the development of the private sector, and the development of human resources needed for the industrial sector. Additionally, although strengthening institutional development and public administration is not defined as a strategic objectives, CAP-Ghana does outline two focal cooperation areas for this purpose and articulates their high priority (ibid, Annex i).

The focal cooperation areas in Annex i and ii of CAP-Ghana seem to offer an ideal way to categorize Japanese aid to Ghana in terms of its location in Japan's overall strategic objectives for Ghana, regardless of the modality of the aid—i.e. development study, technical cooperation project, grant-aid, etc. Furthermore, these strategic objectives establish a context for aid in order to evaluate its overall effectiveness in meeting a strategic objective, i.e., how effective was a given project or aid input in meeting the strategic objectives? Although the CAP-Ghana development pillars and strategic objectives are closely related to Ghana's development strategy, and Japan is in fact a signatory of the G-JAS, it may be necessary to evaluate Japanese assistance against the objectives in the GPRS II in order to get a clear picture of how effective Ghana believes Japanese aid to be and how well its aid is harmonized across sectors and among different aid partners.

Japanese aid implementation within Ghana is directed by an in-country ODA task force. The task force is made up of representatives from Japanese government agencies including the Embassy of Japan, the Japan International Cooperation Agency (JICA), the Japan Bank for International Cooperation (JBIC), and the Japan External Trade Organization (JETRO). The task force approach is utilized in order to "foster internal Japanese coordination around a common vision and build synergies among agencies dealing with grants (the Embassy of Japan), technical assistance (JICA), and loans (JBIC) (Ohno 2007, 7). Ghana maintains "All Japan" collaboration among all four of the Japanese government agencies. The ODA task force offers intellectual support for the formulation of the Country Assistance Programs. The success of CAP-Ghana is affected greatly by the ODA Task force's ability to (1) design and implement projects that are commensurate with the program's strategic objectives and (2) procure necessary resources and commitments from both Japanese and Ghanaian ministries and agencies (Ohno 2007, 31).

Japan has also created the NGO-JICA desk, an office that seeks to enhance cooperation between Japanese and Ghanaian NGOs to support Ghana's development agenda. Along with facilitating collaboration among NGOs, this office has an interest in supporting Japanese NGOs and encouraging the involvement of Japanese citizens in Ghanaian development.

Japan's ODA, as the government's main foreign policy tool in Africa, represents a test for the Japanese of their ability to improve aid effectiveness and support growth, development, and human security despite a change in the aid landscape. Japan is a particularly important partner for Ghanaian development, as indicated by the assistance pledged by Japan in the G-JAS.

## Japanese Aid and Ghanaian Development: Challenges, Successes and Lessons

Both Japan and Ghana have sought to understand the challenges of development with regard to foreign aid and detailed their findings in the GPRS II, the G-JAS and CAP-Ghana. The challenges of matching a development agenda with foreign aid center largely around three main themes. The first is project selection; creating projects that contribute to sustained development and reduce dependence on aid is a significant challenge. Aid projects must help to mitigate the structural problems of the economy and real sector and reduce dependence on earnings from a few key exports. The challenges facing Japan as outlined in CAP-Ghana are first how to implement sound and workable ODA that contributes to sustainable development despite a significant reduction in aid to Ghana, and second, how to harmonize aid objectives as Japan and Ghana sustain an active development partnership. The GPRS II is the central policy framework to ensure ongoing continuity between Japanese objectives and Ghana's own development agenda. A third challenge is monitoring the successes of new aid approaches, such as general budgetary support and pool funds, and proper harmonization of agendas and assistance (Government of Japan 2006, 16). Japan also foresaw challenges in scaling projects to maximize benefits and efficiency. Neither Japan nor Ghana has the capacity to quickly institutionalize and scale successful projects to a level that maximizes efficiency and responds to Ghanaian needs. Other challenges stem from the fact that Japan has not signed on as a partner for Multi-donor Budget Support, which has ongoing dialogues with Ghana and its development partners. This means that policy dialogue is essentially on an ad-hoc basis in and constrained by the project identification cycle. This deficiency promotes additional challenges such as the modality of policy dialogues; being centered on a project-by-project basis means that it is difficult for both Japan and Ghana to easily focus on a given project's context in a sector-wide perspective or within the overall development plan. Given that Japanese aid is largely project-based, predictability of aid and Japanese strategic intentions are difficult to ascertain or rely upon.

Furthermore, while Japan has produced a series of four strategic objectives to support its two pillars of development, it is difficult to define success as the objectives do not offer any additional metrics beyond themselves. A project defined in a given sector is a truism in its own success; it is successful by definition as it is categorized as fulfilling a given strategic objective.

Japan has also dealt with structural challenges in implementing ODA. The vertical isolation of each government ministry involved in ODA creates an additional hurdle in harmonizing overall Japanese strategic objectives with the missions of the individual government ministries. This is the primary reason for the creation of in-country ODA task forces. Yet, while making an effort at coordination offers a good policy for creating a cohesive understanding of Ghanaian needs, it cannot serve as a platform for policy-making that takes into account greater strategic interests and objectives beyond Ghanaian aid. An anecdote of this vertical isolation and lack of real cohesiveness above the country level in its ODA is represented on the websites of the Ministry of Foreign Affairs (MOFA), JICA, JBIC, and JETRO. Each website offers statistics and information about Japanese ODA that may or may not be available on the others websites, making it difficult to navigate the ODA landscape. I have not seen any other evidence of real coordination of ODA above the country level, which makes it difficult to make decisions on prioritization and resource allocation—one of the primary challenges outlined by Ohno (2007, 26).

With greater emphasis on aid effectiveness since the Paris Declaration and the subsequent Accra Agenda for Action, the OECD has published several reports outlining aid effectiveness in Ghana. The most relevant report is the *2008 Survey on Monitoring the Paris Declaration*. The country chapter on Ghana discusses five dimensions of aid effectiveness in overall ODA to Ghana. These are *ownership, alignment, harmonization, managing for results,* and *mutual accountability.* This report is helpful in understanding the role of Japanese aid vis-à-vis other donor countries as well as general concerns and improvements to be made by the Ghanaian government on the five dimensions. One important factor that the survey emphasizes is the need for sharing of analysis between the donor country and the partner government. Often times, the donor countries demand much from the host country in relation to their limited resources (OECD 2008, 16). The report offers insights on how much analysis is coordinated and the need for joint analysis to increase effectiveness, reduce overlap, increase transparency, and set priorities. The report also details the progress made since 2005 and its relation to the goals and priorities of 2010 (ibid, 19).

One of the most difficult assessments of Japanese aid to Africa is fleshing out its role in overall Ghanaian development. The reasons are several fold. The first is that development is rationed out over several sectors. A project-based approach makes it necessary to compare a single development project through the sector or against a given development objective, but also against other Japanese projects across sectors as well as the actions of other donors. This analysis must concurrently be met with understanding the priorities of the host country's development agenda and analyzing their effects from a qualitative and quantitative perspective. This leads to additional problems such as the cost of information, the difficulty of finding information, and the necessity of relying on statistical information and interviews.

The Japanese do lay out a methodology in their reports. JICA's main evaluation tool is the four-step Plan-Do-Check-Act (PDCA) management cycle, which "promotes continuous improvement of project activities." This general outline supports all schemes, programs, and project evaluations. The Japanese also evaluate their efforts cross-sectionally in order to obtain a clearer picture of JICA's operations in the strategic sense (JICA 2008).

JICA also seeks impartiality, transparency and objectivity in its methodology. The last step is to emphasize the utilization of evaluation results; feedback is sought on the program and project levels as well as in reference to JICA's basic policy for the country in order to improve all aspects of ODA assistance. Japan also maintains a third party evaluation system from the Japan Evaluation Society.

It is important to go beyond the scope of JICA analyses of Japan's projects. Although Japan has harmonized its goals with the GPRS II development agenda, an accurate assessment must also look from additional angles, evaluating effectiveness of aid to Ghana from all possible perspectives: Ghanaian and Japanese, and that of the OECD, to begin to synthesize a comprehensive and fair evaluation.

## Conclusion

Japan currently is struggling to maintain its status as a distinctive Asian donor to African countries while being pressured by other foreign donors to coordinate its policies with other governments and funding agencies. The historical dominance of key themes in Japan's national economic identity, at the macro level, frame the implementation of its foreign aid policy to Ghana at the micro level. The case of Japan's aid policy in Ghana highlights the challenges Japan faces as it seeks to carve out its unique status as an Asian donor with emphasis on long-term infrastructural development, production goals, and self-help. The discussion and analysis of the GPRSII, the G-JAS, and CAP-Ghana documents suggest the difficulties in implementing Japan's foreign aid policy.

An analysis of Japan's aid policy suggests that the policy reflects patterns associated with Japan's national identity. However, Japan is faced with numerous challenges as it seeks to maintain its foreign aid presence in Africa. First, Japan uneasily recognizes the growing and influential existence of China on the continent. As China emerges as a powerful economic force, the pressure builds on Japan to respond in kind. Yet Japanese policy is constrained by domestic political pressures and by its image as a democratic nation seeking to promote humanitarian efforts. Second, the current debate within Japanese ministries is how to increase the quantity of aid without incurring the displeasure of its citizens. For many Japanese people, Africa is essentially marginal to Japan's economic and political interests. One outcome of this is the selective provision of aid to only a few countries. As one analyst has written, "such a strategy [is] more pragmatic and politically acceptable within Japan, and could provide a demonstrative effect" (Court 2005, 26). Third, although this stands at odds with other donors who emphasize social sector development, Japan will continue to focus its aid on infrastructural development. Japan has been committed to this form of development for a very long time. Court (2005, 27) observes that "this is a big opportunity: it is an area where Japan has a comparative advantage and an issue to which it can bring its experience from East Asia." Fourth, the Japanese government is in the process of reorganizing its aid agencies to align their structure with the new aid agenda. In part, there is an expectation that its policy will support governance issues in African countries. Yet Japan has shown reluctance to work with societal groups in order to create a better governing environment. Traditionally, Japan has shown more interest in the technical aspect of foreign aid or in expanding capacity than in building political governance. Finally, Japan is continually faced with questions regarding its experience with East Asian countries and how that experience can be applied to African cases.

## References


Adem, S. 2005. "Is Japan's Cultural Experience Relevant for Africa's Development?" *African and Asian Studies*, 4:4, 629–664.

Akira, N., and S. Yazutami. 1999. *The Economics of Development Assistance: Japan's ODA in a Symbiotic World*. Tokyo: LTCB International Library Foundation.

Court, J., ed. 2005. Aid to Africa and the UK's "2005 Agenda": Perspectives of European Donors and Implications for Japan. *Final Report*, JICA, ODI, December.

Development Assistance Committee (DAC). 2010. *Japan: Peer Review*. Paris: OECD.

Government of Ghana. 2005. Growth and Poverty Reduction Strategy (GPRS II) 2006–2009. November. Accra: National Development Planning Commission.

Government of Japan. 2006. Japan's Country Assistance Programme for Republic of Ghana. Tokyo, September.

Government of Ghana. 2007a. Ghana Joint Assistance Strategy (G-JAS), February, 27. Accra.

—. 2007b. Ghana Partnership Results Matrix Accra. Accessed September 6, 2009, at: http://siteresources.worldbank.org/INTGHANA/Resources /cg_results_matrix.pdf

Grant, R. 1998. "Japan: A Foreign Superpower," In *The Global Crisis in Foreign Aid,* eds. R. Grant and J. Nijman. Syracuse: Syracuse University Press, 44–60.

Harsch, E. 2004. "Africa and Asia Forge Stronger Alliances." *Africa Recovery*, 18:1, April.

Hayami, Y. 2003. "From the Washington Consensus to the Post-Washington Consensus," *Asian Development Review* 20:2, 40–65.

Hino, H., and A. Iimi. 2006. "Aid as Catalyst for Private Investment: A Lesson from Asia to Africa." Unpublished paper, February 2006.

Hook, S., and G. Zhang. 1998. "Japan's Aid Policy Since the Cold War." *Asian Survey*, 38: 1, November.

Inoguchi, Takashi. 2004. "The Evolving Dynamics of Japan's National Identity and Foreign Policy Role." In *Global Governance,* ed. S. Katada. London: Ashgate, 31–49.

Inukai, I. 1995. "Why Aid and Why Not? Japan and Sub-Saharan Africa." In *Japan's Foreign Aid,* eds. B. Koppel and R. Orr, Jr. Boulder: Westview Press, 252–274.

Ishikawa, S. 2005. "Supporting Growth and Poverty Reduction: Toward Mutual Learning from the British Model in Africa and the Japanese Model in East Asia." Discussion Paper no. 8, JBIC Discussion Paper Series, March.

Japan International Cooperation Agency (JICA). 2008. *Annual Evaluation Report.* Tokyo.

*Japan Times*. 2005. "Development Vital to International Security, Says Japanese Envoy to UN." February 12.

Jayasuriya, K., and a. Rosser. 2001. "Economic Orthodoxy and the Asian Economic Crisis." *Third World Quarterly*, 22: 3: 381–396.

Kohama, H. 1998. "A Review of Systemic Transition," in *Japanese Views on Economic Development,* eds. K. Ohno and I. Ohno. London: Routledge, 53–60.

Koizumi, J. 2005a. "Japan's Policy for African Development." Message to Africa in the Context of the G8 Summit, July 6.
—. 2005b. Speech, April 22, 2005.
Lehman, H. 2005. "Japan's Foreign Aid Policy to Africa: An Assessment of Ten Years of the Tokyo International Conference on African Development." *Pacific Affairs* 78:3 (Fall): 423–442.
Ministry of Foreign Affairs. 2005. "Japan's Medium-Term Policy on Official Development Assistance." February.
—. 2006. *Japan's Official Development Assistance, White Paper.* Tokyo.
—. 2011. *Japan's Official Development Assistance, White Paper.* Tokyo.
Nafziger, E. W. 1995. *Learning from the Japanese.* Armonk, NY: M.E. Sharpe.
—. 2005. "Meiji Japan as a Model for Africa's Economic Development." *African and Asian Studies,* 4:4, 443–464.
ODI. 2005. *Aid to Africa and the UK's "2005 Agenda": Perspectives of European Donors and Implications for Japan.* London: ODI, March 31.
Ogata, S. 2007. "Japan's Development Assistance is at a Crossroads." JICA, June 22.
Ohno, I. 2007. "Country-Specific Growth Support in East Asia and Africa: Japan's ODA to Vietnam and Ghana." *GRIPS Development Forum Discussion Paper no. 16,* January.
Okita, S. 1980. *The Developing Economies and Japan.* Tokyo: University of Tokyo Press.
Organization for Economic Cooperation and Development. 2008. *2008 Survey on Monitoring the Paris Declaration.* Paris: OECD.
Preston, P.W. 2000. *Understanding Modern Japan.* London: Sage Publications.
Sunaga, K. 2004. *The Reshaping of Japan's Official Development Assistance Charter.* Discussion Paper on Development Assistance no. 3. Tokyo: FASID, November.
TICAD-NEPAD. 2004. Joint Policy Framework for the Promotion of Trade and Investment between Africa and Asia. Bandung, November2.
Vestal, J. 1993. *Planning for Change: Industrial Policy and Japanese Economic Development, 1945–1990.* Oxford: Clarendon Press.
Williamson, J. 1989. "What Washington Means by Policy Reform." In *Latin American Readjustment: How Much Has Happened,* ed. John Williamson. Washington: Institute for International Economics.
Yamauchi, M. 2003. "Trends in Development Aid in Major Developed Countries." In *Global ODA Since the Monterrey Conference,* eds. T. Akiyama and M. Kondo. Tokyo: FASID.

# INDEX